ANGLO SAXON MYTHS

ANGLO-SAXON MYTHS

STATE AND CHURCH
400–1066

NICHOLAS BROOKS

THE HAMBLEDON PRESS
LONDON AND RIO GRANDE

First published by The Hambledon Press, 2000
102 Gloucester Avenue, London NW1 8HX (UK)
PO Box 162, Rio Grande, Ohio 45674 (USA)

ISBN 1 85285 154 6

A description of this book is available from the
British Library and from the Library of Congress

Typeset by John Saunders Design & Production
Printed in Great Britain at the University Press, Cambridge

Contents

Figures

Acknowledgements

These essays first appeared in the following publications and are here reprinted with their accompanying illustrations by the kind permission of the publishers who remain the copyright holders.

1. 'History and Myth, Forgery and Truth', *Inaugural Lecture delivered in the University of Birmingham, 23 January 1986*, pp. 1–20.

2. *The Making of England: Anglo-Saxon Art and Culture AD 600–900*, ed. L. Webster and J. Backhouse (British Museum Publications, 1991), pp. 9–14. By permission of the Trustees of the British Museum and of the British Library Board.

3. *The Origins of Anglo-Saxon Kingdoms*, ed. S.R. Bassett (Leicester University Press, 1989), pp. 55–74, 250–4.

4. *The Origins of Anglo-Saxon Kingdoms*, ed.S.R. Bassett (Leicester University Press, 1989), pp. 159–70, 275–7.

5. This appears here for the first time.

6. *European Towns: Their Archaeology and Early History*, ed. M.W. Barley (Academic Press Ltd., London, 1977), pp. 487–98. [By permission of Academic Press Ltd.]

7. *The History of Canterbury Cathedral*, ed. P. Collinson and N. Ramsay (Oxford University Press, 1995), pp. 1–37. By permission of Oxford University Press.

8. *St Dunstan: Life and Times*, ed. N.J. Ramsay, M. Sparks and T. Tatton-Brown (Boydell & Brewer, Woodbridge, 1992), pp. 1–22.

9. *Anglo-Saxon England*, 3 (Cambridge University Press, 1974), pp. 211–34. [The postscript on pp. 202–215, below, appears here for the first time.]

10. *Anglo-Saxon England*, 13 (Cambridge University Press, 1984), pp. 137–57.

11. *Winchester College: Sixth-Century Essays*, ed. R.A. Custance (Oxford University Press, 1981), pp. 189–228. By permission of Oxford University Press.

12. *Romney Marsh: Evolution, Occupation and Reclamation*, ed. J. Eddison and C. Green (Oxford Committee for Archaeology, monograph 24, 1988), pp. 128–59.

Abbreviations

ASC	Anglo-Saxon Chronicle.
BAR	British Archaeological Reports.
BCS	*Cartularium Saxonicum: A Collection of Charters Relating to Anglo-Saxon History*, ed. W. de G. Birch, 3 vols (London 1885–93). References are to document numbers.
BL	British Library.
DB	Domesday Book.
EHD	*English Historical Documents*, i, *c. 500–1042*, ed. D. Whitelock (London, 1955, 1979).
KCD	*Codex diplomaticus aevi Saxonici*, ed. J.M. Kemble, 6 vols (London, 1839–48). References are to document numbers.
MGH	Monumenta Germaniae Historia.
S	P.H. Sawyer, *Anglo-Saxon Charters: An Annotated List and Bibliography* (London, 1968). References are to document numbers.

Preface

This book is a companion to *Communications and Warfare, 700–1400* (London and Rio Grande OH, Hambledon Press, 2000); in the two volumes are gathered my principal studies on English history, which have been scattered in a wide variety of publications and some of which are now difficult to obtain. The essays reprinted here were first published at various times in the last twenty-five years and they reflect my long-standing fascination with the quality of the evidence for early English history. All historians have, of course, to develop the skill to detect the bias of their sources before they can set out their own interpretation of the past. But most of the written evidence for the early Middle Ages has been preserved by later writers with their own dynastic, monastic or antiquarian agendas, whether conscious or unconscious. Early medievalists therefore have to be expert in the thought-world of later periods, if they are to avoid being misled by the anachronisms of those who have transmitted the evidence; their researches may only throw light upon these later agendas and tell little or nothing of their chosen period. Some of the evidence has indeed been deliberately forged or adapted in order to provide a bogus antiquity and legality for particular claims; and much of it has been recorded selectively, or out of context, so as to create a misleading impression of Anglo-Saxon realities. Understanding why the extant evidence has been preserved and what may have been lost is therefore the constant preoccupation of the early medievalist, who has to steer a personal course between the Scylla of a self-defeating minimalist rigour and the Charybdis of blind acceptance of 'tradition' or maximalist interpretations of fragmentary evidence.

My 'inaugural lecture' at Birmingham sought to show how historians may elucidate myth and forgery and to link the world of the monastic forgers of the ninth and twelfth centuries with the literary, historical, archaeological or fine art forgers of our own age (Chapter 1). Myth has a central role in defining core beliefs about national and ethnic origins. Since in all periods the study of history has been closely associated with the development of national and local patriotisms, an English early medievalist has an obligation to consider the 'roots' of the English people and of the English language and culture (Chapter 2). When my colleague, Steven Bassett, gathered a team of scholars together to re-examine the origins of Anglo-Saxon kingdoms, I therefore had an opportunity to pursue these issues in relation both to the kingdom of Kent (Chapter 3) – which was claimed to have been formed during the

Adventus Saxonum itself, the first 'arrival' of migrant Germans in Britain – and to the Mercian kingdom, whose origins cannot be investigated through Mercian origin myths or heroic tales but only through the eyes of their neighbours and enemies (Chapter 4). The fact that in Kent and Mercia, as in other Anglo-Saxon kingdoms, the definition of the historical kingdom appears to belong to the generation before the conversion to Christianity may tell us more about the threshold of the historical evidence than the actual chronology of state-formation. For this reason it is worth re-examining the legend of Hengest and Horsa, the core story of the English origin legend, in order to see whether it is possible to detect, even in its later forms, traces of the praise of earlier rulers and their kingdoms (Chapter 5).

A trio of papers (Chapters 6, 7 and 8) are devoted to the Christian history of Canterbury. In Chapter 6 an early attempt was made to set out before an audience of European archaeologists how the early traditions of the Canterbury churches and their location in relation to what was then known of the topography of the Roman city suggested that Canterbury might provide an English example where the church formed the bridge between the late-Roman town and the medieval and modern city. It therefore helped to create the climate of opinion which led to the establishment of the Canterbury Archaeological Trust and to its series of dramatic excavations in the city. In Chapter 7 I sought (in 1993) not merely to summarize in a single chapter my interpretation of the early history of Canterbury cathedral (which I had first attempted in book length a decade earlier), but also to revise it in the light of subsequent archaeological excavations and of numerous studies of early manuscripts, charters, liturgical, legal and conciliar texts. Throughout my aim was to reconstruct the history from contemporary sources, manuscripts or from extant remains (architectural or archaeological) in order to test the later monastic versions of Canterbury's Anglo-Saxon history. A similar 'demythologising' aim underlies my attempt (Chapter 8) to use the evidence of contemporary or reliable charters to correct the picture of the career of St Dunstan which had hitherto been concocted on the basis of a pastiche of hagiographical sources of varying dates.

The study of Anglo-Saxon charters has indeed been a central interest of my researches since I first embarked on doctoral research on the charters of Christ Church Canterbury and discovered the joys of the light they throw on the growth of royal government, on ceremonial and political occasions, on the development of Latin learning, on the work of forgers (both skilled and unskilled) and on a host of fascinating problems of English topography. It was therefore a great honour to be invited to review modern scholarship on the charters for the new journal *Anglo-Saxon England* and to provide a guide through the many traps that await the novice or uncritical studies (Chapter 9). Since 1973, however, the pace of work in this field has dramatically quickened, so I have sought to bring this chapter up-to-date with an extended postscript, in the belief that an introduction to charter studies is as much needed today as it was twenty-five years ago. The remaining three chapters show something of the excitement that the study of charters can generate. The deposit in Stafford Record Office of an antiquarian transcript of a charter of King Edgar provided a rare opportunity to add to the corpus of known Anglo-Saxon charters (Chapter 10); it proved to throw light on the king's continued use of a Mercian draftsman for some of his charters, on that writer's stylistic ambitions and on a remarkable assembly of northern nobles at Edgar's court; it also provided some clues to the estate history and toponymic riches of the Black Peak. The purported grant of 100 hides at Micheldever (Hampshire) by King Edward the Elder to the New Minster, Winchester (Chapter 11) provided, by contrast, an opportunity both to see a great monastic house protecting (or creating) its eleventh-century immunity with a superb forgery, and to explore some of the lasting features of the Hampshire landscape. Finally, in Chapter 12, an attempt was made to show how the evidence of charters can be combined with the evidence of geology and of archaeology to reconstruct the Anglo-Saxon landscape (and something of the estate history) of Romney Marsh. At least from the early eighth century, the marshland pastures were normally attached to distant Kentish estates, and a distinctive *Merscware* ('Marsh-people' was developing a sense of identity, in part perhaps from their common quest to protect their lands from floods induced both by climatic change and by their own drainage schemes.

These essays are here reprinted essentially as they were first published, apart from some correction of minor slips and misprints. They show the development of my thought successively as a postgraduate at Oxford, a lecturer at St Andrews and a professor at Birmingham. It has been a relief to find that their argument has very largely commanded support in subsequent scholarship and that large-scale revision is not (so far as I can judge) needed. As in the companion volume, however, I have added a postscript to some chapters, indicating the gist of subsequent work on the issues broached here. Twice, however, I have departed from this policy. One entirely new essay has been included (Chapter 5), because there seemed to be a gap in scholarly treatment of the legend of Hengest and Horsa (which I had hinted at in Chapter 4), which was so central to the theme of this volume that it were best filled here. It also seemed highly desirable to update my 1973 survey of charter scholarship (Chapter 9) with a brief analysis of the main currents of subsequent scholarship, if its judgements were to be of more than historiographical interest for those who embark on the study of the charters today.

Thanks are due to Margaret Gelling and Douglas Johnson, my co-authors in Chapter 10, for agreeing to its reprint here; to the Universities of St Andrews and of Birmingham for support with study leave and travel grants to facilitate my researches and for the able assistance of their library staffs, and to Martin Sheppard for his patience during this book's gestation and his care with its production. It is dedicated to my colleagues and pupils in two departments of Medieval History, who have been a constant stimulus to new avenues of thought and challenge to old ones.

University of Birmingham   Nicholas Brooks

For my Colleagues and Pupils in
the Departments of Medieval History
in the Universities of
St Andrews and Birmingham

1

History and Myth,
Forgery and Truth[1]

IN A TYPICALLY baroque and epigrammatical aside in his essay 'Oper und Drama' the composer Richard Wagner asserted that 'Myth is the beginning and end of History', in the same way as 'Song is the beginning and end of language' and 'sentiment (*das Gefühl*) the beginning and end of understanding'.[2] I am very happy to leave to the inaugurals of future professors of Music or Linguistics Wagner's dictum on song and language, and to professors of Philosophy or even of Psychology that on sentiment and understanding – such are the advantages for inaugural lecturers of the narrowing specialization of modern education! But I would like to pursue Wagner's triptych in as far as it concerns myth and history. For nineteenth-century thinkers, for whom history was very largely the political history of nation-states, or of nations in the making, it was clear enough that history 'began' with myth: the origin-stories of Germanic (as of Greek and Roman) peoples abounded in legend, and early history might therefore be thought to comprise the ordering and elucidation of myth. To a German in the generation after 1870 when the nineteenth-century nationalist interpretations of the legend of the sleeping Emperor Frederick in the Kyffhäuser mountain seemed to have been vindicated by the reunification of Germany, it might seem particularly apparent that myth was also 'the end of history'. Indeed this might well be the theme for a professor of Contemporary History, were such a chair to exist at Birmingham. Where indeed does history end and myth (politics or journalism) begin? If I seem to insult students of politics and the followers of the noble journalistic profession, it is as well to remember that we live in a society wherein the PR man is all powerful in laundering the 'image' (the television myth?) of the rulers and the powerful institutions (and even of universities), and we live in a society in which politicians no sooner retire than they (or their ghost-writers) launch their memoirs upon the long-suffering readers of the Sunday newspapers in an attempt to perpetuate their own image of

---

[1] Inaugural lecture delivered in the University of Birmingham on 23 January 1986 and first printed as ISBN 0 7044 0861 9.

[2] R. Wagner, *Gesammelte Schriften und Dichtungen* (Berlin, 1914), iv, p. 69.

history, the myth that they wish to leave to posterity. Myth, then, might in various senses be said to be 'the end of History'. But if we are not to accept Napoleon Bonaparte's ironic and bitter comment from his island exile that 'History is a myth that men agree to believe' [the irony is particularly acute since Napoleon is known to have attempted to forge some of his own letters],[3] then we must conclude that the role of the historian is to puncture such myths and to explain the purposes that they have been devised to serve – in ancient, in medieval or in modern times. Myth then is not so much 'the beginning and end of History', as History is the elucidation and dispersal of Myth. For this reason what determines the quality of history is the historian's skill in detecting the motives and the assumptions of those who have left their record for posterity. For this same reason I shall not be too concerned tonight with the traditional chronological limits of the Middle Ages, nor with traditional thematic divisions within history (social, economic, political, religious, intellectual and so forth). I prefer to regard history as a 'seamless web', and to assert that the historian who is most aware of his own place in contemporary society and of the factors which have determined the survival to this day of his evidence is most likely to produce the most illuminating history.

In a typically seminal and incisive essay my predecessor, Ralph Davis, drew attention to the fact that the Normans (of whose military, political and architectural achievements in the eleventh and twelfth centuries medieval historians, especially British medieval historians, have waxed lyrical) were in fact only an identifiable nation because of the conscious fabrication of a Norman 'myth' by a succession of monastic and ecclesiastical authors from Dudo of St Quentin in the 1020s to Wace and Benoıt of Sainte Maure in the 1160s and 1170s.[4] So far as we can tell the myth that the Normans were indeed 'Northmen', that is Scandinavian Vikings, was only put into writing at a time when the distinctively Scandinavian characteristics of the Norman ruling dynasty and aristocracy had (in so far as they had ever existed) entirely disappeared. The 'Normans' of the eleventh and twelfth centuries were in fact Christians not pagans; they spoke French, not Old Norse; and they fought as knights on horseback with the growing chivalric code of northern France, not on foot with round shield and axe in the time-honoured Viking fashion. It was therefore a myth to suppose that the people of Normandy at this time were in any real sense 'Norman'. Yet there was a characteristic, hitherto largely ignored, which did help to distinguish the Normans, and which does seem to derive from the Scandinavian Viking past. I refer, of course, to the Norman hairstyle! If

---

[3] Lord Acton, *Historical Essays and Studies* (London, 1907), pp. 363–4.
[4] R.H.C. Davis, *The Normans and their Myth* (London, 1976), pp. 49–69; for a critical assessment, see G.A. Loud, 'The *Gens Normannorum* – Myth or Reality', *Proceedings of the Battle Conference on Anglo-Norman Studies*, 4 (1981), pp. 104–16.

we may trust the evidence of the Bayeux Tapestry (as here we surely may), not only the Norman knightly aristocracy but even Norman servants and grooms shared a distinctive hairstyle that was not found elsewhere in the Christian West.[5] Norman men shaved the back half of their heads entirely – everything behind a line drawn over the crown from ear to ear. On the front half of the head, forward of this line, the hair was left to grow long. By adopting this grotesque style – or at least it seemed grotesque to modern eyes until very recent years when we have grown accustomed to the self-mutilation of 'skinheads' or of 'punk' multicoloured cockatoos – the Normans were in fact proclaiming their Scandinavian 'roots'. Thus at the beginning of the eleventh-century an English writer wrote a letter in Old English chiding his 'brother' Edward:[6]

> by abandoning the English practices which your fathers followed and by loving the practices of heathen men who begrudge you life . . . [you show] that you despise your race and your ancestors, since in insult to them you dress in Danish fashion with *bared neck* and *blinded eyes* . . . I will say no more about this shameful mode . . . except that he will be accursed who follows heathen practices in his life and dishonours his own race.

In adopting this 'Danish' or rather Viking hairstyle we must therefore recognize that the Normans were making a conscious statement about their origins, however bogus. Any parent of a teenage son or daughter today is very conscious of the danger that the pressures of the child's peer-group may outweigh those of the family, and that hair-style is a particularly effective symbol of allegiance, a means of demonstrating membership of a particular community. The medieval world, like the ancient and like primitive societies the world over today, knew this well too. Hence the totally shaven heads of slaves (as of girls who collaborate with the enemy), hence the largely shaven heads of monks ('slaves of God'), and hence the long hair of free men and women and the ultra-long hair of king-worthy Merovingian princes. The Normans (like all the peoples of northern France) were in reality a mongrel stock of Celtic, Romance and Germanic elements. But since they liked to proclaim the national myth of their Norman origins and to reinforce it with a highly distinctive 'Northman' hair-style it is not surprising that they and their neighbours soon accepted their distinctiveness.

For a century and a half at least, the Normans enjoyed a successful national myth, though they had already abandoned the hairstyle in favour of 'effeminate' long hair before the end of the eleventh century.[7] But what of the English? Had they no national myth? Though the

---

[5] *The Bayeux Tapestry*, ed. D.M. Wilson (London, 1985), plates 9–20.
[6] F. Kluge, 'Fragment eines angelsachsischen Briefes', *Englische Studien*, 8 (1885), pp. 62–3; translated in *EHD*, no. 232, pp. 895–6.

discussion of English origins has not ben couched in Professor Davis's terms, it has recently been powerfully argued that the concept of a single English people (*gens*) was in fact a convenient and potent 'myth' foisted upon the politically fragmented Anglo-Saxons by the early medieval church – in the first place by Pope Gregory I, then by the church of Canterbury and most influentially of all by the Northumbrian monk and historian, Bede.[8] Bede's *Ecclesiastical History of the English People (gentis)* was therefore not only a *tour de force* of research and organization which achieved immediate and deserved popularity; it also gave to all the Anglo-Saxon peoples a share in 'English' history and it provided other peoples with an influential model for national history. I confess, however, that I have my doubts how far this line of argument should be pursued and whether myth and historical reality have yet been success-fully disentangled. Part of the problem lies in *our* inability to decide whether we ought to translate the single Latin word *Angli* as 'the Angles' or 'the English'. I sometimes perversely think that it would help us to avoid seeing early medieval history through the perspective of our modern nationalist preconceptions if we regarded Bede's great work as the *Ecclesiastical History of the Anglian People*. Such a version of Bede's title would make it clearer that this was the work of a Northumbrian Angle; it might also help to explain the extreme uncertainty of other early writers whether their subjects were Anglian or Saxon.[9] We might then be less surprised that the western and northern neighbours of the so-called 'Angles' of Mercia and Northumbria uniformly thought of them as 'Saxons' [and Sassenachs they remain to this day]; conversely, across the channel Pope Gregory I thought of the 'Saxon' or 'Jutish' inhabitants of southern England as *Angli*.[10] Since archaeologists have found no practical means of distinguishing Angles from Saxons in England, despite the acres of print devoted to the subject,[11] it seems to

[7] Ordericus Vitalis, *Ecclesiastical History*, viii.10, ed. M. Chibnall (Oxford, 1973), iv, pp. 186–90; F. Barlow, *William Rufus* (London, 1983), pp. 105–8.

[8] C.P. Wormald, 'Bede, the Bretwaldas and the Origins of the *Gens Anglorum*', in C.P. Wormald et al., eds, *Ideal and Reality: Studies in Frankish and Anglo-Saxon History presented to J.M. Wallace-Hadrill* (Oxford, 1983), pp. 99–129.

[9] Bede, *Historia Eccleasiastica Gentis Anglorum*, ed. R.A.B. Mynors and B. Colgrave (Oxford, 1969), passim. For other eighth-century writers' usage compare 'Eddius' Stephanus, *Vita Wilfridi*, ed. B. Colgrave (Cambridge, 1927), ch. xxi where 'Saxons' refers to the men of Lindsey, and ch. xxx where Wilfrid calls himself 'bishop of the Saxons', with Felix's *Vita Guthlaci*, ed. B. Colgrave (Cambridge, 1956), ch. xxxiv where the Mercians are referred to first as 'Angles', then as 'Saxons'.

[10] For the usage of continental and papal writers, see W. Levison, *England and the Continent in the Eighth Century* (Oxford, 1946), pp. 92–3 and C.P. Wormald, 'Bretwaldas and the *Gens Anglorum*', pp. 122–4; for Welsh and Scottish usage, see *Annales Cambriae* in *Nennius' British History and the Welsh Annals*, ed. J. Morris (Chichester, 1980), pp. 85–91 and Adomnan, *Vita S. Columbae*, ed. A.O. and M.O. Anderson (Edinburgh, 1961), passim.

me hazardous to suppose that the church for its own purposes imposed a myth of a single English *gens* upon divergent ethnic stocks. On the contrary it is likely to have been the warrior-kings and dynasties of the sixth, seventh and eighth centuries that imposed their own myths asserting that their peoples were distinctively Angle, or Saxon or Jutish when in fact this was at most true only of their own dynasties. The confusion of the English sources may rather reflect the fact that the Anglo-Saxons were a more or less uniform mongrel stock from the start; many of the crucial differences, linguistic, material and ethnic, only developed long after their settlement in Britain. If so, we must be very careful how we identify which are the myths that need to be explained.

The myths of other peoples have had fluctuating histories. It is difficult to know what the original function of the myth of the sleeping Emperor Frederick in the Kyffhäuser Mountain was.[12] In the fifteenth and early sixteenth centuries, it was held that the Emperor would return to reform and prune a corrupt church. That may not have been the first form of the myth; it is certainly a far cry thence to the nineteenth-century assumption that the Emperor in question was Frederick I Barbarossa and that he would awake to reunite the German *Volk* and recreate a German Empire. It is a feature of certain myths to be infinitely adaptable. In the mid-1980s when German reunification and German nationalism were uneasy subjects, however, Frederick seemed to sleep very soundly in his East German mountain, effectively buried it seemed by myths of much more recent origin controlled by the regime. By contrast the legends of King Arthur of Britain are known to have enjoyed enormous popularity already in the twelfth century, particularly once Geoffrey of Monmouth had dressed up as serious history what William of Malmesbury had dismissed as 'ditties burbled by Britons'.[13] The *History of the Kings of Britain* is a brilliantly conceived pastiche of myth, song and outright invention masquerading as straightforward history. But its effect was not significantly to strengthen a British belief that they would rise again and oust the Saxons under the leadership of a new Arthur recovered from his long healing in the Isle of Avalon. As British national myth it failed in the face of the realities of the political disunity and the relative poverty of British and Breton principalities. The phenomenal popularity of Geoffrey's *Historia* and of the songs of the Arthurian cycle was a reflection not of their success as a national

---

[11] For recent discussions, see J.N.L. Myres, 'The Angles, Saxons and Jutes', *Proceedings of the British Academy*, 56 (1972), pp. 145–74; C. Hills, 'The Archaeology of Anglo-Saxon England in the Pagan Period', *Anglo-Saxon England*, 8 (1979), pp. 313–17.

[12] P. Munz, *Frederick Barbarossa* (London, 1969), pp. 3–22.

[13] Geoffrey of Monmouth, *Historia Regum Britanniae*, ed. A. Griscom (New York, 1929); William of Malmsbury, *Gesta Regum*, Rolls Series (London, 1887–9), i, p. 11. For the development of the legend see R.S. Loomis, *The Development of Arthurian Romance* (London, 1963).

myth but as an international or class myth. The Arthurian myths
became the literature of the knightly class throughout the Romance and
Germanic speaking worlds and (whatever Geoffrey's intention) this
myth was acceptable to courts and to noble halls both in England and
throughout *le douce France*, as well as across the Alps and the Rhine,
precisely because its political message was defused.

It is easy to adopt a patronizing attitude to the more outlandish
adoptions of myth that we find in the early Middle Ages – such as the
seventh-century Fredegar's use of the legends of ancient Troy to create
a mythical antiquity for the Franks,[14] or the inclusion of Caesar in the
genealogy of an eighth-century ruler of East Anglia, or the claim that
virtually all the eighth-century royal dynasties in England were
descended from the mythical warrior-god Woden.[15] We may be good
enough historians to reject such absurdities but we need to recognize
that new or young nations in our own day still feel the need for myths
that justify the present. Fortunes are being made today, as never before,
by those who are inventing a history for the American people before
Christopher Columbus, with even less material evidence than was available to Geoffrey of Monmouth. Though the Kensington Stone and the
Vinland Map are now known in the scholarly world to be forgeries,[16]
the pace of 'discovery' of supposed runic inscriptions in the USA and
of claimed decipherments of nonexistent runes grows year by year and
is spread over an ever larger proportion of the North American continent. Not content with developing a Viking myth for the Americans,
'Professor' B. Fell and his associates – despite their total lack of philo-
logical or epigraphical expertise – have gone on to 'discover' Ogam,
Punic and hieroglyphic inscriptions throughout the Americas and thus
to add entirely mythical Celtic, Carthaginian and Egyptian settlers to
the proto-American mix.[17] The lunatic fringe of archaeology and of
history is rich indeed and it is but a short step thence to the visitations
of extra-terrestrial inter-galactic beings championed by Erik van
Daniken and his ilk. Nor should we suppose that it is only the
Americans who have an inexhaustible taste for myth. Last Sunday a
full-page advertisement was placed in the Observer magazine for a

[14] Fredegar, *Chronicarum Libri IV*, ed. B. Krush, (MGH, Scriptores rerum
merovingicarum, II (Hanover, 1885) ii.4–8, iii.2.
[15] D.N. Dumville, 'The Anglian Collection of Royal Genealogies and King-Lists',
Anglo-Saxon England, 5 (1976), pp. 23–50.
[16] E. Wahlgren, *The Kensington Stone: A Mystery Solved* (Columbia, 1958); J.R.
Redmond, *Viking Hoaxes in North America* (New York, 1980).
[17] B. Fell, *America BC* (New York, 1976); idem, *Saga America* (New York, 1980);
idem, *Bronze-Age America* (New York, 1982) and the 'Occasional Publications' of the so-
called 'Epigraphical Society of America'. For some critical assessments, see *Antiquity*, 54
(1980) pp. 154–5, 57 (1983) pp. 84–5.

volume entitled *Did the Virgin Mary Live and Die in England?*[18] With bold wishful thinking the author claims to be a millionaire and author of numerous books on business psychology. He calls himself Victor Dunstan thereby linking with Glastonbury's greatest abbot. In a series of improbable assertations about the maternal kin of Jesus being resident in 'England' (which did not exist at the time) he claims the authority of ancient manuscripts and unpublished documents in a variety of English and continental libraries. So far as can be seen from this advertisement – a splendid subject for a first-year School of History 'Principles and Methods' seminar – this example of the genre is heavily based upon the 'Glastonbury legends' which were invented in the twelfth and thirteenth centuries as the need of the largest monastery in England to develop itself as a prime centre of pilgrimage led to ever more implausible claims for its Christian antiquity.[19] But at least the medieval Glastonbury myth-makers knew and respected their bibles, unlike Mr Dunstan. Human gullibility, then, takes different forms in different ages. The skill of the myth-maker lies in attuning the myth so closely to the desires and standards of the age that it is accepted, however improbable: *Mundus vult decepi, ergo decipiatur* – the world wishes to be deceived, and therefore is deceived.[20]

I have mentioned in passing the Kensington stone and the Vinland map, two forgeries which played a crucial role in consolidating the idea that America had been settled by western European peoples long before Columbus. Here then we pass to forgery, and we find it most effective when it is in the service of a potent myth.

Amidst the numerous archaeological forgeries of the last hundred years, by far the most successful was the dramatic 'discovery' and reconstruction between 1908 and 1913 of the so-called 'Piltdown Man' (*Eoanthropus Dawsoni*) which seemed to provide the 'Missing Link' between ape and man for which palaeontologists had been looking ever since Darwin's *Origin of the Species* (1859) and *the Descent of Man* (1871).[21] 'Piltdown Man' would have been inconceivable without the

[18] *Observer* 'Magazine Section', 19 January 1986.

[19] J. Armitage Robinson, *Two Glastonbury Legends: King Arthur and St. Joseph of Arimathea* (Cambridge, 1926); R.F. Treharne, *The Glastonbury Legends* (London, 1967); A. Gransden, 'The Growth of Glastonbury Traditions and Legends', *Journal of Ecclesiastical History*, 27 (1976), pp. 339–46.

[20] For the antiquity, but uncertain origins of this epigram, see G. Constable, 'Forgery and Plagiarism in the Middle Ages', *Archiv für Diplomatik*, 29 (1983), pp. 1–41 at 1.

[21] C. Dawson and A.S. Woodward, 'On the Discovery of a Palaeolithic Skull and Mandible in a Flint Bearing Gravel Overlying the Wealden (Hasting) Beds at Piltdown, Sussex', *Quarterly Journal of the Geological Society of London*, 69 (1913), pp. 117–44. For the exposure of the forgery, see J.S. Weiner, K.P. Oakley and W.E. Le Gros Clark, 'The Solution of the Piltdown Problem', *Bulletin of the British Museum (Natural History) Geology*, 2, no. 3 (1953), pp. 225–87 and also J.S. Weiner's popular account in *The Piltdown Forgery* (London, 1955) to which I am heavily indebted for what follows.

intellectual tumult stirred up by Darwin which had converted two generations of Victorian and Edwardian gentlemen into avid fossil-collectors, geologists and archaeologists. Not until 1953, when the fashion for fossil-collecting had subsided in Britain and the leading participants (both the duper and the duped) had long passed into the grave did three scientists pool their expertise and collaborate in a series of tests that quickly exposed the fraudulent association of a semi-petri-fied human skull with an artificially stained and hardened orang-utan jaw which had had its most distinctive features removed. Not until 1955 in J.S. Weiner's popular account was the finger of suspicion tentatively pointed at Charles Dawson, the respected Uckfield solicitor and antiquarian polymath known as the 'Wizard of Sussex' from the amazing series of discoveries with which he was associated. Even now doubts remain, and it has been suggested that Dawson was an innocent enthusiast who was duped by his colleague – the hitherto irreprochable Sam Woodhead, schoolmaster and Public Analyst in Brighton.[22]

When new theories are about to be presented, caution might be advised. But I must confess that the preliminary publication of the attempt to clear Dawson seems to me utterly unconvincing. It was Dawson who identified the stratum of gravel in the road-workings beside the Piltdown road as a potential fossil-bearing level and who warned the workmen in 1908 to keep their eyes skinned for fossils. It was Dawson who then collected the broken skull fragments when they had duly turned up, and who asserted that the level was of Pleistocene or Pliocene formation. It was Dawson who found the jaw, and it was he who involved the learned palaeontologist Arthur Smith Woodward and the young Teilhard de Chardin in the excavations where they discovered other vital fragments, and who enthused Woodward to produce the reconstruction of the head of Piltdown Man and to publish the find jointly with him. None of this proves his guilt – merely that he had the opportunity. Nor should we pay too much attention to the fact that Dawson was distrusted throughout Sussex archaeological and geological circles.[23] *Odium academicum* for the apparently successful amateur is not unknown even today. Dawson was certainly a notable geologist and a justly-famed fossil-collector,[24] though doubts are today beginning to be expressed about some of his 'discoveries'. Nor should we necessarily

---

[22] See the preliminary statement of P. Costello, 'The Piltdown Hoax Reconsidered', *Antiquity*, 59 (1985), pp. 167–73. For further speculation on the identity of the hoaxer(s), see G. Daniel, 'Piltdown and Professor Hewitt', *Antiquity*, 60 (1986), pp. 59–60.

[23] Weiner, *Piltdown Forgery*, pp. 155–9, 169–88. Compare L.G. Salzman's acid footnote in *Sussex Archaeological Collections*, p. 85 (1946), 38, n.. 1: 'His name was later given to the Piltdown Man (*Eoanthropus Dawsoni*), the lowest known form of human being, with the discovery of whose remains he was associated.'

[24] Weiner, *Piltdown Forgery*, pp. 82–5.

convict Dawson because even by the standards of the day he was a poor archaeologist whose chaotic excavation of the Lavant caves (1893) produced (or were said to have produced) Neolithic flints, Roman finds and medieval woolseals, but were never published.[25] Nor should we convict Dawson because he published in his own name a *History of Hastings Castle* some of which copies verbatim an unpublished manuscript of the antiquary, William Herbert;[26] nor should we be disturbed if his account of the Wealden iron industry for his exhibition of 1903 proves to be (like many exhibition catalogues) second-hand and hasty work.[27] Hasty scholars with too many irons in too many fires are not necessarily forgers!

Two things damn Dawson in my eyes. Firstly he was associated not just with Piltdown Man but with an astonishing series of 'discoveries' between 1893 and 1913. Some were published by others from material provided by Dawson, some were published by Dawson but were said to have been discovered by others who had died meantime. Several were said to have disintegrated shortly after discovery but not before they had been conveniently drawn by Dawson or by their finder. All are odd; several are incredible; and no less than four have been proved independently to be forgeries.

In 1893 Dawson exhibited a supposedly Roman cast-iron figurine reputedly found 20 years earlier with Hadrianic coins; it was dismissed at the time and seems to have been a nineteenth-century casting.[28] In 1894 he published a boat exposed on the Sussex coast after storms. This extraordinary boat was, Dawson boldly claimed, 'transitional' between a British coracle and a Viking long-ship, but it had disintegrated soon after he had drawn it.[29] In the same year he published a neolithic axe with its carbonized and decorated wooden haft (handle) still intact, but this too had conveniently disintegrated after drawing.[30] Dawson's interest in Sussex iron-work led him to acquire about the turn of the century the Ashburnham ironworks clock, which at some stage in

[25] Hadrian Allcroft's critical account of Dawson's excavation in *Sussex Archaeological Collections*, 57 (1916), p. 65, was delivered in July 1916 when Dawson was on his deathbed (he died on 10 August 1916).

[26] C. Dawson *History of Hastings Castle*, 2 vols (London, 1909) which was critically reviewed in *Sussex Archaeological Collections*, 53 (1910), p. 282. For Manwaring-Baines discovery of the plagiarism, see Weiner, *Piltdown Forgery*, pp. 176–7. Costello's brief defence of Dawson ('Piltdown Hoax', p. 168) does not meet the criticisms.

[27] C. Dawson, 'Sussex Iron-Work', *Sussex Archaeological Collections*, 46 (1903), pp. 1–54, see further Weiner, *Piltdown Forgery*, pp. 181–2.

[28] Ibid., pp. 182–3; despite its reception it was exhibited by Dawson again in 1903 (*Sussex Archaeological Collections*, 46 (1903), pp. 4–5).

[29] C. Dawson, 'Ancient Boat Found at Bexhill', *Sussex Archaeological Collections*, 39 (1894), pp. 161–3.

[30] 'Neolithic Flint Weapon in a Wooden Haft', *ibid.*, pp. 97–8.

its history received an engraved face now known to be an anachronistic forgery rather than a contemporary depiction of remarkable ironworking techniques.[31] In 1906 he was associated with the discovery of forged 'Roman' tiles which had been planted in the excavation of the Roman Saxon Shore fort of Pevensey and which bore stamped inscriptions with the name of the Emperor Honorius.[32] A supposed Norman prick-spur which is now believed to be nothing of the sort and a remarkable fossil fish claimed to be a 'cross' between a carp and a goldfish followed in 1909,[33] and a supposedly eighteenth-century (but actually forged) map of Maresfield forge in 1911.[34] In this cumulatively incredible list we can find patterns that recur at Piltdown: a concern with evolutionary or technical advances, original discovery by 'workmen', a 'shepherd', 'fisherman' or the like, recognition by Dawson, the association of established scholars in the ultimate discovery or in the publication, and the planting of forged evidence on excavation sites. If Dawson were indeed duped at Piltdown in 1911–12, then we should also need to suppose that skilled hoaxers had been deceiving him for the previous twenty years.

The second piece of damning evidence lies in that work of Dawson's where I first encountered him. In 1907 Dawson published an article on the restorations of the Bayeux Tapestry.[35] Dawson here had hit upon a most important problem: how do we establish the authority of the Tapestry today when it does not conform with the earliest (eighteenth-century) engravings? Dawson's solution – to charge the antiquarian artist Stothard and the 1842 restorers who followed his designs with fraudulent forgery – in fact proves to be totally unacceptable when one compares the earliest engravings and the nineteenth-century drawings with the Tapestry itself.[36] Again and again the eighteenth-century

---

[31] J.H. Cambridge, 'The Ashburnham Ironworks Clock', *Antiquarian Horology*, Autumn 1977; J.G. McDonnell, 'The Ashburnham Clock', *Ryedale Historian*, 8 (1976), pp. 44–5. The clock is illustrated in E. Straker, *Wealden Iron* (London, 1932), pp. 75–7.

[32] The Pevensey tiles were published in good faith by L.F. Salzmann in *Sussex Archaeological Collections*, 51 (1908), pp. 112–13. For their exposure as forgeries, see D.P.S. Peacock, 'Forged Brick-Stamps from Pevensey', *Antiquity*, 47 (1973), pp. 138–40.

[33] Weiner, *Piltdown Forgery*, p. 186.

[34] P.B.S. Andrews, 'A Fictitious Purported Historical Map', *Sussex Archaeological Collections*, 112 (1974), pp. 165–7; see also J. Petit, 'No absolution [for C. Dawson]', *Sussex Archaeological Newsletter*, 15 (1975).

[35] C. Dawson, *The 'Restorations' of the Bayeux Tapestry* (London, 1907).

[36] N.P. Brooks and the late H.E. Walker, 'The Authority and Interpretation of the Bayeux Tapestry', *Proceedings of the Battle Conference on Anglo-Norman Studies*, 1 (1978), pp. 24–6 (reprinted in Brooks, *Communities and Warfare 700–1400* (London, 2000), pp. 175–218, at 205–6). In D.M. Wilson's magnificent full-colour reproduction (*Bayeux Tapestry*, London, 1985) it is possible to distinguish original work from the principal restorations.

engravings can be shown to be inaccurate by comparison with the unrestored parts of the Tapestry. Again and again detailed comparison confirms Stothard's scholarly accuracy. Dawson did not have the advantage of the recent superb colour reproductions of the Tapestry, but in his article we can surely see the mentality of the compulsive forger who himself flings out accusations because that is exactly the way his own mind works.

The climate of gentlemanly scholarship and of public fame that kept Dawson immune from exposure long after his death in 1916 despite the individual resentments and suspicions of local scholars can be almost exactly paralleled in the career of Dawson's younger contemporary, Sir Edward Backhouse, as indeed can many of their methods of work.[37] Backhouse with a brilliant oriental linguist and an amazing charlatan. Just as Dawson was a most generous benefactor of museums, so Backhouse made the Bodleian Library the richest Western European repository of Chinese manuscripts and printed books (not to mention of forgeries). Like Dawson, Backhouse denounced the forgeries published by other Sinologists. Like Dawson, Backhouse made sure that his most extravagant and successful forgery was published not just in his own name but also in that of the respected journalist, J.O.P. Bland – namely the diary of the Chinese courtier Ching-San, which formed the principal source of Bland and Backhouse's *China under the Empress Dowager* (1910). Like Dawson, Backhouse perpetrated an ever growing series of hoaxes – spurious ship-building contracts for the long suffering John Brown & Co. of Clydeside, spurious and huge arms deals as a secret agent of the British Government in the Great War, spurious currency deals for the American Bank Note Company and so on and so on. Those he duped proved to be so embarrassed that he was never publicly denounced. He was not indeed exposed until the manuscript of his deathbed memoirs – full of plausible but excessive sexual adventures with the literary figures of his youth in England and France and with all the Chinese politicians of his maturity – came into the sceptical hands of the Regius Professor of Modern History in the University of Oxford for safe transfer to the Bodleian. H. Trevor-Roper (now Lord Dacre) could not read a single Chinese character, but he could piece together an amazingly damning picture from the papers of those who knew and suffered from Backhouse's fraudulent schemes.

Similar lessons can be drawn from the careers of other warped and thwarted near-geniuses who also worked in fields where public interest was great but expertise was very rare. We may cite fine-art forgers like Van Meegeren and his bogus Vermeers or Tom Keating and his

[37] H. Trevor-Roper, *A Hidden Life* (London, 1976).

Samuel Palmers;[38] or Thomas Wise, book collector and book thief, and compulsive forger of 'first editions' of English poets;[39] or the great forger of classical texts and inscriptions François Lenormant;[40] and it is not without irony that it should have been Trevor-Roper, the brilliant exposer of Backhouse's frenetic Walter Mitty career of endless hoaxes, who should recently have given his tentative blessing to the publication of the forged *Diaries of Adolf Hitler*. With the pressures and temptations of television and in areas beyond our true competence, which of us would not prove equally credulous?

For the modern historian forgery of documents or of texts is a rare phenomenon amongst the enormous mass of the surviving archival and narrative records; when forgery is detected, I suspect it provides a pleasant diversion along unusual paths. For medievalists, however, or more correctly for the early medievalist, forgery is an ever present problem, affecting a high proportion of the surviving evidence. Thus for example the great German student of diplomatic, Heinrich Bresslau, pointed out that over 50 per cent of the extant diplomas in the names of the Merovingian Frankish kings [that is those of the seventh and eighth centuries] are in fact forgeries.[41] In England Dr Clanchy has drawn attention to the fact that of the writs and charters attributed to the eleventh-century ruler, Edward the Confessor, scarcely 40 per cent are generally accepted as being authentic.[42] Of course certain famous kings and popes were particularly favoured by forgers [and Edward was amongst these], but it is otherwise broadly true that the older a medieval document claims to be, the more likely it is to be forged. This is not because age was in itself a desirable quality, but because few people in the Middle Ages knew (or could prove) what an early document ought to look like. The risk of detection was therefore proportionately less the older it claimed to be.

The pattern of the incidence of medieval forgery has been well studied in recent years by British and continental scholars and there is general agreement that whilst we can find forgeries of various types in every medieval century, the pattern is not an even one.[43] A brief but

[38] P. Coremans, *Van Meegeren's Faked Vermeers and De Hooghs* (London, 1949); T. Keating, *The Fake's Progress* (London, 1977).

[39] J. Carter and G. Pollard, *An Enquiry into the Nature of Certain Nineteenth-Century Pamphlets* (London, 1934).

[40] H. Roehl, 'In Franciscum Lenormant inscriptionum falsarium', *Hermes*, 17 (1882), pp. 460–6 and 18 (1883), pp. 97–103.

[41] H. Bresslau, *Handbuch der Urkundenlehre* (3rd edn., Berlin, 1958–60), i, p. 15.

[42] M.T. Clanchy, *From Memory to Written Record* (London, 1979), pp. 248–9 citing the evidence gathered in P.H. Sawyer, *Anglo-Saxon Charters: An Annotated List and Bibliography* (London, 1968), pp. 298–343.

[43] H. Silvestre, 'Le problème des faux au moyen age', *Moyen Age*, 66 (1960), pp. 362–6. C.N.L. Brooke, 'Approaches to Medieval Forgery', *Journal of the Society of*

dramatic peak is reached in the ninth century with a group of astonishing forgeries: the Donation of Constantine (as we now have it)
forged by John the Deacon 'of the maimed fingers' in order to promote
the independence and the burgeoning territorial claims of the Papacy;[44]
or the 'Pseudo-Isidoran' collection of bogus papal decretals produced in
a north-French episcopal centre [?Rheims];[45] or the great series of
multifarious forged texts and documents produced at Le Mans to
support its bishops' territorial ambition.[46] But the great age of forgery is
agreed to lie between the late eleventh and the late twelfth century.

At this time, as Morey and Brooke have written: 'Respectable men
and respectable communities forged as they had not forged before and
would never forge again.'[47] The phenomenon is Europe-wide, not
limited to any one kingdom, province or region. It is undoubtedly a
reflection of the growing use of written records and therefore of the
growing awareness of the inadequacy of the records already possessed.
The enormous growth in the provision of every level of schooling in
twelfth-century Western Europe and the consequent growth of literacy
and development in the keeping of archives are all, as Clanchy has
taught us, part and parcel of a major transformation of medieval
society: the gradual switch from reliance predominantly on human
memory to reliance predominantly on the written record.[48] Initially this
development gave a great boost to forgery as churches found that their
records no longer satisfied the requirements of a new age, and they
sought to provide what was lacking. But in the longer run, the twelfth-
century renaissance contained the seeds of the decline of forgery. As
governments and courts became more used to written records they
devised means of making documents more difficult to forge; they later
went on to ensure that a record was maintained of settlements and
judgements reached and of documents issued. Of course bureaucracies
were by no means always efficient in finding particular documents in

Archivists, 3(8) (1968), pp. 377–86 reprinted in idem, *Medieval Church and Society:
Collected Essays* (London, 1971), pp. 100–20; H. Fuhrmann et al., 'Die Falschungen im
Mittelalter', *Historische Zeitschrift*, 197 (1963), pp. 529–601; Clanchy *Memory to Written
Record*, pp. 119–20, 248 ff; G. Constable, 'Forgery and Plagiarism', *Archiv für
Diplomatik*, 29 (1983), pp. 1–41.

[44] H. Fuhrmann (ed.), *Constitutum Constantini*, MGH Fontes iuris Germanici
antiqui, X (Hanover, 1968); for the identity of the forger, see the donation of Otto III to
the Roman church in 1001 which is conveniently translated by B. Pullan, *Sources for the
History of Medieval Europe* (Oxford, 1966), pp. 121–2.

[45] H. Fuhrmann, *Einfluss und Verbreitung der pseudoisidorischen Fälschungen*, MGH
Schriften, XXIV (Stuttgart, 1972–4).

[46] W. Goffart, *The Le Mans Forgeries* (Cambridge, MA, 1966).

[47] A. Morey and C.N.L. Brooke, *Gilbert Foliot and his Letters* (Cambridge, 1965), p.
127.

[48] Clanchy, *Memory to Written Record*.

their registers and rolls; but the mere fact that such records were known to exist made documentary forgery less safe. The tide of forgery of charters, then, reflects broad developments in European cultural history. It is clear that the new 'age of government records' – which in England, France and at the papal curia begins at the very beginning of the thirteenth century or just before – marked the end of the great age of forgery, or at least it partially closed certain avenues for the forgers.

If we turn from the broad pattern of medieval forgery to the individual forgers, then we immediately encounter a great contrast to the forgers of the modern era. Medieval forgers – in so far as we can yet know them – were not quirky intellectual misfits with giant chips on their shoulders. There were some professional forgers in the Middle Ages and there were also forgers of coinage to parallel the normally faceless forgers of banknotes or credit cards of today. But forgery was a serious crime, both in secular and in canon law, and for laymen it was a very dangerous one. At his Christmas court in 1124 Henry I had all the moneyers of England gathered together and mutilated by cutting off their right hands and by castrating them – a radical means of demonstrating his wrath – because many of them had been forging or debasing the coinage. He thereby enforced a penalty that went back to late-Roman legislation on counterfeiting gold coins and to the laws of the Lombard kings of Italy of the seventh and eighth centuries;[49] but forgers who were in holy orders avoided mutilatory sentences by virtue of their cloth. They faced simply loss of office and of their orders. Gregory of Tours records how Bishop Egidius of Rheims was deposed when the documents he had presented to a court of bishops at Metz were shown to be forgeries by the referendary; and in 1095 Pope Urban II deposed Bishop Humbald of Limoges for forgery.[50] If forgery was then a serious crime, it is difficult for the scholar of today not to be shocked by the realization that the vast majority of extant medieval forgeries were fabricated by, or on behalf of, monks. The 'servants of God' prove to have included amongst their number a significant proportion of master criminals. We may mitigate our shock by pointing out that monastic archives of the twelfth century have survived rather better than episcopal, let alone than secular, muniments. But we should surely be cautious before deducing from the proliferation of twelfth-century forgery that it was lightly regarded, that everyone knew that it

[49] ASC, E. s.a. 1125, ed and trans D. Whitelock et al. (London, 1961), 191. P. Grierson, 'The Roman Law of Counterfeiting', in R.A.G. Carson and C.H.V. Sutherland, eds, *Essays in Roman Coinage presented to H. Mattingly*, (Oxford, 1956), pp. 255–6. See further Constable, 'Forgery and Plagiarism', p. 17, n. 82.
[50] Gregory of Tours, *Historia Francorum*, B. Krusch and W. Levison, MGH Scriptores Rerum Merovingicarum, I, x.19; for Humbert of Limoges, see H.E.J. Cowdrey, *The Cluniacs and the Gregorian Reform* (Oxford, 1970), p. 94.

went on and conspired to turn a blind eye to it. German scholars indeed have championed the view that medieval forgers intended through their work to realize God's plan on earth and to establish or restore things to their proper order. Forgery in Fuhrmann's view was an effort to establish order, to protect and assert what was held to be truth and justice.[51] But there is, surely, a danger that in seeking to understand the forger and his self-delusions, we minimize the extent of the deceptions he perpetrated.

That the majority of monastic forgers were working for the glorification and defence of their own order or of their own house rather than for direct personal profit is clear enough. The monk Guerno whose famous deathbed confession, sometime between 1119 and 1131, revealed that he had forged charters for the monasteries of St Medard of Soissons, of St Ouen at Rouen and also for St Augustine's at Canterbury, also confessed that he had received some precious ornaments for his work and that he had kept them to the end at St Medard.[52] But it is difficult to regard these ornaments – even in the communal world of the Benedictine monastery – as in any real sense 'payment' for his work. Moreover, a very high proportion of the medieval forgers who have been identified, turn out to be drawn from the very highest ranks of ecclesiastical and monastic society. They were not men who needed private gain to further their careers. Thus Professor Cronne showed that when Robert de Sigillo ('of the Seal') who had headed Henry I's chancery and kept his seal, retired to spend his last days as a monk at Reading Abbey, he was soon engaged in forging a royal charter for the Reading brethren.[53] Clearly the arrival of a new brother with specialist knowledge of exactly how royal charters were drawn up was too great an opportunity to be missed. Dr Eleanor Searle has shown that Abbot Walter of Battle Abbey – the Conqueror's foundation – was himself responsible for the series of forgeries to buttress Battle's struggle to free itself from episcopal control in the mid-twelfth century.[54] Even more dramatic is the example of Osbert de Clare, the reforming and critical prior of Westminster who completed the first full Westminster version of the *Life of St Edward the Confessor* in 1138 and who in the following year set out for Rome to secure papal approval for the cult. Osbert took with him three vast charters written in gold letters and attributed to Edward in order to reinforce the case for the king's sanctity. But the charters were forged and Dr P. Chaplais has

[51] H. Fuhrmann, 'Die Falschungen im Mittelalter', p. 553.

[52] Levison, *England and the Continent*, pp. 207–8.

[53] H.A. Cronne and R.H.C. Davis, eds, *Regesta Regum Anglo-Normannorum*, 4 (1969), pp. 5–6 and plate X.

[54] E. Searle, 'Battle Abbey and Exemption: The Forged Charters', *English Historical Review*, 83 (1968), pp. 449–80.

shown that, like many others in the Westminster archive, their stylistic and verbal parallels establish that the forger was Prior Osbert himself.[55] Moving up the ecclesiastical hierarchy, I may be permitted to cite the example of Archbishop Wulfred of Canterbury who in the early ninth century engaged in a heroic struggle to wrest control of the Kentish monasteries from the Mercian rulers of Kent and from their kinsfolk. There is good reason to think that in the face of both royal and papal pressure, the archbishop himself forged the charters which purported to show that earlier Mercian and Kentish kings had granted to the archbishops exactly the rights in dispute.[56]

Such eminent forgers, already at the peak of their monastic or ecclesiastical careers, cannot be compared with the compulsive forgers and hoaxers of the modern era who sought academic or artistic recognition or else private gain. Medieval forgery derived not so much from the personal psychological inadequacies of the forger as from the pressures upon his institution and from the formidable internally generated pressures that can develop in celibate communities of highly educated monks or nuns. No one can be unaware of these pressures who reads Thomas of Marlborough's fascinating but tortuous account in the *Evesham Chronicle* of the pressures which led him to lead the prolonged rebellion of the stronger-minded monks against the dissolute and tyrannical Abbot Roger Norreys.[57] But when the bishop of Worcester attempted to intervene to settle the dispute and to restore proper monastic order, the rebels and the hated abbot made common cause to resist the episcopal intruder. Eventually they took their joint case against episcopal visitation to Rome. There in 1205 the papal curia examined the forged papal bulls that the Evesham deputation, led by Thomas, produced to support its case for exemption. Pope Innocent III, who had himself drawn up sophisticated guidelines for detecting forgeries of papal documents, could not in this case refer to the papal registers – for no register of the early-eighth-century pope, Constantine I, survived. So pope and cardinals handed the privileges around, tugged at the threads by which the leaden bulls were attached and pronounced them genuine. Here then we see why so many forgeries were ascribed to early medieval rulers and popes. Even the best organized of chanceries, even the pope most aware of the threat of forgery, could not detect a

[55] P. Chaplais, 'The Original Charters of Herbert and Gervase, Abbots of Westminster (1121–1157)', in P.M. Barnes and C.F. Slade, eds, *A Medieval Miscellany for D.M. Stenton*, Pipe Roll Society, new series, 36 (1960), pp. 89–110.

[56] N.P. Brooks, *The Early History of the Church of Canterbury* (Leicester, 1984), pp. 191–7.

[57] *Chronicon Abbatiae de Evesham*, ed. W. Macray, Rolls Series (London, 1863). The best modern account remains that of D. Knowles, *The Monastic Order in England* (Cambridge, 1941), pp. 331–45.

competent forgery if it claimed to be old enough. It is, I believe, for this reason that such a high proportion of medieval forgery was committed by monks of old-established houses, that is by 'Black' or Benedictine monks from monasteries founded in the early medieval centuries. There is no reason to suppose that such houses had a greater proportion of criminals than the newer reformed orders of the twelfth and thirteenth centuries. But only the long-established orders had the opportunity to claim that they had received grants from early kings or popes. Moreover, only they could realistically fell intense frustration that their earliest records were so maddeningly vague or silent about the vital issues of privilege, land and jurisdiction that were now in dispute in the twelfth century.

Having defeated the bishops of Worcester, Thomas of Marlborough went back to the struggle with Abbot Roger. When Roger was eventually removed in 1213, Thomas's own path to promotion, first as prior and then in 1229 as abbot, was clear. It is already known that the marvellously detailed account of these struggles and of the history of his house that he has left us in the *Evesham Chronicle* involved doctoring earlier Evesham narratives.[58] What has yet to be determined is whether he was personally responsible for the forged bulls presented at Rome in 1205 and which of his twelfth-century precursors was responsible for the astonishing series of forged charters claiming to be grants to Evesham by Anglo-Saxon kings. Amongst some twenty-eight extant diplomas, not one seems to be a copy of an authentic charter.[59] A marvellous research topic awaits a diligent researcher.

It is, of course, possible in the accounts of the 'discovery' of medieval forgeries to find close parallels to the excuses that modern forgers like Backhouse or Dawson have used to explain the circumstances of the appearance of the forgery. Fire at Canterbury cathedral in 1067 and at the abbey of Croyland in 1091 provided a convenient excuse for the community's inability to produce properly sealed papal bulls or royal writs.[60] The discovery of the 'copies' (which we can recognize as forgeries) in some suitably forgotten spot might be said to be attended by miraculous revelations. The Canterbury monk, historian, and perhaps forger Eadmer, describes how in 1120 the Canterbury case for

[58] A. Gransden, *Historical Writing in England, 550–1307* (London, 1974), pp. 111–14. M. Lapidge, 'Dominic of Evesham's *Vita S. Ecgwini*', *Analecta Bollandiana*, 96 (1978), pp. 65–104.

[59] S 54, 78, 79, 80, 81, 83, 97, 112, 115, 191, 203, 226, 873, 935, 957, 991, 1026, 1052, 1053, 1057, 1058, 1174, 1175, 1214, 1123, 1238, 1398, 1479. Important work on the Evesham cartularies has been done by H.B. Clark, 'Early Surveys of Evesham Abbey' (unpublished Ph.D. thesis, University of Birmingham, 1977).

[60] Eadmer, *Historia Novorum in Anglia*, ed. M. Rule, Rolls Series (London, 1884), p. 261, *Ingulph's Chronicle*, trans H.T. Riley (1854), p. 201.

primatial authority over the see of York and all other sees in Britain appeared to be being lost; the monks therefore put their trust in God and by divine revelation after long searches discovered in some ancient gospel-books almost a dozen papal bulls of various dates from the seventh to the eleventh century, which in Canterbury eyes confirmed their claims.[61]

At least one of the gospel-books in question survives to this day, though it has been insufficiently studied because it was broken up by Sir Robert Cotton in the early seventeenth century and the leaves on which the papal letters were written are now bound up in separate volumes. Thanks to the codicological detective work of the late N.R. Ker, however, it is possible to reconstruct the contents of the so-called 'Athelstan Gospels' in the form in which they had lain upon the high altar in the cathedral at Canterbury. This beautiful book with its classical Carolingian minuscule script and golden initials seems to have once belonged to the German king Otto I and to his mother Matilda, and to have been given by King Athelstan to Christ Church, Canterbury.[62] The inscriptions with the names of Otto and Matilda and those recording Athelstan's gift of the book to Christ Church in prose and verse were entered by different scribes of the second quarter of the tenth century in available spaces of blank parchment between the end of one gospel and the beginning of the next. At some date before *c.* 1030 the volume was rebound – perhaps to provide a more handsome binding – and at the same time the opportunity was taken to insert additional blank leaves between each of the four gospels. It is possible that the original intention was to provide prefatory illuminated pages before each gospel and thus to make the book conform to the pattern of the most sumptuous English altar-books. If so, the plan was never fulfilled. The example of the insertion of the notices of Athelstan's gift of the book proved too seductive. Between *c.* 1030 and 1125 a series of charters and privileges as well as numerous brief notes of bequests to the cathedral church were inserted into every inch of the space that had been made available in this sacred and royal book.[63] Because of their brevity we cannot determine the authenticity of the short notes of grants and bequests, but every royal charter and every

[61] Eadmer, *Historia Novorum*, pp. 261–76.

[62] For this gospel-book (BL, Cotton Tiberius A. ii), see S.D. Keynes, 'King Athelstan's Books', in M. Lapidge and H. Gneuss, eds, *Learning and Literature in Anglo-Saxon England: Studies presented to Peter Clemoes on the Occasion of his Sixty-Fifth Birthday* (Cambridge, 1985), pp. 147–53. For the correct placing of the leaves that once formed part of this manuscript but were removed by Sir Robert Cotton, see N.R. Ker, 'Membra Disiecta', *British Museum Quarterly*, 12 (1937–8), pp. 130–1.

[63] N.P. Brooks, 'The Pre-Conquest Charters of Christ Church Canterbury' (unpublished D.Phil. thesis, University of Oxford, 1969), pp. 73–102, 313–16.

papal bull that was recorded in this gospel-book in full is in fact a forgery. The dismal series starts with the very first inserted document which was entered between the gospels of Luke and John by the master-scribe of the Christ Church community, the monk Eadui Basan.[64] This charter purported to be a refoundation by King Æthelred II of the monastic chapter of the cathedral in the year 1006 together with the king's confirmation of all the landed possessions (which are listed at length) of the reformed community. Following this example the blank spaces between the gospels seem to act acted as a magnet to Canterbury forgers, and at least eight different scribes entered a further nineteen forged documents in the course of the following century.[65] These forgeries include the famous Canterbury 'primacy forgeries', which were finally denounced at the papal curia in 1123, though they were not all written in the gospel-book at one time nor by the same scribe. In some of the entries we can detect traces of revision and redrafting, seemingly by the forger himself; in others we appear to have a fair copy. But in this sacred volume which was kept on the altar of Christ at Canterbury, we can detect, not the work of a single compulsive forger, but a volume whose unassailable authority, both holy and royal, made it the ideal place for entering forgeries and giving them status to compensate for the absence of genuine documents with genuine wax seals or leaden bulls.

Interestingly (though not without justice), almost none of these forgeries seems in the long run to have secured for the monks and the see of Canterbury the rights or privileges that were in dispute. Despite the efforts of monastic forgers, it would seem that the lying pen was not always stronger than the blunt sword, and that the world did not always wish to be deceived. There was still room for historical truth, if only because the monks' opponents retained greater influence than they. The historian has a duty to the public to expose myths, to reveal and explain forgeries and to show what interests – private, institutional or governmental – lie behind them. Whether the world will notice or will continue to be deceived must depend upon our ability to present the case in a form that attracts rather than repels the world, that is upon how we profess our subject. I hope that my words tonight have indicated that the search for historical truth involves the exposure of forgery and myth, whether in medieval chronicles and charters, in archaeological museums and excavation reports, or in the popular literature and the purported memoirs and diaries of our own age. It is an exciting and important quest.

[64] KCD 715 (= S 914). For its forgery by Eadui Basan, see Brooks, *Early History*, pp. 257–9.

[65] Listed in Brooks, 'Pre-Conquest Charters', pp. 314–16.

2

Introduction to
'The Making of England'

T HE ANGLO-SAXONS, whose artistic, technological and cultural achievements in the seventh, eighth and ninth centuries were displayed in the exhibition 'The Making of England' (British Museum, 1991), were the true ancestors of the English of today. At the time these works were produced, there were several rival Anglo-Saxon kingdoms, each of which had its own dynasty, its own aristocracy and its own separate traditions and loyalties. Spoken English already showed wide regional variations of dialect. None the less the Anglo-Saxons had a sense that they were one people. Thus their greatest historian, the Northumbrian monk, Bede, chose to write the 'Ecclesiastical History' of the single 'English people', not of separate English kingdoms. This overriding sense of belonging to a common race derived from a shared experience of migration from the continent and of winning land from the native British population. It also derived from a common past allegiance to pagan Germanic gods (Woden, Thor, Frig and many others) and from having accepted Christianity in a manner that tied the Anglo-Saxons closely to the authority of Rome. It therefore made sense to view the greatest surviving examples of their artistic skills in jewellery, sculpture and manuscript illumination in one exhibition. It is also instructive to examine the books they wrote, or the gold and silver coins they produced or their workmanship in bone, leather and textile, in one overall sequence. But if we are to understand and appreciate their achievement fully, we must know something of who the Anglo-Saxons really were and how they actually lived.

Britain by 600

In the fifth and sixth centuries Britian had undergone astonishing polit-ical, economic and cultural changes. Political control of the island came to be split between the indigenous Celtic peoples, who retained or acquired power in the western and highland areas of the island, and Germanic 'Anglo-Saxon' invaders, who took over much of the east and south, that is those regions more suited to arable than to pastoral agriculture. Unlike the other provinces of the Roman Empire, Britain reverted to barbarianism, that is to an essentially prehistoric warrior culture. After the Roman legions had been withdrawn and the Emperor Honorius had in 410 instructed the British cities to provide for their own defences, the whole structure of the Roman state rapidly disintegrated: the army and civil service immediately, the cities and villas more slowly.

With the demise of the Roman state, the Latin language was also gradually abandoned (except by the Christian church) in favour of British (or 'Primitive Welsh'). This triumph of Celtic over Romance speech sets Britain in striking contrast to the continent. The British kings, 'tyrants' or war-lords, who can be briefly seen in the fifth century in the writings of St Patrick and in the sixth in those of the Welsh monk Gildas, were not Roman senatorial aristocrats aping a Roman lifestyle in surviving Roman villas. They were rather British-speaking leaders of war-bands of aristocratic warriors, who had carved principalities for themselves out of the maelstrom of the collapse of imperial authority. Their power depended upon raiding the territories of their neighbours for gold or silver, for cattle and for captives who could be enslaved.

The economy of Roman Britain had collapsed in these so-called 'Dark Ages'. Without a paid Roman army and a paid Roman civil service, there was no longer a need for Roman currency, so the supply of new coins from Roman mints on the continent quickly dried up. Without the need to equip, feed and clothe the troops and officials of the Empire, not only the Romano-British pottery industries but also a whole range of urban crafts in metal, bone and leather died or decayed. The cities of Roman Britain had always been artificial creations superimposed upon an Iron Age economy. Many of them had already been in decay in the later fourth century; all now went into rapid decline, though their walls and ditches retained military significance. Sometimes Roman imperial or municipal authority may have passed to British kings, such as the three who seem to have been associated with Gloucester, Circencester and Bath in 577. In other towns churches may have continued to serve a Christian population of British origin. But urban marketing and trade seem to have withered with the collapse of the currency; town-buildings decayed and were replaced either in timber or not at all, so that the Roman street-layouts and Roman property boundaries were lost almost everywhere. The economy of sub-Roman Celtic Britain was a far more primitive one than its Roman predecessor: a tiny warrior aristocracy extracted treasure and tribute from a rural population, whether free or unfree, who were engaged in subsistence agriculture, predominantly pastoral.

Whilst these dramatic changes were in train, the large part of lowland Britain was passing from British to Anglo-Saxon control, and the language of the southern and eastern half of the island was in the process of becoming English and its culture pagan. Written sources preserve only the most rudimentary information about these cataclysmic changes. The British monk Gildas, in the mid-sixth century, wrote of the 'Saxons' being invited to Britain as mercenary troops to defend the British communities from attacks by their northern enemies. He told how the Saxons rebelled against their paymasters over the issue of rations, and of their subsequent bloody conquests 'from sea to sea'. This Saxon rising and conquest of much of Britain is dated to the year 441–2 by a contemporary chronicler in Gaul. In English tradition, as recorded in 731 by Bede, the invaders were said to be 'from the three most powerful races of Germany: the Saxons, the Angles and the Jutes'. The origin-stories of the Anglo-Saxon dynasties ruling Kent, Sussex and Wessex in the eighth and ninth centuries claimed that their royal lineages had been founded by successful invaders leading small war-bands carried in three to five ships around the middle or in the second half of the fifth century. According to Gildas a generation of warfare with fluctuating fortunes culminated in a major British victory at Mons Badonicus. Unfortunately this battle cannot be located, nor can it be dated more precisely than *c.* 500. But the result of the British revival is clear. The advance of Anglo-Saxon conquest and settlement was checked for the first half of the sixth century. In medieval Welsh tradition this was the time of the legendary 'King Arthur'. Be that as it may, it was not until the second half of the sixth century that Anglo-Saxon conquests resumed and it is not until that period that the majority of the known Anglo-Saxon kingdoms seem to have been formed.

The Anglo-Saxon invasions were, of course, part of the wider Germanic migrations which changed the political map of the whole of Europe in the fifth and sixth centuries. But only in Britain did the language and religion of the Germanic incomers triumph. The English language today contains astonishingly few words taken over during the 'Dark Ages' by the Anglo-Saxons from the Celtic and Latin languages of the indigenous population. The place-names of England include a number of river, forest and hill names of Celtic origin (the proportion increases in the more westerly regions); they also include some names incorporating Latin terms for visible relics of the Roman past, such as walled fortifications or stone-lined springs (*-chester/-caster*, *-font*). Such survivals point to an era when the British and Old English languages existed side by side. But the majority of the topographical names in England and virtually all the names for actual settlements (farms, enclosures etc.) and for groups of settlers are English. The comprehensive nature of the linguistic change in lowland Britain must reflect the scale of the Anglo-Saxon settlements; it shows that we are dealing with a true migration of settler farmers, whose experience in their north German homeland had been of mixed arable farming. The totality of the ultimate replacement of the British language by English also, however, reflects the continued military dominance of the Anglo-Saxons and the consequent gap in the social and political status of the two languages. The British language had none of the aura of imperial Rome which so attracted continental barbarians; it was simply the language of those whose land the Anglo-Saxons were taking over. The fate of much of the British population of the south and east is revealed in the English word for a Briton, *wealh* ('Welshman'), which also served as a normal Old English term for a slave. Except in frontier areas, it was as slaves that most Britons probably survived under Anglo-Saxon rule. They would have been in no position to influence the way in which the Anglo-Saxons spoke English.

The Anglo-Saxons also brought with them their own pagan gods whose cult appears to have very largely replaced Christianity in lowland Britain by the end of the sixth century. The war-gods, Tiw and Woden, the thunder-god, Thor, and the goddess, Frig, have left traces of their worship in place names and in the days of the week (Tuesday, Wednesday, Thursday and Friday). Astonishingly the fertility goddess, Eostre, has given us the English name for the greatest Christian festival, that is Easter, and has caused us to celebrate that springtime feast with egg symbolism. But the most obvious change that Anglo-Saxon paganism wrought was to introduce new burial practices. Some early Anglo-Saxon settlers cremated their dead and deposited their ashes in distinctive funerary urns; others were buried in the ground with clothing and equipment to accompany them to the next world. Both rites make pagan Anglo-Saxon cemeteries distinct. By contrast the graves of Britons, who under the influence of Christianity followed the practice of inhumation without grave goods, are very difficult to identify. Many burials without grave goods in pagan Anglo-Saxon inhumation cemeteries may well be the graves of Britons rather than of poor Anglo-Saxons; indeed some of those with grave goods may be of Britons who had begun to follow Anglo-Saxon burial practices. What is clear, however, is that as in Frankish Gaul barbarian conquest led to the establishment of new burial grounds. The distribution of pagan Anglo-Saxon cemeteries therefore provides the best indication of the extent of Anglo-Saxon settlement up until the time in the seventh or eighth centuries when their adoption of Christian ideas about death caused the Anglo-Saxons to cease placing jewellery and weapons in the grave and eventually to establish new Christian cemeteries.

England 600–900

Our understanding of the political and social development of the Anglo-Saxon peoples in the seventh and eighth centuries is transformed by their conversion to Christianity. In 596 Pope Gregory I despatched a party of forty Roman monks to Kent to commence the missionary task there. In 634 Oswald returned from exile among the Gaelic peoples of western Scotland to seize the Northumbrian throne. Within a year he had invited a party of monks from Iona to Lindisfarne to begin converting the peoples subject to his rule. The work of these 'Roman' and 'Celtic' missions was assisted in piecemeal fashion by others from Frankish Gaul such as St Felix, from Ireland such as St Fursey, and in the border kingdoms very probably by British clergy. By the last decade of the seventh century the process had been so successful that all the royal courts of Anglo-Saxon England had adopted Christianity; bishoprics and monasteries had been established in most kingdoms, and the work of training English clergy and setting up a network of churches to bring effective pastoral care to a rural population was well under way.

'The Making of England' highlighted the dramatic impact of Christianity upon the English: on the one hand, the new openings that the church provided for artistic and technical expression, and on the other, the pagan forms that it brought to an end. Not that the old pagan cemeteries and burial practices were abandoned suddenly; indeed, some of them continued in use until well into the eighth century. But the restriction and eventual abandonment of the practice of placing weapons and even jewellery in the grave means that our knowledge of the skills of Anglo-Saxon metalworkers and of the work they undertook for secular patrons is interrupted and greatly diminished. Occasionally, as in the magnificent helmets from Coppergate in York and from Benty Grange in Derbyshire, we can see that Christian noble warriors were just as sumptuously armed or bedecked as their pagan predecessors had been. Similarly an episcopal pectoral cross shows that Anglo-Saxon jewellers found that churchmen now required jewellery with garnet and other stones set in fine gold- or silverwork of comparable quality to that demanded by their lay clients. But in general it is true that our knowledge of the skills of Anglo-Saxon jewellers, goldsmiths and silversmiths no longer derives from burials. Increasingly for the eighth and ninth centuries it comes instead from treasure hoards, ecclesiastical or secular, that were buried in the ground for safe-keeping in times of danger, but which were never recovered by their owners; it also comes from the growing body of finds of individual items recovered either in archaeological excavations or by chance in building work or with metal detectors. Such discoveries give us a more balanced impression of the variety of the work of English craftsmen than do the weapons and personal ornaments from pagan cemeteries.

The greatest change that Christianity introduced, however, was the art of reading and writing. Christian missionaries brought with them from Italy, from Gaul and from Ireland the manuscripts that were essential for their pastoral work and for training monks and priests: namely the books of the Bible, especially the Gospels, and also liturgical and patristic works. As the numbers of converts grew, so copies were urgently needed, and scriptoria or writing offices were set up in all major churches. In time distinctive forms of Anglo-Saxon script were developed from Roman and Irish models. Christian traditions in art that derived from the Roman and Mediterranean world were introduced to decorate the most prestigious books, and there were opportunities too for indigenous Celtic and Germanic styles to be adapted to new Christian purposes. Churches needed to be adorned with sculpture in stone and wood, with plasterwork, wall-paintings and with textile hangings; crosses were needed of stone or of precious metals; chalices, relics and other church treasures had to be ornamented. In the seventh, eighth and ninth centuries the church in England became enormously wealthy through donations of land and treasure by pious kings, queens and nobles. Wealth enabled the church to become a dominant, perhaps the dominant, patron. What survives today is, of course, a tiny fraction of what must once have existed. But it does convey some idea of the rich inspiration of Anglo-Saxon artists and of their technical mastery of their craft in the service of the church.

The churches established in every kingdom by kings and nobles also served as centres where the memory of these benefactors and of their dynasties was preserved. In other words, with Christianity came historical records. As a result, and thanks above all to the *Ecclesiastical History of the English People*, which the Venerable Bede completed in 731, we are very much better informed about the political development of Anglo-Saxon England in the seventh and early eighth centuries than we are about the preceding 'Dark Ages'. It was a turbulent period in which the political map was constantly being redrawn by the activities of warrior-kings and of their followers. Bede tells us of the more substantial Anglo-Saxon kingdoms, but it is clear that each of them was an amalgamation, forged by warfare, of smaller tribal groupings. The leading families of these small groups may each have once had ambitions to become powerful war-lords and to progress from cattle-raiding to the exaction of tribute of gold and silver, and thence to the conquest of an enlarged territory. Those who were most successful in this internecine warfare were able to attract a growing army of followers by the prospect of rewards of arms, treasure and land. Thus they founded enlarged kingdoms and turned their heterogeneous war-bands into landed aristocracies who took their ethnic or folk identity from the origins of their founders. The descendants of such successful war-lords ruled the kingdom as long as it survived as an independent unit.

In the course of the century from *c.* 550 to *c.* 650 about a dozen kingdoms formed in this manner can be recognized: in Kent and the Isle of Wight there were kingdoms that considered themselves Jutish; the Saxon kingdoms of the East, South and West Saxons have left their trace in the modern Essex, Sussex and Wessex; whilst to the north were the Anglian kingdoms of the East Angles, the Hwicce (in Worcestershire and Gloucestershire), the Mercians, Lindsey, and (north of the river Humber) Deira and Bernicia (Figure 1). The east midlands seem still to have been divided among some twenty tiny peoples, but they were shortly to be formed into a province of the Middle Angles. It remains uncertain whether the Middle Angles and the Middle Saxons (Middlesex) with their 'southern province' (Surrey) had been ancient kingdoms with their own royal dynasties or were simply administrative provinces formed in the later seventh or early eighth century from the enlarged Mercian kingdom. Similar uncertainties surround the origins in the mid or late seventh century of the territories of the Wreocensæte ('the dwellers near the Wrekin') in Shropshire and the Magonsæte in Herefordshire.

The wealth and fortunes of these kingdoms in the seventh, eighth and ninth centuries depended upon three factors: the exploitation of their landed resources, their external trade, and their seizure by military force of treasure and of new land from neighbouring kingdoms. To exploit their own resources kings and their military retainers toured their kingdoms ceaselessly from one royal estate to the next. In part this was in order to consume the surpluses of perishable food brought there by their subjects as a form of rent or tax; in part it was to provide occasions to gather the people of the district and to display royal power and magnificence, to distribute gifts, to enforce justice and to issue laws. Like the contemporary Celtic rulers among the Welsh or the Dalriadic Scots, English kings exacted payments and services from their subjects on the basis of notional assessments of the number of peasant households ('hides') that particular communities contained. It was a rough and ready system – round figures of tens and hundreds of hides were the norm – but it enabled kings to define what food renders should be demanded from a fixed number of hides or to calculate the military resources of their kingdoms.

Trade with the continent began to play a role in the life of these early medieval states. The first coins produced in Anglo-Saxon England were gold coins minted in Kent and in London intermittently from the late sixth century in imitation of the contemporary 'tremisses' of the

Figure 1. Map of Anglo-Saxon kingdoms *c.* 550–650.

northern parts of Frankish Gaul. Their first function was to facilitate trade, though they were soon also used in the law as a means of reckoning fines and composition-payments. From the 670s English mints followed the Frankish and Frisian example in abandoning the use of gold in favour of silver. The new silver 'pennies' were produced from a growing number of southern and eastern mints and they circulated throughout the Anglo-Saxon kingdoms. Coinciding with the new silver coins were new trading centres established in the major kingdoms. These planned but undefended estuarine settlements – such as those at Southampton (*Hamwic*), London (*Lundenwic*), Ipswich and York (*Eoforwic*) – were the first truly urban communities in Anglo-Saxon England. They suggest that the kings of Wessex, Mercia, East Anglia and Northumbria were seeking to break the near monopoly of long-distance trade which Kent's proximity to the continent had hitherto secured for that kingdom. By channelling the trade of their own kingdoms through their own ports, they cold exact tolls on goods and ships for their own benefit. Royal control was made even more evident from the later eighth century when English pennies, imitating the reforms of the Carolingian ruler Pippin III, were increased in size and weight and henceforth always bore the name of the king on one side. Coinage was now explicitly a royal right, and we may presume that it was a highly profitable one.

But it was the fortunes of war, rather than agricultural wealth or the profits of trade, that determined the political shape of Anglo-Saxon England. War-leaders of genius, such as Æthelberht of Kent (*c.* 580–616), Rædwald of East Anglia (*c.* 610–27), and three successive Northumbrian kings – Edwin (616–33), Oswald (634–42) and Oswiu (642–71) – consolidated their own kingdoms and for short periods pushed themselves into prominence as powerful overlords, who took tribute from the other English kings south of the river Humber and compelled subject rulers to attend their courts. The Northumbrians extended their kingdom northwards to the Forth and westwards across the Pennines to the Irish Sea, bringing under their rule large areas where English rule and settlement was only a thin aristocratic veneer. But it was the Mercians whose long-lived and powerful rulers – Penda (*c.* 626–55), Wulfhere (658–74), Æthelbald (716–57), Offa (757–96) and Cœnwulf (796–821) – most frequently dominated the politics and warfare of seventh- and eighth-century England. Their control of the huge tract of midland England and of the port of London, their exploitation of their long border with the Welsh, and their gradual annexation of neighbouring kingdoms – the Hwicce, Lindsey, Essex, Sussex and Kent – appeared to mark them out as the English kingdom with the greatest potential.

In this turbulent world the church worked for English unity by discouraging kings from attacking each other, and by insisting on the payment of compensation – *wergeld* or 'blood-price' – whenever an Anglo-Saxon king or prince had been slain so that prolonged feuds did not develop between kingdoms. No such forbearance was extended towards the neighbouring British states. Anglo-Saxon churchmen regarded the Welsh with scorn, in part because they claimed the Britons had neglected to convert the English to Christianity and in part because until the ninth century the Welsh church refused to accept Roman authority on the date of the Easter festival. English kings were therefore encouraged to pillage British churches and to use the confiscated properties to enrich and endow English monasteries. This was the racialist climate of opinion in which military leadership passed in the seventh and eighth centuries to those Anglo-Saxon kingdoms (Northumbria, Mercia and Wessex) which had a frontier with the Britons where new conquests could be made and punitive tributes exacted.

A less unattractive aspect of English nationalism was the missionary work that Anglo-Saxon churchmen undertook among the continental Germans in the eighth century. They combined the Celtic ideal of holy exile with the Anglo-Saxon awareness that their continental kinsmen were still pagans. Northumbrians such as St Wilfrid and St Willibrord attempted to commence the conversion of the Frisians of the Low Countries; West Saxons, including St Boniface and Lul, reorganized the church among the Rhineland Franks and the Bavarians so that it could provide a base for missionary work among their pagan neighbours, the Hessians and Thuringians. The flow of English monks who made careers for themselves in the new sees and monasteries was soon matched by a flow of English works of art: illuminated gospels, books of all shorts, crosses and chalices, embroideries for altars and vestments. It is a paradox that, because of such Englishmen overseas throughout the eighth century, more of the finest examples of English workmanship of the period have survived on the continent than in England.

The loss of many of the contemporary works of art that remained in England can be attributed to the Viking raids and invasions of the ninth century. The Norse and Danish bands were not only pagan, they were also equipped with the best ships known in the early medieval world. They were therefore able to subject the royal and ecclesiastical centres of the Anglo-Saxons to the sorts of terror that the English had long visited upon the Welsh: increasingly systematic raiding, exaction of tribute, and (in the later ninth century) conquest and the establishment of Viking kingdoms. Where in 850 England had been divided between four large and wealthy Anglo-Saxon kingdoms (Northumbria, Mercia, Wessex and East Anglia), by the end of the century only Wessex and a fragment of western Mercia and of northern Northumbria survived under English control. In their place powerful Viking kingdoms had been established in East Anglia and in the north at York when the larger Danish armies had ceased campaigning, had settled on the land and established Scandinavian colonies based upon fortified boroughs. The wealth extorted from Anglo-Saxon communities and churches made these Scandinavian settlements by 900 the most prosperous parts of

England and fuelled the economies of new urban settlements at York, Lincoln, Norwich and elsewhere.

The effect on the English church and on Christian culture was cataclysmic. The archiepiscopal church at York maintained a precarious existence under pagan kings, and the community of St Cuthbert retained its cohesion, along with its most important relics and treasures – the body of St Cuthbert and the Lindisfarne Gospels – through years of flight until they gained permission to settle at Chester-le-Street in 883. But most bishoprics and monasteries and almost all libraries in eastern and northern England came to an end through destruction or decay. Even in Wessex there was very little inclination to follow an ecclesiastical or monastic vocation when churches were so vulnerable. Latin literacy declined disastrously so that even in major churches, like the archiepiscopal see of Canterbury, the production of books, the writing of charters and the training of clergy were at risk. In the eyes of the West Saxon king, Alfred (871–99), and of his advisers, the Vikings were God's punishment for a people who had neglected their religious duties. He therefore set about military transformation, reforming his army and building garrisoned boroughs, but also inspired a religious renaissance He attracted to his court scholars and craftsmen from the continent and from Mercia and began an ambitious programme of education, of translation into English of the works he held to be most essential for the propagation of Christian values, and of copying and dissemination of manuscripts of these works to the major churches of his kingdom. By the time of his death in 899 it was very far from clear how successful these measures had been. No one could predict whether political and cultural power would lie with the West Saxon descendants of King Alfred or with the rich Viking kingdoms of the east and north.

3

The Creation and Early Structure of the Kingdom of Kent

ISTORIANS of Anglo-Saxon England have been strangely reluctant to produce any general model of state formation. Interest in the creation of the early Anglo-Saxon kingdoms has been largely or solely in their role as precursors of the single (West Saxon) kingdom of England, rather than in the process of state formation itself, and has been limited to political and military developments. The early Middle Ages in England have been interpreted in terms of 'progress' towards a single monarchy. There has been virtually no expression here of the concern of Marxist historians to relate the rise of the state to the emergence of the feudal mode of production, that is to the rise of a land-owning aristocratic élite living off the rents or labour of an increasingly tied peasantry.[1] Eastern European historians[2] or 'new' archaeologists,[3] who are both accustomed to working with far less evidence, would find our lack of interest in theoretical models extraordinary. One would be more confident of justifying our empirical concentration upon the extant evidence and our rejection of models, were it not a reflection of the insularity of much English scholarship.

In any account of Anglo-Saxon state formation Kent will inevitably have a prominent place, since it was claimed to be the first English kingdom in existence. It was also the first to be converted to Christianity and has therefore an earlier 'historical threshold' – that is the period from which written sources first survive – than any other. The Kentish origin myth is preserved in various forms by Bede, by the *Historia Brittonum* and by the Anglo-Saxon Chronicle, whilst the Kentish royal genealogy is found in these same sources and in the

---

[1] For a survey ranging over much of Europe, see C.J. Wickham, 'The Other Transition: From the Ancient World to Feudalism', *Past & Present*, 106 (1985), pp. 3–36.

[2] See, for example, A. Dorpalen, *German History in Marxist Perspective* (London, 1985).

[3] R. Hodges, 'State Formation and the Role of Trade in Middle Saxon England', *Social Organization and Settlement*, BAR, British series, 47, 1978), pp. 438–53; idem, *Dark Age Economics* (London, 1982); C.J. Arnold, *From Roman Britain to Saxon England* (London, 1984).

'Anglian Collection' of genealogies.[4] It has even been claimed that fragments of Kentish annals of seventh-century origin survive in later continental annals.[5] More certainly the law codes of seventh-century Kentish rulers – Æthelberht, Hlothhere and Eadric, and Wihtred – allow us to see the Kentish state in operation earlier than any other English kingdom.[6] Similarly Kent has preserved by far the largest number of early (seventh- and eighth-century) royal diplomas, both in contemporary form and in later copies,[7] which show something of how the ecclesiastical and lay aristocracy secured their hold on the land. If we add to all this the Kentish royal hagiographical legend whose eighth-century origins have recently been traced by Dr Rollason and the fact that Kent was predominant in the production of early coinage in England,[8] then it is clear that, relatively speaking, there is no shortage of written evidence for the early Kentish kingdom.

The unwritten sources for early Kent are equally impressive: namely the archaeological record and the evidence of the Kentish landscape itself. The pagan Anglo-Saxon cemeteries of Kent with their rich inhumation burials have long attracted scholarly study and thankfully are still graced by archaeologists who use the study of grave-goods to suggest answers to historical questions about the origins and chronology of invasions and about the development of social and political structures.[9] Most recently Kent's landscape and settlement history have been brilliantly analysed by Professor A. Everitt.[10] By distinguishing the six contrasting *pays* of Kent whose exploitation has been so very different throughout Kentish history (Figure 2), he has given us a key to an

---

[4] Bede, *Ecclesiastical History of the English People*, ed. B. Colgrave and R.A.B. Mynors (Oxford, 1969); *Historia Brittonum*, ed. T. Mommsen (*Chronica Minora*, III, MGH Auctores antiquissimi, XIII, Berlin, 1898); *The Anglo-Saxon Chronicle*, trans. D. Whitelock et al. (London, 1961); D.N. Dumville, 'The Anglian Collection of Royal Genealogies and Regnal Lists', *Anglo-Saxon England*, 5 (1976), pp. 23–50.

[5] W. Levison, *England and the Continent in the Eighth Century* (Oxford, 1946), pp. 270–3, 277, citing *Annales iuv. mai.* (MGH SS, i), 87; *Ann. Lind. et Cant.* (MGH SS, iv), 2; and Fleury annals in L. Delisle, *Catalogue des mss des fonds Libri et Barrois* (Paris, 1888), pp. 70–1.

[6] *Die Gesetze der Angelsachsen*, F. Liebermann, 3 vols, (Halle, 1903–16), i, pp. 3–14.

[7] P.H. Sawyer, *Anglo-Saxon Charters: An Annotated List and Bibliography* (London, 1968) BCS; *Charters of Rochester*, ed. A. Campbell (*Anglo-Saxon Charters*, i, London, 1973).

[8] D.W. Rollason, *The Mildrith Legend* (Leicester, 1982); P. Grierson and M. Blackburn, *Medieval European Coinage*, i, Early Middle Ages (Leicester, 1986), pp. 155–89.

[9] S.C. Hawkes, 'Anglo-Saxon Kent c. 425–725', in P. Leach, ed., *Archaeology in Kent to AD 1500* (London, 1982), pp. 64–78; V.I. Evison, *The Fifth Century Invasions South of the Thames* (London, 1965).

[10] A. Everitt, *Continuity and Colonization: The Evolution of Kentish Settlement* (Leicester, 1986).

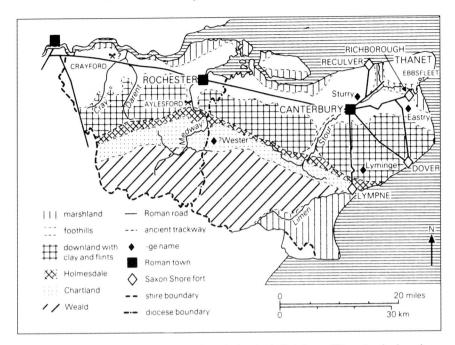

Figure 2. Early Kent: physical and ecclesiastical divisions. The physical regions or *pays* are taken from A. Everitt, *Continuity and Colonization: The Evolution of Kentish Settlement* (Leicester, 1986). The earliest evidence for the boundary between the dioceses of Rochester and Canterbury is of the mid-eleventh century (S1564).

understanding of the peculiarities of Kent's early medieval archaeology and agriculture and of its political and administrative geography.

A true synthesis of all these categories of evidence is much needed but would have to be of monograph length. Here it may be more useful to re-examine the written sources for the creation of the kingdom and for its early structure. Some of them have been subjected to critical, even hypercritical, analysis in recent years; others have come to bear an enormous superstructure of interpretation and conjecture that has been accepted widely and has been built into current models of settlement history. There is a need for a new assessment.

The Name 'Kent' and the Origins of the Kingdom

Alone of the southern English kingdoms Kent was already a kingdom, a state, long before the *adventus Saxonum*. It had indeed been a Celtic (Belgic) Iron Age principality and thereafter a Romano-British *civitas* with its capital at *Durovernum Cantiacorum* (Canterbury), which was the focus of the Roman road system of Kent.[11] The survival of Kent as a distinct political unit is paralleled by the survival of the name. Καντιον, *Cantium* and *Cantia* are the learned forms known to Ptolemy, Caesar and Bede respectively, but they probably all represent a monosyllabic ⋆ *C(h)ant* or *Cænt* in the vernacular, whether British or Old English.[12] The survival of the name, perhaps paralleled in the northern English kingdoms of Deira and Bernicia,[13] may suggest that the Anglo-Saxon kingdom had been formed not simply by the coalescing of groups of English settlers, but that it had also inherited something of its structure from the Celtic and Roman past. The concentration of early Anglo-Saxon settlement in exactly those areas – the 'Foothills' and the 'Holmesdale' (Figure 2) as defined by Everitt – where the major Romano-British sites had been located reinforces the possibility of such continuity. So does the emergence of centres of Anglo-Saxon royal government at places like Lyminge, Wingham and Faversham which had been the sites of villas or temples or of metal-working in the Roman era.[14] So too does the influence of the Roman theatre in Canterbury on the emerging topography of the town in the early Middle Ages.[15] In this context it is also perhaps worth recalling the story in the *Historia Brittonum* of how the kingdom of Kent was transferred from the British king Gwyrangon to Hengist as the bride-price for Vortigern's marriage to Hengist's daughter.[16] This story may indeed be entirely mythical, but it is perhaps significant that it is a story of the transfer of a kingdom from British to English control by legal means, not a story of the forging of an English kingdom by warfare.

The name Kent was known to Strabo and Diodorus Siculus in the first century BC and it is probable that Kent had already been mentioned some three centuries earlier by the navigator Pytheas. At least as a geographical term 'Kent' is therefore very ancient.[17] According to Caesar the inhabitants of Kent in 55–4 BC were ruled by four kings, whom he names. Whether scholars have been correct to deduce that at this time Kent was divided into four territories which can be identified from the distribution of coins, pottery or hillforts seems very doubtful. Joint rule is surely equally possible. Rule by a single king well before the Claudian

---

[11] A. Detsicas, *The Cantiaci* (Gloucester, 1983).

[12] A.L.F. Rivet and C. Smith, *Place-Names of Roman Britain* (London, 1979), s.v.; K. Jackson, *Language and History in Early Britain* (Edinburgh, 1953), pp. 600, 603.

[13] Jackson, *Language and History*, pp. 419–20, 701–5; J.G.F. Hind, 'Elmet and Deira – Forest-Names in Yorkshire?', *Bulletin of the Celtic Studies* 28 (1978–80), pp. 541–52.

[14] Everitt, *Continuity*, pp. 93–117.

[15] N.P. Brooks, *The Early History of the Church of Canterbury* (Leicester, 1984), pp. 24–5.

[16] *Historia Brittonum*, c. 37.

[17] Strabo, *Geography*, ed. G. Aujac (Paris, 1969), iv.3.3 and iv.5.1; Diodorus Siculus, *History*, ed. C.H. Oldfather (London, 1939), v.21.3.

conquest of AD 43 is certainly suggested by the distribution of coins of one of the Belgic rulers named Dumnovellaunus.[18] It must be stressed, however, that there is really no evidence of the western extent either of the Celtic kingdom of Kent or of the Romano-British *civitas* of *Cantium*. Ptolemy indeed attributes three towns to the *Cantii*: London, *Durovernum* and *Rutupiae* (Richborough).[19] Scholars have unanimously refused to include London, but in rejecting it we are left without any proof that Romano-British *Cantium* included West Kent at all. Several have supposed that the Roman *civitas* was divided into two *pagi* based on the towns of Rochester and Canterbury, but that is no more than a guess derived from the existence of the towns and the later division of Kent into two halves. We have in fact no evidence of where the boundary between the *Cantiaci* and the *Regni* lay, though the Weald is certainly the only single geographical feature that could have served the purpose.

Whatever the extent of the pre-Anglo-Saxon unit, however, by the fifth century AD 'Kent' had had several centuries' existence both as a geographical term and as a tribal territory, and it may still have retained some memories of rule by Celtic kings. Two principal ways in which the name might then have been transmitted to the Anglo-Saxons can be suggested: (i) after the withdrawal of Roman armies, 'tyrants' or kings may have emerged once more as rulers in Kent, and their power may then have been transferred to, or seized by, English rulers; (ii) alternatively 'Kent' may simply have been known to 'Saxon' seafarers in the fourth century and have passed into the Germanic languages as a geographical expression. In this sense it could have served as a suitable name for an English kingdom when political and military developments created a unit of comparable extent.

The Kentish Origin Myth

Bede

It may well be doubted after the devastating criticism of Turville-Petre, De Vries, Dumville and Sims-Williams[20] whether the historian can find anything usable in the traditional stories of the arrival in Britain of the

[18] Caesar, *De Bello Gallico*, ed. R. du Pontet (Oxford, 1900–1), v.22; B. Cunliffe, 'Social and Economic Development in Kent in the Pre-Roman Iron Age', in Leach, ed., *Archaeology in Kent*, pp. 40–50; W. Rodwell, 'Coinage *Oppida* and the Rise of Belgic Power in SE Britain', in B. Cunliffe and T. Rowley, eds, *Oppida in Barbarian Europe*, BAR International series, 11, 1976), pp. 187–367. However, the coins of Tasciovaunus (who seems to have preceded Dumnovellaunus) are limited to the area east of the Medway, and it is there that the 'Belgic' pottery is concentrated.

[19] Ptolemy, *Geography*, ed. C. Müller, 2 vols. (Paris, 1883–1901), ii, pp. 3, 12–13.

[20] J.E. Turville-Petre, 'Hengest and Horsa', *Saga Book of the Viking Society*, 14 (1953–7), pp. 273–90; J. De Vries, 'Die Ursprungssage der Sachsen', *Niedersächsisches*

founders of the Kentish dynasty. But whilst the stories of Hengist and Horsa and of Oisc/Æsc and of their relations with Vortigern and his sons may be myth, it is important to locate, to date and to understand the various mythical elements as fully as possible. The first witness is Bede, writing in 731 in the famous Book I chapter 15 of his Ecclesiastical History. He begins by repeating Gildas's account of the British invitation to the *Saxones* to settle in 'the eastern part of the island', ostensibly to defend the Britons against their northern enemies. After a famous passage on the continental origin of the English, which was probably a late addition, Bede then says, 'Their first rulers are said (*perhibentur*) to have been two brothers Hengist and Horsa'. Bede goes on to record Horsa's death in battle and the existence in East Kent of a notable monument in his name, and he traces their descent from the Germanic war god, Woden (Uoden–Uecta–Uitta–Uictgisl–Hengist).[21] In a later chapter he gives the genealogy of the Kentish king Æthelberht, which traces his descent back to Oeric *cognomento* Oisc, the son of Hengist, and he states that Hengist and Oisc first entered Britain at the invitation of Vortigern as he had already related (*ut supra retulimus*).[22]

In fact, however, this is Bede's first mention of Oeric/Oisc; he has hitherto written of Hengist and *Horsa* as the first leaders of the 'Saxons' who arrived in response to Vortigern's invitation. Bede was here being uncharacteristically slipshod, but it is likely that he knew more stories about Hengist, Horsa and Oisc than he actually tells us. His concern after all was with *ecclesiastical* history; he needed only to say enough about them to explain the presence of pagan Anglo-Saxons in Britain. His use of the word *perhibentur* suggests that he was indeed following oral tradition, whose authority he could not check, rather than a written source of a first-hand witness whose personal authority was unimpeachable.[23] Technically Sims-Williams is correct to insist that Bede does not state that Hengist and Horsa landed, or even fought, in Kent.[24] He only asserts that Horsa's *monumentum* was there and that the kings of Kent were descended from Oisc, son of Hengist. It is therefore theoretically conceivable that the stories in the *Historia Brittonum* and the Anglo-Saxon Chronicle of the battles of Hengist, Horsa and Oisc with the

---

Jahrb. f. Landesgesch. 31 (1959), pp. 20–37; D.N. Dumville, 'Sub-Roman Britain: History and Legend', *History*, n.s. 62 (1977), pp. 173–92; idem, 'Kingship, Genealogies and Regnal Lists', in P.H. Sawyer and I.N. Wood, eds, *Early Medieval Kingship* (Leeds, 1977), pp. 72–104; P. Sims-Williams, 'The Settlement of England in Bede and the *Chronicle*', *Anglo-Saxon England*, 12 (1983), pp. 1–41.

[21] *HE* i.15.

[22] *HE* i.5.

[23] Bede's use of *perhibentur* can be traced in P.F. Jones, *Concordance to the Historia Ecclesiastica of Bede* (Cambridge, MA, 1929), s.v.

[24] Sims-Williams, 'Settlement of England', p. 21.

Britons in Kent are simply post-Bedan inventions of later eighth-century or ninth-century authors, who jumped to the wrong conclusions from Bede's account.

But it is difficult to conceive who, apart from Bede's Kentish informants, would have been concerned about Hengist's and Oisc's descent from Woden, about Horsa's monument in East Kent and about the descent of the Kentish royal dynasty. Some version of the Kentish origin myth known to us from the later sources is therefore likely to have already been known in Kent in Bede's day. Moreover even in the story as we have it in Bede there are mythical elements already present. I refer here not just to the supposed ancestors of Hengist and Horse – Uihtgisl, Uitta and Uecta – who, as Sims-Williams has argued, may represent a Kentish claim to the 'Jutish' settlement of the Isle of Wight (Latin *Uecta/Uectis*; OE *Uiht*);[25] nor just to the surely fictitious doubleton Hengist and Horsa (OE 'stallion' and 'horse'); nor to Hengist's fame in the Old English poetic record; but rather to Oisc. Bede reports that Oisc was the *cognomentum*, the distinguishing family name, of Oeric, Hengist's son, and that from him the Kentish kings were called *Oiscingas* ('the descendants of Oisc'). We are given no indication how an apparently undistinguished Eric acquired this surname, or why the dynasty should have remembered themselves as the sons of Oisc rather than of Oeric or indeed of Hengist. If *Oiscingas* was the dynastic family name, what was the force of Oeric's *cognomentum* Oisc? There is reason to suspect that at some early stage in the transmission of the Kentish origin myth Oeric has been identified with a divine founder figure, for philologists equate the name Oisc with (i) the *princeps* Ansehis, who according to the Ravenna Cosmographer had brought the 'Saxons' to Britain; (ii) the Norse word for a god *áss* and the OE personal-name element Os-; and (iii) the Gothic demi-gods *Ansis* whom Jordanes tells us stood at the head of the royal genealogies of the Goths. Indeed 'Hengist' may be a further (and later) duplication of the same god name,[26] or may have been borrowed from heroic tales originally quite distinct. Claims of descent from divine progenitors and the identification of the 'Founding Fathers' as gods are of course standard elements in the dynastic praise or 'oral tradition' of early Germanic peoples, as they are of many tribes throughout the world today.[27] It may be that the identification of Oeric

---

[25] *ibid* 24–25

[26] H.M. Chadwick, *The Origin of the English Nation* (Cambridge, 1907), pp. 44–5; H. Moisl, 'Anglo-Saxon genealogies and Germanic oral tradition', *Journal of Medieval History*, 7 (1981), pp. 219–23, 235–6; Sims-Williams, 'Settlement of England', pp. 21–4.

[27] A. Faulkes, 'Descent from the Gods', *Mediaeval Scandinavia*, 11 (1978–9), pp. 92–125; Moisl, 'Anglo-Saxon Genealogies', pp. 215–48; E. Leach, *Genesis as Myth and Other Essays* (London, 1969), pp. 25–83; B.A. Agiri, 'Early Oyo History Reconsidered', *History in Africa*, ii (1975), pp. 1–16; R. Law, 'Early Yoruba historiography', ibid., iii (1976), pp. 68–89.

as Oisc represents one stage in the evolution of the Kentish royal genealogy before the supposed generations from Hengist to Woden, another divine progenitor, were added. The dynasty would have been known as *Oiscingas* before descent from Woden, or from Hengist, was claimed.

In the form recorded by Bede the Kentish royal genealogy can therefore be seen to be a fiction of epic heroes, gods and demi-gods and of eponymous but invented Wight-men. It is likely to reflect the stories that were cultivated at the royal court of Kent by English court poets (*scopas*) in the early eighth century and which were passed on to Bede by his informant on Kentish matters, Abbot Albinus of St Augustine's. Indeed if we were to accept Moisl's argument that descent from pagan gods is unlikely to be a feature of dynastic tradition that was invented after the conversion to Christianity, then some version of the descent of the *Oiscingas* from Woden and other gods may have existed in oral tradition at the Kentish court of Æthelberht before the arrival there of St Augustine in 597.[28] A case might be made that Oeric and Octha are less clearly mythical than the other names in the genealogy, but where our evidence is so slight no weight can be attached to that. If, then, the *dramatis personae* of the Kentish origin legend are largely or entirely fictional, we need to go on to consider whether any credence can be given to the elaborate details of their deeds recorded in the *Historia Brittonum* and the Anglo-Saxon Chronicle.

The Anglo-Saxon Chronicle

At first sight the Chronicle's account of the foundation of the kingdom, set in a brief annalistic framework, seems more credible. In essence it is a story of a landing, of four battles (three of which are named), of the death of Horsa and the succession of Hengist (in 455, that is) six years after the landing, and of the succession of his son Æsc (in 488) seemingly in the fortieth year after the landing. The chronology is attached to a first landing in 449, which was the year in which Bede recorded the accession of Marcian and Valentinian in whose time he believed the arrival of the English to have occurred. As Sims-Williams has pointed out,[29] the Chronicle's pattern of landing, of creation of the kingdom after five or six years, of three named battles and of the succession of the son some forty years later is exactly matched in its duplicated and equally artificial account of the origins of the West Saxon kingdom. Indeed elements of the same pattern recur in the

[28] Moisl, 'Anglo-Saxon Genealogies', pp. 215–48. The argument is normally countered by the suggestion that Christians were prepared to invent descent from euhemerized men.
[29] Sims-Williams, 'Settlement of England', p. 35.

account of the supposed establishment of Ælle (a warrior whose wider fame was known to Bede) and his sons in Sussex. There is little sense in attempting to determine whether the Kentish account is modelled upon the West Saxon, or the West Saxon upon the Kentish. The pattern is likely to have once been far more widely spread than our extant examples indicate. We are here in the presence of a recurrent origin myth,[30] whose form owes more to the court poet's, or *scop*'s, concept of what a dynastic origin story ought to contain (and to the annalist's attempt to fit that concept into a chronological scheme) than it does to historical reality.

A number of loose ends in the Chronicle's story of the beginnings of Kent suggest that it is a late and composite account. Thus after the supposed battle of *Ægelesthrep* and the death there of Horsa (455), Hengist *and Æsc* are said to have 'succeeded to the kingdom' or 'taken power' (*feng to rice*). Yet in 488 Æsc 'succeeded to the kingdom' (*feng to rice*) apparently for a second time and then reigned a further twenty-four years. The Kentish place-names of the Chronicle's account are worrying too, since they just fail to be satisfactory forms of well-known Kentish places. The landing takes place at *Ypwinesfleot* (*Heopwinesfleot*) which seems to be significantly close to, but not the same as, *Yppelesfleot*, that is Ebbsfleet on Thanet; the first battle occurs at *Ægelesthrep*, an improbable place-name form where we might expect *Ægelesford* for Aylesford; the next takes place at *Crecganford* which is close to, but not an acceptable form of, *Cræganford*, Crayford (Figure 2). The third battle, *Wippedesfleot*, cannot be identified but gains no credibility from the reputed death there of the eponymous thegn Wipped. We may regard all these four places as genuine but unidentifiable sites, but it is surely more likely – as Wallenberg argued[31] – that the first three are all mangled forms of the names Ebbsfleet, Aylesford and Crayford. Such consistent error suggests that the compilers of the Anglo-Saxon Chronicle were not following a Kentish written account of the origins of the dynasty, but rather drawing on oral tradition, which after the demise of the independent Kentish kingdom would have been kept alive through the ninth century only in a West Saxon context. The West Saxon dynasty of Egbert (802–39) may have had ancestors in the Kentish royal family,[32] and a West Saxon *scop*, ignorant of Kentish

[30] For various approaches see B. Malinowski, 'Myth in Primitive Psychology', *Magic, Science and Religion* (Glencoe, IL, 1948), pp. 72–124; C. Levi-Strauss, *The Savage Mind* (London, 1966); L. De Heusch, *Le roi ivre ou l'origine de l'état* (Paris, 1972); *The African Past Speaks*, ed. J.C. Miller (Folkestone, 1980); R. Law, 'How Many Times Can History Repeat Itself?, *International Journal of African Historical Studies*, 18(1) (1985), pp. 33–51.

[31] J.K. Wallenberg, *Kentish Place-Names* (Uppsala, 1931), pp. 83–4, 286–8, 320–3.

[32] F.M. Stenton, *Anglo-Saxon England* (3rd edn., Oxford, 1971), p. 207, identified Egbert's father Ealhmund as the Kentish ruler 'Ealmundus' who is the donor of S 38 (= BCS 243); but see my cautionary note: Brooks, *Early History*, p. 349, n. 15.

geography, could have garbled the place-name forms in a way that would not have been acceptable to a Kentish audience.

Indeed the closer we search the common stock of the Anglo-Saxon Chronicle for authoritative information about the early kingdom of Kent, the more it vanishes before our eyes. There is indeed some record of West Saxon–Kentish hostilities: in 568 Ceawlin and Cutha are said to have defeated King Æthelberht of Kent in battle at *Wibbandun*; in 686 Cædwalla and his brother Mul are said to have ravaged Kent; and in 687 Mul is burnt there and Cædwalla takes his revenge. The weighting of this information suggests, as we might expect, that it derives from West Saxon rather than Kentish sources. Otherwise the only information that the Chronicle has about Kent before 731 was drawn from Bede's Ecclesiastical History and in particular from the chronological recapitulation in the final chapter.[33]

The inference would seem to be that the compilers had no Kentish written sources for the early kingdom at all. That reinforces the conclusion that the Chronicle's version of the Kentish origin story is oral tradition, and that it is an account of mythical founders creating a kingdom according to a set formula at dates and places that deserve no credence. That does not of course mean that dynastic oral tradition could not preserve memories of actual events, or even that written sources are necessarily more authoritative or less liable to manipulation than the oral record. It only means that the early medievalist does not normally possess the tools, sometimes available to the anthropologist/historian in modern Africa, to establish which parts of the tradition may be historical rather than mythical.[34]

The Historia Brittonum

In Kent, however, we are remarkably fortunate that we have another control on the Kentish origin myth in the version recorded in the *Historia Brittonum* of the early ninth century.[35] This account was claimed by John Morris to be 'a sixth-century source', which he termed 'the Kentish Chronicle' and which he believed to have been incorporated lock, stock and barrel by 'Nennius' into the *Historia* in the 820s.[36] David Dumville has since taught us to disbelieve every element of this interpretation: the author of the *Historia* was not 'Nennius'; he did not simply incorporate earlier written sources by 'making a heap of what he

---

[33] *HE* v.24. After 731 the Chronicle records archiepiscopal successions, the fire at Canterbury in 756 and some eighth-century Kentish royal successions.

[34] *The African Past Speaks*, ed. Miller; J. Vansina, *Oral Tradition as History* (London, 1985).

[35] *Historia Brittonum* cc. 31, 36–8, 43–6.

[36] J. Morris, *Age of Arthur* (Chichester, 1973), pp. 37, 80–1.

found'; there is no reason to suppose that the *Historia*'s chronological calculations were made in the sixth century rather than in the ninth.[37] None the less the relationship of the *Historia*'s account to that of the Anglo-Saxon Chronicle is of interest, and Morris was quite right to stress that there is a connection between the two:

Anglo-Saxon Chronicle	*Historia Brittonum*
449 Hengist and Horsa, invited by Vortigern, land at *Ypwinesfleot*.	*c.* 31 Vortigern invites Hengist and Horsa and gives them Thanet.
	c. 44 Vortemir son of Vortigern fights four battles against Hengist and Horsa:
455 Hengist and Horsa fight against Vortigern at *Ægelesthrep* (? Aylesford). Horsa killed; Hengist and Æsc succeed to kingdom.	Second battle at ford called *Episford* (Brit. *Rithergabail*). Horsa killed and also Categirn, Vortigern's son.
456 Hengist and Æsc fight Britons at *Crecganford* (? Crayford) and kill 4000; Britons flee from Kent to London.	First battle on river *Derguentid* (Darent).
465 Hengist and Æsc fight Britons at *Wippedesfleot* and slay twelve British elders. Thegn Wipped also slain.	Third battle in field by shore of Gallic sea *iuxta lapidem tituli*. Barbarians flee to ships.
473 Hengist and Æsc fight Britons, capture spoils. Britons flee.	
488 Æsc succeeds to the kingdom and reigns twenty-four years.	*c.* 45 After Vortemir's death, barbarians return through Vortigern's friendship. Treacherous slaying of 300 British elders. Vortigern cedes Essex, Sussex and Middlesex.

Like the Chronicle the *Historia Brittonum* tells of the arrival of Hengist and Horsa in East Kent; like the Chronicle it tells of four battles, but names only three; like the Chronicle it records the death of Horsa in one of the named battles; and like the Chronicle it records a series of battles which ends with the enemy fleeing. But beyond these similarities which indicate a common origin, the overall effect of the *Historia*'s account is of course the reverse of that in the Anglo-Saxon

[37] Dumville, 'Sub-Roman Britain', pp. 176–8; idem, 'Some Aspects of the Chronology of the *Historia Brittonum*', *Bulletin of the Celtic Studies*, 25 (1974), pp. 439–48; idem, ' "Nennius" and the *Historia Brittonum*', *Studia Celtica*, 10–11 (1975–6), pp. 78–95.

Chronicle. When the sequence of battles starts, the English (*Saxones*) are already in control of Kent as a result of Vortigern's marriage to Hengist's daughter (*c.* 37); Vortemir fights them first in the extreme west of Kent at the river Darent – the Chronicler's second battle at Crayford is just two and a half miles from the Darent (Figure 2); then Vortemir fights them at the ford site, *Episford*,[38] perhaps equivalent to the Chronicle's *Ægelesthrep* (? Aylesford) since Horsa is killed at each; and the last named battle is on the English Channel (*mare Gallicum*), which may be identical with the battle that the Chronicle calls *Wippedesfleot* since the element *-fleot* in Kentish place-names is the standard term for a tidal creek in coastal marshes. The site could be in the marshes of the Wantsum channel or possibly in Romney Marsh.[39] The overall contrast between the two accounts is stark: the Chronicle has landing and battles apparently involving movement from east to west, and has the Britons fleeing to London; the *Historia Brittonum*'s three battles progress from west to east and culminate in the flight of the Saxons to their ships on the Channel.

Clearly we have here a single tradition which in one version has been slanted for the benefit of an English audience, in the other for a British audience. It is a splendid example of how myth can be adapted to serve diametrically opposed purposes by a relatively minor reordering of the chronology, the location of key events or the motivation of the key participants. Yet, as H.M. Chadwick pointed out long ago,[40] there can be no doubt that the *Historia*'s version of the story is of English origin. Hence we are given the English form of names first, followed by their British equivalents: *Tænet – Ruoihin* (*c.* 31), *Cantguaraland – Cent* (*c.* 37), *Episford – Rit her gabail* (*c.* 42); hence too the story of Vortigern's 300 counsellors being treacherously murdered by Hengist's Saxons at the conference/feast when Hengist ordered his men to produce their hidden knives with the cry, *Eure nimath seaxas* ('Draw your knives'). The *Historia*'s use of Old English here would itself suggest the origin, but it is confirmed when the same story is found with the same punch line, but with different participants, in the origin myth of the continental Saxons as recorded in part by Widukind of Corvey and more fully in the *Annales Stadenses*.[41] This is clearly a familiar Germanic

[38] For possible explanations of this name, see Sims-Williams, 'Settlement of England', p. 29, n. 124.

[39] Wallenberg, *Kentish Place-Names*, passim; N.P. Brooks, 'Romney Marsh in the Early Middle Ages', in R.T. Rowley, ed., *Evolution of Marshland Landscapes* (University of Oxford, Department for External Studies, 1981), pp. 74–94 (= below, pp. 275–300).

[40] Chadwick, *Origin*, pp. 39–44.

[41] Widukind of Corvey, *Res Gestae Saxonicae*, ed. K.A. Kehr (MGH, Script. rer. Germ. in us. schol., 1904), i, 6–7; *Annales Stadenses* s.a. 917, ed. M. Lappenberg (MGH, SS, xvi, 1925), 317. See de Vries, 'Ursprungssage d. Sachsen', pp. 20–37.

folktale or formulaic myth which, suitably adapted, is likely to have been part of the stock repertoire of many an Anglo-Saxon or Germanic court *scop* or praise singer. That it is a story of treachery and could therefore readily serve British interests in the *Historia* does not weigh against its English or Saxon origin. The gap between base treachery and admirable cunning was not great, for earlier wrongs by the enemy could always be held to justify deception.

In the *Historia Brittonum*, then, we find English myth adapted for a British audience, but this does not mean that its evidence should simply be rejected in favour of the Anglo-Saxon Chronicle's seemingly more straightforward account. It may be significant that the flight of the Britons to London in the Chronicle follows only the second of the battles (*Crecganford*). Our impression of the westward progress of the English relies upon the fact that *Wippedesfleot* cannot be identified and that the fourth battle is unnamed. The oral tradition upon which the Chronicle's sparse annals draw may have been much more tumultuous and complex. Similarly we have already seen that both Bede and the Chronicle make Oisc (Æsc) the son of Hengist, which is difficult to square with the name *Oiscingas* for the Kentish royal dynasty and with the fact that the warrior king Oisc appears to be the name of a god. It is therefore of interest that in the *Historia* Oisc does not figure in the stories of the struggles of Vortigern and his sons with Hengist and his 'Saxons'. Moreover in its version of the Kentish royal genealogy, which the *Historia* draws from the so-called 'Anglian collection' of genealogies, the descent is given in the sequence: Hengist–Octha(Ocga)–Ossa (Oese), rather than: Hengist–Oisc(Æsc)–Octa as found in Bede and the Chronicle. If we bear in mind that these genealogies are also an essential part of the court praise preserved and developed orally by Anglo-Saxon *scopas*,[42] then we should not seek to explain one or other version as a product of a simple error in transmission, whether written or oral. Rather each may stand witness to different versions of the Kentish/English origin legends.[43] In this light the *Historia Brittonum* may be seen to preserve the fullest version of the sort of dynastic stories that were first told in the court of the Anglo-Saxon kings of Kent. They have been transmitted to us immediately by a British writer, and perhaps intermediately through a wider 'Anglian' context, and it remains difficult to be sure how much they may have been changed in the process. Their function, however, is clear. They serve to explain the tenure of the kingdom of Kent by Hengist and Octa, and therefore also

[42] Dumville, 'Genealogies and Regnal Lists', pp. 72–104; Moisl, Anglo-Saxon Royal Genealogies', pp. 215–48.

[43] For a bold suggestion of when these versions may have been current see D.P. Kirby, 'Vortigern', *Bulletin of the Board of Celtic Studies*, 23 (1968–70), pp. 37–59 at 47–8.

by those whom the genealogy showed to be descended from them. Genealogy and origin story are together the essential constituents of the court propaganda of the Kentish kingdom.

The Anglo-Saxon Kingdom

Irminric

If we move on down the Kentish royal genealogy (Hengist–Oeric/ Oisc–Octa–Irminric–Ædilberct), we leave the realms of dynastic myth and approach those of history with Irminric or Iurminric, who bore the same name as Ermanaric, the Gothic warrior king of the fourth century, and is said to be the son of Octa in one version and of Oese (? = Oisc) in the other.[44] Writing in the early 590s Gregory of Tours refers to Irminric (without naming him) as 'a certain king in Kent' at a date which, as we shall see, seems to be in the late 570s or early 580s.[45] Beyond the divergent claims made for his ancestry in the genealogy nothing is known of Irminric's origin. It should be noted, however, that Irmin-/Eormen- is an uncommon element in Anglo-Saxon personal names. Apart from the infamous Northumbrian queen, Iurminburh, who fell out with St Wilfrid but whose origins are unknown, the only Anglo-Saxons whose names contain the element are from Kent, and almost all of them can be shown to have been members of the Kentish ruling house and therefore descendants of Irminric.[46] Through rare in England, Irmin- is a very common element in continental personal names, especially among the Franks.[47] Archaeologists have long recognized amongst the grave-goods from sixth-century Kentish burials a significant Frankish element, particularly of luxury items such as belt fittings, garnet jewellery, glassware and bronze bowls. Their significance and chronology have been much disputed;[48] but if we were looking for a moment when a Frankish element first entered Kentish dynastic history, it should perhaps be reckoned to have been under Irminric rather than his better-known son. Indeed to be accurate, this

[44] *HE* ii.5; Dumville, 'Anglian Collection', pp. 23–50.

[45] Gregory of Tours, *Decem Libri Historiarum*, ed. B. Krusch and W. Levison (MGH, Script. rer. merov., i (1), Hannover, 1951), ix, 26.

[46] See the names listed by W.G. Searle, *Onomasticon Saxonicum* (Cambridge, 1897).

[47] M.T. Morlet, *Les noms de personne sur la territorie de l'ancienne Gaule dès vi au xii siècle*, i (Paris, 1968), s.v.; E. Förstemann, *Altdeutsches Namenbuch*, i, *Personennamen* (Nordhausen, 1856), s.v.

[48] E.T. Leeds, *Early Anglo-Saxon Art and Archaeology* (Oxford, 1936), pp. 41–78; C.F.C. Hawkes, 'The Jutes of Kent', in D.B. Harden, ed., *Dark-Age Britain: Studies to E.T. Leeds* (Oxford, 1956), pp. 91–111; Evison, *Fifth-century Invasions*; J.M. Wallace-Hadrill, *Early Germanic Kingship in England and the Continent* (Oxford, 1971), pp. 24–32; Hawkes, 'Anglo-Saxon Kent', pp. 72–4.

continental Germanic element presumably began with the parents who chose his name. Even so it is difficult to suppose that the naming of Irminric can (unless he were unusually long lived) have been quite as early as *c.* 500, the date preferred by Sonia Chadwick Hawkes for the beginning of the Frankish phase in the Kentish archaeological record. A date for Irminric's birth in the second quarter of the sixth century would seem most likely in view of the redating of the reign of his son Æthelberht that the contemporary evidence requires. But since we cannot identify Irminric's parents, and since archaeological dating is necessarily hazardous, to have brought the two categories of evidence within a generation of each other is as much as could be hoped.

Æthelberht

With King Æthelberht we cross the historical threshold more definitely. As the first Anglo-Saxon king to be baptized, as the most powerful English ruler of his day and as the progenitor of the later kings of Kent, there were good reasons for Æthelberht to be remembered. Moreover Bede, our principal but not our only informant, derived his information about Kent from Albinus, the abbot of the monastery of St Peter and St Paul at Canterbury – the church where Æthelberht and the subsequent Christian kings of Kent were buried.[49] It is therefore no surprise that Bede should be well informed about the deaths of Kentish kings of the seventh and early eighth centuries. That was above all the information that a royal burial-church like St Augustine's (as it was later to be called) would preserve. We must therefore take Bede's information about the length and dates of Æthelberht's reign seriously.

Bede tells us that Æthelberht died in 616, 'the twenty-first year from the sending of Augustine and his companions to preach to the English people'.[50] It is likely that Bede himself supplied the incarnation year, as was his practice in the Ecclesiastical History. There is no reason to suppose that Bede, or his informants, had calculated all the incarnation dates of sixth- and seventh-century Kentish kings from a regnal list in the manner that Bede was able to reckon the dates of every Northumbrian ruler back to the supposed accession of the dynastic founder Ida in 547.[51] Neither Bede nor the compilers of the Anglo-

---

[49] *HE* preface; K.H. Krüger, *Königsgrabkirchen der Franken, Angelsachsen und Langobarden bis zum Mitte des 8, Jahrhunderts* (Münstersche Mittelalterschriften, 4, 1971).

[50] *HE* ii.5: 'qui est annus uicesimus primus ex quo Augustinus cum sociis ad praedicandum genti Anglorum missus est'.

[51] P.H. Blair, 'The Moore memoranda on Northumbrian history', in C. Fox and B. Dickins, eds, *The Early cultures of North-West Europe [H.M. Chadwick Memorial Studies]* (Cambridge, 1950), pp. 243–59. For Bede's practice in calculating incarnation dates and regnal years, see S. Wood, 'Bede's Northumbrian Dates Again', *English Historical Review*, 98 (1983), pp. 280–96.

Saxon Chronicle seem to have had access to any such Kentish regnal list. Bede did indeed know that Egbert I, who died in the year of the synod of Hertford (673), had reigned for nine years and that his predecessor Earconberht's rule lasted twenty-four.[52] But unless he knew the length of Eadbald's reign, which he does not state, he could not have calculated the year of Æthelberht's death by working backwards in this fashion. In fact it would have been far simpler for Bede to reckon forward twenty completed years from the sending of Augustine in 596 and thus to reach 616. That Æthelberht's death and burial were indeed remembered at Canterbury in terms of the chronology of the mission is confirmed later in the same chapter when Bede returns to the subject: 'King Æthelberht died on 24 February, 21 years after receiving the faith, and was buried in the *porticus* of St Martin within the church of the blessed apostles Peter and Paul.'[53]

While the interest in the mission of Augustine and in the location of the king's burial was natural enough for Bede's informant, abbot Albinus, it must be observed that this second presentation of the facts might lead us to calculate the king's death as 597 + 21 = 618, since Augustine probably actually arrived in Kent in Spring 597. 618 is indeed the year of Æthelberht's obit in the fragmentary early Kentish and Northumbrian annals preserved in later continental chronicles from St Germain des Prés, Fleury and elsewhere.[54] 618 also seems to be indicted by the 'E' version of the Anglo-Saxon Chronicle when it places Æthelberht's accession in 565 and attributes a reign of fifty-three years to him [though most scholars have preferred to suppose the annal misplaced and *liii* to be a misreading for *lvi*).[55] But Bede's confusion whether the *xxi* years after the mission should be an ordinal or a cardinal number, and whether they should be reckoned from the sending or the arrival of the Gregorian mission, certainly warns us against accepting his calculated date of 616 too firmly. 616 × 618 would seem a wiser estimate of Æthelberht's death.

In his first references to Æthelberht's death Bede also tells us the length of his reign: '. . . after the temporal kingdom which he had held most gloriously for 56 years, he attained the eternal joys of the heavenly

[52] *HE* iii.8; iv.1, 5.

[53] *HE* ii.5; 'Defunctus uero est rex Ædilberct die xxiiii mensis Februarii post xx et unum annos acceptum fidei atque in porticu sancti Martini intra ecclesiam beatorum apostolorum Petri et Pauli sepultus.' For the chronology of the Augustinian mission, see Brooks, *Early History*, pp. 3–11.

[54] Fleury annals in Delisle, *Cat. des mss des fonds Libri et Barrois* (Paris, 1880), pp. 70–1; *Ann. Lind. et Cant.* (MGH, SS, iv, 2).

[55] *Venerabilis Baedae Historia Ecclesiastica*, ed. C. Plummer (Oxford, 1896), ii, p. 85; ASC s.a. 565, 616; *Annals of St Neots*, s.a. 565, ed. D.N. Dumville and M. Lapidge (*Anglo-Saxon Chronicle*, ed. Dumville and S.D. Keynes, 17 (Cambridge, 1985), p. 8.

kingdom.'[56] G.H. Wheeler sought to suggest that Bede is here contrasting Æthelberht's *life* on earth with his everlasting *life* in heaven,[57] and is therefore telling us that Æthelberht was fifty-six years old when he died. But the contrast between the earthly *rule* of kings and the eternal *rule* of God in heaven is such a favourite theme of monastic writers, and of Bede in particular,[58] that it is more probable that Bede meant that Æthelberht had *reigned* for fifty-six years. Whether he was correctly informed, or had understood his information correctly, is another matter. Fifty-six years would indeed be a reign of unusual length, some fifteen years more than the longest Anglo-Saxon reign otherwise known, that of Æthelbald of Mercia (716–57).[59] Indeed it would be longer than that of any other English rulers apart from George III (1760–1820) and Victoria (1837–1901).

Such doubts deserve attention because the supposed fifty-six-year reign conflicts with the evidence of a writer who was an exact contemporary of Æthelberht, namely Gregory of Tours. Writing Book IV of his History at some date in or before 581, Gregory described how the Frankish king Charibert had (in 561) succeeded to his share of the kingdom of his father Lothar and had then taken as his wife Ingoberga, by whom he had a daughter who later received a husband in Kent.[60] Reading this passage in the context of Gregory's account of the succession of Lothar's sons, it seems that Charibert was following standard Merovingian practice in taking a wife after acquiring his kingdom. Only the offspring of a king could succeed to the throne in Merovingian Francia, and ambitious Frankish princes therefore delayed marriage until they became king.[61] Gregory mentioned the marriage of

[56] *HE* ii.5: 'Ædilberct rex Cantuariorum post regnum temporale, quod L et sex annis gloriosissime tenuerat, aeterna caelestis regni gaudia subiit.'

[57] G.H. Wheeler, 'Gildas *De Excidio* chapter 26', *English Historical Review*, 41 (1926), p. 521.

[58] See e.g. *HE* ii.5: '. . . Sabercti regis Orientalium Saxonum qui ubi regna perennia petens tres suos filios . . . regni temporalis heredes reliquit . . .'; *HE* iii.18: 'Tantumque rex ille [= *Sigberct*] caelestis regni amator factus est ut ad ultimum . . . intraret monastrium . . .'; *HE* iv.14: '. . . regis Osualdi, qui quondam genti Nordanhymbrorum et regni temporalis auctoritate et Christianae pietatis quae ad regnum perenne ducit . . . praefuit . . .'; *HE* v.21 (letter of abbot Ceolfrith to king Nechtan): 'Sic enim fit ut post acceptam temporalis regni potentiam ipse beatissimus apostolorum princeps caelesti regni tibi . . . pandat introitum.'

[59] For a comparable muddle over Penda's age at his accession and at his death, see below, pp. 67–72.

[60] *Decem Libri Historiarum* iv.26: 'Porro Charibertus rex Ingobergam accepit uxorem de qua filiam habuit, quae postea in Ganthia uirum accipiens est deducta.' For the date of composition see Gregor v. Tours, *Fränkische Geschichte*, ed. R. Büchner (Deutscher Verlag der Wissenschaften, *c.* 1955), p. xxi.

[61] P. Stafford, *Queens, Concubines and Dowagers: The King's Wife in the Early Middle Ages* (Athens, GA, 1983), pp. 35–6, 38, 67–8, 73–4.

Ingoberga's daughter again, when in the early 590s he described in Book IX how he had attended Ingoberga on her deathbed in 588–9 in order to hear her will. He explains her generous benefactions to the poor and to the church of Tours by the fact that she had no descendants save a single daughter whom 'the son of a certain king in Kent had married'.[62]

If historians have been correct in identifying this daughter as Bertha, the Frankish princess whose marriage to Æthelberht of Kent is recorded by Bede, then the chronological implications are clear. Bertha must have been born between late 561 and 568, since her father Charibert had died in 567. She would not have been old enough to marry Æthelberht before the mid-570s at the earliest, and she had evidently done so in or by 581, when Gregory first noted the fact. At the time of the marriage (*c.* 575 × 581) Æthelberht was apparently only 'the son of a certain king in Kent', a description inconceivable if he were already on the Kentish throne, let alone if he had been ruling since 560 × 562 as acceptance of Bede's fifty-six-year reign would imply. However, all the chronological problems disappear if Bede's '56 years' had originally applied not to Æthelberht's reign but to his age at death. Æthelberht would then have been born in 560 × 562 and have been of very much the same age as his wife Bertha. Married when he was about eighteen–twenty years of age, he had certainly gained the Kentish throne before the death of Ceawlin of Wessex in *c.* 593 since he had earlier been defeated by him at *Wibbandun* and driven back to Kent.[63] It is possible that Æthelberht may still not have been king in 588–9 when Ingoberga did not know of (or did not remember!) her son-in-law's accession; unfortunately we cannot tell how regularly Bertha had kept in contact with her mother in Tours or be sure that Gregory's ignorance therefore means that Æthelberht was not yet then king.

Thus the evidence of the contemporary Gregory of Tours enables us to correct Bede's interpretation of Kentish chronology and to assign the following dates to the first Christian king of Kent: born 560 × 562, married to Bertha *c.* 580, succeeded to the Kentish kingdom *c.* 580 × 593, became overlord *c.* 593 × 597, received the Augustinian mission 597, died 616 x 618. Here surely is a credible career, which does not

---

[62] *Decem Libri Historiarum* ix.26: 'Anno quoque quarto decimo Childeberti regis [588–9], Ingoberga regina Chariberti quondam relicta migrauit a saeculo . . . relinquens filiam unicam, quam in Canthia regis cuiusdam filius matrimonio copulauit.' My interpretation of the details of the chronology was reached independently (cf. Brooks, *Early History*, pp. 5–6) but is largely parallel to that of I.N. Wood, 'The Merovingian North Sea', *Occasional Papers on Medieval Topics*, i (1983), pp. 15–16, though I am not inclined to follow him in thinking that Frankish court praise means that Frankish overlordship was real.

[63] ASC s.a. 568, 593. For Æthelberht's overlordship after Ceawlin see *HE* ii.5.

compel us either to attribute to Æthelberht an entirely improbable longevity or to prefer the second-hand and later tradition recorded by Bede to the evidence of a disinterested and well placed foreign contemporary. One final point emerges from Gregory's evidence: nothing suggests that the marriage of Bertha and Æthelberht was of great significance at the time it was contracted. With the division of the Frankish kingdom in 511 and again in 561, and with so many Merovingian rulers entering successive marriages or alliances of whatever sort, Frankish royal princesses were not in short supply. Ingoberga, indeed, seems not to have retained Charibert's favour for very long, and after his death in 567 and the dismemberment of his kingdom it must have been clear that Bertha would have neither great inherited wealth nor significant political clout.[64] Similarly we do not know that Æthelberht was Irminric's only son or whether there were elder brothers, let alone uncles or cousins, to dispute his path to the Kentish throne. We must constantly beware the temptation to assume that a royal genealogy is in fact a regnal list of successive kings passing the throne from father to son. At the time of his marriage to Bertha Æthelberht was simply one Kentish *filius regis*. We cannot be sure how far the marriage enhanced his political prospects, since we do not know what other brides might have been available. Marriage to a West Saxon princess during the overlordship of Ceawlin might have been a far more ambitious act.

The Structure of the Kentish Kingdom

Already in the laws of king Æthelberht we can see something of the structure of the early Kentish state. Amongst the compensations and penalties prescribed for a great range of injuries and offences, the laws specify the payment due to the king when one of his followers (*leode*) was injured; they also protect all those at a royal vill (*cyninges tun*) and those drinking with the king at the *ham* of one of his subjects. An itinerant royal household eating and drinking the food surpluses collected at his own estates and those of his subjects therefore lies at the core of the Kentish kingdom as of other early medieval states.[65] Thanks to the researches of Professor Everitt a high proportion of these early estate centres in Kent can be identified and their location in the 'old arable lands' of the county, the so-called 'Foothills' and 'Holmesdale', established.[66]

[64] Wood, 'Merovingian North Sea', p. 16.

[65] *Laws of Æthelberht*, cc. 2, 3, 5 (*Gesetze*, ed. Liebermann, i, pp. 3–8). For the organization of itinerating royal households see T. Charles-Edwards, 'Early Medieval Kingships in the British Isles', in S.R. Bassett, ed., *The Origins of Anglo-Saxon Kingdoms* (Leicester, 1989), pp. 28–39, at 28–33.

[66] Everitt, *Continuity*, pp. 69–92.

The king's protection or *mund*, whose breach led to a fine of fifty gold shillings, was also used to prevent the violation of his slave girls (*c.* 10) and of the 'best' widows of noble rank (*c.* 75). Even more remarkably the same sum was exacted by the king as 'lord-ring' (*drihtinbeage*) when a free man was slain (*c.* 6), and probably also when a free man was the victim of robbery (*c.* 9). Clearly royal lordship was already dominant in Kent and was being exercised over both the noble and the free classes. Both *eorls* and *ceorls* in Kent had their own estates (*tunas*), however, staffed by their own 'loaf-eaters' (dependants) and female slaves who came under their *mund* of 12 and 6 shillings respectively (*cc.* 13–17, 25, 27). Both the Kentish king and the noble and free lords therefore had a financial interest in doing justice. In the laws of Hlothhere and Eadric we hear of the court (*mædel þing*) where the judges of the Kentish people (*Cantwara deman*) imposed right on plaintiffs and defendants (*c.* 8); we also meet the king's hall (*sele*) in the trading port of *Lundenwic* where witnesses could be brought before the king's *wic*-reeve to warrant disputed property that had been bought in the town (*c.* 16). Presumably the kings had halls at other centres where reeves could fulfil the same function. In Canterbury it seems likely that the great Roman theatre, whose vast bulk dominated the early medieval town, long served as the assembly place for the Cantware.[67] The overall impression is of a highly centralized kingdom on which royal lordship had been firmly imposed.

However strongly governed Æthelberht's Kent may have been, it seems likely to have been an amalgamation of two kingdoms that had once been distinct. The creation of a second Kentish bishopric at Rochester as early as 604 is difficult to understand, unless there was a real sense in which the inhabitants of West Kent were still at that time a separate *gens*. No other seventh-century English kingdom had two sees until Archbishop Theodore deliberately set out in the 670s to divide the vast East Anglian, Northumbrian, Mercian and West Saxon bishoprics. Until then diocese and kingdom were coterminous. Yet in the seventh and eighth centuries Kent was frequently ruled by two joint-kings and, as Dr Yorke has recently shown, it was common for one of these kings to be subordinate and sometimes (perhaps normally) to have authority only in West Kent. Some of these minor rulers in Kent were the sons or brothers of the king of the whole of Kent; others, such as Sæbbi, Sigehere and Swæfheard in the late 680s and early 690s, and Sigered in the early 760s, seem to have been either the contemporary kings of Essex or else cadets of the East Saxon royal house.[68] If we compare this

[67] Brooks, *Early History*, pp. 24–5.
[68] B.A.E. Yorke, 'Joint Kingship in Kent, *c.* 560–785', *Archaeologia Cantiana*, 99 (1983), pp. 1–20. There are some important revisions of the order and dates of early eighth-century Kentish kings in *Charters of St Augustine's Abbey Canterbury*, ed. S.E. Kelly, Anglo-Saxon Charters, 4 (London, 1995), pp. 195–203.

evidence with that for the seventh-century subordinate Northumbrian kingdom of Deira, which – thanks to Bede – is somewhat better evidenced, then it is difficult to resist the suggestion that West Kent had been either a separate kingdom for which the rulers of (East) Kent and of Essex had competed or a part of a once larger East Saxon kingdom.

In this connection we need to remember that archaeologists have long recognized that the pagan archaeology of West Kent is distinct from that of the richer East; its links are with the cemeteries of the lower Thames valley, especially those of Surrey and Essex, not with those of East Kent with their Jutish and Frankish connections.[69] One further indication of the early separation of East and West Kent may be found in the place-name Wester in the parish of Linton in East Kent (Figure 2). If this name indeed contains the primitive element -*ge* (cf. German *Gau*), then this 'western district' was an exact parallel to Eastry ('the eastern *ge*').[70] A kingdom whose 'western *ge*' had its administrative centre at Wester cannot have included West Kent. The implication would seem to be that the earliest Anglo-Saxon kingdom of Kent, presumably before the reign of Æthelberht, only comprised what is today East Kent, that is the medieval diocese of Canterbury. Hence *Durovernum* (Canterbury) could properly be termed in Old English *Cantwaraburh*, 'the borough of the people of Kent', that is of this smaller kingdom in the east. Whether West Kent was an autonomous kingdom for long or whether it was always disputed between the Kentish and East Saxon dynasties cannot be known. We may suspect, however, that a function of the Kentish origin legend was to show Æthelberht's purported ancestors operating in West Kent and in the vicinity of London so as to justify his claim to that half of the kingdom too.

If we wish to pursue the substructure of the early Kentish kingdom more deeply, then we have to tackle the thorny problem of the Kentish lathes. Domesday Book shows that in 1086 Kent was divided into administrative and jurisdictional districts whole Old English name, *læð*, was latinized by the Anglo-Norman scribes as *lest(um)*. In East Kent there were four lathes: *Wiwarlest* from *Wiwaralæð*, 'the lathe of the men of Wye'; *Borowartlest* from *Burhwaralæð*, 'the late of the men of the borough (i.e. Canterbury)'; *Limowarlest* from *Limenwaralæð*, 'the lathe of the men of Lympne' (or 'of the river *Limen*'); and *lest de Estrei*, 'the lathe of Eastry'. In West Kent there was one whole lathe of Aylesford (*lest de Elesford*) and two 'half lathes' of Sutton-at-Hone and Milton Regis (*dimidium lest de Sudtone, dimidium lest de Middeltune*). The

---

[69] S.C. Hawkes, 'Anglo-Saxon Kent', pp. 70–4.

[70] J.K. Wallenberg, *Place-Names of Kent* (Uppsala, 1934), p. 139, was cautious; A.H. Smith, 'Place-names and the Anglo-Saxon settlement', *Proceedings of the British Academy*, 42 (1956), p. 82, and idem, *English Place-Name Elements* (English Place-Name Society, 26, 1956), ii, p. 256, accepts derivation from -*ge*.

geographical reality of the division of Kent into lathes is revealed by the fact that almost every Kentish manor in the survey is said to lie in a certain lathe and a certain hundred. Hence the Domesday lathes can be mapped (Figure 3). The men of the four lathes of East Kent sometimes met together as a single court, for they were asked by the Domesday commissioners to declare what laws or rights the king had over the *alodiarii* (the free peasants or gavelkinders) of the whole county. They replied that the king had a fine of 100 shillings for encroachments upon the king's highway (*publica via regis*), that he had *grithbryce* (the fine for breach of his especial peace) of £8 when the offence occurred on the road, but that all other royal fines (*forisfacturae*) were of 100 shillings.[71] Allowing for the differences in the units of account, we may surely see these eleventh-century 100 shilling fines as the successors of the fines of 50 Kentish gold shillings for *mundbryce* and *drihtinbeage* in Æthelberht's laws and as fulfilling much the same function. Whether we should place any weight upon the fact that the men of the lathes of East Kent appear to declare the law for the whole county and whether we may suppose that some form of lathe and lathe court already existed in Æthelberht's day for the exaction of such fines are more problematic issues.

The word *læð* is in fact only rarely found in pre-Conquest documents. Like OE *soc* ('soke') it may mean either 'jurisdiction' or a 'court' or the area over which authority is exercised. The one document where names lathes occur is the Rochester bridgework list of *c.* 975.[72] The identification of all the contributory estates listed there, however, shows that 'Aylesford and all the lathe that belongs thereto' cannot refer to the Domesday lathe of Aylesford, but only to the royal manor of Aylesford itself; whilst the reference to 'Hollingbourne and all the lathe that belongs to it' is to the area that was later the Domesday hundred of Eyhorne. It seems clear that 'lathe' was not a technical term for a district of a particular size and function. Despite the richness of our documentation for Anglo-Saxon Kent, it would be foolish to attach much weight to the absence of any explicit reference to administrative territories that can be identified with the Domesday lathes. If the courts of the lathes are correctly understood as courts of the free peasants, the gavelkinders, of Kent,[73] then we should not expect our extant Kentish charters and dispute settlements, which only concern the nobility and

[71] *Domesday Book seu Liber censualis Willelmi Primi Regis*, ed. A. Farley, 2 vols (London, 1783), i, fo. 1a.
[72] J. Bosworth and T.N. Toller, *Anglo-Saxon Dictionary* (rev. edn A. Campbell, Oxford, 1975), s.v.; the Rochester bridgework document is A.J. Robertson, *Anglo-Saxon Charters* (1st edn, Cambridge, 1939), no. 52, and the estates and territorial units assigned to the repair of sections of the bridge are identified by G. Ward. 'The lathe of Aylesford in 975', *Archaeologia Cantiana*, 46 (1934), pp. 7–26.
[73] J.E.A. Jolliffe, *Pre-Feudal England: The Jutes* (Oxford, 1933), pp. 39–72.

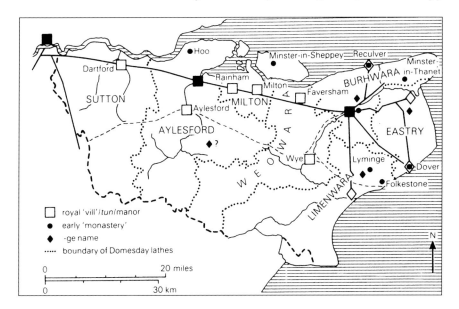

Figure 3. Early Kent: administrative divisions. The boundaries of the Domesday lathes in the Weald are largely conjectural. The royal 'vills' or manors are those recorded in Domesday Book or in pre-Conquest charters; the monasteries are those recorded before 900.

emanate from the shire court(s) of East and West Kent, to refer to them.

The principle evidence that the Domesday system of lathes is indeed ancient is found in a number of diplomas of the eighth century granting estates in various parts of Kent that have detached woodland pastures ('denns') in the Weald ('the common wood'), which are said to lie *on limenweara wealde, on weowera wealde, in limen wero wealdo et in burh waro uualdo, in cæstruuarouualth, on cæstersæta walda* and so forth.[74] By that time substantial areas of the Weald would seem to have already been assigned to the lathes of the *limenwara*, the *burhwara* and the *weowara* as commons for the pannage of herds of pigs; it would also seem that the *cæsterwara* or *cæstersæte*, 'the people of the chester' (i.e. of Rochester), may be an early name for a West Kentish lathe which in Domesday Book is apparently represented in whole or in part by the 'lathe of Aylesford'. In other charters we meet estates located *in regione eastrgena, in regione easterege* and *in regione caestruuara*.[75] Such phrases might be translated as 'in the lathe of Eastry' and 'in the lathe of the

---

[74] S 1180 (= BCS 141); S 125 (= BCS 248); S 30 (= Campbell, *Rochester*, no. 4); S 157 (= Campbell, *Rochester*, no. 16).

[75] S 128 (= BCS 254); S 1264 (BCS 332); S 31 (= BCS 199).

men of Rochester', if *regio* here refers to a precise administrative district rather just the general vicinity.

Our understanding of such references and of the working and origins of the lathe system in Kent is dominated by the interpretation of J.E.A. Jolliffe, who approached the lathe from the legal and estate records of the thirteenth century and regarded it as a relic of the pre-feudal age.[76] For him the lathe was 'an embodied folk' administering customary law in its court and regulating customary communal use of outlying wealden and marshland pastures. At the centre of each lathe was a royal vill, adminis-tered by a *praefectus* or reeve, where the dues of the free peasantry were collected without the intervention of any intermediate lords. By analysing the assessment of Kentish manors in Domesday Book, Jolliffe deduced that each lathe was a territorial unit assessed at a round number of 80 or 160 sulungs for the purpose of securing the payment of food rents to the king.[77] This assessment was ancient, being already traceable in the reckoning of estates in terms of *aratra* in the earliest Kentish charters of the late seventh century. It followed that the five lathes and two half lathes of Domesday Book had in the seventh century been represented by some eleven or twelve original lathes with a uniform assessment in sulungs. Jolliffe believed that these original units could also be traced through the use of the Latin term *regio* and the vernacula *-ware* in early sources, as well as through the occurrence of the primitive element *-ge* in Kentish place-names (Eastry, Sturry and Lyminge). Thus for example it was possible to recognize early references to lathes of Sturry, Lyminge, Hoo, Rainham and Faversham.[78] The further back one traced the lathe, the smaller and more regular it became.

Jolliffe's interpretation of the lathe has been enormously influential. As he foresaw, scholars have detected similar pre-feudal territorial units based on royal vills very widely elsewhere in Britain: in the sokes of East Anglia, the 'shires' and 'thanages' of northern England and Scotland, in the 'multiple' or 'discrete' estates beloved by geographers and in primi-tive *regiones* in many parts of Anglo-Saxon England.[79] In Kent K.P. Witney, building on Jolliffe's work, identified a high proportion of the 500-odd outlying wealden 'denns' of Kentish manors and was able to

[76] Jolliffe, *Pre-Feudal England.*

[77] J.E.A. Jolliffe, 'The Hidation of Kent', *English Historical Review*, 44 (1929), pp. 613–14; and *Pre-Feudal England*, pp. 44–6.

[78] Ibid., p. 46.

[79] R.H.C. Davis, *Kalendar of Abbot Samson* (Royal Historical Society, Camden 3rd series, 84, 1954); G.W.S. Barrow, 'Pre-feudal Scotland: Shires and Thanes', in *The Kingdom of the Scots* (London, 1973), pp. 7–68; G.R.J. Jones, 'Multiple Estates and Early Settlement', in P.H. Sawyer, ed., *English Medieval Settlement*, ed. (London, 1979), pp. 9–34; W.J. Ford, 'Some Settlement Patterns in the Central Region of the Warwickshire Avon', ibid., pp. 143–63.

go on to conjecture how the Weald had been divided between nine of the supposed twelve original lathes.[80] Before this dominant model is inscribed on the tablets, however, its foundations need to be examined.

The counting of sulungs (as of hides) is a horrible task on which no two scholars agree, and it is not surprising that before the age of the computer Jolliffe made slips and that his desire to find eighty-sulung units sometimes overrode the evidence or the geographical probabilities. K.P. Witney has corrected the grosser errors but his successive emendations of the details mean that there is no longer any clear overall pattern and therefore put the reality of the eighty-sulung units into question. Even more fundamentally, however, neither Jolliffe nor Witney sought to establish the antiquity of the Domesday assessments. Domesday Book itself shows that there were major changes in the assessment of estates between 1066 and 1086; yet we are asked to believe that the 1066 assessment was that of the seventh century, substantially without change. Whenever we examine particular estates in detail, we find evidence to the contrary. A single example must suffice. The cathedral church of Canterbury claimed to have been given twenty-six sulungs at Reculver by King Eadred in a charter which survives in a tenth-century manuscript. The detailed boundary clause establishes that the estate by then comprised the ecclesiastical parishes of Herne, Reculver and Hoath, as did the archiepiscopal manor of Reculver in the thirteenth century and subsequently.[81] Yet the assessment of the manor in Domesday Book and subsequently was only eight sulungs, not twenty-six. In fact amongst the authentic pre-Conquest charters of Christ Church, Canterbury, there is not one where the assessment of the estate is identical with that of the Domesday manor of the same name. Reductions of varying proportions are the rule.[82] Yet unless they were uniform and systematic throughout the county, such reductions will have made any attempt to reconstruct the seventh-century units from the Domesday assessments hazardous.

Equally unsatisfactory, as Gordon Ward demonstrated,[83] was

---

[80] K.P. Witney, *The Jutish Forest* (London, 1976), especially pp. 31–55. Witney's further revisions of Jolliffe's 'original lathes' are in his *Kingdom of Kent* (Chichester, 1982), pp. 52–60, 236–8. For an early vigorous and for the most part well-justified criticism of Jolliffe's use of sources see G. Ward's review in *Archaeologia Cantiana*, 45 (1933), pp. 290–4.

[81] S 546 (= BCS 880); for the later manorial history of Reculver see K.H. McIntosh and H.E. Gough, eds, *Hoath and Herne: The Last of the Forest* (Canterbury, 1984). For my understanding of the details of the bounds I am indebted to information from Mr Gough, Mr P.R. Kitson, Mr T. Tatton-Brown and Mrs M. Sparks.

[82] e.g. Ickham: 14 sulungs in S 123 (= BCS 247), 4 in DB; Mersham: 5 sul. in S 328 (= BCS 496) + 9 in S 332 (= BCS 507), 6 in DB; Teynham: 30 hides in S 1258 (= BCS 291), 12 sul. in S 1613 (= BCS 301), 5½ in DB; Warehorne: 5 sul. in S 282 (= BCS 396), 1 in DB.

[83] *Archaeologia Cantiana*, 45 (1933), pp. 290–4.

Jolliffe's incomplete and selective discussion of the use of the term *regio* in early charters. When a charter states that a property is *in regione quae vocatur cert, in regione vocabulo bromgeheg* or *in regione quae dicitur westan widde*,[84] there can be little doubt that it is simply locating the land by reference to the nearest estate centre or notable topographical feature. We do not need to start inventing early lathes of Chart, Broomy or Westwood. For the same reason we should hesitate before accepting the reality of the supposed early lathes of Rainham or Faversham, unless we suppose that every royal estate had its lathe.[85] When the *regio* is a folk name – *in regione caestruuara, in regione merscuuariorum* – the case for regarding it as a 'lathe' is clearly stronger, particularly since we find the former people to have had woodland commons in the Weald, whilst the *Merscware* ('the people of Romney Marsh') were of sufficient importance for their devastation by King Coenwulf of Mercia to be mentioned alongside that of the *Cantware*.[86] We can only guess, however, whether the *Merscware* were a subdivision of the *Limenware*, an alternative name for the same lathe or a separate folk and lathe in their own right. More instructive is the case of the Hoo peninsula: the Domesday hundred of Hoo, which comprised estates assessed at fifty-seven sulungs, seems to have been the territory of *Howare* in the Rochester bridgework list and may be identical with the *regio* in which the neighbouring estate of Stoke lay in a charter of 738.[87] It would seem that *-ware*, like *læð* and *regio*, could be applied to areas or peoples of different size and different status.

There is therefore good reason to be much more cautious how we reconstruct the primitive *regiones* of Kent. A new analysis of the Domesday assessments without Jolliffe's preconceptions, a study of the parish and hundredal boundaries along the lines now proving so fruitful elsewhere, and the testing of the wide range of evidence that Professor Everitt has brought to bear on the development of Kentish settlement – all these are needed before we can hope to identify the early territorial units of Kent or to understand their role with any confidence. For the present it may be most helpful to summarize present knowledge in diagrammatic form (Figure 4).

This presentation of the evidence suggests that the four lathes of East Kent existed from the early days of the kingdom. Each was based upon a major royal vill; three of the four had a single *-ge* name in their territory; and three had woodland commons in the Weald mentioned in

---

[84] S 25 (= BCS 191); S 36 (= Campbell, *Rochester*, no. 10); S 177 (= BCS 348).

[85] Jolliffe, *Pre-Feudal England*, 46, and Witney, *Kingdom of Kent*, p. 236, arguing from S 128 (= BCS 254) and S 168 (= BCS 335).

[86] S 31 (= BCS 199); the *regio* of the *Merscuare* appears in a tenth-century interpolation to the text of S 168 (= BCS 335); ASC s.a. (796 for) 798.

[87] Robertson, *Anglo-Saxon Charters*, 52; S 27 (= Campbell, *Rochester*, no. 3).

Figure 4. The primitive *regiones* of Kent.

Domesday Lathe	Royal Vill	*Ge*	*Wara* name	Monastery	*Regio*
Wiwaralæð	Wye (Faversham)		Wiwaraweald	Minster-in-Sheppey	
Burhwaralæð	Canterbury	(Sturry)	Burhwaraweald	St Augustine's Minster-in-Thanet Reculver	
Limenwaralæð	Lympne	(Lyminge)	Limenwaraweald	Lyminge Folkestone	
Eastry	Eastry	Eastry		Dover	Eastry
Aylesford	Aylesford (Rochester)	(?Wester)	Cæsterware	(Hoo)	Cæsterware
Sutton (½)	Dartford				
Milton (½)	Milton (Rainham)				
			Merscware Howare	Hoo	Merscware Hoo
	Rainham Faversham				Rainham Faversham

early charters. At present there does not seem to be any good evidence that there were ever more than four lathes in the East. A case has indeed been made for a lathe of Faversham; but it amounts to no more than that (i) there was a royal estate there in the ninth century as in Domesday; (ii) a nearby property could be described as 'in the region suburban to the king's *oppidum* which is called by the inhabitants there Faversham'; and (iii) Faversham had a detached wood at Kingsnoad in Ulcombe.[88] In West Kent there seems to be no evidence that the lathe of Aylesford or the half lathes of Sutton and Milton were ancient administrative units. We hear instead in pre-Conquest charters of a single unit based on Rochester, that is of the *Cæsterware*; later, perhaps when the kings had given away all their property in the city to the bishops, West Kent was reorganized into three unequal territories based upon the king's chief manors.

Such an interpretation of the early lathe system of East and West Kent is very much less ambitious than that of Jolliffe, but it does not do

---

[88] Jolliffe, *Pre-Feudal England*, pp. 45–50, and Witney, *Jutish Forest*, pp. 32, 35, 42, 249–51, citing S 168 (BCS 335), S 169 (= BCS 341), S 170 (= BCS 340), S 178 (= BCS 353) and S 300 (= BCS 459).

violence to the sources. It has the merit too of pointing to yet another way in which West Kent differed from the East. 'Men of Kent' and 'Kentishmen' were, it would seem, distinct in their organization, and the differences may go back to the incorporation of West Kent under the rule of the East Kentish dynasty – a process that is likely to have been prolonged, but to have reached a decisive stage in the reign of Æthelberht. It may have been at that time too that the Kentish origin legends and the Kentish royal genealogy were first formulated for the gratification of the itinerant king and his *leode*. The court of an ambitious and initially pagan overlord is exactly the place where we would expect there to be cultivated stories of his heroic and divine ancestors, claims of his descent from the first Anglo-Saxon leaders and accounts of their glorious activities in the most recently acquired part of his kingdom. In the English origin legend in its various forms may we not detect some of the political cement of the kingdom of Æthelberht?[89]

[89] I am most grateful to David Dumville, Simon Keynes, David Kirby, Chris Wickham and Patrick Wormald for their comments on earlier drafts of this chapter, which have helped me to make many corrections and improvements. I remain alone responsible for the views expressed and for errors that persist.

4

The Formation of the Mercian Kingdom

THE MERCIANS stand out as by far the most successful of the various early Anglo-Saxon peoples until the later ninth century when they succumbed to the Viking military threat. Yet precisely because Mercia eventually failed, its history remains obscure. Indeed, despite the kingdom's early political prominence there are virtually no Mercian written sources. Not only is there no Mercian chronicle but there was not even a single Mercian among the informants whom Bede consulted when preparing his Ecclesiastical History.[1] Some fragments of annals, purportedly of seventh- or eighth-century origin, recording the creation of the Mercian kingdom have indeed been rescued by Professor Wendy Davies from oblivion among the later compilations of Henry of Huntingdon, Roger of Wendover and Matthew Paris in which they had been incorporated; but they seem to be East Anglian rather than Mercian in their focus, and the date of their composition remains to be determined.[2] No Mercian ecclesiastic has left us a letter collection, as have the West Saxon Boniface and the Northumbrian Alcuin, though both of these on occasion corresponded with Mercians. We might indeed consider that the 159 Latin diplomas issued in the name of Mercian rulers should qualify as Mercian sources, but almost all of them concern estates in kingdoms that fell under Mercian rule – Kent and the territory of the Hwicce above all – rather than in Mercia itself, and they seem to have been drafted and written by local ecclesiastics rather than by Mercians.[3] Even the coins which bear

---

[1] *Bede's Ecclesiastical History of the English People*, ed. B. Colgrave and R.A.B. Mynors (Oxford, 1969), preface. This chapter follows Bede's chronology as interpreted by S. Wood, 'Bede's Northumbrian Dates Again', *English Historical Review*, 98 (1983), pp. 280–96.

[2] W. Davies, 'Annals and the Origin of Mercia', in A. Dornier, ed., *Mercian Studies* (Leicester, 1977), pp. 17–29.

[3] P.H. Sawyer, *Anglo-Saxon Charters: An Annotated List and Bibliography* (London, 1968), nos 67–226. For local production of early charters, see P. Chaplais, 'The Origin and Authenticity of the Royal Anglo-Saxon Diploma', *Journal of the Society of Archivists*, 3 (1965–9), pp. 48–61, and N.P. Brooks, *The Early History of the Church of Canterbury* (Leicester, 1984), pp. 167–70, 327–30.

the names of Mercian kings were minted in south-eastern England or in East Anglia. Their circulation was indeed much wider, but what they can tell us of the Mercian kingdom, though important, is limited.[4] The Anglo-Saxon royal genealogies, which used to be attributed to the court of King Offa, were rebaptized the 'Anglian Collection' by Dr Dumville and with some important caveats accorded a Northumbrian provenance.[5] Finally there is the mysterious Tribal Hidage. Though historians have disputed its date and interpretation, there has been some consensus that it is a Mercian tribute list.[6] Yet if it is indeed a tribute list rather than a general register of hidage assessments capable of serving a variety of purposes, then it seems unlikely to have been Mercian; for the first people whose hidage assessment is listed are the Mercians themselves – 30,000 hides'. An early medieval king did not impose tribute upon his own kingdom. A Northumbrian origin for the Tribal Hidage deserves consideration since it could explain both the document's overall form and the fact that the Elmetsaete are included while both the Deirans and the Bernicians are omitted.

Be that as it may, our knowledge of the Mercians certainly depends to an astonishing degree upon information preserved by their neighbours, their enemies and those whom they conquered. Such people had little reason to record or to develop any coherent account of the origin of the Mercian kingdom. The historian investigating Mercian origins has therefore to draw conclusions from uncertain, incomplete and hazardous materials.

Locating the Mercians

The people known to us as the Mercians (OE *Mierce*, Latin *Mercii*), the 'borderers' or 'dwellers on the march', have certainly been so-called since the early eighth century. That is, for example, the only name

---

[4] A convenient modern survey with full references may be found in P. Grierson and M. Blackburn, *Medieval European Coinage, i, Early Middle Ages (Fifth–Tenth Centuries)* (Cambridge, 1986), pp. 155–89, 270–93.

[5] D.N. Dumville, 'The Anglian Collection of Royal Genealogies and Regnal Lists', *Anglo-Saxon England*, 5 (1976), pp. 23–50.

[6] D. Dumville, 'The Tribal Hidage: an Introduction to its Texts and their History', in *The Origins of Anglo-Saxon Kingdoms*, ed. S.R. Bassett (Leicester, 1989), pp. 225–30, at 227, and in BCS 297. The principal modern discussions are C.R. Hart, 'The Tribal Hidage', *Transactions of the Royal Historical Society*, fifth series, 21 (1971), pp. 133–57; W. Davies and H. Vierck, 'The Contexts of Tribal Hidage: Social Aggregates and Settlement Patterns', *Frühmittelalterliche Studien*, 8 (1974), pp. 223–93; H.R. Loyn, *The Governance of Anglo-Saxon England 500–1087* (London, 1984), pp. 34–40. For tribute see T. Reuter, 'Plunder and Tribute in the Carolingian Empire', *Transactions of the Royal Historical Society*, fifth series, 35 (1985), pp. 75–94.

known to Bede. It is true that the late Dr Hunter Blair argued that the term *Suþanhymbre* (Southumbrians'), which is used sparingly by annals which derive from a Northumbrian compilation of the early eighth century, was indeed an early name for the Mercians;[7] but there is no reason to suppose that the name ever had any currency outside Northumbria. It seems more likely to have been coined late in response to the name *Norðanhymbre* for the Deiran and Bernician peoples when united in one kingdom. Thus the legends on Mercian coins describe their kings only as *Rex* or *Rex Merciorum*, never as 'kings of the Southumbrians'.[8] Similarly the drafters of Mercian charters did not, it would seem, know of this or any other antique name when they sought to vary the regnal styles of Mercian kings. (We may contrast the way that West Saxons occasionally refer to their rulers as kings 'of the Gewisse').[9] Similarly Bede, 'Eddius' Stephanus and the Anglo-Saxon Chronicle all confidently refer to the 'Mercians' from the very first occasion that they need to mention them.[10] So far as we can tell, therefore, 'the Mercians' is the only and the original name of the people. To understand their origin we therefore need to locate the boundary from which they took their name.

When Bede described Rædwald of East Anglia's defeat of Æthelfrith in 616 by the river Idle, he stated that the battle on the east bank of the river was *in finibus gentis Merciorum* (Figure 5).[11] But the location of the north-eastern boundary of the Mercian kingdom there in Bede's day is no indication of the whereabouts of the original *mearc* from which they were named. At first sight the Tribal Hidage provides a better chance of resolving the problem, since in allotting 30,000 hides to the land of the Mercians it goes on to specify the territory as that 'which is called the first (land) of the Mercians' (*þær mon ærest myrcna hæt*). By identifying the neighbouring peoples on all sides that are listed in the Tribal Hidage we can therefore locate the territory that the compiler considered to be 'original Mercia'. On the west we appear to have the Wreocensæte and

[7] P.H. Blair, 'The Northumbrians and their Southern Frontier', *Archaeologia Aeliana*, fourth series, 26 (1948), pp. 98–126 at 105–12, citing the Anglo-Saxon Chronicle (ed. D. Whitelock et al., London, 1961), E s.a. 449, 641, 697, 702.

[8] Grierson and Blackburn, *Medieval European Coinage, i*, p. 279; H. Pagan, 'Coinage in Southern England, 796–874', in M. Blackburn, ed., *Anglo-Saxon Monetary History* (Leicester, 1986), p. 46.

[9] H.E. Walker, 'Bede and the Gewisse', *Cambridge Historical Journal*, 12 (1956), pp. 174–86. For *rex Geuis(s)orum* in early West Saxon charters, see Sawyer, *Charters*, nos 256, 262 whose authenticity is discussed by H. Edwards, 'The Authority of the Earliest West Saxon Charters' (unpublished Ph.D. thesis, University of Glasgow, 1985), pp. 407–8.

[10] *Historia ecclesiastica*, ii.12, 14, 20; *The Life of Bishop Wilfrid by Eddius Stephanus*, ed. B. Colgrave (Cambridge, 1927), c. 14; ASC s.a. 655, 657.

[11] *Historia ecclesiastica*, ii.12.

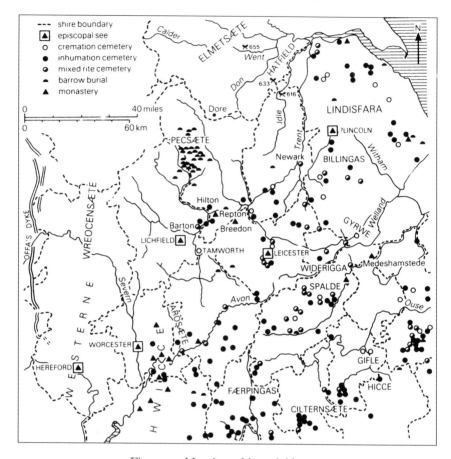

Figure 5. Mercia and its neighbours.

Westerne; on the north the Pecsæte, the Elmetsæte and the Lindesfaran with Hatfield; on the east a host of small East Midland peoples including the Gyrwe, Spalde, Gifle, Hicce and so forth; and on the south the Hwicce, the Arosæte and the Færpingas (Figure 5). Few scholars believe that it is now possible to define the boundaries of these peoples (and therefore of 'original Mercia') exactly, but there is a measure of agreement on their general location.[12] Though some substantial peoples, such as the *Wigesta* (900 hides), the *Nox* and *Oht*

---

[12] C.R. Hart's bold attempt ('Tribal Hidage') to define the boundaries has not been accepted, but there is much common ground between him and the work of Davies and Vierck and of Loyn, of D. Hill, *Atlas of Anglo-Saxon England* (Oxford, 1981), map 136, and of D. Hooke, *Anglo-Saxon Territorial Organization: The Western Margins of Mercia* (University of Birmingham, Department of Geography, Occasional Paper 22, 1986), pp. 1–45.

gaga (5000 and 2000 hides), the *Hendrica* (3500 hides), and the *Unecungga* (1200 hides), still defy identification, it would seem that the 'original Mercia' of the Tribal Hidage may have comprised much of the modern counties of Staffordshire, Leicestershire and Nottinghamshire together with south Derbyshire and northern Warwickshire. Whether it extended any further would be disputed. This extensive tract of Midland England, this 'first Mercia', may, however, itself have already been an agglomeration of earlier unrecorded peoples created primarily by military means. It is certainly difficult to envisage when or how the whole of this area was a frontier.

More helpful perhaps is Bede's statement that, at the time of the brief supremacy of Oswiu of Northumbria following his victory at the river *Winwæd* in 655, the 'North Mercians' were divided by the river Trent from the 'South Mercians', and that the two groups were assessed at 7000 and 5000 hides respectively.[13] We cannot tell whether the North and South Mercians together occupied a smaller territory than the 'original Mercia' of the Tribal Hidage or were merely less heavily assessed. Nor are we told whether the division of the Mercians was ancient or was a temporary arrangement imposed by Oswiu; but the fact of the division does suggest that the Trent flowed through the heart of the Mercian kingdom. Moreover it is in the vicinity of the Middle Trent that the principal historical foci of the Mercian kingdom are to be found (Figure 5). Thus the Mercian bishopric was established at Lichfield under Chad *c.* 669 (and it remained there until the Norman Conquest even though Lichfield was itself neither a former Roman town nor an Anglo-Saxon one). Also in the Middle Trent was the Mercian royal monastery of Repton, apparently already established by the late seventh century; and it was nearby at the royal vill of Tamworth that successive eighth- and ninth-century Mercian kings most frequently gathered their *fideles* to celebrate the major Christian festivals.[14] In the absence of evidence for earlier foci elsewhere it is surely in or near this Mercian heartland that we must locate the 'march' from which the Mercians were named. For this reason it seems best to side with Stenton and earlier scholars in supposing that the Mercians were originally a 'border people' because they were settled on the frontier with the Welsh Britons. Hunter Blair's iconoclastic notion that the *Mierce* somehow took their

[13] *Historia ecclesiastica*, ii.24.
[14] For Lichfield see *Historia ecclesiastica*, iv.3 and *Life of Wilfrid*, ed. Colgrave, c. 15, and below, p. 000 and n. 46. For Repton see the grant of Frithuric of 675 × 692, Sawyer, *Charters*, no. 1805 which is discussed above by J. Blair (above, ch. 7) and also by A. Dornier and by A. Rumble in Dornier, ed., *Mercian Studies*, pp. 158, 169–92. Early charters whose witness lists indicate meetings of the Mercian witan at Tamworth in 781, 790, 799, 808, 840, 841, 845, 849, 855 and 857 are S 121, s 133, S 155, S 163, S 192, S 193, S 198, S 199, S 207, S 208.

name from the important boundary between the Northumbrians and the *Sutangli*—that is the no man's land in North Derbyshire and South Yorkshire from Dore to the river Don, then to the Idle and the Humber (Figure 5), an area that is singularly devoid of pagan Anglo-Saxon cemeteries – has held the field for a generation.[15] But it entirely lacks positive supporting evidence – whether toponymic, historical or archaeological – and should therefore be set aside.

By contrast the Middle Trent valley is an area with numerous pagan Anglo-Saxon cemeteries, not only cremation cemeteries but also several of mixed rite and a number of inhumation cemeteries as well. They stretch from Newark, Holme Pierrepoint and Cotgrave (Nottinghamshire) in the east via Kingston-upon-Soar (Nottinghamshire) and Melbourne and Hilton (Derbyshire) in the centre and then to Caves Inn and Stapenhill (Leicestershire), Barton-under-Needwood and Stretton (Staffordshire) in the west. Unfortunately the river Trent cuts through the modern and medieval administrative boundaries – of counties and municipalities – which determined the establishment of museums and archaeological societies in Victorian times and more recently of archaeological units. As a result the Trent valley cemeteries have never been studied as a group. Such work as has been done in the last generation suggests that these proto-Mercian settlements were relatively small, relatively late (beginning in the sixth century rather than the fifth) and relatively poor. It has also suggested that the settlers reached the Middle Trent mainly from the east via such valleys as that of the Leicestershire river Soar and ultimately from the rivers that drain into the Wash.[16]

Kingdom and Dynasty

This conclusion, uncertain though it must be in the absence of any systematic modern study, has the merit of having been propounded *before* Professor Davies so boldly reconstructed various entries in

[15] Blair, 'Southern Frontier', pp. 112–26.

[16] A. Meaney, *A Gazetteer of Early Anglo-Saxon Burial Sites* (London, 1964), passim; M. Fowler, 'Anglian Settlement of the Derbyshire–Staffordshire Peak District', *Derbyshire Archaeological Journal*, 74 (1954), pp. 134–51; A. Ozanne, 'The Peak Dwellers', *Medieval Archaeology*, 6–7 (1962–3), pp. 15–52; T.H. McK. Clough, A. Dornier and R.A. Rutland, *Anglo-Saxon and Viking Leicestershire* (Leicester Museum, 1975). For more recent work see M.W. Bishop, 'An Anglian Cemetery at Cotgrave, Notts.', *Transactions of the Thoroton Society*, 88 (1984), pp. 16–17; S Losco-Bradley and H.M. Wheeler, 'Anglo-Saxon Settlement in the Trent Valley: Some Aspects', in M.L. Faull, ed., *Studies in Late Anglo-Saxon Settlement* (Oxford, 1984), pp. 101–14. J.N.L. Myres, *The English Settlements* (2nd edn, Oxford, 1986), pp. 182–6, largely follows his original account of 1935.

twelfth- and thirteenth-century annalistic compilations into a coherent account of the settlement and conquest of both East Anglia and Mercia under numerous chiefs (*proceres*) in the early sixth century, that is initially in 527 (or rather in 515, as she would have us correct it).[17] So far as Mercia is concerned, subsequent entries in these compilations purport to record the foundation of a Mercian kingdom by Crida (Creoda) in 585 and the succession of his son Pypba on Crida's death in 588, of Cearl (the first Mercian king mentioned by Bede) in 594 or 597, and of Penda by the year 610. Despite Professor Davies's tentative advocacy of the historicity of this material, it cannot be said that it is yet clear that what lies behind these scattered entries in the works of Henry of Huntingdon, Roger of Wendover and Matthew Paris is anything more important than some inventive conjectures by an English monk, perhaps as late as the early twelfth century, on the basis of the names available in Bede, the Mercian royal genealogy and the Anglo-Saxon Chronicle. On such an interpretation it would not be surprising that they should more or less fit the fragments of information that we have on the early history of Mercia; for the compiler of these entries may have had access to the same sources as are available to us.

The family (*egregia stirps*) to which Creoda, Pypba and Penda belonged traced their descent in the early eighth century from Icel and therefore came to be known as Iclingas.[18] Icel may have been regarded as the founder of the line because he was the first member of the family in Britain. According to the Mercian royal genealogies preserved in the 'Anglian Collection' of the end of the eighth century there were just five generations spanning the period from Icel to that of the Mercian brothers Penda and Eowa in the first half of the seventh century (Icel–Cnebba–Cynewald–Crida (Creoda)–Pypba–Penda).[19] Depending upon how we resolve the chronological *cruces* of Penda's reign and on whether we allow twenty-five or thirty years per generation we could therefore calculate a *floruit* for Icel at any time of our choice between *c.* 450 and 525. According to the genealogy the Iclingas were descended (via a number of heroes of poetry and myth) from the Germanic war god Woden. Such a claim was presumably an assertion of the Mercian dynasty's martial qualities. As in other kingdoms descent from Woden was part of the propaganda that accompanied the process by which certain dynasties brutally arrogated the kingly title and status to themselves and demoted other families whose past was no less presti-

[17] Davies, 'Annals', pp. 22–3.
[18] *Felix's Life of Saint Guthlac*, ed. B. Colgrave (Cambridge, 1956), c. 2.
[19] Dumville, 'Anglian Collection', p. 33. For the earlier (pre-Icel) stages of this genealogy, see idem, 'Kingship, Genealogies and Regnal Lists', in P. Sawyer and I. Wood, eds, *Early Medieval Kingship* (Leeds, 1977), pp. 72–104 at 93, and H.M. Chadwick, *The Origin of the English Nation* (Cambridge, 1907), pp. 111–43.

gious to be merely *principes, reguli, subreguli, praefecti, duces, ealdormen* and the like.[20] These centralizing and aggrandizing tendencies seem to have been stronger in England than they were in early medieval Ireland with its 150-odd *tuatha*, each with its own *rí* (king), or in Wales where we have evidence for about a dozen early kingdoms. Be that as it may, Midland England at the beginning of the seventh century is likely to have had much more in common with the multiplicity of rulers and states in the contemporary Celtic world than it was to have in the eighth or ninth centuries. There is no reason to suppose that the Iclinga dynasty, until it produced a war leader of genius, namely the pagan king Penda, was necessarily any more (or any less) royal than the ruling houses of any of the small Midland peoples which were separately recorded in the Tribal Hidage and assessed at 300 or 600 hides each.[21]

There is one other potential clue to the early activity of the Iclinga dynasty which has been strangely neglected in recent years. In 1927 Stenton drew attention to the concentration of place names in Worcestershire and Warwickshire which apparently preserve the rare personal names of Penda and his father Pypba.[22] In more recent times scholarly fashion has swung against the early emphasis on interpreting place-names in terms of personal names. Topographical names now arouse greater interest and topographical explanations tend to be sought when etymologies are uncertain. Stenton, however, had already warned his readers against the automatic association of these place-names with the Mercian leaders known to us. But their regional distribution is unlikely to be accidental and some such explanation as Stenton's, that these personal names must have become popular among Anglian settlers and lords in the West Midlands because of the success of the dynasty, is necessary. At least at second-hand the place-names are therefore likely to reflect the activities of the Iclinga dynasty, and it is worth extending the enquiry to all the names in the Mercian royal genealogy between the eponymous Icel and Penda:

Icel   Ickleton (Cambs.), Ickleford (Herts.) and Icklesham
            (Sussex).
Cnebba   Knebworth (Herts.).
Cynewald   Kinwalsey (Warwicks.).

---

[20] J. Campbell, *Bede's Reges and Principes* (Jarrow Lecture for 1979) (reprinted in idem, *Essays in Anglo-Saxon History* (London, 1986), pp. 85–98).

[21] Davies and Vierck, 'Tribal Hidage', pp. 224–41. For Ireland see F.J. Byrne, *Irish Kings and High-Kings* (London, 1973), and G. MacNiocaill, *Ireland before the Vikings* (Dublin, 1972); for Wales, W. Davies, *Wales in the Early Middle Ages* (Leicester, 1981), pp. 85–116.

[22] *The Place-Names of Worcestershire*, ed. A. Mawer and F.M. Stenton (English Place-Name Society, 4, 1927), 22.

Creoda	Credenhill (Herefs. and Wilts.), Curbridge (Oxon.), Curdworth (Warwicks.) and Kersoe and *Creodan ac* (Worcs.).
Pypba	Publow (Somerset), Pedmore, Pepper Wood and Pepwell (Worcs.) and possible Peplow (Shropshire).
Penda	Penley (Flintshire), Pinbury (Gloucs.), Peddimore (Warwicks.) and Pinvin and *Pendiford* (Worcs.).

Such a list must be used with caution.[23] Where there is only a single extant place-name, as is the case for Cnebba and Cynewald, its location is unlikely to be significant – particularly when the second element (for example, *gehæg* in Kinwalsey) suggests a much later origin than the sixth or seventh century. Equally the temptation to build elaborate conjectures about the origins of the dynasty upon the existence of two Icel names in the East Midlands should be resisted, since the location of both places on the Icknield Way warns us that alternative etymologies are possible. None the less it is clear that place-names formed from Creoda, Pypba and Penda are concentrated in the West Midlands, especially in the south-west (that is in, or on the fringes of, the later territory of the Hwicce). They are not found elsewhere. Such a distribution may suggest that the late accounts of the creation of a Mercian kingdom by Creoda and of its subsequent rule by Pypba and Penda do indeed represent some form of dynastic tradition, as Professor Davies has suggested. For the place-names certainly indicate that these three personal names achieved a unique popularity in this area, whilst the earlier names in the genealogy did not. The names may commemorate a particular and early phase of Anglian colonization.

Penda *c.* 626–655

Thus far we may dimly and very tentatively hope to pierce the gloom of Mercian origins. The achievement of Penda in forging a greater Mercian kingdom stands out more clearly from the sources. It cannot, however, be placed in its proper historical context unless some attempt is made to understand and explain the conflicting evidence for the duration of his reign. While there is unanimity that Penda met his death in battle against the Northumbrian king Oswiu, we have three separate dates for the commencement of his reign vouched for by independent authorities. Indeed we might have a fourth were we to accept Professor

---

[23] It has been compiled on the basis of the volumes of the English Place-Name Society supplemented by E. Ekwall, *The Concise Oxford Dictionary of English Place-Names* (4th edn, Oxford, 1960). I am most grateful to Margaret Gelling for advice on these names.

Davies's conjecture that behind the Anglo-Saxon Chronicle, Henry of Huntingdon and Roger of Wendover lies a source (either an annal or a regnal list) which allotted him a reign of fifty years and therefore supposed that Penda's reign began in 605 or 606.[24] That, however, would be to build a hypothesis upon the most improbable element in the latest of our three principal sources for Penda's reign. Since there are, as we shall see, simpler explanations available, it is best to concentrate attention upon the three sources that do exist:

1. The Anglo-Saxon Chronicle, compiled at the end of the ninth century, states under the year 626: 'And Penda held his kingdom for 30 years and he was 50 years old when he succeeded to the kingdom.'[25] Since the same source records that Penda 'perished' (*forwearþ*) in 655 (rather than 656), it is clear that we should not press the '30 years' too exactly.

2. In his Ecclesiastical History Bede described Cadwallon's defeat of Edwin of Northumbria at the battle of Hatfield in 633 and recounted that Penda, a *vir strenuissimus* of the Mercian royal line, had aided Cadwallon and from that time had himself ruled the Mercians for twenty-two years with varying fortune (*varia sorte*).[26]

3. Finally the *Historia Brittonum* in its so-called 'Northern British' section records: 'Penda, the son of Pypba, reigned ten years. He first freed (*separavit*) the kingdom of the Mercians from the kingdom of the Northerners (*Nordorum*) . . . He fought the battle of *Cocboy*, in which fell his brother Eowa, king of the Mercians (and) son of Pypba, and Oswald king of the Northerners.'[27]

Here then we have three independent and apparently contradictory versions of Penda's reign – namely that it lasted thirty, twenty-two or ten years respectively. Given that it is difficult to accept the Chronicle's assertion that Penda was already fifty years old in 626, given the low opinion in which the *Historia Brittonum* has been held by historians, and given the difficulty in reckoning only ten years from the battle of *Maserfelth/Cocboy* where Oswald was slain to that of *Winwæd/Campus Gai* where Penda himself fell, it is perhaps not surprising that historians have tended to stick to Bede's account. The other dates have been largely forgotten and Eowa has been neglected, except by Professor Davies who wrote of Penda and Eowa as joint rulers. But if we bear in mind that none of these sources is Mercian, then we should be less surprised that they record contradictory information about Penda. Not

---

[24] Davies, 'Annals', p. 21.

[25] ASC s.a. 626.

[26] *Historia ecclesiastica*, ii.20.

[27] *Historia Brittonum*, ed. T. Mommsen, *Chronica Minora Saec. IV–VII*, iii, MGH Auctores Antiquissimi, XIII (Berlin, 1898), c. 65.

only may his reign have been perceived differently by his West Saxon, Northumbrian and Welsh neighbours, but they also only had reason to record those of his activities which brought him into military contact with their own peoples. We should also observe that Bede's statement that after Hatfield (633) Penda ruled the Mercians with mixed fortune could indicate that his reign was intermittent, which would allow it to have had a new beginning after his defeat of Oswald at *Maserfelth/Cocboy* (642).

Greater difficulties are presented by the 626 annal in the Anglo-Saxon Chronicle. As H.M. Chadwick pointed out long ago, if Penda had indeed been aged fifty in 626 he would have been almost eighty at the battle of the *Winwæd*. Yet it is difficult to believe that he could have been termed *vir strenuissimus* at Hatfield in 633 when he would already have been fifty-seven, or that his eldest son Peada should have been a young man (*iuvenis*) in 653, or that another son, Wulfhere, should have still been *adulescens* when he was brought out of hiding in 658, while a third son, Æthelred, who was to retire to a monastery as late as 704, was apparently even younger still, it would be strange too that Penda's sister should have married Cenwalh of Wessex between 642 and 645 at a time when her brother was nearly seventy.[28] Individually none of these items is impossible, but cumulatively they suggest that the Chronicle's chronology has had the effect of making Penda a generation too old.

If we re-examine the 626 annal with this in mind it becomes significant that, although its purpose ought to be to record Penda's accession, in fact it only states the length of his reign and his age, both of which more naturally belong to a record of the end of his reign or to a regnal list. The Chronicle's source may have recorded this information in some such brief form as: *Penda mortuus est xxx^{mo} anno regni sui, aetate L.* In calculating from his death at the *winwæd* (655) that Penda must have acquired the throne in 626, the chronicler could simply have misapplied Penda's age to his accession. In other words what the Chronicle should have written under 626 was: 'Penda (succeeded to the kingdom and) reigned 30 years and was 50 years old *when he died.*' This simple emendation would solve all the chronological problems of Penda's career and would have him reigning (intermittently) from the age of about twenty until his death in battle aged fifty. It is easier to suppose that the *strenuissimus vir* who was an ally of Cadwallon in the defeat of Edwin at Hatfield was twenty-seven years of age than that he was already fifty-seven; by the same token it is easier to believe that the victor of *Maserfelth* was thirty-six rather than sixty-six, and that the great warrior king who led thirty *duces regii* to the *Winwæd* and left

[28] Chadwick, *Origin*, p. 15, referring to *Historia ecclesiastica*, ii.20, iii.7, 21, 24, and v, 13.

young children among his heirs was a man of fifty, not a doddering octogenarian.

There is a little more information to be elicited from the evidence for his accession. The Welsh sources, that is both the *Historia Brittonum* and the *Annales Cambriae*, regard Penda's reign as lasting from his victory at *Cocboy/Maserfelth* to his defeat at the battle of the field of *Gai* (that is Bede's *Winwæd*).[29] Hence when the *Historia* states that at *Cocboy* Oswald king of the Northerners and Eowa king of the Mercians were killed, its assumption is probably that Eowa was ruling the Mercians until his death in that battle and that Penda succeeded him as a result. We should therefore hesitate to follow Professor Davies in supposing that Eowa had ruled jointly with his brother Penda – common though shared kingship was in the Anglo-Saxon kingdoms of the seventh and eighth centuries. Rather Eowa's reign may have been one of the periods in Bede's twenty-two years when Penda's fortunes were low. Here we need to bear in mind the *Historia*'s statement that Penda first *separavit* the kingdom of the Mercians from the Northerners. There is some exaggeration of Penda's achievement here, for the Mercian king Cearl can scarcely have been subject to the Northumbrian Æthelfrith when he allowed his daughter Cwenburh to marry the exiled Deiran prince Edwin.[30] None the less the author of the *Historia* would seem to have believed that before the battle of *Cocboy/Maserfelth* the Mercians and their king Eowa had indeed been subject to control by the Northumbrian king Oswald. We should therefore beware assuming that Eowa was killed fighting alongside his brother Penda. If Eowa had indeed been a Northumbrian puppet, it is more probable that he fought alongside his overlord to maintain his throne against his brother.

By such means the bare bones of Penda's career begin to emerge. There seems no reason to reject the Chronicle's suggestion that Penda had acquired the Mercian throne in (or about) 626, for the West Saxons had reason to remember him. The battle which he fought against the pagan West Saxon kings, Cynegils and Cwichelm, at Cirencester in 628 (according to the Chronicle) is likely to have been a West Saxon defeat since they then 'came to terms'.[31] Thereafter the people alter known as the Hwicce were under Mercian rather than West Saxon lordship. It may have been then that the personal names Creoda, Pypba and Penda became popular in this territory.

By 633 Penda was extending his and his people's ambitions as a junior client of the great British war-lord Cadwallon of Gwynedd. It

---

[29] *Historia Brittonum*, cc. 64–5; *Annales Cambriae*, s.a. CC, CCXII (= 644, 656), ed. E. Phillimore, *Y Cymmrodor*, 9 (1888), pp. 141–83.
[30] *Historia ecclesiastica*, ii.14.
[31] ASC s.a. 628.

was presumably Penda's Mercians who were the 'pagans' who after Edwin had been killed at Hatfield burnt his royal vill of *Campodonum* and the church that had been newly built there.[32] The Hatfield campaign and its brutal aftermath were indeed what first caused Penda's rule to be remembered in Northumbria.

How long Penda enjoyed the spoils of that campaign, however, how long, that is, he survived in power after Oswald's destruction of Cadwallon at 'Heavenfield' in the following year, is uncertain. He certainly attempted to ingratiate himself with Oswald by murdering Edwin's son Osfrith who had fled to his protection; but we do not know that Penda was still ruling the Mercians in 635 when Oswald sponsored the baptism of Cynegils of Wessex at Dorchester and married Cynegils's daughter.[33] Other recorded activities of Penda – such as his slaying of the East Anglian kings Ecgric and Sigberht in battle, or the marriage of his sister to Cenwalh of Wessex, or his devastation of Northumbria and of the royal centres of Bamburgh and Yeavering[34] – cannot be precisely dated. They may all have occurred after his defeat of Oswald at *Maserfelth/Cocboy* and should perhaps be seen as attempts to undo the Northumbrian regime step by step and to replace it with Mercian lordship. Certainly it was his overthrowing of Northumbrian control and his victory at *Cocboy* that impressed themselves upon Welsh memories as marking the beginning of Penda's rule.

Eowa's rule of the Mercians, which we have interpreted as belonging to the political system of Oswald, may therefore have lasted from *c.* 635 to his death at *Cocboy/Maserfelth* in 642. Nothing is known of his reign, but it provides a possible historical context for some evidence that is otherwise difficult to explain. Thus it may have been at this time and under Oswald's direction that the territory of the Hwicce was established under a dynasty whose members' personal names over several generations could indicate that they were linked to, or descended from, the Bernician royal dynasty, that is Oswald's own family.[35] Pushing conjecture even further we might suggest that the establishment of a kingdom of the Hwicce had the corollary that Eowa was not allowed the whole territory that Penda had been ruling before 634 × 635; his

---

[32] *Historia ecclesiastica*, ii.14. Compare Bede's use of the term 'pagan' in *Historia ecclesiastica*, ii.20.

[33] *Historia ecclesiastica*, ii. 20, iii.7.

[34] For Bamburgh see *Historia ecclesiastica*, iii.16; for Yeavering *Historia ecclesiastica*, ii.14 and B. Hope-Taylor, *Yeavering: An Anglo-British Centre of Northumbria* (London, 1977).

[35] W. Stubbs, 'The Cathedral, Diocese and Monasteries of Worcester in the 8th Century', *Archaeological Journal*, 19 (1862), pp. 237–8; H.P.R. Finberg, 'The Princes of the Hwicce', in idem, *Early Charters of the West Midlands* (Leicester, 1961), pp. 167–80. But compare the argument of S.R. Bassett, 'In Search of the Origins of Anglo-Saxon Kingdoms', in *The Origins of Anglo-Saxon Kingdoms*, p. 238, n. 19.

reduced kingdom may have been restricted to the 'first land of the Mercians' which the Tribal Hidage assessed at 30,000 hides.[36] One of the functions of the Tribal Hidage, indeed, in allocating 7000 hides to such peoples as the Hwicce (*Hwinca*), the Wrekin-dwellers (*Wocen sætna*), the Westerne and the Lindisfaran, and multiples of 300 hides to a host of smaller Midland peoples, would seem to be to assert that such peoples were no longer part of the Mercian kingdom. No longer were the Mercians to be a great and growing warrior folk on the border; but henceforth, restricted to their previous boundaries, they would just be one Anglo-Saxon kingdom surrounded by others. Divide and rule is the apparent philosophy underlying the Tribal Hidage. The assessment of this remaining core of the Mercian kingdom at a massive 30,000 hides, however, suggests that there was also a penal element in the exactions of the Northumbrian overlord, whether this was Oswald himself (634–42) or one of his successors Oswiu or Ecgfrith, who were briefly dominant in the south from 655 to 658 and from *c.* 674 to *c.* 678 respectively.

Finally and most hesitantly we need to take some account here of Old Welsh poetry. It is unlikely that there will ever be a consensus on how to interpret and evaluate poems that are only extant in manuscripts of the thirteenth century and later, but whose subject matter concerns heroes and warfare of the sixth or seventh century. The date of original composition, the length of the oral transmission and the period when these poems were first written down are all highly uncertain. Those who go 'in search of' the true songs of Aneirin, Taliesin or Llywarch Hen meet problems in every way comparable to those encountered in the search for the historical Troy or Roland or indeed Arthur. Poetry and legend make dangerous tools for the historian when they have been subject to adaptation and corruption over so long a period and when the context of the composition of the extant works is so uncertain.[37] Widely accepted rules of thumb, such as that poems in which the enemy are the English must reflect the conditions of the ninth century or later, clearly rest upon the shakiest of historical and critical foundations. Moreover those like the present writer who have no command of

[36] BCS 297A.

[37] For varying assessments see I. Williams, 'The Poems of Llywarch Hen', *Proceedings of the British Academy*, 18 (1932), pp. 269–301; reprinted in idem, *The Beginnings of Welsh Poetry*, ed. and trans. R. Bromwich (Cardiff, 1972); R. Bromwich, 'The Character of Early Welsh Tradition', in N.K. Chadwick, ed., *Studies in Early British History* (Cambridge, 1954), pp. 83–136; D.P. Kirby, 'Welsh Bards and the Border', in Dornier, ed., *Mercian Studies*, pp. 31–42; D.N. Dumville, 'Palaeographical Considerations in the Dating of Early Welsh Verse', *Bulletin of the Board of Celtic Studies*, 27 (1976–8), pp. 246–52; idem, 'Sub-Roman Britain: History and Legend', *History*, 62 (1977), pp. 173–92; Davies, *Wales in Early Middle Ages*, pp. 209–12.

the Welsh language, old or modern, seek to assess the evidence and the scholarly debate at their peril.

When all the necessary reservations have been made, however, it deserves to be noted that the battle of *Cocboy* long continued to be of interest to Welsh poets. A poem attributed to the late eleventh- or early twelfth-century poet Cynddelw depicted it as a struggle between Oswald and the men of Powys;[38] while a stanza of the *Canu Llywarch Hen*, dated by some to the ninth century, has Cynddylan (of Powys) present at the battle as an ally.[39] More important is the *Marwynad Cynddylan* or lament for Cynddylan whose death in battle had brought an end to his dynasty. If Dr Rowland is correct in claiming that this elegy was composed very shortly after Cynddylan's death, then its statement that 'When the son of Pyb [that is, *either Penda or Eowa*] desired, how ready he [*Cynddylan*] was!' could provide a welcome early support for the alliance between Cynddylan and Penda that might be deduced from the later poetry.[40] Whether she is right to suppose that Cynddylan's death was at the battle of *Gai/Winwæd* rather than at *Cocboy/Maserfelth*, it is certainly clear that Welsh support played a part in determining Penda's fortunes at the critical moments of his career. In 633 he had attached his Mercians to the cause of Cadwallon of Gwynedd; in 642 he regained his kingdom at *Cocboy* probably with the support of Cynddylan of Powys; and in 655 Cadafael of Gwynedd was certainly, and Cynddylan possibly, among the thirty *duces regii* whom he led to the disaster of the *Winwæd*.[41]

We do not know whether the alliance between Mercia and certain Welsh kingdoms survived Penda's death. The absence of any record of Mercian–Welsh hostilities until the Welsh victories of the early eighth century[42] does not indicate that peace was the norm. Lacking Mercian sources we have no record of how the territories of the Magonsæte and the Wreocensæte were established under English rule;[43] the silence of

[38] I. Williams, 'A Reference to the Nennian Bellum Cocboy', *Bulletin of the Board of Celtic Studies*, 3 (1926–7), pp. 59–62; for the earlier date see J. Rowland, *Early Welsh Saga Poetry* (Bury St Edmunds, 1990), p. 124.

[39] *Canu Llywarch Hen*, ed. I. Williams (Cardiff, 1935), p. 48.

[40] *Marwynad Cynddylan*, in ibid., pp. 50–2; a widely available translation is in J.P. Clancy, *Earliest Welsh Poetry* (London, 1970), pp. 87–9, and a much more scholarly text and translation in Rowland, *Saga Poetry*, pp. 174–89. Dr Dumville dated the poem no earlier than the ninth century: 'Sub-Roman Britain', p. 186.

[41] *Historia Brittonum* c. 65: 'Solus autem Catgabail, rex Guenedotae regionis, cum exercitu suo evasit de nocte consurgens; quapropter uocatus est Catgabail Catguommed.'

[42] F.M. Stenton, *Preparatory to Anglo-Saxon England: Collected Papers*, ed. D.M. Stenton (Oxford, 1970), pp. 357–63.

[43] For attempts to bring archaeological and onomastic evidence to bear, see K. Pretty, 'Defining the Magonsæte', in Bassett, ed., *The Origins of Anglo-Saxon England*, pp. 171–83, and M. Gelling, 'The Early History of Western Mercia', ibid., pp. 184–201.

the *Annales Cambriae* may only reflect their sparse record for that period (or their natural reluctance to record Welsh defeats). Nor need we suppose that King Eowa had shared his brother's close relations with the Welsh. Indeed Eowa's reign provides a possible context for Morfael's great raid on *Caer Lwytgoed* which is recounted in a difficult passage of the *Marwynad Cynddylan*. We learn that Morfael carried off 1500 cattle and five herds of swine and gave no protection to the bishop or the book-holding monks there.[44] Such swashbuckling raiding from which even the churches of one's enemies were not exempt remained typical of Welsh princely activity as late as the twelfth and early thirteenth centuries when the extant manuscript of the poem was written.[45] But if the Morfael episode genuinely belongs to the lament for Cynddylan and if the poem was indeed composed in the mid-seventh century, then its account of a Welsh raid on Mercia is of prime importance. The name *Llwytgoed* ('grey wood') refers to the woodland from which both the Romano-British fortified town of *Letocetum* (now Wall, Staffordshire) and the nearby Anglo-Saxon episcopal see of Lichfield (Bede's *Liccidfelth*) take their name. But *Caer Lwytgoed* ('the fort of the grey wood') must refer to *Letocetum*, whose Roman walls still stood some twelve feet high in places in the eighteenth century, rather than to Lichfield which could not have been a *caer* since its defences are no earlier than the twelfth century.[46] Morfael was, however, raiding right into the heart of the Mercian kingdom and carrying off much of its movable wealth. If he were a contemporary of Cynddylan and there-fore of the pagan Mercian king Penda, it is difficult to understand the presence at Wall of a bishop and monks. It is conceivable that Penda might have permitted British clergy to continue at Wall to serve the needs of any British subjects of his kingdom; but the poet is unlikely to have reported so glowingly an attack on Penda's Mercia, that is on his hero's ally. Nor is there any hint that the raid was subsequent to (and in revenge for) the deaths of Cynddylan and Penda. Mercia under King Eowa, the puppet of the Northumbrian overlord who had slain Cadwallon and was the enemy of Cynddylan, is a much more probable target for Morfael's raid. In that event the bishop and monks at Wall are

---

[44] *Marwynad Cynddylan*, in *Canu Llywarch Hen*, ed. Williams, p. 11.

[45] Welsh politics of that later period are now superbly analysed by R.R. Davies, *Conquest, Coexistence and Change: Wales 1063–1415* (Oxford, 1987).

[46] For *Lwytgoed*, Lichfield and *Letocetum* see M. Gelling, *Signposts to the Past* (London, 1978), p. 57, and A.L.F. Rivet and C. Smith, *The Place-Names of Roman Britain* (London, 1979), pp. 436–7; for *Letocetum* see J. Gould, 'Letocetum, Christianity and Lichfield', *Transactions of the South Staffordshire Archaeological and Historical Society*, 14 (1973), pp. 29–31; for Lichfield see C.C. Taylor, 'Origins of Lichfield, Staffs.', ibid., 10 (1968–9), pp. 43–52, S.R. Bassett, 'Medieval Lichfield: A Topographical Review', ibid., 22 (1982), pp. 93–121 at 112–13, and J. Campbell, 'The Church in Anglo-Saxon Towns', *Studies in Church History*, 16 (1979), pp. 119–35 at 120.

likely to have been Northumbrians or 'Scots' installed by Oswald.[47]

Such are the sorts of conjecture to which the *Marwynad Cynddylan* may lead us if we accept it as an early source. It suggests that Wall (*Letocetum*) had some role in the early development of Christianity in Mercia, and this may help to explain both the choice of Lichfield by Chad and Wilfrid as the site for the Mercian see and Theodore's acceptance of it. Girt by forest and marsh Lichfield was perhaps the nearest approximation Chad could find to an island 'Lindisfarne' in the sea-less Mercian kingdom. But it is at Wall rather than at Lichfield that archaeologists should seek the sub-Roman and early Christian roots of the Mercian kingdom. Above all, however, the *Marwynad Cynddylan* supports the conclusion that has emerged from our re-examination of the exiguous sources, namely that Penda's fortunes and in consequence relations between Mercia and the Welsh kingdoms in his day were more uneven and tortuous than has hitherto been supposed. Amid much uncertainty we can none the less recognize that Penda of Mercia bestrode the political stage like a Colossus. He it was who made the *Mierce* into a great kingdom dominating the whole of Midland England. He it was who found new ways of exploiting their frontier situation. Had the eventual demise of Mercia and his own paganism not combined to prevent his memory from being cultivated, Penda might have been known to us in English poetry, like some early El Cid, as a great war leader who had made nonsense of the ethnic and religious divisions of his day.[48]

[47] A similar suggestion but in the context of Oswiu's recovery of Oswald's relics is made by Rowland (*Saga Poetry*, pp. 133–5).

[48] This chapter benefited greatly from the comments of Steven Bassett, David Dumville, Margaret Gelling and Patrick Wormald. I am, however, alone responsible for any errors and for the form of the argument.

5

The English Origin Myth

HISTORIANS examining the origins of the English have long been accustomed to draw attention to the fact that there are no well-informed contemporary sources for the Anglo-Saxon conquest of lowland Britain in the fifth century and that the earliest English sources derive from the eighth and ninth centuries. In the last twenty years there has developed the further understanding that not only these narrative sources for the invasions but also the extant Anglo-Saxon royal genealogies (which purport to trace the descent of English royal dynasties back to Germanic heroes and gods) are relics of the praise-singing and story-telling in honour of Anglo-Saxon dynasts of the seventh, eighth and ninth centuries.[1] Both are constructs reflecting the wish of royal households to define a kernel of 'tradition' which would provide an identity for the people under the leadership of the ruling house. We need not assume these heroic tales and origin myths to be total fictions, but we certainly cannot establish what element of historical truth they may contain. We can therefore learn something of the stories which kings and courts liked to hear, but have no means of knowing how far an Anglo-Saxon *scop* or court-poet may have both possessed and exercised a freedom to invent (or to adapt) his stories to suit the gullibility (or the ambitions) of his audience.

In these circumstances little value can now be attached to the traditional historical technique[2] of concentrating upon the earliest or the simplest versions of the tales whilst rejecting fuller or more bizarre

---

[1] For the genealogies, see K. Sisam, 'Anglo-Saxon Royal Genealogies', *Proceedings of the British Academy*, 39 (1953), pp. 287–348; D.N. Dumville, 'Kingship, Genealogies and Regnal Lists', in P.H. Sawyer and I.N. Wood eds, *Early Medieval Kingship* (Leeds, 1977), pp. 72–104; idem, 'The Anglian Collection of Royal Genealogies and Regnal Lists', *Anglo-Saxon England* 5 (1976), pp. 23–50; H. Moisl, 'Anglo-Saxon Royal Genealogies and Germanic Oral Tradition', *Journal of Medieval History*, 7 (1981), pp. 215–48; C.R. Davis, 'Cultural Assimilation in the Anglo-Saxon Royal Genealogies', *Anglo-Saxon England*, 21 (1992), pp. 23–36. For the narratives, see P. Sims-Williams, 'The Settlement of England in Bede and the Chronicle', *Anglo-Saxon England*, 12 (1983), pp. 1–41; N.P. Brooks, 'The Creation and Early Structure of the Kingdom of Kent', in S.A. Bassett, ed., *The Origins of Anglo-Saxon Kingdoms* (Leicester, 1989), pp. 55–74; B. Yorke, *Kings and Kingdoms of Early Anglo-Saxon England* (London, 1990), pp. 1–25.

[2] F.M. Stenton, *Anglo-Saxon England* (3rd edn, Oxford, 1971), pp. 1–31; P. Hunter-Blair, *Introduction to Anglo-Saxon England* (Cambridge, 1956), pp. 13–18; J. Campbell et al., *The Anglo-Saxons* (London, 1982), pp. 23–7.

stories as unhistorical poetic elaborations. The old approach had allowed some credit to Bede's statement that the first Anglo-Saxon leaders were 'said to have been Hengist and Horsa' and to his association of them with Kent and with the Kentish royal dynasty;[3] credit had even been attached to the brief annals of the Anglo-Saxon Chronicle purporting to record the arrival of Hengist and Horsa in 449 and subsequent battles against the Britons to establish the Kentish kingdom attributed to the years 455, 456, 465 and 473 (despite the admitted unreliability of the dates);[4] but there was general agreement in rejecting the elaborate tales of Hengist and his kinsmen's dealings with Vortigern (Gwrtheyrn) and his son Vortemir (Gwrthefyr), in the *Historia Brittonum* which was seen as a concoction of fictional tales.[5] Today the *Historia* is rather considered to preserve one version of the Hengist and Horsa legend, a myth which Bede and the Anglo-Saxon Chronicle treat more sparingly purely because of the particular requirements of ecclesiastical history or of the annalistic form.[6] We are not entitled to assume that the brevity of Bede or of the Chronicle makes what they say of Hengist and Horsa any more (or any less) credible.

A more helpful approach is to examine the Hengist stories in the *Historia* in order to see whether their functions and components can be analysed and explained. Remarkably there has been little detailed study of them, since the important but widely neglected work of H.M. Chadwick,[7] written long before the impact of studies by anthropologists and oral historians on ethnicity, oral tradition and origin stories had begun to influence early medieval historians' understanding of their sources.[8] We may therefore begin by summarizing the content of the account in the *Historia Brittonum*.

[3] *Bede's Ecclesiastical History of the English People*, ed. B. Colgrave and R.A.B. Mynors (Oxford, 1969), i.15, ii.5.

[4] Anglo-Saxon Chronicle, s.a. [The Chronicle is generally quoted from the translation in *EHD*, pp. 145–261.]

[5] *Historia Brittonum*, cc. 31, 36–8, 43–6, 56, ed. Th. Mommsen, *Chonica minora*, III, MGH, Auctores Antiquissimi, xiii (Berlin, 1894–8). There is a convenient translation by J. Morris, *Nennius* (Chichester, 1980). A multi-volume edition of the different recensions of this text has been initiated by Professor D.N. Dumville; but the principle witness to the first recension of 829–30, BL, Harley 3859 (a manuscript of *saec. xi/xii*, possibly from St Davids) has not yet been published, and Mommsen's edition makes it difficult to separate the versions.

[6] Brooks, 'Creation of Kent', pp. 58–64; I.N. Wood, 'Before and After Migration to Britain', in J. Hines, ed., *The Anglo-Saxons from the Migration Period to the 8th Century* (Woodbridge, 1997), pp. 41–51, at 43–4 and discussion on pp. 58–60.

[7] H.M. Chadwick, *The Origin of the English Nation* (Cambridge, 1907), pp. 33–50. See, however, the comparison of the Anglo-Saxon Chronicle's account of Hengist's conquest with the *Historia Brittonum's* account of his battles with Vortimer in J. Morris, *Age of Arthur* (1973), pp. 37, 80–1, which is interpreted rather differently in Brooks, 'Creation of Kent', pp. 60–4 (above, pp. 40–6).

[8] J. Vansina, *Oral Tradition as History* (London, 1985); *The African Past Speaks*, ed. J.C. Miller (1980); R. Law, 'How many times can history repeat itself?', *International Journal of African History*, 18(I) (1985), pp. 33–51; A. Smith, *The Ethnic Origin of Nations* (Oxford, 1986); R. Wenskus, *Stammesbildung und Verfassung: das Werden der frühmittelalterlichen Gentes*

c. 31 For forty years after the death of Maximus and the ending of Roman rule, the Britons lived in fear. During the reign of Vortigern (*Guorthigirnus*) – who was oppressed by fear of the Picts and 'Scots', of a Roman invasion and of Ambrosius – Hors and Hengist, brothers exiled from Germany, arrived in three 'keels' and were given the island of Thanet/*Ruoihm*. They were the sons of Guictgils, son of Guitta, son of Guectha, son of Woden, son of Frealaf, son of Fredulf, son of Finn, son of Folcwald, son of Geta who (they said) was a son of a god. Vortigern received the Saxons during Gratian's second rule with Equitius, 347 years from the passion of Christ.

c. 36 Encamped on Thanet the Saxons agreed to fight against Vortigern's enemies in return for supplies of food and clothing; as their numbers increased, the Britons could no longer provide sufficient supplies. Invited to depart, they took counsel with their elders to break the peace.

c. 37 With Vortigern's consent, the crafty and bold Hengist, seeing how defenceless and unarmed were the Britons, summoned reinforcements from his homeland across the sea. Sixteen keels arrived with their crews of chosen warriors, in one of which was Hengist's beautiful daughter. At a banquet for Vortigern, his warriors and his interpreter, Ceretic, the king fell in love with her as she served the wine and cider and asked Hengist for her hand, offering up to half his kingdom. On the advice of his elders, who had come with him from the island of *Oghgul* [Angeln], Hengist requested the *regio* of Kent, which Vortigern granted to him (even though his son, *Guoyrancgonus*, had ruled there until then) before Vortigern married the girl, whom he loved dearly.

c. 38 Hengist advised Vortigern to invite his son and cousin to fight against the 'Scots' and to grant them the northern regions next to the Wall. Octha and Ebissa duly arrived with 40 keels; they sailed around the Picts, laid waste the Orkney islands and occupied many *regiones* beyond the 'Frisian Sea' as far as the frontier of the Picts. Inviting further keels little by little, so that they might leave the island(s), to which they had come, uninhabited, Hengist's forces grew in strength and they attained the city of the men of Kent.

c. 43 Vortigern's son, Vortemir (*Guorthemir*), fought with Hengist and Hors and their men, expelling them back to Thanet where they were thrice besieged, imperilled and terrified. They summoned further keels from Germany with a huge force of armed men, so that their fortunes of battle varied thereafter.

(2nd edn, Graz, 1977); H. Wolfram, '*Origo et Religio*: Ethnic Tradition and Literature in Early Medieval Texts', *Early Medieval Europe*, 3 (1994), pp. 19–38; D. Ó Corráin, 'Irish Origin Legends and Genealogy: Recurrent Aetiologies', in T. Nyberg et al., eds, *History and Heroic Tale: A Symposium* (Odense, 1985), pp. 51–96; P.P. Sims-Williams, 'Some Functions of Origin Stories in Early Medieval Wales', in Nyberg et al., eds, *History and Heroic tale*, pp. 97–132.

c. 44 Vortemir fought four battles against them: the first at the river *Derguentid*, the second at the ford *Episford/Rit her gabail*, where both Hors and Vortigern's son, Categirn, fell; the third on the field by the stone of the inscription [of Titul ?] on the shore of the Gallic Sea. The barbarians were defeated and fled to their keels like women. But Vortemir soon died, having requested his family that his tomb be built in the port on the sea shore whence they had departed. But they ignored his command. [He was buried at Lincoln; had they respected his order, they would have obtained their wishes through the prayers of St Germanus.]

c. 45 The barbarians returned in force through the offices of Vortigern and of his wife, and none then dared to drive them out. Who can resist the will of God? After their return, Hengist planned to trick Vortigern and his army. His envoys proposed a peace treaty and a conference was arranged where the two parties, Britons and Saxons, would meet unarmed to confirm the peace.

c. 46 Hengist instructed his following to hide their daggers in their boots and on the command, 'Draw your *sæxas*', to attack them all fiercely, saving the life of the king for the sake of his daughter and in the hope of a ransom. So the conference assembled and the Saxons sat down, man beside man, in friendship. On Hengist's call, the throats of all three hundred of Vortigern's *seniores* were cut; the king alone being taken captive. To redeem his life he ceded several *regiones* to them, that is of the East Saxons, the South Saxons, the Middle Saxons, with other regions of their choice.

c. 56 At that time the numbers of the Saxons in Britain grew, and on Hengist's death, his son Octha came from the north to the kingdom of the men of Kent and from him are sprung the kings of the men of Kent. Then Arthur fought against them . . .

The *Historia Brittonum* is a synthesis of British history and myth put together in its earliest form in the territory of kings of Gwynedd at the end of the third decade of the ninth century and which was much revised in subsequent centuries.[9] It is natural in such a work that the overall bias and much of the terminology in its account of Hengist and Horsa should be patently British or Welsh. Thus Hengist's followers are uniformly described as *Saxones*, the normal term for any variety of Anglo-Saxons in Welsh and Irish sources and notwithstanding the fact

---

[9] D.N. Dumville, ' "Nennius" and the *Historia Brittonum*', *Studia Celtica* 10–11 (1975–6), pp. 78–95; idem, 'Some Aspects of the Chronology of the *Historia Brittonum*', *Bulletin of the Board of Celtic Studies*, 25 (1972–4), pp. 439–48; idem, 'The Historical Value of the *Historia Brittonum*', *Arthurian Literature*, 6 (1986), pp. 1–26; idem, '*Historia Brittonum*: An Insular History from the Carolingian Age', *Historiographie im frühen Mittelalter*, ed. A. Scharer and G. Scheibelreiter (1994), pp. 406–34. The attribution to Nennius, rejected by Dumville, has been plausibly reasserted by P.J.C. Field, 'Nennius and his History', *Studia Celtica*, 30 (1996), pp. 159–65.

that they are said (c. 37) to have come from the 'island' of *Oghgul*; they are also referred to as 'barbarians' (cc. 44, 45), 'pagans' (c. 37) and as 'friendly in word, but wolfish in intent and deed' (c. 46). English place-names are said to be in 'their tongue' whereas British is *nostra lingua* (cc. 37, 44) and British forms of English place-names are added in order to help the reader (*Ruoihm* c. 31, *Chent* c. 37, *Rit her gabail* c. 44). A Welsh geographical perception of northern Britain is apparent when Octha and Ebissa's journey from their settlement near Hadrian's Wall to Kent is described as 'from the left-hand side of Britain' (c. 56). Moreover whilst there are generalized references to Hengist's men 'sometimes victoriously advancing their frontiers, sometimes being defeated and expelled' (c. 43), all the specific military engagements mentioned are either British victories over them (c. 44) or record their expulsion to Thanet (c. 43) and from the shores of Britain (c. 44). Conversely the 'Saxons' do not acquire British territory by victory in battle, but only by terms of an agreement to fight Vortigern's enemies (cc. 31, 38), of the marriage settlement following Vortigern's wedding Hengist's daughter (c. 37) and of the redemption of Vortigern after the treacherous murder of his 300 *seniores* at the peace-feast (c. 46); the pagan Saxons indeed occupy Britain by 'the will of God' (c. 45) rather than by feats of arms.

This, then, is an English origin myth presented for a Welsh audience in a form which supports British identity. It is scarcely surprising that the *Historia's* account of Hengist and Horsa stands at the head of a long tradition of Welsh story-telling both in the vernacular and in Latin, in which this original Saxon treachery would one day be avenged by a renascent British people.[10] But despite this British colouring, there can be no doubt (as Chadwick argued in 1907) that the author of the *Historia* was here adapting a story of English origin, whether he received it in oral or (more probably) in written form. Clues to this English source may be found in the fact that place-names are given first in English; that Hengist's command (*Nimath eure sæxas*) is given in Old English; that the account of four battles with Hengist's men (in the second of which Horsa is killed, but only the first three of which are named) is remarkably paralleled in the Anglo-Saxon Chronicle's version of the conquest of Kent;[11] and that Hengist and his elders are said to come from the island of *Oghgul* (c. 37) whilst the 'islands' to which the reinforcements came were left without an inhabitant (c. 38) – which may be compared with Bede's assertion in *Historia ecclesiastica,*

[10] E.g. in the tenth-century prophetic poem *Armes Prydein Vawr*, ed. and trans. I. Williams and R. Bromwich (Dublin, 1972), ll. 134–6, 184–90 and in Geoffrey of Monmouth, *Historia Regum Brittanniae*, ed. N. Wright, I (Woodbridge, 1985).
[11] Brooks, 'Creation of Kent', pp. 61–4 (= above, 40–5).

I.15 that the Angles came from the homeland called *Angulus* which was said to have remained deserted thereafter up to Bede's own day.

We should indeed not be surprised to find this Welsh compiler adapting English sources for his own purposes here, for later in the *Historia* (cc. 57–61) he included a set of Anglo-Saxon royal genealogies of the so-called 'Anglian collection' of the late eighth century, and also (cc. 62–5) merged a Northumbrian regnal list with information that may derive from a set of northern British annals,[12] perhaps produced in an area under Anglo-Saxon control. We do not know whether or not the eleventh-century recension of the *Historia* had any good reason to add a preface attributing the composition of the hitherto anonymous work to 'Nennius', the *discipulus* of Bishop Elfoddw of Bangor (d. 809). But something of the same Anglo-Welsh interests and rivalries in early ninth-century Gwynedd certainly can be seen in the 'Alphabet of Nemniuus', a parody found in a manuscript written in 817 × 835, which rebuts English allegations of Welsh illiteracy by ascribing Welsh names to the English runic letters of the futhorc.[13] The church of Bangor and the court of the powerful king of Gwynedd, Merfyn Frych (826–44), are exactly the place where we might expect to find English myth recast to serve the purpose of strengthening Welsh national identity.

Is it possible to remove this Welsh surface-coat and to analyse the function of the underlying Hengist and Horsa myth in the *Historia* for its earlier English audience? Given that we cannot be certain how much the Guenedotan compiler may have invented, there are evident dangers in any such process. In a previous chapter[14] it was argued that there is no certainty that the four battles by which the *Historia* depicts Vortemir driving Hengist and Horsa from Kent to the English Channel ('Gallic sea') derived from an English source in which, as in the Anglo-Saxon Chronicle, Hengist and Horsa and Æsc make steady progress eastwards from Thanet to the environs of London. It is possible that the *Historia's* English source may have described the initial settlement by treaty with Vortigern, the marriage settlement and even (as we shall see) the massacre of Vortigern's counsellors; it may have told of fluctuating fortunes of battle (which the Alfredian annalist chose to obscure) even if it is perhaps unlikely that it described English defeats in any detail.

Much more clear, however, is the fact that (like Bede and the *Anglo-Saxon Chronicle*) the *Historia's* English exemplar associated Hengist with

---

[12] D.N. Dumville, 'On the Northern British Section of the *Historia Brittonum*', *Welsh History Review*, 8 (1976–7), pp. 345–54.

[13] Oxford, Bodleian Library, Auct. F. 4. 32, fo. 20r discussed by I. Williams, 'Notes on Nennius', *Bulletin of the Board of Celtic Studies*, 7 (1935), pp. 380–9; Dumville, 'Historical Value', *Arthurian Literature*, 6 (1986), pp. 1–26 at 24–5, and Field, 'Nennius', *Studia Celtica* 30 (1996), pp. 159–65.

[14] Above, p. 45.

an initial establishment in Thanet, with battles in Kent and also made him the father of the alleged progenitor of the Kentish royal dynasty. On that all three sources are agreed; so there is no question of the Welsh author having invented any of these elements. They must have been brought together before 731, when Bede completed his *Ecclesiastical History*. Moreover the disagreement between Bede and the Chronicle on the one hand and the *Historia* and the Anglian collection of genealogies on the other as to whether Hengist's son, from whom the kings of the *Cantware* claimed descent, was Oisc/Æsc or Octa/Octha does not take away from the fact that the function of the myth in either form is to assert the primacy of Kent among English dynasties. The claim that the kings of Kent were alone descended from the first Anglo-Saxon leader to arrive in Britain might conceivably have been made when Kent Wihtred (691–725) was an independent ruler; it could scarcely have originated when Kent was under the authority of a Northumbrian, Mercian or West Saxon overlord. We might rather expect such a claim to have been first made by a *scop* at the court of King Æthelberht (c. 585–616/8), the only Kentish king to have exercised an overlordship over other southern English kingdoms. With the conversion of Kent to Christianity in his reign and with all other English kingdoms coming, in the course of the seventh century, to accept the authority of the metropolitan church of Canterbury, a written culture developed in all kingdoms, which may have helped to stabilize English myth and to make it difficult for other dynasties to claim descent from Hengist. There seems to have been no English parallel to the Welsh or Scottish origin legends in which different dynasties descend from different sons of the mythical founding leader.[15]

The context of the court of King Æthelberht might best explain other features of the Hengist myth as we find it in the *Historia*. Thus in c. 38 we read that Hengist's growing forces enabled them to come to the *civitas Cantiorum*, evidently representing OE *Cantwaraburh* (Canterbury). Moreover the royal genealogies of Bernician, Kentish, East Anglian, Mercian and Deiran dynasties (cc. 57–61) all trace their descent from the Germanic god, Woden, with the exception of the Kentish which in c. 58 only lists the ancestors of King Ecgberht I

---

[15] For the supposed migration of Cunedda to Wales from the land of the Votadini to establish the kingdom of Gwynedd, with his eight sons founding either other Welsh kingdoms, see *Historia Brittonum*, c. 62; and for discussion, W. Davies, *Wales in the Early Middle Ages* (Leicester, 1982), pp. 89, 98–102. For the supposed role of the sons of Erc in establishing the Dalriadic *cenéla* of western Scotland at the start of the sixth century, see *Senchus Fer nAlban*, ed. J. Bannerman, in his *Studies in the History of Dalriada* (Edinburgh, 1974), pp. 27–156. Hints that there may have been comparable English myths may be found in the reference in *Historia Brittonum*, cc. 57 and 60 to Ida of the Bernicians and Pybba of Mercians each having twelve sons. For the suggestion that the claim that English kings were descended from Woden is of Kentish origin, see E. John, 'The Point of Woden', *Anglo-Saxon Studies in Archaeology and History*, 5 (1992), pp. 127–34, at 129–30.

(664–73) from Hengist, because in c. 31 Hengist and Horsa's pedigree has already been traced back not only to Woden (as had Bede in *Historia ecclesiastica*, I.15) but a further five generations to Geat (Woden–Frealaf–Frioðulf–Finn–Geat) 'who was, as they say, a son of a god' (*filius dei*). Geat or *Gautr* was, it would seem, both a Norse by-name for Woden (Oðinn)[16] and the eponymous ancestor of the *Gautar* (OE *Geatas*) of southern Sweden, the people to whom the dragon-slaying hero of the great Old English poem, *Beowulf*, belonged and who were neighbours of and sometimes confused with the Jutes.[17] Here, then, the Kentish dynasty is being given a longer and grander pedigree than other royal families, and one that particularly stressed its Scandinavian roots.

It is difficult to suppose that any southern English overlord of the eighth century would have been keen to encourage this sort of exaltation of the Kentish dynasty, but we must hesitate before supposing that the claim to descent from Geat therefore goes back to the days of Æthelberht. Bede, whose links with Abbot Albinus of Canterbury made him well informed on the Kentish royal house, tells only of Hengist's descent from Woden, so the extension back to Geat may postdate the *Ecclesiastical History*. Moreover the genealogies in the *Historia* are an early version of the so-called 'Anglian collection' and were probably first compiled in Northumbria between 765 and 779.[18] Northumbrian kings of that era, who had long given up any hope of dominance south of the Humber, may have been keen to associate the northern English with Hengist's family – hence the *Historia's* story of the settlement between the wall and the Picts by Hengist's son, Octa, and Ebissa (cc. 38, 56). A Bernician *scop* would have had no political difficulty in attributing priority of descent to the Kentish dynasty. Indeed we might see the *Historia's* version of the Hengist myth as originally a Northumbrian version honouring the Kentish dynasty in very much the same way as Bede's *Ecclesiastical History* had honoured the Kentish church, recognizing its chronological priority (and, for Bede, its consequent authority). It is therefore particularly instructive to find that, in those versions of the Anglian collection of genealogies that seem to have

[16] C.R. Davis, 'Cultural Assimilation', *Anglo-Saxon England*, 21 (1992), p. 29 citing *Edda: Prologue and Gylfaginning*, ed. A. Faulkes (Oxford, 1982), l. 15 (trans. A. Faulkes, *Edda* (London, 1987), p. 22); Moisl, 'Genealogies and Oral Tradition', *Journal of Medieval History*, 7 (1981), 219–23.
[17] R.W. Chambers, *Beowulf: An Introduction . . . with a Discussion of the Stories of Offa and Finn*, 3rd edn with supplement by C.L. Wrenn (Cambridge, 1959), p. 320; Sisam, 'Royal Genealogies', *Proceedings of the British Academy*, 39 (1953), pp. 308–21.
[18] Dumville, 'Anglian Collection', *Anglo-Saxon England*, 5 (1976), pp. 48–50. For the political situation in eighth-century Kent, see N.P. Brooks, *The Early History of the Church of Canterbury* (Leicester, 1984), pp. 111–32 and S.D. Keynes, 'The Control of Kent in the 9th Century', *Early Medieval Europe*, 2(ii) (1993), pp. 111–31.

been revised at the courts of Kings Ecgfrith (796) and Coenwulf of Mercia (796–821), the dynasty whose ancestry is traced back from Woden Frealafing to Geat is *not* that of Kent, but of Lindsey![19] Both King Offa (757–96) and Coenwulf had personal experience of the resistance of the Kentish dynasty to Mercian rule, which may have made a Mercian *scop* reluctant to attribute to that line a divine ancestry superior to all other English lineages.

It would therefore seem that behind the Welsh version of the Hengist and Horsa legend in the *Historia Brittonum* there may lie a late-eighth-century Northumbrian Anglian version of an original story told at the court of the Kentish kings, most probably first in the time of Æthelberht I. There remain, however, certain features of the *Historia's* version still to be accounted for, in particular the elaborate tale of the slaughter of Vortigern's counsellors at the peace-feast by Hengist's men using their short swords (*seaxas*) hidden in their footwear. There can be no doubt that this is specifically a Saxon (rather than an Anglian or Jutish) story. It depends upon the pun between *seaxas* and *Seaxe* 'Saxons'; the Saxons are 'sword-people' as is stated explicitly in the version of the same story (with different participants) in the origin-myth of the Old or continental Saxons.[20] The fact that c. 46 of the *Historia* ends with Vortigern's cession of Essex and Sussex (and in some versions Middlesex) to Hengist confirms that this is a Saxon tale, whose function is indeed to justify the rule of the Saxon peoples of south-east England by Hengist's descendants. The account of Hengist's entry into Canterbury (c. 38) and the four Kentish battles that underly both the *Historia's* account of Vortemir's campaign and the Chronicle's account of Hengist and Æsc's victories may likewise have served as 'charter-myths', justifying the dynasty's control of both the eastern Jutish half and the western Saxon half of Kent.[21] Some claim to control the Saxon peoples of the South-East must certainly have been made when Æthelberht was able to install a Mellitus as bishop of London and may even have been thinking of transferring the seat of his power to London.[22] Conceivably we might rather look to the brief time in the later 660s and early 670s when Ecgberht I of Kent was founding the abbey of Chertsey and Eorcenwold, perhaps a kinsman, was becoming bishop of London (c. 672–93) when such Saxon stories might have been generated for a Kentish royal audience.[23]

[19] Dumville, 'Anglian Collection', pp. 31, 33, 37.
[20] Brooks, 'Creation of Kent', p. 63 (= above, p. 45).
[21] Ibid., pp. 60–4, 73–4 (= above pp. 40–6, 60).
[22] Brooks, *Early History*, pp. 8–11.
[23] W.J. Blair, 'Frithuwald's Kingdom and the Origins of Surrey', in Bassett, ed., *Origins of Anglo-Saxon Kingdoms*, pp. 97–107.

We need to ask whether a Kentish audience would have experienced any difficulty with Hengist as the hero of this *Saxon* origin myth, if he were regarded as the founder of the *Jutish* dynasty of Kent and of no others. Hengist, however, may have been a relatively late intrusion into the Kentish royal legends. Bede tells us that the kings of Kent were customarily known as *Oiscingas*, 'the sons of Oisc'. The fact that they were not known as *Hengestingas* suggests that Oisc – whose name has links with other Germanic divine progenitors and may derive from **ans*, 'god' – had become established as the founder of the Kentish dynasty *before* Hengist came to be regarded as Oisc's father.[24] This might indicate that the story of Hengist and the *seaxas* had been transposed from a Saxon dynastic legend to that of Kent, perhaps in order to justify the incorporation of western Kent into the 'Jutish' kingdom under Æthelberht and his successors. We may note here the assertion of the sixth-century Ravenna Cosmographer that Britain is inhabited by the nation of the Saxons, 'which came long ago from Old Saxony with their chief, Ansehis by name'. Unfortunately it remains uncertain whether *Ansehis* should be regarded as an attempt at the name, Hengist, or at Oisc – or indeed whether the two have the same origin.[25] Finally it should be observed that the warrior and exile (*wrecca*) Hengest, who figures prominently in the Finnsburh episode in *Beowulf*, is the leader of a band, not of Saxons, probably not of *Eotenas* (Jutes), but of 'Half-Danes'.[26]

Hengist's changing ethnicity whenever he appears in our sources is a sign of the adaptability of myth in the hands of Anglo-Saxon *scopas* working for different lords, not of a multiplicity of historical Hengists. They wove some splendid tales. In Old English *hengest* means a 'stallion' – a particularly suitable name for the supposed first Anglo-Saxon warrior to arrive in Britain and especially for the founder of the first English dynasty; OE *hors* is a 'horse'. There is no reason to suppose that either term had any currency as a personal name,but horses were associated with the cult of a number of Germanic gods including, it would seem, Woden.[27] Moreover as founder-heroes Hengist and Horsa belong to a huge Germanic and Indo-European family of pairs of brothers with alliterating names and divine or semi-

---

[24] *Historia ecclesiastica*, ii.5; P. Sims-Williams, 'Settlement of England', *Anglo-Saxon England*, 12 (1983), pp. 22–3.

[25] 'In oceano vero occidentale est insula quae dicitur Britania, ubi olim gens Saxonum veniens ab antiqua Saxonia cum principe suo Ansehis modo habitare videtur.' (ed. J. Schnetz, *Itineraria Romana*, ii (Leipzig, 1940), p. 105; Sims-Williams, 'Settlement', p. 22.

[26] *Beowulf*, ed. F. Klaeber (3rd edn, Boston, 1950), ll. 1068–1159. For the debates about whether the Jutes were Hengist's men or his opponents, see R.W. Chambers, *Beowulf: an Introduction* (Cambridge, 1959), pp. 245–68, 333–44, 543–5.

[27] Davis, 'Cultural Assimilation', *Anglo-Saxon England*, 21 (1992), p. 27.

divine associations; apart from Romulus and Remus, we know of Ibor and Agio of the Lombards, Ambri and Assi of the Vandals, Raos and Raptos of the Hastingi, the twins Castor and Polydeuces of the Spartans, and so forth.[28] There is every reason to suppose that suitable names for the 'sire' of the English race and for his brother have been invented by a resourceful and knowledgeable poet/singer to fit an established pattern of origin myths.

Because our sources for Hengist and Horsa, though fragmentary, are far more varied than those for most other such legendary founders, we can indulge in a little of the archaeology of English myth and can seek to distinguish the different layers and functions of these tales in the Anglo-Saxon and Celtic worlds of seventh, eighth- and ninth-century Britain. It is for those centuries that historians can attempt to make Hengist and Horsa reveal their secrets, *not* for the Dark Ages. We can certainly see something of the use of this myth in the service of Merfyn Frych, king of Gwynedd, to rally his people on a diet of Saxon treachery; beyond that, we may glimpse something of late eighth-century Northumbrian interests in promoting a sense of English (or Anglian) unity and in stressing the links between Kent and Northumbria; and beyond that we seem to see myths developed at the court of the Kentish kings to justify their rule in West as well as East Kent and to provide a foundation for Kentish claims to rule over the South and East Saxons. To what extent these myths were invented in Kent or were filched from the praise of other courts and peoples, we cannot tell. Whilst it would be absurd to claim to date their composition with any probability, they certainly fit the context of the court of King Æthelberht better than that of any other Kentish king. If we can reconstruct something of the life of the household of Æthelberht and his *leode*, the study of the *Historia Brittonum* may prove to have been more worthwhile than earlier historians had supposed likely.[29]

[28] J.E. Turville-Petre, 'Hengest and Horsa', *Saga Book of the Viking Club*, 14 (1953–7), pp. 273–90.

[29] I am grateful to David Dumville and Eric John for their comments on an early draft of this chapter. I am alone responsible for any remaining errors.

6

The Ecclesiastical Topography of Early Medieval Canterbury

T HE CRUCIAL ROLE played by the church during the early Middle Ages in providing an institutional and economic link between the *civitates* of the late-Roman Empire and the emergent towns of the tenth, eleventh and twelfth centuries is a well-recognized feature of European urban history. In Britain however, where the hiatus of the 'Dark Ages' broke the continuity of religious and economic life in towns more thoroughly than in most parts of the Roman world, this aspect of urban history has (save at Winchester) received little attention. More than any other English city, Canterbury owes its historical importance to the church. The city was uniquely well documented during the early Middle Ages, and its topography still bears the imprint of the ecclesiastical institutions that had been established by the seventh century. Moreover, although the limited post-war excavations on bomb-damaged sites concentrated on recovering evidence of Canterbury's Roman past, they also revealed something about the immediately succeeding centuries.[1] There is therefore a greater opportunity at Canterbury than elsewhere in Britain to bring together historical, topographical and archaeological evidence about the emergence of the town as an ecclesiastical centre. There is also a chance to draw attention to the questions that urgently need to be answered by research and rescue excavations in Canterbury, before the evidence is destroyed by urban redevelopment.

Under Roman rule Canterbury was a *civitas*-capital, *Durovernum Cantiacorum*, and its role as the administrative centre of a tribal region was repeated in the Anglo-Saxon period when Canterbury was apparently a *Volksburg–Cantwaraburh* being the borough of the people of Kent. We do not yet know what (if anything) this meant for the economy, the buildings and the layout of the Dark Age and early medieval town. When Augustine arrived in 597 to convert the pagan English to Christianity, Canterbury is said to have been the *metropolis* of

---

[1] S.S. Frere, *Roman Canterbury* (4th edn, Canterbury, 1965).

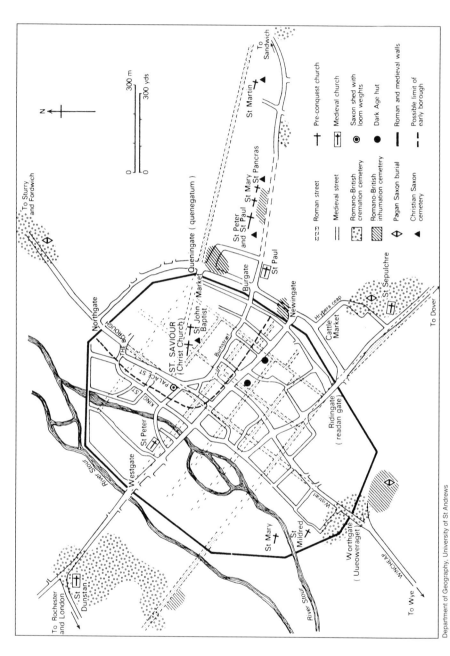

6. Anglo-Saxon Canterbury.

Department of Geography, University of St Andrews

To Rochester
and London

St Dunstan

River Stour

Westgate

St Peter

KING ST
PALACE ST

THE BOROUGH

Northgate

To Sturry
and Fordwich

ST. SAVIOUR
(Christ Church)

St John,
Baptist
Burhstret

Market
Queningate (quenegatum)

St Peter
and St Paul

St Paul

Burgate

St Mary
St Pancras

St Martin

To
Sandwich

Newingate

Hrydena ceap

Cattle
Market

St Sepulchre

To Dover

Ridingate
(readan gate)

Wistret

River Stour

St Mary

St
Mildred

Worthgate
(Uueoweraget)

WINCHEAP

To Wye

N

0   300 m
0   300 yds

Roman street
Medieval street
Romano-British cremation cemetery
Romano-British inhumation cemetery
Pagan Saxon burial
Christian Saxon cemetery

Pre-conquest church
Medieval church
Saxon shed with loom weights
Dark Age hut
Roman and medieval walls
Possible limit of early borough

King Æthelberht's *imperium*.[2] To some degree therefore, it must have been a seat of secular power and residence. Until a royal residence or palace is located and excavated in Canterbury however, we cannot know whether the barbarian Anglo-Saxon rulers of Kent made use of Roman buildings or sought to continue anything of Roman civic administration. Something of the physical structure of Roman Durovernum certainly did survive to give shape to the city's medieval successor.[3] The walls of late-Roman Canterbury provided the line for the medieval defences. The main Roman roads survived leading to the city from Reculver, from Richborough, from Dover and from Lympne, and four or five of the Roman gates of the town seem to have remained in use since they were succeeded by medieval gates on the same site (Worthgate, Ridingate, Queningate, Northgate and possibly Westgate). Thus the physical remains of the Roman town helped to predetermine the topography of the early medieval city.

It is therefore all the more remarkable that the intra-mural layout of the Roman city did not survive, despite the survival of walls and gates. The Roman street-grid which has been revealed by excavations in the central and eastern area of the city, and whose main elements elsewhere can be conjectured, bears almost no relation to the streets as they have been known in modern times. The modern street plan has been traced back at least as far as the twelfth century, and certain streets can be shown to have been in existence some centuries earlier; it is likely that the street-plan is largely the product of the Anglo-Saxon period.[4]

There is one other area where we might look for physical continuity from the Roman era – namely in the churches of Canterbury. We do not know whether *Durovernum* was an episcopal see in the fourth century. Certainly that was not the reason for the choice of Canterbury as the first of the two metropolitan sees of the English *gentes* some two centuries later. Rather Canterbury was chosen (despite Pope Gregory I's instructions that the see be at London) because it was the chief place, the *metropolis*, of the kingdom of Æthelberht of Kent, who happened to be the dominant English ruler when Augustine arrived in 597. None the less we know that there were Roman churches standing in Canterbury at that time. When the king had been converted, Augustine was given permission to build or to restore churches throughout the kingdom, and Bede specifically mentions two such Roman churches in Canterbury: St Martin's, where Æthelberht's

[2] Bede, *Historia ecclesiastica*, i.25: *Bede's Ecclesiastical History of the English People*, ed. R.A.B. Mynors and B. Colgrave (Oxford, 1969).

[3] J.S. Wacher, *The Towns of Roman Britain* (London, 1975).

[4] W. Urry, *Canterbury under the Angevin Kings* (London, 1967), pp. 185–92, 202–4; N.P. Brooks, *The Early History of the Church of Canterbury* (Leicester, 1984), pp. 21–5.

Christian wife, Bertha, had long been accustomed to pray and where Augustine and his companions first worshipped before Æthelberht's conversion, and the church in the city which Augustine 'recovered' for use as his episcopal see and which he then dedicated to the Holy Saviour (that is, Christ Church).[5] These two Roman churches are known to us because they were relevant to the theme of Bede's *Ecclesiastical History*. They are unlikely to have been the only Roman churches standing in Canterbury in 597. Indeed Frere has drawn attention to the possibility that St Peter's may preserve the site of a Roman church; although no early fabric is now detectable, the location and alignment of this church seem to relate to the Roman rather than to the medieval street grid.[6] But in view of the great variation in the orientation of the churches of Canterbury, the hypothesis of a Roman origin for St Peter's needs to be tested by excavation.

Indeed a programme of excavation within and around all the medieval churches of Canterbury, as opportunities occur through modern repairs or when churches become redundant, is essential if we are to understand their origins and to assess the degree of Christian continuity from Roman times. The excavations at Winchester have taught us that it is normal for urban churches there to be many centuries older than the visible fabric or the extant documentation.[7] We cannot therefore afford to ignore the fact that at Canterbury there appears to be an interesting relationship between the extra-mural parish churches as they are known in the twelfth century and the location of the cemeteries of the Romano-British town. The medieval parish churches of St Dunstan and Holy Sepulchre and their adjacent graveyards lie on the site of Romano-British cremation cemeteries. At St Sepulchre the gap has been narrowed by the discovery amongst the Roman cremation urns of a fifth-century 'Jutish' pot.[8] The other two extra-mural parish churches, St Paul's and St Martin's, both lie within 2–300 m of Roman cemeteries. The relationship may indeed be more exact, for the Roman cemeteries are known from poorly recorded chance finds rather than from systematic excavation; their extent and their period of use remain very uncertain. The question raised by the apparent coincidence of parish church and Roman cemetery is whether any or all of these four churches represent a British parallel to the familiar continental development: *cella memoriae* in a Roman extra-

[5] *Historia ecclesiastica*, I.26, 33.

[6] S.S. Frere, 'The End of Towns in Roman Britain', in *The Civitas Capitals of Roman Britain*, ed. J.S. Wacher (Leicester, 1966), pp. 87–100.

[7] M. Biddle, 'Excavations at Winchester, 1970', *Antiquaries Journal*, 52 (1972), pp. 93–131.

[8] D.B. Kelly and J.N.L. Myres, 'A Fifth-Century Anglo-Saxon Pot from Canterbury', *Anitquaries Journal*, 53 (1973), pp. 77–8.

mural cemetery → early medieval *locus sanctus* → medieval parish church.

At St Martin's indeed some such development can already be postulated. Bede tells us that the church in honour of St Martin had been built while the Romans still remained in Britain ('*Erat autem prope ipsam civitatem ad orientem ecclesia in honorem sancti Martini antiquitus facta, dum adhuc Romani Brittaniam incolerent . . .*'.[9] Though the dedication to St Martin is likely to derive from the Frankish connections of Queen Bertha,[10] there is no good reason to doubt Bede's statement about the antiquity of the church. Bede was writing from information provided by Albinus, abbot of the monastery of St Peter and St Paul, only a few yards from St Martin's down the Roman road into Canterbury. His assertion that the queen used to worship there is confirmed by the discovery in the graveyard to the south of St Martin's of a necklace of Frankish coins of mid-sixth-century date; the necklace included one 'medalet' of English manufacture inscribed with the name of Bishop Liudhard, that is Bertha's Frankish chaplain.[11] Piecemeal excavations over many years at St Martin's have established that the chancel of the present church incorporates a small rectangular building built of Roman materials, to which a nave was added probably at an early date in the Anglo-Saxon period.[12] Nothing in the excavation evidence precludes a late-Roman date for this building, and the discovery of a closely comparable late-Roman structure incorporated into the medieval church at Stone-by-Faversham renders it more likely.[13] Indeed it would be difficult to understand why Bertha and Liudhard should have chosen so distant a site for worship when she arrived in Kent to marry Æthelberht (before 565),[14] unless the building was then known to be, or to have been, a centre of Christian cult.

St Martin's is therefore best understood as an extra-mural *cella memoriae* or *martyrium* of the fourth or early fifth century, reused as a church and associated with St Martin by Bertha and Liudhard in the second half of the sixth century. By the mid-ninth century it was an important church with at least one stall (*sedes, setl*) endowed by the

[9] *Historia ecclesiastica*, i.26.

[10] O. Chadwick, 'The Evidence of Dedications in the Early History of the Welsh Church', in *Studies in Early British History*, ed. N.K. Chadwick (Cambridge, 1954), pp. 000–00, at 173–81.

[11] P. Grierson, 'The Canterbury (St Martin's) Hoard of Frankish and Anglo-Saxon Coin-Ornaments', *British Numismatic Journal*, 27 (1952), pp. 39–51, at 41–3.

[12] F. Jenkins, 'St Martin's Church at Canterbury', *Medieval Archaeology*, 9 (1965), pp. 11–15.

[13] Sir E. Fletcher and G.W. Meates, 'The Ruined Church of Stone-by-Faversham', *Antiquaries Journal*, 49 (1969), pp. 273–94.

[14] But for the chronology of Æthelberht's reign and marriage, see now ch. 3 above, pp. 47–51.

West Saxon king, and a century later we hear if 'those who serve God there';[15] in the early eleventh century St Martin's was the seat of the assistant bishops who deputized for Archbishops Æthelnoth and Eadsige when they became too old or too inform to fulfil their duties. By the twelfth century St Martin's had full parochial functions.[16] Little weight can be placed upon the gaps in the recorded history of this church from Roman times. It is true that we cannot suppose that the church had already been dedicated to St Martin from the late fourth or early fifth century – unless with Morris we are prepared to rewrite the known history both of dedications to saints in the west and of the development of the cult of St Martin.[17] However this does not mean that there was necessarily a total break in Christian worship on the site in the fifth and early sixth centuries. For the text known as the *Obsecratio Augustini* is evidence that, in the area of Augustine's missionary activity, there was at least one shrine of a Romano-British saint (Sixtus) whose cult had been maintained, although the ruling Anglo-Saxons were not impressed by any miracles there or by any acceptable *ordo passionis*.[18] Pope Gregory I on Augustine's request sent 'authentic' relics from Rome, so that worship could be continued there in a form agreeable to the newly converted Anglo-Saxons. We cannot therefore rule out the possibility that a small Christian or sub-Christian population of British origin still maintained a semblance of Christian worship in the ruins of Roman churches and at Roman shrines in and around Canterbury in the late sixth century. Their traditions may have been of little interest to the English. Some link, however tenuous, with such a population, or some memory of them, is the least that must be assumed to explain how Liudhard and Augustine came to know that certain buildings in and around Canterbury had been Roman churches and shrines. Excavation in the churches of Canterbury, especially in the extra-mural parish churches of St Paul, St Dunstan and Holy Sepulchre, would resolve such uncertainties and help to determine the extent of the debt to Romano-British Christianity at Canterbury.

The second church in Canterbury which Bede mentions as being of Roman origin was the Saxon cathedral itself dedicated by Augustine to the Holy Saviour in evident imitation of the papal cathedral in Rome, the later St John Lateran. The renewed controversies of recent years about the form and development of the pre-conquest cathedral need not

---

[15] BCS 516, 426.

[16] Urry, *Canterbury*, pp. 210–11.

[17] J. Morris, *The Age of Arthur* (London, 1973)

[18] M. Deanesly and P. Grosjean, 'The Canterbury Edition of the Answers of Pope Gregory I to Augustine', *Journal of Ecclesiastical History*, 10 (1959), pp. 1–49, at 28–9; Brooks, *Early History* p.20.

concern us here.[19] What is important however is the belief of the English monk Eadmer, our chief informant about the late-Saxon cathedral, that the church that he remembered from his childhood was indeed the church built by the Romans which Bede mentions.[20] It would be foolish to disregard Eadmer's clear statement, for we know how at Glastonbury, Winchester and at the monastery of St Peter and St Paul in Canterbury the earliest church remained in use for all or most of the Anglo-Saxon period as a place of especial veneration. Though Eadmer was but a child when the Saxon cathedral was destroyed by the fire of 1067, the main elements of his account can be controlled from pre-conquest sources,[21] and on matters of detailed local tradition the post-Conquest Canterbury writers such as Osbern, Eadmer and Goscelin command considerable respect.[22] Whatever alterations and extensions there may have been to the cathedral during almost five centuries of Anglo-Saxon Christianity, we must presume that the Saxon cathedral had a Romano-British core unless and until excavation proves the contrary. The situation and the alignment of the late-Saxon cathedral would therefore have been determined by that of the original Roman church. Though the exact size of the Saxon cathedral is uncertain, we do know that it was on the same site as its Norman successor. It is therefore of interest that the Norman and Gothic cathedral lay athwart the presumed grid of the Roman streets in this area; it would however – as Biddle has pointed out to me – relate to the Roman pattern if, as is possible, the Roman road from Richborough continued into the town on the same line as it approaches Queningate. Here too we seem to detect how the Roman past may have influenced the emergence of Christian and medieval Canterbury, and once again excavation is needed to establish the point.

Outside the walls of Canterbury and just to the south of the Roman road to Richborough lay the monastery of St Peter and St Paul, later known as St Augustine's. Here there is no question of a Romano-British origin. The monastery was founded by Æthelberht and Augustine. Together they built the church of St Peter and St Paul to serve *inter alia* as a burial-place for the archbishops and the Kentish kings; Æthelberht's successor, Eadbald, added the church of St Mary on the

[19] D. Parsons, 'The Pre-Conquest Cathedral at Canterbury', *Archaeologia Cantiana*, 84 (1969), pp. 175–84; H.M. Taylor, 'The Anglo-Saxon Cathedral Church at Canterbury', *Archaeological Journal*, 126 (1969), pp. 101–30; R.D.H. Gem, 'The Anglo-Saxon Cathedral Church at Canterbury', *Archaeological Journal*, 127 (1970), pp. 196–201; E.C. Gilbert, 'The Date of the late-Saxon Cathedral at Canterbury', *Archaeological Journal*, 127 (1970), pp. 202–10. See also, below pp. 149–54 for later excavations.

[20] Taylor, 'Anglo-Saxon Cathedral Church', p. 128.

[21] Brooks, *Early History* pp. 37–59.

[22] R.W. Southern, *St Anselm and his Biographer* (Cambridge, 1963).

same alignment but immediately to the east.[23] The location of the monastery outside the walls of the city reflects its purpose as a burial-place. Under Roman law burials were not permitted within the settled area of a town, nor according to the canons could Christians be buried within the body of a church – hence the early proliferation of *porticus* around the church of St Peter and St Paul to accommodate the royal and pontifical graves. The positions of the burials of the early Kentish kings and archbishops were recorded at the time of their translation in the 1090s by the St Augustine's monk, Goscelin, and have been confirmed by the excavations of the 1920s.[24] St Augustine's was there-fore one of the great royal burial churches of early medieval Europe,[25] but it was also a general cemetery as well. The 'lay cemetery' extended to the south of the monastic church throughout the Middle Ages. Until burials within the town walls became permissible, apparently in the time of Archbishop Cuthbert (740–60), it is likely that St Augustine's was the sole cemetery for the lay Christian population of Canterbury.[26] This may help to explain the need for the third of the family of early churches at St Augustine's, the church of St Pancras. Whatever we may make of the tradition first recorded by the late-medieval St Augustine's writer William Thorne that the building had been a pagan temple used by King Æthelberht, the dedication of the building – as of other seventh-century churches in Canterbury – follows a Roman model. At Rome, as Professor D.A. Bullough has reminded me, and probably therefore at Canterbury (and perhaps at London too?), the church of St Pancras began its life as an extra-mural cemetery church.

There is yet more to be learnt from the siting of the monastery of St Augustine's. Sherlock kindly told me that his limited trial excavations in 1974 in the lay cemetery to the south of the Saxon churches revealed Roman inhumation burials of the second century AD.[27] Roman pagan inhumations of the same period are also known outside the Newingate and in Lady Wootton's Green, just outside the gate of the monastery.[28] The monastery therefore seems to have been situated on part of an extensive Roman inhumation cemetery. Only systematic excavation with sophisticated dating techniques can establish whether this cemetery was

[23] *Historia ecclesiastica*, i.33, ii.6.

[24] C.R. Peers and A.W. Clapham, 'St Augustine's Abbey Church before the Norman Conquest', *Archaeologia*, 77 (1927), pp. 201–18.

[25] K.H. Kruger, 'Königsgrabkirchen der Franken, Angelsächsen und Langobarden bis z. Mitte d. 8 Jahrhunderts', *Münstersche Mittelalter-Schriften*, 4 (Munich, 1971).

[26] A.L. Meaney and S.C. Hawkes, *Two Anglo-Saxon Cemeteries at Winnall* (London, 1970), pp. 50–5; Brooks, *Early History*, p. 21.

[27] D. Sherlock and H. Woods, *St Augustines Abbey, Report on Excavations, 1960–8*, Kent Archaeological Society, monograph series, 4 (Maidstone, 1988).

[28] Frere, *Roman Canterbury*.

in use in the late-Roman and sub-Roman periods, for it must not be assumed that oriented burials here without grave goods must necessarily be the graves of Christian Anglo-Saxons. Æthelberht and Augustine may have built their royal and pontifical burial-church here precisely because it was, or had been, the city's Christian burial-ground.

Setting conjecture aside, it is at least clear that the Christian cemeteries of Canterbury had a part in determining the city's medieval topography. In the mid-eighth century Archbishop Cuthbert built a church of St John the Baptist immediately to the east of the cathedral to serve both as a baptistery for the inhabitants of the town and as a burial-place for future archbishops.[29] The building of this church created a 'family' or 'cluster' of churches at the cathedral like that at St Augustine's. It was also probably at this time that a cemetery for the laity was established south of the cathedral church,[30] the first of many infringements of the monopoly of burial-rights hitherto held by the monastery of St Augustine's. Such developments at the cathedral must also have necessitated extensions of the cathedral precincts and therefore must have affected the layout of streets around the cathedral – just as comparable but better documented extensions were to do in later centuries.[31]

The known early churches of Canterbury are concentrated in the north-east of the city and along the Roman road to Richborough. It is unlikely that this grouping is fortuitous; it could reflect the pattern of Christian settlement in late-Roman or sub-Roman Canterbury. Be that as it may, the loss of the Roman street pattern and the emergence of the medieval streets are mostly readily explained in terms of a severe contraction of settlement in Canterbury during the Dark Ages, followed by the gradual emergence of a new layout related to the cathedral complex. In particular we notice that the main Roman routes through the town, east–west from the London gate to Ridingate and north–south from Northgate to Worthgate, were lost. The new road out of the town southwards, already known as Wistræt in the ninth century,[32] is clearly intended to provide access to and from the cathedral rather than a route through the town. Even more significant are the street-names around the cathedral precinct itself. Palace Street, which departs from the line of the Roman street entering the town from the north, is known to have been diverted when Archbishop Lanfranc built the Norman archiepiscopal palace some time between the years 1070 and 1086.[33] On the other hand the short stretch of street immediately

[29] Taylor, 'Anglo-Saxon Cathedral Church', p. 126.
[30] Brooks, *Early History*, p. 36.
[31] Urry, *Canterbury*, pp. 204–7.
[32] BCS 519.
[33] Urry, *Canterbury*, pp. 73, 190; E.W. Parkin, 'No 17 Palace St, Canterbury', *Archaeologia Cantiana*, 87 (1972), pp. 183–90.

within Northgate is still on the original alignment and is called The Borough. Since the street to the south of the cathedral (now Burgate Street) was already called burhstræt in the late-Saxon period and since the gate by which it leaves the town is Burgate (borough gate), we seem to have a situation preserved in these street names in which the *burh* defines a limited area in the north-eastern quarter of the town immediately around the cathedral complex. In Canterbury therefore, as in early medieval Trier,[34] there seems to have been a period when the area of settlement within the Roman walls had contracted and was restricted to the area around the cathedral immunity. Whether as the name might indicate this restricted borough was fortified by earthwork and timber defences within the Roman circuit can only be determined by excavation. Already in the ninth century there is evidence at Canterbury of communities of *innan burhwara* and *utan burhwara* who may perhaps be understood as the inhabitants who lived within and without this restricted borough around the cathedral, rather than those living within and without the Roman walls.[35]

Hence the topography of early medieval Canterbury is seen to have been determined by its churches, especially by the metropolitan church itself. It is not until the laying out of a new east–west street through the town, which involved the building of a new gate (Newingate – from *æt þæm neowan gate*), and the development of a somewhat irregular grid of streets parallel and at right angles to this street and to Wistræt, that a more secular element enters the planning of the medieval city. The laying out of these streets had certainly been accomplished by the twelfth century. Until direct archaeological evidence is forthcoming it is probably best understood as another example of late-Saxon planning, perhaps to be attributed to the early tenth century.[36]

Here, as throughout this survey of the topography of early medieval Canterbury, the historian and topographer may conjecture; but only the archaeologist can hope to resolve the problems of interpreting the influence of the Roman past and of the Church on the emergence of the medieval city. Surely Canterbury deserves a long-term programme of excavation to elucidate its entire history through both research and rescue excavations. This paper will have served its purpose if it draws attention to some of the questions that the archaeologists need to be asking.

---

[34] K. Böhner, 'Urban and Rural Settlement in the Frankish Kingdom', in *European Towns: Their Archaeology and Early History*, ed. M.W. Barley (London, 1977), pp. 185–202.

[35] Cf. Brooks, *Early History*, pp. 22–30 for a different interpretation.

[36] M. Biddle and D. Hill, 'Late Saxon Planned Towns', *Antiquaries Journal*, 51 (1971), pp. 70–85.

7

The Cathedral Community at Canterbury, 597–1070

The Foundation

THE ROMAN CITY of Canterbury (Durovernum Cantiacorum) was the capital of the tribal province or *civitas* of Kent. It is likely that during the fourth century AD there was already a Christian element in its population and an episcopal church in the city, but unfortunately we do not know even the name of any of the Romano-British bishops. A rich silver-hoard buried just outside the west wall of the town in the early fifth century is a testimony to the wealth of some of the Christian inhabitants (Figure 7); but it remains uncertain how long a British Christian population may have remained in the town once Kent came under the rule of pagan Anglo-Saxons in the mid-fifth century.[1] The archaeological evidence suggests that in the later fifth and early sixth centuries there was a real hiatus in the economic and civic life of the town and that any continuing occupation was at a minimal level and confined to inhabitants of low status. Most of the western half of the town became uninhabitable through repeated flooding and was later to be used only as water-meadows; in the east, Roman buildings and streets fell into disuse and into varying degrees of ruin. In the present state of our knowledge, the emergence of Canterbury as the first see of Anglo-Saxon England and as the metro-politan church therefore seems to have owed relatively little either to its Roman past or to any living Christian tradition maintained by inhabitants of British descent. Rather, it was the product of the particular

---

[1] For possible Christian survivals, see N.P. Brooks, 'The Ecclesiastical Topography of Early Medieval Canterbury', in M.W. Barley, ed., *European Towns: Their Archaeology ad Early History* (London, 1977), pp. 487–98 (= above, pp. 91–100); for a less sanguine view, see C. Thomas, *Christianity in Roman Britain to AD 500* (London, 1981), pp. 170–4, 183–4. For the hiatus in civic life in Dark Age Canterbury, see T. Tatton-Brown, 'The Towns of Kent', in J. Haslam, ed., *Anglo-Saxon Towns in Southern England*, ed. J. Haslam (Chichester, 1984), pp. 1–36, and D.A. Brooks, 'The Case for Continuity in 5th-century Canterbury', *Oxford Journal of Archaeology*, 5 (1988), pp. 99–114; for the Christian silver-hoard, see C.M. Johns and T.W. Potter, 'The Canterbury Late Roman Treasure', *Antiquaries Journal* 65 (1985), pp. 312–52.

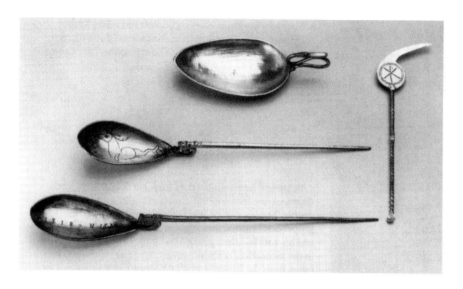

Figure 7. Part of the late-Roman hoard of Christian silver from Canterbury. (Canterbury Museums.)

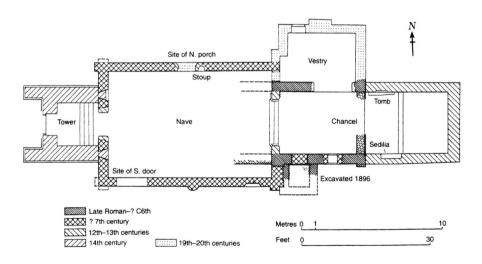

Figure 8. Plan of St Martin's Church, Canterbury. Reproduced by permission of T. Tatton-Brown.

circumstances of the closing years of the sixth century.

In 596 Pope Gregory I dispatched to Britain a group of forty monks from his own monastery of St Andrew on the Caelian Hill in Rome to convert the pagan English. The missionary party was led by their prior, Augustine, who was promoted by Gregory to be abbot and was subsequently consecrated as bishop by Frankish prelates in the course of his journey to England.[2] The arrival of the group, reinforced by Frankish interpreters, in Kent in the following year was not simply dictated by the convenience of the short sea-crossing. Kent had long-established ties through settlement, trade, and diplomacy with the Frankish kingdoms and may sometimes have been subject to Frankish lordship. King Æthelberht of Kent (*c.* 580–616 × 618) was certainly married to a Christian Frankish princess, Bertha, the daughter of Clovis's grandson, King Charibert of Paris.[3] For a decade or more, Bertha had been accompanied at the Kentish court by her Frankish chaplain, Bishop Liudhard, and had been accustomed to worship in the church of St Martin, a building believed to have been a Roman church and lying just to the east of the city (Figure 8). Augustine and his companions were therefore assured of a hospitable welcome in Kent and may have had reason to believe that the king was ready to consider conversion. Even more advantageous was the fact that Æthelberht was at that time the most powerful English king, exercising dominion over all the Anglo-Saxon rulers south of the river Humber. His lordship proved to be of short duration, but in 597 a mission had to start in Kent if it was to have the prospect of expansion into subordinate kingdoms.

It was therefore in Kent that Augustine's mission began its work, and in Canterbury, the principal Roman town of Æthelberht's kingdom, that they were first given a former Roman church as an episcopal see. Christ Church, the cathedral church of Canterbury, has occupied the same site in the north-eastern sector of the city ever since the king's original grant to Augustine (Figure 9). The dedication of this church to Jesus Christ, the Holy Saviour, in imitation of the papal cathedral on

---

[2] The principal sources for the Gregorian mission are the letters of Gregory himself (*S. Gregorii Magni Registrum Epistularum*, ed. D. Norberg (Corpus Christianorum Series Latina 140–140A; Turnhout, 1982), pp. vi, 51–7, 59–60; xi, 34–42, 45, 47–8, 50–1, 56) and the account in Bede, *Historia ecclesiastica*, i. 23–33; ii. 1–8. For a recent critical assessment, see N.P. Brooks, *The Early History of the Church of Canterbury* (Leicester, 1984), pp. 1–36, 63–7, 87–91.

[3] For the dates of Æthelberht's reign and of his marriage to Bertha, see N.P. Brooks, 'The Creation and Early Structure of the Kingdom of Kent', in S.R. Bassett, ed., *The Origin of the Anglo-Saxon Kingdoms* (Leicester, 1989), pp. 65–7 (= above, pp. 000–00). For the possibility of Frankish lordship, see I.N. Wood, 'The Merovingian North Sea', *Occasional Papers on Medieval Topics*, i (Alingsås, 1983), pp. 15–16, and J.M. Wallace-Hadrill, *Early Germanic Kingship in England and on the Continent* (Oxford, 1971), pp. 24–32; for a minimalist interpretation see Brooks, *Early History*, pp. 6–7.

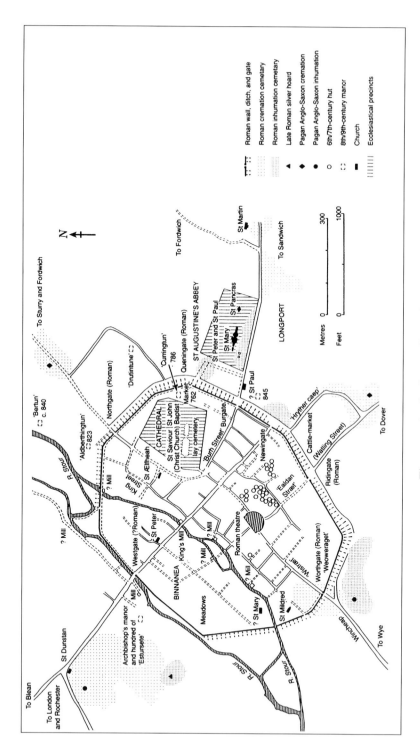

Figure 9. Anglo-Saxon Canterbury.

the Lateran, helped to create in Canterbury a little Rome. So did the relics and books which the missionary-monks had brought from Rome with them. At Christ Church the Roman monks sent by Gregory retained the leadership of the English mission as long as any of them still lived, that is until the death of Bishop Honorius, in 653.

Æthelberht's overlordship over other English kingdoms made far-reaching plans for the extension of the mission seem feasible. In 601 Gregory therefore sent to Kent a further band of Roman monks bearing instructions for the organization of the English church. He proposed metropolitan sees at London and at York, each with twelve suffragan bishops.[4] This ambitious plan was premature with regard both to York and to London. Though new sees were established at Rochester and at London in 604, King Æthelberht is not known to have made London the focus of his authority. Augustine and his successors as metropolitan bishops of the embryonic English church (Laurence 604 × 609–619, Mellitus 619–24, Justus 624–627 × 631, and Honorius 627 × 631–653) seem to have remained at Canterbury. Gregory's scheme still stood as the authoritative guidance on such matters as the number of metropolitan and suffragan sees that ought to be established. But paradoxically Canterbury's authority was reinforced when King Æthelberht died, in 616 or 618. In the pagan reaction that followed his death, both Mellitus, bishop of London, and Justus, bishop of Rochester, fled to Frankish Gaul. For a time, Canterbury was once more the only English see. Thereafter, its fame, as the first English see and as the sole surviving church of the disciples of St Gregory, helped to ensure its continued pre-eminence.

Bede records that Æthelberht had given Augustine and his companions 'the necessary possessions of various types'; later he tells us that the king endowed the sees of Rochester and London with many estates and possessions 'as at Canterbury'.[5] Unfortunately, we cannot determine the extent or location of the initial endowment at Canterbury, since the surviving series of authentic early charters granting lands to Christ Church begins only in the closing years of the eighth century. Yet there is good reason to believe that the cathedral church of Canterbury, like the other major Kentish churches, acquired a landed lordship of phenomenal wealth during the period when Kent was ruled by its own dynasty, that is from 597 until 764. By comparing the estates of the archbishops and community as they existed in 1066 with those that are known to have been acquired in the ninth, tenth, and eleventh centuries, we can deduce that many of the larger manors in Kent may

---

[4] *Greg. Epist.*, XI. 39.
[5] Bede, *Historia ecclesiastica*, i. 26, ii. 3. For what follows on the Christ Church endowment, see Brooks, *Early History*, pp. 100–7.

have formed part of the early endowment of the see. By 1066 almost a quarter of the landed wealth of Kent was to belong to the cathedral church, and it is likely that the bulk of this endowment had been acquired before 764. The independent kings of Kent had sacrificed their dynasty's fortune by the scale of their pious benefactions. By the eighth century, moreover, the church of Canterbury was also receiving grants of huge estates beyond Kent from the powerful overlords of the southern English. One such grant was King Æthelbald of Mercia's gift of the monastery of Cookham in Berkshire, with 100 hides of land, at some date between 740 and 756; another was the acquisition, on an unknown occasion, of 300 hides at *Iognes homme*, perhaps Eynsham in Oxfordshire. Despite the gaps in our evidence, it is clear that during the first century and a half of its existence, the cathedral church of Canterbury received a massive endowment, spread over much of south-eastern England.

It was indeed Canterbury's wealth, together with its links with Rome and with St Gregory, 'the apostle of the English', which made its ecclesiastical dominance acceptable throughout England in an age of fluctuating political fortunes. As Northumbrian, Mercian, and West Saxon rulers sought to extend their power over the southern English in the course of the seventh and eighth centuries, the metropolitan bishops of Canterbury (or '*arch*bishops', as they were styled at least from the year 679[6]) cultivated an aura of Roman authority. In England, as on the Continent, *romanitas* had an unfailing attraction for barbarian Germanic rulers. Pope Gregory I, himself adapting Roman imperial precedents, had sent to Augustine a *pallium* or 'pall', that is a long band of white wool marked with crosses, to be worn when celebrating mass. He intended it to authorize Augustine to consecrate suffragan bishops.[7] This concept of the papal *pallium* as the symbol and prerequisite of metropolitan authority took root in England when palls were granted to Justus, Honorius, and subsequent archbishops. Thereafter, whenever an archbishop of Canterbury died, it was necessary to secure a *pallium* from Rome for his successor. The papacy was thus able to maintain contact with the nascent English Church, and at least by the early

---

[6] Theodore was 'bishop of the church' of Canterbury' at the synod of Hertford (672), but 'archbishop' in an original charter of 679 and 'archbishop of the island of Britain and the city of Canterbury' in the synod of Hatfield (679). See Bede, *Historia ecclesiastica*, iv .5, 17, and BCS 45 (S 8). For the wider significance of these terms, see E. Lesne, *La Hiérarchie épiscopale* (Lille, 1905), pp. 31–5; F. Kempf, 'Primatiale und episcopal-synodale Struktur de Kirche vor der gregorianischen Reform', *Archivum Historiae Pontificiae*, 16 (1978), pp. 47–66; H. Vollrath, *Die Synoden Englands bis 1066* (Konziliengeschichte, Reihe A; Paderborn, 1985), pp. 28–30.

[7] For the pall, see Brooks, *Early History*, pp. 66–7; Th. Gottlob, *Der kirchliche Amtseid der Bischöfe* (Kanonistische Studien und Texte, 9; Bonn, 1936), pp. 26–30.

eighth century popes were accustomed to require from the archbishops-elect a written profession of faith before they would send the *pallium*.

Occasionally, in times of dispute or crisis in the English church, as with the elevation of Wigheard in 666–8, Berhtwald in 690–2, and perhaps of Cuthbert in 740, an archbishop-elect himself travelled to Rome to receive the pall in person, and sometimes even for consecration. Personally endorsed by the bishop of Rome in this way, an archbishop of Canterbury could be sure of his authority in England. If, as happened with Wigheard in 668, the elect died in Rome, a pope might even appoint and consecrate his successor. When Theodore, a Greek-speaking native of Tarsus, arrived in Canterbury in 669, he had been chosen directly by Pope Vitalian I for the task of reviving the English Church. Theodore's vigorous assertion of the metropolitan authority of the see of Canterbury – by holding regular annual synods, by appointing and even deposing bishops, and by creating new sees and dividing old ones – could not have been carried out had it not been axiomatic that an archbishop sent from Rome was entitled so to act. Even Bishop Wilfrid of York, the ablest and most determined opponent of the hierarchical policies of Archbishops Theodore and Berhtwald, could hope to resist only if he could secure from Rome explicit support upon the disputed issues.[8] But when Wilfrid returned to England with the necessary privileges from Popes Agatho, Sergius I, and John VI, he found on each occasion that the Northumbrian church and the Northumbrian kings preferred to stick with the decisions that had been reached under the aegis of the arch bishops of Canterbury. Compromises were possible only after the deaths of leading protagonists and in such a way as left the authority of the see of Canterbury intact.

By such means, the young English church achieved in the later seventh century a far more effective and hierarchical structure than was to be found at that time in the contemporary Frankish or Lombard kingdoms. Bishops had fixed sees, and their authority was restricted to their own, clearly defined dioceses. They were consecrated by their metropolitan, the archbishop of Canterbury, who presided over synods which were intended to be annual gatherings of the whole English church; there, matters of faith, discipline, and organization could be settled and enforced. The *pallium* served to emphasize the authority of the metropolitan and thence ultimately of Rome in such matters. In the early eighth century the Anglo-Saxon missionaries on the Continent, Willibrord and Boniface, took such concepts of ecclesiastical hierarchy,

---

[8] Bede, *Historia ecclesiastica*, v. 19. 'Eddius' Stephanus, *Life of Bishop Wilfrid*, ed. B. Colgrave (Cambridge, 1927); H. Mayr-Harting, *The Coming of Christianity to Anglo-Saxon England* (London, 1972), pp. 129–47; G. Isenberg, 'Die Würdigung Wilfrieds von York' (Ph.D. thesis, University of Münster, 1978); Vollrath, *Die Synoden*, pp. 66–123.

metropolitan authority, and ultimate dependence upon papal decisions into the new ecclesiastical provinces that they established east of the Rhine; from there they were to be adopted throughout the Frankish Church and to form a foundation for the medieval growth of the authority of the Holy See.[9]

The Early Community

The Christian community established in Canterbury under Augustine comprised about forty Roman monks, reinforced in 601 by a further band under Mellitus; there were also Franks, in the household of the queen, and others recruited by Augustine on his journey to England. The traditions which Bede recorded about the way of life of these missionaries derived from Albinus, Abbot of the monastery of St Peter and St Paul, which Augustine and Æthelberht had founded just outside the walls of the city. These traditions centred upon the activities of the Roman monks and on the links with Rome. They remembered nothing, for example, of the activities of Liudhard, Bertha's Frankish chaplain. Yet Liudhard had been a bishop, not simply a household priest. This suggests that he had been intended to have a missionary role and to consecrate priests. Bede tells of the 'apostolic' life of Augustine and his companions, serving God with assiduous prayers, vigils, and fasts, preaching *to whom they could* and despising everything of this world.[10] Several of the Roman monks are indeed known to have become priests. Though their disciplined and ascetic way of life and their Latin scriptures and liturgy may have seemed a strange and potent magic to their pagan Kentish hosts, we may suspect that preaching and pastoral work would have been more effectively undertaken by Franks (whose vernacular speech was closer to Kentish) than by Romans.

Had Bede's information derived from Christ Church, we might be better informed about the Frankish role in the conversion of the English, since the Frankish clergy are likely to have been based there, leaving the monastery of St Peter and St Paul (the later St Augustine's) as a separate establishment, principally for the Roman monks. We know that Augustine was concerned about his relations with his clergy and that Gregory instructed him to follow the monastic or 'apostolic' tradition to which he was accustomed, that is to live communally and without private property. Only clerks in minor orders could take wives or have individual stipends, though they too were to be under ecclesias-

[9] Th. Schieffer, *Winfrid-Bonifatius und die christliche Grundlegung Europas* (2nd edn, Darmstadt, 1972).

[10] Bede, *Historia ecclesiastica*, i. 26.

tical discipline.[11] In recommending that the priests and deacons of the Cathedral at Canterbury should adopt a monastic regime, Gregory was seeking to establish in the English church the high standards that many of the early Fathers of the western church had sought to impose on their clergy: Augustine at Hippo, Eusebius at Vercelli, Ambrose at Milan, and Martin at Tours, to name only the best known.[12] He was not enjoining that the Canterbury clergy should all be monks, observing a full monastic liturgical regime and seeking a secluded communal life. That was, however, to be the interpretation adopted both by tenth-century monastic reformers and by later Canterbury forgers in an age when the future of the monastic chapter was in doubt.[13] Rather, the great pope was seeking to bring the life of the Canterbury clergy closer to that of Roman monks and to his own personal practice. Indeed, the arrangement of cathedral and separate monastery which Augustine set up in Canterbury suggests that the intention was to mirror arrange-ments in Rome, where monks from the monasteries of the city joined the cathedral clergy for the morning and evening offices (lauds and vespers), but were alone responsible for the regular recitation of the shorter daytime offices and for the long night-vigil (nocturns).

Such liturgical co-operation helped to make the 'church of the people of Kent' famous in the seventh and eighth centuries as a source of choirmasters skilled in chanting the Office 'according to Roman custom', a tradition maintained at Canterbury first by 'the disciples of St Gregory' and then by their pupils.[14] Augustine had indeed been authorized to adopt any liturgical practices of the Frankish Church which met with his approval, but his loyalties must have remained predominantly with Rome. Certainly, when, in the eighth century, we first have detailed evidence of the practice at Canterbury, we find that Rome and Gregory remained the models. It was the Roman, not the Gallican, psalter text that was used,[15] while Archbishop Cuthbert's synod of *Clofesho* of 747 prescribed the general use of a written exemplar from the church of Rome in the office of baptism, in the mass, and in liturgical chant; it also advocated the adoption of an

[11] Ibid., i. 27 (Resp. 1), pp. 78–80. For the authenticity of the *Responsiones*, see P. Meyvaert, 'Les *Responsiones* de S. Grégoire le Grand à S. Augustin de Cantorbéry', *Revue d'histoire ecclésiastique*, 54 (1959), pp. 879–94.

[12] G. Lawless, *Augustine of Hippo and His Monastic Rule* (Oxford, 1987); M. Zacherl, 'Die *Vita Communis* als Lebensform des Klerus in her Zeit zwischen Augustinus und Karl dem Großen', *Zeitschrift für katholische Theologie*, 92 (1970), pp. 385–424.

[13] Brooks, *Early History*, pp. 90–1.

[14] Ibid., pp. 91–3; Bede, *Historia ecclesiastica*, ii. 20; iv. 2; v. 20. 'Eddius' Stephanus, *Life of Wilfrid*, ed. Colgrave, ch. 14.

[15] *Le Psautier romain et les autres psautiers latins*, ed. Dom R. Weber (Collectanea Biblica, 10; Rome, 1953), pp. ix–xxii; *The Vespasian Psalter*, ed. D.H. Wright and A. Campbell (Early English Manuscripts in Facsimile, 14; Copenhagen, 1967).

annual cycle of observance of saints' festivals according to the martyrology of the Roman church, with the appropriate psalmody.[16] Rome, then, continued to be the model that the church of Canterbury sought to imitate.

In monastic observance it is unlikely that the Gregorian missionaries were bound by one single code or rule. This was the age of the *regula mixta*, when abbots had an eclectic attitude to monastic practice. But Gregory the Great had devoted the whole of the second book of his *Dialogues* to the miracles of St Benedict, so it is likely that his disciples in Canterbury would have had a very high regard for Benedict's authority. An early interpolated text of the Rule of St Benedict is known to have been extensively studied and glossed in seventh-century Canterbury. So too were Gregory's *Dialogues*.[17] It is therefore likely that the Anglo-Saxon veneration for the Rule, so evident in the careers of men like St Wilfrid and St Boniface, owed something to the honour in which the Rule was held in the English metropolitan see.

The establishment of a school at Canterbury, to train young English clerks to read and to understand both the Latin Scriptures and the Church's liturgy, must have been among Augustine's first concerns. Already by 631 or 632 Canterbury was able to send teachers and masters to East Anglia to establish a comparable school there. But it was under Archbishop Theodore (668–90) and Abbot Hadrian of St Augustine's (670–708) that Canterbury became an outstanding centre of instruction, famous above all for their teaching of the Scriptures, but also for the training they provided in other essential ecclesiastical skills: metre (the rules for the composition of Latin poetry), the computus (the workings of the calendar), law, and astronomy.[18] Many of the outstanding English churchmen of the early eighth century acquired a foundation in Greek and deepened their Latin learning from the teaching of these two scholars. Unfortunately, none of the library books from the Canterbury of Theodore and Hadrian's day has survived; nor have any library catalogues. But we can attribute to the pen of Augustine of Canterbury two sermons preserved in a manuscript from Mainz, and to Theodore some octosyllabic verse and an extensive body of judgements on penitential discipline.[19] Moreover, collections of glosses which survive in

---

[16] Synod of Clofesho, 747, c. 13; *Councils and Ecclesiastical Documents Relating to Britain and Ireland*, ed. A.W. Haddan and W. Stubbs (Oxford, 1869–78), iii. 367.

[17] M. Lapidge, 'The School of Theodore and Hadrian', *Anglo-Saxon England*, 15 (1986), pp. 45–72. For the authenticity of the *Dialogues*, see P. Meyvaert, 'The enigma of Gregory the Great's *Dialogues*: A Response to Francis Clark', *Journal of Ecclesiastical History*, 39 (1988), pp. 335–81.

[18] Brooks, *Early History*, pp. 94–9; Lapidge, 'School of Theodore', pp. 45–72.

numerous continental manuscripts have been shown to derive from a collection first made at Canterbury in the late seventh century. They establish that a wide range of Latin authors, both patristic and monastic, were studied there. The extensive biblical glosses in these collections have preserved something of Theodore's exegesis of the Pentateuch and of the gospels.[20] It is clear that what made Canterbury virtually unique in the Latin West was that Theodore followed the eastern or Antiochene style of commentary: that is to say, he used the Greek Fathers in preference to the Latin, and adopted factual and literal interpretations rather than following the western allegorical tradition.

Under Theodore's successors the ephemeral pre-eminence of the school of Canterbury in the study of Greek slipped away, probably because texts of the Greek Fathers were lacking. But several of the archbishops of the first half of the eighth century were competent Latin scholars. Tatwine (731–4) was the author both of a grammar and of a collection of riddles; Cuthbert (740–60) has left us some skilled inscriptions in hexameters.[21] Such men are likely to have maintained a good level of Latin scholarship in their cathedral church.

King Offa and the Imposition of Mercian Rule (764–805)

The second half of the eighth century proved to be a decisive watershed in the history of the Church of Canterbury.[22] At that time, all the southern English kingdoms came under the increasing domination of the rulers of Mercia, with the result that the archbishop's responsibilities for the province necessarily involved difficult adjustments to changing political realities. Moreover, in Kent itself the rule of the native dynasty, which had established and endowed Christ Church so

[19] L. Machielson, 'Fragments patristiques non-identifiés du ms. Vat. Pal. 577', *Sacris Eruditi*, 12 (1961), pp. 488–539; Lapidge, 'School of Theodore', pp. 46–9; P. Finsterwalder, *Die Canones Theodori Cantuariensis und ihre Überlieferungsformen* (Weimar, 1929).

[20] Lapidge, 'School of Theodore', pp. 53–67; B. Bischoff, 'Wendepunkte in her Geschichte der lateinischen Exegese im Frühmittelalter', *Sacris Eruditi*, 6 (1954), pp. 187–279, at 191–5, trans. as 'Turning-points in the History of Latin Exegesis in the Early Middle Ages', in M. McNamara, ed., *Biblical Studies: The Medieval Irish Contribution* (Dublin, 1976), pp. 73–160.

[21] M. Lapidge, 'Some Remnants of Bede's Lost *Liber Epigrammaticum*', *English Historical Review*, 90 (1975), pp. 812–14.

[22] The fundamental studies of the Mercian kingdom are F.M. Stenton, *Anglo-Saxon England* (3rd edn, Oxford, 1971), pp. 202–38, and the chs. of C.P. Wormald in J. Campbell, ed., *The Anglo-Saxons* (London, 1982), pp. 70–128. See also Brooks, *Early History*, pp. 111–27.

handsomely, came to an end, after a prolonged and fluctuating struggle. From the year 764, when Offa of Mercia (757–96) first intervened directly in Kent at the head of a large Mercian following, the Kentish kings, Egbert and Heahberht, came under increased pressure. They gained some respite in 776, when the men of Kent seem to have defeated the Mercians in a battle at Otford, but at least by 785 Offa was ruling Kent as 'King of the Mercians', without reference to any local king. On Offa's death, in 796, the rising of Eadberht Præn briefly re-established Kent as an independent kingdom. But from 798 King Cenwulf had imposed Mercian rule once more, though initially he set up his brother Cuthred (798–807) as a subordinate king there.

These political changes had obvious dangers for the archbishops and for the community of Christ Church. Victorious kings could annul the bequests of defeated kings to a church, as grants either of rebellious nobles or of unjust foreign invaders. To a Mercian king, the major Kentish churches would need to be purged of any residual loyalty to the dynasty which had founded and enriched them. The two Kentish bishoprics and the Kentish 'minister' churches were therefore obvious targets after the dynasty had been suppressed, particularly since both Offa and Cenwulf needed land and offices to reward the nobles on whom their victories had depended. But they also needed the support of the ecclesiastical hierarchy. Each claimed descent from the Mercian royal house, but neither Offa nor Cenwulf could number a king among their immediate or near ancestors. They were both well aware of the contemporary example set by the Carolingian dynasty's successful usurpation of the Frankish throne, which had depended upon episcopal and papal support and had utilized new rituals of royal 'ordination' or consecration. Like the Carolingians, both Offa and Cenwulf sought to legalize their extended rule and to pass it on to their descendants. They therefore hoped to control the metropolitan church of Canterbury. Otherwise they might need to transfer its metropolitan authority to a see which was more easily dominated from the Mercian heartland. The stage was set for a titanic struggle, whose outlines can be only dimly discerned in the extant sources.

The conflict began during the archiepiscopate of Jænberht (765–92). Though consecrated in Offa's presence, Jænberht had previously been abbot of St Augustine's, and his ties were with the Kentish dynasty and nobility. Through friendship with King Egbert II and kinship with Aldhun, reeve in Canterbury, he secured for Christ Church in 780 or thereabouts three valuable manors in East Kent: Charing, Great Chart, and Bishopsbourne. Offa, however, soon annulled Egbert's grants on the grounds that 'it was unlawful for his thegn [*minister*] to give away land granted to him by his lord without his lord's testimony'.[23] It seems clear that the Mercian king regarded the church of Canterbury as one of the centres of opposition to his rule and was determined to punish it. In 779, when he had won control of the upper Thames valley, after defeating the West Saxons in battle at Bensington, he acquired the wealthy minster of Cookham (Berkshire), which his predecessor, King Æthelbald, had once granted to Christ Church. Despite the evidence of Æthelbald's charter, and despite the best efforts of both Jænberht and his successor, Æthelheard (792–805), Offa retained Cookham in his own hands and passed it on to his widow, Queen Cynethryth, to rule as abbess.[24] Not until 798–9, when the Mercian throne had passed from Offa's kin to Cenwulf, was Æthelheard able to recover (at a price) Charing, Chart, and Bishopsbourne, and to secure some recompense in Kent for the loss of Cookham's extensive properties.

The conflict of church and state was not limited to these property disputes and to Jænberht's support for Kentish independence. From 781 (the year in which Charlemagne had had his sons, Pippin and Louis, anointed by the Pope) Offa began to attend the annual synods of the Canterbury province, perhaps as a means of pressurizing Jænberht or of countering his influence. Moreover, the Mercian king also sought to secure the succession of his only son, Ecgfrith, to his enlarged kingdom. The papal legates, Bishops George of Ostia and Theophylact of Todi, who visited England in 786, are known to have concerned themselves with the 'ordination' of legitimate kings.[25] But it would seem that Archbishop Jænberht was determined to avoid consecrating Ecgfrith, lest that might appear to legitimize Ecgfrith's rule throughout the province of Canterbury, that is over all the kingdoms south of the Humber. To resolve the issue, a 'contentious synod' was held in 787 at Chelsea, where two momentous steps were taken. Not only was Ecgfrith consecrated as king during his father's lifetime, seemingly by the Mercian Bishop Hygeberht of Lichfield, but the province of Canterbury was also divided in such a way that London and all the sees south of the Thames remained subject to Jænberht, while Dunwich, Elmham, Lindsey, Leicester, Lichfield, Worcester, and Hereford were formed into a new province of Lichfield under Hygeberht, who

---

[23] BCS 293 (S 155) and cf. BCS 319, 332 (S 1259, 1264). For differing interpretations of Offa's confiscations, see E. John, *Land Tenure in Early England* (Leicester, 1960), p. 48; H. Vollrath, *Königsgedanke und Königtum bei den Angelsachsen* (Köln, 1971), pp. 163–8; C.P. Wormald, 'Bede, the Bretwaldas and the Origins of the *Gens Anglorum*', in idem, ed., *Ideal and Reality in Frankish and Anglo-Saxon Society*, idem (Oxford, 1983), pp. 115–16; Brooks, *Early History*, pp. 114–15.

[24] BCS 291 (S 1258); Brooks, *Early History*, pp. 116–17.

[25] *Councils*, ed. Haddan & Stubbs, iii. 453–4. The best discussion of the report of the papal legates and of the relations of Mercian rulers with English synods is now C.R.E. Cubitt, *Anglo-Saxon Church Councils c. 650–c. 850* (Leicester, 1995), pp. 153–234.

received a *pallium* and metropolitan rank from Pope Hadrian I.[26]

The church of Canterbury had suffered a heavy price for Jænberht's determination to resist Offa's consolidation of his power. It had failed to secure the right to consecrate the most powerful English king. Its metropolitan authority was now restricted to the Kentish and Saxon bishoprics (Canterbury, Rochester, London, Selsey, Winchester, and Sherborne). Its endowment had been severely pruned. When Archbishop Jænberht died, in 792, he was replaced by an abbot from the new province, that is by Æthelheard of Louth in the subkingdom of Lindsey. Offa was clearly not prepared to tolerate another Kentish archbishop of Canterbury, and he continued to attend the synodal assemblies of the two provinces, over which the two archbishops now presided jointly.[27] At Christ Church, Æthelheard seems to have been regarded as a foreign intruder, for on Offa's death he fled, on the community's advice, to the Mercian court. His flight may not have safeguarded his church, for either during or after the rising of Eadberht Præn (796–8) Christ Church seems to have lost all its early archives.[28] Meanwhile King Cenwulf negotiated with Rome in order to transfer metropolitan authority from Canterbury to the vacant see of London, but when Pope Leo III refused to allow any further tampering with the structure of the English Church, Cenwulf re-established Æthelheard at Canterbury by force of arms. Thereafter, the Mercian king and the archbishop worked together to restore the confiscated Canterbury properties and, with papal support, to secure the abolition of the metropolitan see of Lichfield and the restoration of Canterbury's authority over its province (803).[29]

At Christ Church, from 798 and for most of the ninth century, a careful record was kept of the professions of faith and of obedience to the archbishop made by bishops-elect of the Canterbury province. The terms in which some pledged their loyalty were indeed deliberately reminiscent of secular oaths of fealty:

> I declare that whatever thou, father, whatever thy successors as prelates of the holy church of Canterbury, affirm in truth I shall lovingly affirm; whatever they shun as unjust, that I too shall hasten to shun in every way.[30]

Thus the church of Canterbury sought to buttress its metropolitan

---

[26] *Anglo-Saxon Chronicle: A Revised Translation*, ed. and trans. D. Whitelock and D.C. Douglas and S.I. Tucker (London, 1961), s.a. 787. For the division of the sees, see Brooks, *Early History*, pp. 118–20.

[27] At Chelsea in 789 (BCS 255, 256, 257; S 131, 1430, 130), and in 793 (BCS 267; S 136); at *Clofesho* in 794 × 796 (BCS 274; S 139) and 798 (BCS 289, 291; S 153, 1258); at Tamworth in 799 (BCS 293; S 155).

[28] Brooks, *Early History*, p. 121.

[29] BCS 310; Brooks, *Early History*, pp. 123–7.

[30] *Canterbury Professions*, ed. M. Richter (CYS, 67; Torquay, 1973), no. 28.

authority by maintaining the earliest record of such professions of obedience to survive in Europe. They serve as a reminder that the see had survived the greatest threat to its status, but at the cost of accepting a Mercian archbishop. Never again would the church of Canterbury work for Kentish independence.

Archbishop Wulfred (805–32)

In 805 Wulfred, who had served as archdeacon during the later years of Æthelheard's archiepiscopate, was chosen to succeed him. The election of a member of the Christ Church community accorded with the advice that Alcuin had given during Æthelheard's flight, and doubtless served to satisfy local pride. But the new archbishop was in fact a member of a noble Middle Saxon family;[31] his elevation may reflect the introduction of Mercian clergy into the community by Archbishop Æthelheard. Be that as it may, Wulfred's pontificate is surprisingly well documented, thanks to a splendid series of Canterbury charters and episcopal professions of faith, as well as the canons of his great reforming synod, held at Chelsea in 816. From such sources, we can show Archbishop Wulfred to have been a dynamic leader and reformer who made a major impact on the whole English church.

Fundamental to his work was the reform of his cathedral community at Christ Church along lines very similar to those that had been pioneered at Metz by Bishop Chrodegang and which were to form the standard for cathedral clergy that Louis the Pious and Benedict of Aniane sought to impose throughout the Frankish realms in a series of reforming councils of the years 813–16. In a former charter of 808 × 813, Wulfred announced that he had 'revived the holy monastery of the church of Canterbury by renewing, restoring and rebuilding it': he insisted that the Christ Church community maintain the Office at the canonical hours, eat their meals in a communal refectory, and sleep in a communal dormitory, and that any property owned by individual members be bequeathed to the community.[32] His reforms represented a marked tightening of the regime at Christ Church, a return to some of the monastic ideals that Pope Gregory the Great had recommended to Augustine and his clergy. In referring to the priests and deacons of

[31] Brooks, *Early History*, p. 132 for Wulfred's family. For Alcuin's advice that the archbishop be elected from the community, see *Alcuini Epistolae*, ed. E. Dümmler, MGH Epist., IV (Berlin, 1895), no. 128, trans. in *EHD*, no. 203.
[32] BCS 342 (S 1265); Brooks, *Early History*, pp. 153–60; R. Schieffer, *Die Entstehung von Domkapiteln in Deutschland* (Bonner Historische Forschungen, 43; Bonn, 1976), pp. 262–78.

Christ Church as being subject 'to the rule of the life of monastic discipline', rather than calling them cathedral 'canons' subject to a 'canonical' rule, Wulfred was sticking to the terminology of an older tradition and avoiding the new language of the Carolingian reforms. The difference, however, was one of nomenclature rather than of substance.

As archbishop, Wulfred enjoyed fluctuating relations with the secular powers. He quarrelled with King Cenwulf early in his period of office and again more dramatically from *c.* 815 to 821; thereafter, the rapid changes in the Mercian royal succession and, from *c.* 825, the subjection of Kent to the rule of the West Saxon Kings Egbert and his son Æthelwulf, all required nimble political footwork.[33] None the less, the evidence suggests that as far as circumstances allowed, Wulfred allowed a consistent and vigorous territorial policy in the acquisition of estates for his own use and in reorganizing and extending the properties of the community. By spending a considerable personal fortune, he purchased estates in Kent and in Middlesex and disposed of properties (or claims to properties) in the Thames valley or even further afield. By a series of exchanges and planned purchases, he accumulated adjacent properties, both for himself and (separately) for the community, which could be efficiently administered as single manors. Indeed, many of the great medieval manors of the archbishops and of Christ Church (Bishopsbourne, Eastry, Lympne, Graveney, Harrow, Otford, and Petham) seem to have taken their definitive form in his time. He also insisted that grants made to Christ Church were inalienable and permanent gifts, so long as the community maintained the reformed life that he had established for them.

By contrast, Wulfred was careful to insist that he himself had full powers of disposal over the huge lordship that he accumulated for his own use. Indeed, in one charter he expressed resentment at the idea that he should be any more restricted in the disposition of his own booklands than other men were in the disposition of theirs.[34] Wulfred's will has not survived, but while he certainly used some properties to help build up a permanent endowment for the archbishops, he is known to have passed on the bulk of his estates to his kinsman the priest Werhard, who can be shown to have risen very rapidly in the Christ Church community: a deacon in 824 and only a junior priest in 825, Werhard was presiding over the community as 'priest-abbot' by the mid-830s. Indeed, if, as seems likely, other members of the same Middle Saxon family may be recognized in the Wulfhard who had been the senior priest at Christ Church from 803–13, and in the Wernoth who was 'priest-abbot' in 811 and 813 then Wulfred's kin may be seen

---

[33] Brooks, *Early History*, pp. 132–7.
[34] S 1622, discussed and quoted ibid., p. 139.

to have dominated the Christ Church community from the beginning of the century until after our last record of 'priest-abbot' Werhard, in 845.[35] Though Wulfred had indeed observed his own regulation that individual members of the community should not grant their lands outside it, his immediate concern would seem to have been to exalt the members of his own family.

Little is known of the life of the community during Wulfred's archiepiscopate, except from the charters and books which may, with some probability, be ascribed to the Christ Church scriptorium. During the second and third decades of the ninth century, a number of Christ Church scribes, led and probably trained by Archbishop Wulfred himself, developed a highly calligraphic and mannered variety of insular cursive minuscule. The Canterbury script represents one of the high points in the development of insular minuscule, and they evidently regarded it as suitable for the more formal synodal charters (Figure 10) and for important books. Astonishingly, however, at the very time when Christ Church scribes were attaining the high point of the script's calligraphic potential, their standards of Latin grammar and orthography were at a low ebb. Indeed, the two charters which may plausibly be attributed to the hand of Archbishop Wulfred himself are already replete with false agreements and with spellings affected by the scribe's vernacular pronunciation.[36] It is clear that under Wulfred several of the cathedral clergy were well able to produce a finely written charter or copy a book in a handsome script; they could also compose, utilizing earlier models, elaborate professions of faith for bishops-elect to present to the archbishop, and perhaps for archbishops-elect to send to the pope.[37] Doubtless many of them could comprehend the routine services and familiar passages of the Scriptures; but few, if any, of them appear to have had sufficient command of grammar to be able to compose in Latin for new needs. With standards of learning so low in the metropolitan church, there must have been a danger that the decline would be irreversible and would seriously hamper the routine pastoral work of the church.

Canterbury's metropolitan responsibility for pastoral standards in the English church was also at the root of the major dispute of Wulfred's archiepiscopate. For a century and more, leading English churchmen

[35] Ibid., pp. 139–42.
[36] BCS 370 and 373 (S 186, 187); for the attribution to Wulfred's hand, see Brooks, *Early History*, p. 168.
[37] For Wulfred's charters and the attribution of charters to the Christ Church scriptorium, see Brooks, *Early History*, pp. 164–74; M. Brown, 'Paris BN lat. 10861 and the Scriptorium of Christ Church, Canterbury', *Anglo-Saxon England*, 15 (1985), pp. 119–37; J. Crick, 'Church, Land and Local Nobility in Early Ninth-Century Kent: The Case of Earldorman Oswulf', *Historical Research*, 61 (1988), pp. 251–69.

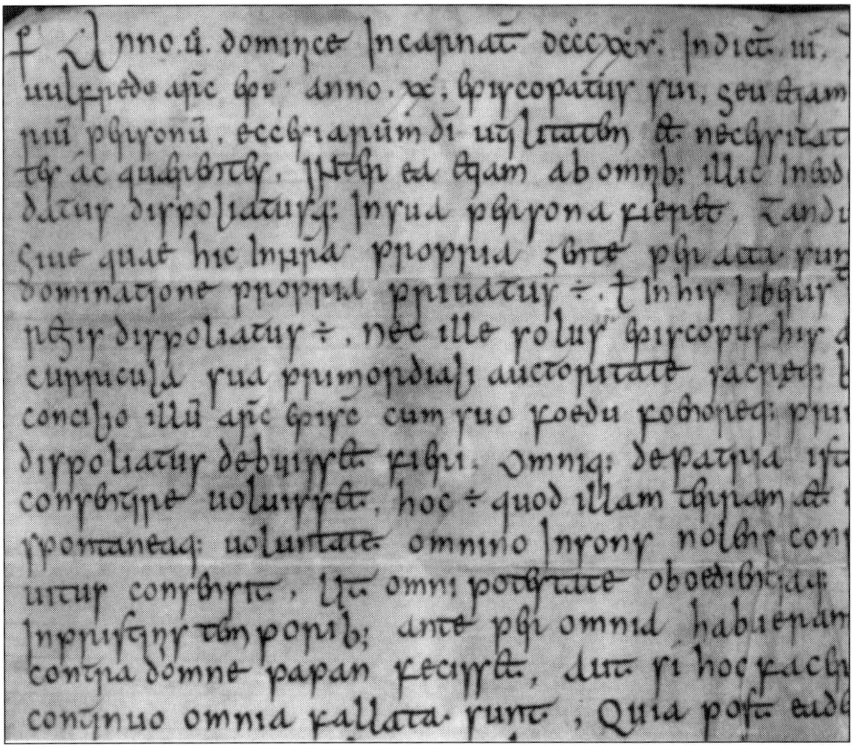

Figure 10. Opening part of the record of the synod of *Clofesho* of 825, written by a contemporary Canterbury scribe (BL, Stowe Charter 15). [By Permission of the of the British Library.]

had been concerned lest 'monasteries' or minster-churches should fall under the hereditary control of the local noble or royal families, to the detriment not only of their 'monastic' discipline, but also of effective pastoral care in their extensive territories or *parochiae*.[38] In 803 Archbishop Æthelheard and the bishops of his province had decreed that minster communities should never choose laymen as their lords and should henceforth observe monastic discipline. But it was left to Wulfred to attempt to enforce such general pronouncements against the entrenched proprietorial rights of lay lords. He presided over the synod of Chelsea (816), which prohibited the alienation of monastic estates for more that a single lifetime (can. 7), asserted the duty of bishops to choose (with the consent of the *familiae*) worthy abbots and abbesses for the minsters of their diocese (can. 4), and finally authorized them to

[38] Brooks, *Early History*, pp. 173–80. Archbishop Æthelheard's decree against lay lordship is BCS 312; the canons of Wulfred's 816 synod of Chelsea are printed in *Councils*, ed. Haddan & Stubbs, iii, pp. 579–85.

intervene to secure the property of communities which were threatened by the rapacity of laymen (can. 8). Thus the synod overrode the traditional canonical restrictions on episcopal interference in monastic elections and property. The stage was set for a major clash of church and state.

Wulfred was immediately embroiled in a bitter test-case with King Cenwulf of Mercia over the lordship of the Kentish 'monasteries' of Reculver and of Minster-in-Thanet. In the course of a long struggle (816–21), the King secured papal privileges confirming his acquired and inherited rights over monasteries, while the church of Canterbury produced forged charters which purported to grant control of monastic elections and property to the archbishops.[39] The King used his influence at Rome and at the court of the emperor, Louis the Pious, to secure the archbishop's suspension from office, and the archbishop may in turn have tried to depose the king. At all events, most of the moneyers of the Canterbury mint preferred in these years to produce a unique series of 'anonymous' coins (Figure 11), bearing the royal or archiepiscopal bust but omitting the king's or archbishop's name. Shortly before his death, in 821, Cenwulf imposed a solution whereby the archbishop retained the lordship of Reculver and Minster, but at the price of ceding to the king 300 hides of land at *Iognes homme* (perhaps Eynsham in Oxfordshire) and of paying a massive fine, equivalent to the *wergild* or blood-price of a king. In Canterbury eyes, however, even this savage settlement did not stick, since from 822 to 824 the king's daughter, Abbess Cwoenthryth of Minster, did not in fact pay the rents and obedience due from her house. After the succession of King Beornwulf of Mercia (823–5), Wulfred reopened the dispute on more favourable terms at a synod at *Clofesho* in 825 and subsequently at *Oslafeshlau*. There the Abbess was compelled to compensate the archbishop for the injuries done him by her father; she gave up control of Minster and in addition ceded an estate of 100 hides at Harrow, Wembley, and Yeadding in Middlesex, which thereafter was to form one of the greatest archiepiscopal manors.[40]

Wulfred's remarkable, though partial, victory was to be short-lived. The days of Mercian rule in Kent were numbered. In 825 Egbert of Wessex defeated Beornwulf's army at Wroughton (Wiltshire) and then

[39] The forged privileges of Wihtred and Æthelbald are BCS 91, 162 (S 22, 90); Cenwulf's papal privileges are BCS 337, 363. See also W. Levison, *England and the Continent in the Eighth Century* (Oxford, 1946), pp. 255–7, and Brooks, *Early History*, pp. 185–6.

[40] The only account of the Reculver and Minster dispute is the Canterbury record of its settlement, BCS 384 (S 1436). For the interpretation followed here, see Brooks, *Early History*, pp. 173–206, at 180–3.

Figure 11. Silver pennies bearing the name of archbishops and produced by moneyers of the Canterbury mint from *c*.770 to *c*.925. 1. King Offa – Archbishop Jænberht. 2. King Offa – Archbishop Æthelheard. 3. King Cenwulf – Archbishop Æthelheard. 4. Archbishop Wulfred – *Doroverniae Civitatis*. 5. Anonymous (Wulfred) Wilnoth *moneta* – *Dorobernia Civitas*. 6. Archbishop Ceolnoth – Biornoth *monet'*. 7. Archbishop Æthelred – Ethered *mon'*. 8. Archbishop Plegmund – Æthelfreth *mon'*. [British Museum, Dept. of Coins and Medals. © Copyright The British Museum.]

sent his son, Æthelwulf, to establish West Saxon power in the south-eastern kingdoms (825 × 827). The new rulers of Kent did not recognize Wulfred as sole lord of the Kentish minsters and they confiscated an estate at 'Malling' (probably East Malling in Kent) which, they claimed, had been given to the church of Canterbury by King Baldred, a Mercian subking, when in flight from the West Saxon forces. The interruption of the archbishops' minting-rights during the initial years of West Saxon rule may be another indication of their strained relations with the metropolitan church. The only acquisition of Wulfred's later years (825–32) – King Wiglaf of Mercia's grant of Botwell, near Hayes (Middlesex) in 831 – suggests that the great archbishop still preferred to operate within the Mercian political stage.[41] His Middle Saxon origins and the political loyalties of a lifetime were not easily set aside.

West Saxon Rule and the Impact of the Vikings (832–923)

It was left to Archbishop Ceolnoth (833–70) to adjust the stance of the church of Canterbury in order to bring it into keeping with a political situation in which the West Saxons ruled south of the Thames and had claims over Essex as well, while the Mercians remained the dominant Midland kingdom. Nothing is known of Ceolnoth's origins, since the late story that he had previously been the 'dean' of the Christ Church community is a typically anachronistic monastic invention.[42] Early in his archiepiscopate, namely in 836, he presided over a provincial synod, which was held at Croft (Leicestershire), deep in Mercian or Middle Anglian territory. This synod was attended by King Wiglaf and his nobles,[43] and was the last known occasion when a Mercian king and his retinue attended such a gathering, as had been the norm since the 780s. Thereafter, Ceolnoth attended the West Saxon court under Egbert (802–38), Æthelwulf (830–58), and his sons, in the company of the southern English bishops; and he also attended, though less frequently, the Mercian court under Kings Berhtwulf (840–55) and Burgred (855–75). As metropolitan, he probably also needed to attend the East Anglian court on occasions during the reigns of the successive Kings Æthelstan, Æthelweard, and Edmund (825–69), but none of their charters has survived. Henceforth, when the bishops of the entire province gathered in synod, as at *Astran* in 839 and London in 845,[44] their meeting was a purely ecclesiastical occasion. We may therefore suspect that the archbishops continued to preside over the annual synods of their province in the second half of the ninth century; but in the absence of any king, these were no longer occasions which produced royal charters, the principal evidence for English synodal activity in the period from 780 to 836. We must therefore hesitate before assuming from the silence of our sources that the archbishops of

[41] BCS 400 (S 188). For Wulfred's relations with the West Saxon kings, see Brooks, *Early History*, p. 138.

[42] Gervase, *Historical Works*, ii. 348; for the reasons to discount this assertion, see Brooks, *Early History*, p. 145.

[43] BCS 416 (S 190); for the interpretation of the changing pattern of English synods in the mid-ninth century, see Cubitt, *Anglo-Saxon Church Councils*, pp. 235–40.

[44] For the synod at *Astran*, see BCS 421 (S 1438); for that at London, BCS 448 (S 1194).

the later ninth century neglected their duty to exercise metropolitan authority through regular provincial synods.

In general the rule of the West Saxon kings seems to have greatly reduced the flow of royal benefactions to the church of Canterbury. It is difficult to be certain whether Archbishop Ceolnoth and his successors were less wealthy and less active in the land market than Wulfred had been, or whether the West Saxon dynasty was less well disposed towards a see which they considered already more than adequately endowed. However, in 838–9 a window of opportunity opened for Ceolnoth, because of King Egbert's desire to secure for his son, Æthelwulf, who was already ruling as subking in Kent, the succession to the whole of his enlarged kingdom. It was almost 200 years since the West Saxon succession had last passed from father to son, so it is not surprising that Egbert was willing to be generous in order to secure ecclesiastical support for his efforts to establish a dynasty. In 838 the archbishop presided over a 'venerable council' of southern bishops, meeting with Kings Egbert and Æthelwulf and their nobles at Kingston in Surrey. There the two kings restored to Christ Church the estate at Malling, which had been confiscated at the time of the West Saxon take-over. They also settled the long-running dispute over the control of minster-churches, by reaching agreement that Æthelwulf and his father had been chosen for (secular) protection and lordship, while the bishops had been constituted as spiritual lords, so that the rule of the monastic life and liberty of election in these 'free monasteries' might thenceforth be preserved.[45] This was a compromise, reflecting similar developments in Carolingian Francia, by which the bishops and the crown attempted to co-operate in a shared lordship in order to protect the minsters from the abuse of local aristocratic power.

Neither in this agreement, nor in grants of a series of properties on the edge of Romney Marsh and of an estate near Lyminge in the closing months of the same year,[46] is there mention of any cash payment by the archbishop or his church to secure these favours from Æthelwulf and his father. What is recorded, however, is a solemn undertaking by the archbishop and the community at Christ Church on their own behalf and that of their successors that they would thence-forth offer firm and unbroken friendship, patronage, and protection to Egbert and Æthelwulf *and to their heirs*. It is unlikely to be an accident that this promise of friendly support was made at Kingston, the place where the river Thames ceases to be tidal and where West Saxon and English kings were normally to be consecrated as king in the tenth

---

[45] BCS 421 (S 1438); for the interpretation of this difficult charter, of which three contemporary copies survive, see Brooks, *Early History*, pp. 145–6, 197–200, 323–5.

[46] BCS 407, 408, 419 (S 323, 1623, 286); Brooks, *Early History*, (cit. in n. 2), p. 145.

century.[47] It may even have been part of this agreement that Archbishop Ceolnoth should consecrate Æthelwulf as king of the Saxons at Kingston during his father's lifetime. Be that as it may, what is clear is that Ceolnoth had tied the fortunes of his church to those of Egbert's dynasty. In the ensuring century, Egbert's lineage was to go on to forge, through its conquests, a unitary English kingdom. The archbishop's choice therefore proved prescient. This time the church of Canterbury had avoided the dangers – implicit in the policies of Wulfred's later years – of committing itself to the losing cause. Ceolnoth was no Jænberht.

Despite his success in steering his church into calmer political waters and recovering confiscated property, Ceolnoth's chief hope of attracting benefactions for Christ Church lay in establishing good relations with the leading nobles of south-eastern England, especially with the ealdormen of Kent and with their wives, daughters, and other kinsfolk. Ceolnoth's friendship with Ealdorman Ealhhere and Ealhhere's powerful kin – his brothers, Ealdorman Æthelmod and (probably) the reeve Abba, his sister Ealhburg, daughter Ealawyn, and grandson Eadwald – brought a steady flow of Kentish estates and of food-rents from Kentish manors into the Christ Church lordship during the 840s and 850s. In the next generation, Archbishop Æthelred's friendship with Ealdorman Ælfred of Kent and Surrey was to prove equally beneficial. Critical too were Ceolnoth's links with a number of the widows of Kentish nobles (Heregyth, widow of reeve Abba, Ealhburg the widow of Ealdred, and Cynethryth the widow of Ealdorman Æthelmod) and with others wishing to devote their lives to God's service, such as Lufu 'handmaiden of God'. Noble testators appreciated the prospect of the archbishop's protection of their widows (who might otherwise be pressurized into unwelcome remarriages) and of their young children. A similar need was met by Ceolnoth's willingness to offer a haven at Christ Church to nobles, such as Badanoth Beotting, who wished to abandon the secular life and end their days in some form of religious observance. Above all, the community's ability to promise to commemorate in perpetuity the anniversaries of their benefactors with prayers and psalmody tied the interests of the local Kentish nobility to their cathedral church. Such were the factors which enabled Christ Church under Ceolnoth's and Æthelred's guidance to acquire substantial estates and food-rents in Kent – at Challock,

---

[47] For consecrations at Kingston, see S.D. Keynes, *The Diplomas of King Æthelred the Unready, 978–1016* (Cambridge, 1980), pp. 270–1, and C.P. Wormald, 'Celtic and Anglo-Saxon Kingship: Some Further Thoughts', in P.E. Szarmach and V.D. Oggins, eds, *Sources of Anglo-Saxon Culture* (Kalamazoo, MT, 1986), pp. 151–83, at 160 and n. 42.

Mongeham, Bishopsbourne, Little Chart, Finglesham, Chartham, Nettlestead, and several properties in and around Canterbury itself.[48]

The benefits of these good relations with the crown and with the lay nobility were put at risk by the growing threat of pagan Viking armies. The sources do not provide an adequate account of Viking activities in south-eastern England in the ninth century. Incidental references in charters show that Viking forces were already active in Kent at the close of the eighth century and were building fortresses there by the second decade of the ninth century.[49] Presumably some Viking armies were by then overwintering in England and constructing camps as bases for their raiding. Moreover, not only is the record of Viking activity in Kent in the *Anglo-Saxon Chronicle* under the years 835, 841, 851, 853, 855, 865, 885, and 892–3 extremely sparse; it also shows no interest in the fortunes of individual churches.[50] None the less, the events of which we are told – the ravaging of Sheppey in 835, the storming of Canterbury itself in 851, the attempt to dislodge a 'heathen army' from Thanet in 853, the wintering of the heathens on Sheppey in 855 and on Thanet in 865, their attempt to besiege Rochester in 885, and their two-pronged attack on Kent in 892–3 – were all likely to have included threats to the major Kentish churches in these places, since they were such easy targets for booty-seeking raiders. The disappearance of the communities of such minsters as Folkestone, Dover, Minster-in-Thanet, Reculver, Minster-in-Sheppey, and Hoo from all records for a century and more after *c.* 850 suggests that these houses were indeed attacked and their communities dispersed and disrupted. The beautifully illuminated eighth-century Kentish gospel-book, the Stockholm *Codex Aureus* (Figure 12), which Ealdorman Ælfred and his wife Werburg purchased from 'the heathen army with much clean gold' and then presented to Christ Church, is itself likely to have been pillaged from one of the Kentish minsters during these raids.[51]

The estates of the major churches, and of Canterbury in particular, must also have suffered from the Viking wasting of the Kentish countryside in order to induce the payment of tribute. Indeed, one of

[48] For archiepiscopal relations with the Kentish nobility and the estates acquired at that time, see Brooks, *Early History*, pp. 147–9, 151–2.

[49] For the charter references to early Viking activity in Kent, see BCS 848, 332, 335, 348, 370 (S 134, 1264, 169, 177, 186); for their interpretation, see N.P. Brooks, 'The Development of Military Obligations in Eighth- and Ninth-Century England', in P. Clemoes and K. Hughes, eds, *England before the Conquest: Studies in Primary Sources Presented to D. Whitelock* (Cambridge, 1971), pp. 69–84, at 79–80; reprinted in Brooks, *Communities and Warfare, 700–1400* (London, 1999), pp. 48–68, at 61.

[50] Brooks, *Early History*, pp. 151, 201–2.

[51] F.E. Harmer, *Select English Historical Documents of the Ninth and Tenth Centuries* (Cambridge, 1914), no. 9.

Figure 12. Begining of the Gospel of St Matthew, with illuminated Chi-rho initial, from the eighth-century *Codex Aureus*. The inscription recording the purchase of the gospel-book from the heathen army by Ealdorman Ælfred and his wife and their gift of it to Christ Church was added in the second half of the ninth century. The reproduction is taken from the facsimilie in J.O. Westwood, *Facsimiles of the Minatures and Ornaments of Anglo-Saxon Manuscripts* (London, 1868), pl.II, which was made before the pages were trimmed and the inscription in part lost. (Stockholm, Kungliga Bibliotek, MS A.135. fo. II.)

Christ Church's benefactors, Ealhburg, when making a bequest to St Augustine's, provided for the eventuality that her estate might be unable to pay any food-rent to the community for three years because of the devastation caused by the 'heathen army'.[52] As major landowners, the archbishops and the Christ Church community would also have had to make substantial contributions to the payments of tribute offered, as in 865, in the hope of persuading the Danish army to move elsewhere. It would therefore be unwise to underestimate the Viking impact upon the economy of the cathedral church. Indeed, we

[52] Ibid., no. 6 (S 1198).

do not even know the fate of Christ Church during the attack on the city in 851. Whilst its early charters certainly survived, none of its library books and altar-books would seem to have done so, since those that are extant all came into its possession after the 851 raid. It therefore seems unlikely that the oldest and most important church in England escaped damage.

More insidious than the immediate financial and physical difficulties, however, was the damage caused to Christian morale by the unchecked activities of armies of pagans. If neither the Kentish minsters nor even the cathedral church itself could provide a secure environment for the pursuit of a religious vocation, it would be surprising had the quality and quantity of recruits not been affected. We have, of course, no means of knowing to what extent the progressive decline in the Latinity of charters produced by the Christ Church scriptorium in the ninth century may have been associated, directly or indirectly, with Viking activity throughout that century. What is clear is that the two processes were coeval and that the low point of Latin learning at Canterbury between *c.* 850 and *c.* 880 coincided with the period when the Viking assaults were at their height. Indeed, the principal Christ Church charter-writer of the 850s and 860s adopted none of the features of the beautiful 'mannered minuscule' of earlier Canterbury scribes. His crude and uneven script eschewed all attempt at calligraphic adornment, and his Latin abounded in mis-spellings and orthographic oddities. He would seem to have joined the Cathedral community soon after the town had been sacked in 851, and to represent a significant lowering of standards there.[53] By the archiepiscopate of Æthelred (870–88), the situation had become critical. By then, charters had apparently to be written either by a scribe who could no longer see what he had written, or by men who had no effective command of Latin grammar at all. To judge by the standards in the metropolitan church, the future of Christian education and worship was indeed in the balance in England in these years. The community was failing to produce men who could read and interpret the Latin Scriptures and services, let alone pass those skills on to the next generation.

The elevation of one of King Alfred's court scholars, the Mercian Plegmund, to the archiepiscopal see in 890 is likely to have been intended to reverse this precipitate decline. Plegmund was one of the

---

[53] For the level of learning at Christ Church and the work of 'scribe 7', see Brooks, *Early History*, pp. 171–4; for a more sanguine interpretation of standards in the whole of england, see J. Morrish, 'King Alfred's Letter as a Source on Learning in England in the 9th Century', in P.E. Szarmach, ed., *Studies in Earlier Old English Prose* (Albany, NY, 1985), pp. 87–107.

scholars who instructed King Alfred in the task of translating Gregory the Great's *Cura Pastoralis* into English. Though the archbishop must therefore have been at court often in his early years, he was clearly well equipped to introduce a new standard of education to the Cathedral clergy. Only two charters written in the Christ Church scriptorium survive in contemporary manuscripts from his long archiepiscopate (890–923), but both show that under his guidance there were scribes in the community who used a handsome rounded version of the insular minuscule script and whose command of Latin grammar was excellent.[54] Though the evidence is certainly slight, it seems clear that Canterbury participated in the Alfredian revival of learning.

It is also likely that Plegmund lent his support to the King's administrative and military reforms. Certainly we find him in 898 assembling in London with Bishop Werferth of Worcester, King Alfred, Ealdorman Æthelred, and Lady Æthelflæd of the Mercians to confer about the laying-out (*instauratio*) of the borough of London.[55] Alfred's programme of burghal foundation, renewal, and garrisoning offered to the church the prospect of secure places where major churches could be built within protective town-walls of stone or of earthwork and timber. Though no detail is yet known of any strengthening of the defences of Canterbury itself at this time, nor of the fate of the city during the double assault on Kent in 892–3, it is likely that the cathedral city had become a garrisoned borough and was in a position to resist attack. The laying-out of a new High Street and the construction of a new gate ('Newingate') may plausibly be attributed to the reign of Alfred or to that of Edward the Elder (899–924).[56] The church of Canterbury will have benefited both from the new security and from the urban revival. As the greatest landlord in east Kent and in the city itself, it will also have made a major contribution to the cost of the work. In an age of Viking attacks, it was more than usually apparent that the interests of church and state coincided.

---

[54] BCS 539, 638(S 1203, 1288); Brooks, *Early History*, pp. 173–4, 214.

[55] BCS 577/8 (S 1628); T. Dyson, 'Two Saxon Land-Grants for Queenhythe', in J. Bird, H. Chapman and J. Clark, eds, *Collectanea Londiniensia: Studies Presented to R.B. Merrifield* (London and Middlesex Archaeological Society, Special paper 2 (1978), pp. 200–15.

[56] Brooks, 'Ecclesiastical Topography', pp. 487–98 = above, pp. 91–100.

Widening Horizons (924–1016)

The political and military success of the descendants of Egbert and of Alfred in the tenth century brought new opportunities and responsibilities. The conquests of Edward the Elder, of Athelstan (924–39), and of their successors extended their rule first to the whole province of Canterbury and then to part of that of York. What was to be Canterbury's role in the unification of the kingdom?

First, it is clear that the archbishops were brought firmly within the West Saxon patronage system. From the appointment of Athelm, bishop of Wells, as archbishop in 923 until that of Lyfing, also of Wells, in 1013, every new archbishop had held one of the southern English sees before his appointment to Canterbury. This was a radical break from previous practice. With the possible exception of Cuthbert, who may have been bishop of Hereford before being transferred to Canterbury in 740, none of the archbishops had been translated from another see since the early days of the Roman mission. Such translations were indeed prohibited by canon law and therefore needed express papal permission. Cuthbert is believed to have travelled to Rome to receive the *pallium* from the Pope in person. Every tenth-century archbishop from Wulfhelm (926–41) onwards is likewise known to have commenced his office by journeying to Rome for the *pallium*, so it is possible that Athelm had already done the same in 923.[57]

The early tenth century was a time when the papacy was beset with local political difficulties, and most of the popes had themselves been translated from other Italian sees. They were scarcely in a position to assert papal authority over the English church by requiring a translated archbishop-elect to come to Rome, instead of themselves sending a pall to England. It is much more likely that the motive for the change came from the English kings, who wanted to appoint to Canterbury men whom they trusted and whose record they knew. As the kingdom grew and royal visits to Kent were necessarily less frequent, the kings dared not risk promoting Kentish clerics trained in the Christ Church community, lest Canterbury should once again be the focus of local antagonisms. Nor could they allow there to be doubt about their metropolitan's status, so the kings' interest was to secure papal support for their archbishops. Wealthy kings may have been prepared to pay substantially to get their way. Certainly by the early

---

[57] Brooks, *Early History*, pp. 216–17; for the evidence for *pallia* sent from Rome and obtained in Rome, see Levison, *England and the Continent*, pp. 241–8; for the Continental development of papal *pallia*, see H. Jedin and J. Dolan, *History of the Church*, iii (London, 1980), pp. 72, 166–9, 288–90.

eleventh century, when resources were tighter, archbishops bitterly objected to being expected to pay in order to secure the *pallium*.[58] The West Saxon bishops whom the English kings promoted to Canterbury were mostly from West Saxon aristocratic families whose interests were closely tied to those of the monarchy.[59] They were also men who, as bishops, had attended the royal court regularly and on whose advice the kings had come to rely. Such men owed their careers entirely to the king. It was a policy designed to cement the alliance of crown and archbishops.

One role that the archbishops fulfilled in return for their promotion was to preside over the English king-making rituals. The earliest English coronation order may have been in use at royal inaugurations from the middle of the ninth century, that is, from the archiepiscopate of Ceolnoth and the consecration of Æthelwulf to succeed his father, Egbert, in 838 or 839.[60] The 'second English *ordo*' seems to have been composed either for the coronation of Edward the Elder (900) or for that of Athelstan (925). It was therefore either Archbishop Plegmund or Archbishop Athelm who introduced into English royal ritual the ring, the crown itself, and much liturgical ceremony that was perhaps of West Frankish origin.[61] Most of the tenth-century coronations took place at Kingston-upon-Thames,[62] and it is clear that they were occasions for all the bishops and leading secular nobles to witness and to join the feasting that followed. In the

[58] The letter of protest against the simonious expenses of the *pallium*-journey is printed in *Councils and Synods Relating to the English Church*, i. *871–1204*, ed. D. Whitelock, M. Brett, and C.N.L. Brooke (Oxford, 1981), pt 1.441–7, no. 61. For its attribution to Archbishop Wulfstan of York, see D. Bethurum, 'A Letter of Protest from the English Bishops against the Expenses of the Pallium Journey', in *Philologica: The Malone Anniversary Studies*. ed. T.A. Kirby and H.B. Woolf (Baltimore, MD, 1949), pp. 97–104.

[59] Brooks, *Early History*, pp. 214–16, 222–3, 237–40, 243–4, 278–9.

[60] J.L. Nelson, 'The Earliest Royal *Ordo*: Some Liturgical and Historical Aspects', in B. Tierney and P. Linehan, eds, *Authority and Power: Studies in Medieval Law and Government Presented to Walter Ullmann* (Cambridge, 1980), pp. 29–48.

[61] C.E. Hohler, 'Some Service Books of the Late Saxon Church', in D.P. Parsons, ed., *Tenth-Century Studies* (Leicester, 1975), pp. 67–9; *The Claudius Pontificals*, ed. D.H. Turner (Henry Bradshaw Society, 97; 1971 for 1964), pp. xxxi–xxxiii; J.L. Nelson, 'The Second English *Ordo*', in her *Politics and Ritual in Early Medieval Europe* (London, 1986), pp. 360–74.

[62] For the coronations of Athelstan (925) and Æthelred (979), see *Anglo-Saxon Chronicle*, trans. Whitelock *et al.*, 924 BCD, 978 E, 979 C. For Eadred (946) and Eawig (956), see *Florentii Wigorniensis Monachi Chronicon ex Chronicis*, ed. B. Thorpe, 2 vols. (*English Historical Society*, London, 1848), i., pp. 134, 136; for Edward the Elder (900), Edmund (939), and Edward the Martyr (976), see Ralph de Diceto, *Pera Historica*, ed. W. Stubbs, 2 vols, Rolls Series, 68 (London, 1876), i, pp. 140, 146, 153, whose authority for tenth-century events is very doubtful.

first half of the tenth century, when Canterbury was the only metropolitan see in the kingdom, such coronations were therefore
occasions when the authority of the see of Canterbury was
manifested. Again in 956 (when Wulfstan of York was close to
death), Archbishop Oda seems to have presided alone. But at Edgar'
'imperial' coronation at Bath, in 973, Archbishop Dunstan officiated
jointly with Oswald of York, and that was to be the normal pattern in
Anglo-Saxon coronations thereafter.[63] A kingdom that now
comprised, as the second English *ordo* stated, 'the sceptres of the
Saxons, the Mercians, and the Northumbrians', could readily accommodate two metropolitan sees.

   The unification of the English kingdom in the tenth century removed
the clear geographical distinction between the assemblies (*witenagemots*), to which kings summoned their nobles and bishops, and ecclesiastical synods, where all the bishops of the province met under the
authority of the metropolitan. Charters show that from the reign of
Athelstan it was normal for there to be at least one royal assembly every
year, and sometimes as many as four, attended by all the bishops of
Canterbury's province. From 928 until 939, from 944 to 950, and again
from 954 or 955, when the Viking kingdom of York had been brought
under English rule, the archbishop of York was also usually present at
the *witan* and was ranked immediately after the archbishop of
Canterbury.[64] Such regular assemblies of all the leading clergy of the
kingdom made purely provincial synods superfluous. The *witan* therefore took over the functions of the synod. The law-codes of Athelstan
and Edmund, issued from such assemblies, include individual laws,
substantial sections, or even whole codes, devoted to ecclesiastical law.
Thus Athelstan's first code concerned the payment of tithes and was
enacted 'on the advice of Wulfhelm, my archbishop, and also of my
other bishops'. Edmund's first code, also devoted to canon-law matters,
declares that the king:

> assembled a great synod [*micelne synoð*] at London in the holy Easter season,
> both of ecclesiastical and secular orders: there Archbishop Oda and

[63] 'Florence' of Worcester names the officiating archbishop(s) in 925, 946, 956, 973,
975, and 979: see *Chronicon*, ed. Thorpe, i. 134, 136, 142, 145–6. For the wider activities
at coronations, see B.'s *Vita Sancti Dunstani*, in *Memorials of Saint Dunstan, Archbishop of
Canterbury*, ed. W. Stubbs, Rolls Series, 63 (London, 1874), pp. 32–4; for the 973
coronation, see Byrhtferth's *Vita S. Oswaldi*, in J. Raine, ed., *Historians of the Church of
York*, 3 vols, Rolls Series, 71 (London, 1879–94), ii, pp. 436–7.
[64] Hrothward attests BCS 663, 664 (S 400, 399) of 928; BCS 667, 669 (S 404, 403)
of 930; Wulfstan's attestations begin in 931: BCS 675, 677, 680, 683 (S 413, 416, 410,
409). For the relationship of synod and *wittenagemot* in the tenth and eleventh centuries,
see *Councils and Synods*, pt 1, pp. vi–vii, and Vollrath, *Die Synoden Englands*, pp.
210–29.

Archbishop Wulfstan and many other bishops were taking thought for the good of their souls and of those subject to them.[65]

That was to be the pattern throughout the late Anglo-Saxon period. When King Æthelred II summoned a *sinodale concilium* to Winchester on Whitsunday 993, those present included not only the bishops and abbots of the entire kingdom, but also 'the other leading magnates of mine', that is the *æthelings*, ealdormen, and king's thegns.[66] Ecclesiastical law (like secular law) was declared at meetings of the *witan* attended by bishops and nobles from the whole kingdom; the leading role of one or both archbishops is often mentioned in the preambles to the extant codes, or is associated with particular enactments on fasting, pledges, tithes, and so forth. But the law that was determined was the king's law, and the assembly was that of the whole kingdom. There can be little doubt that these arrangements represented a deliberate attempt to foster the concept of a single nation and of a single national Church. The kings were concerned to incorporate the Northumbrian kingdom and Church firmly into the institutions of their new state. Though it is possible that when the members of the *witan* were assembled, the English bishops were sometimes able to meet without the king, it is significant that neither in the ecclesiastical codes of the tenth and eleventh centuries nor in the canonical writings of Archbishop Wulfstan of York, is there any indication that the 'synod' or 'the bishops' ever referred to a provincial assembly rather than to a meeting of bishops from the whole kingdom.

Thus the political needs of the kingdom seem to have overridden the traditions of the provincial organization of the English church. The fact that York in the tenth and early eleventh centuries normally had only one suffragan, the bishop of Chester-le-Street (later of Durham), made the integration of the northern province into a national structure seem appropriate. York was never at this time a rival of Canterbury. The two metropolitans were independent and formally of equal status. When one archbishop died, the arrangement laid down by Pope Honorius I in 634 – that the other should be responsible for consecrating the archbishop-elect to the vacant see – was followed faithfully.[67] None the less, the archbishop of Canterbury almost always took precedence in

---

[65] I Athelstan, prologue; I Edmund, prologue (F. Liebermann, *Die Gesetze der Angelsachsen*, 3 vols (Halle, 1903–16), i, pp. 146, 184).

[66] See S 876, a charter of 993, the best edition of which appears in *Councils and Synods*, i, pt 1, no. 39. For a somewhat different interpretation, see Vollrath, *Die Synoden Englands*, pp. 308–10.

[67] Honorius's letter is in Bede, *Historia ecclesiastica*, ii. 17, which is cited in the rubrics for the consecration of an archbishop in the 'Dunstan Pontifical' (Paris, Bibl. Nat., lat. 943) and in later pontificals. See *Canterbury Professions*, p. lxiii and n. 2.

English councils, despite the personal eminence or the seniority in age or appointment of particular archbishops of York. Canterbury was the older see, its province was larger, and it had more suffragans. The establishment of the single kingdom of the English does not seem to have given rise to any rivalry between York and Canterbury before the Norman Conquest.

For the church of Canterbury, however, participation in the making of the English kingdom was not an unmixed blessing. Early in Athelstan's reign, in his Grately code, the king had enacted that there was to be 'one coinage throughout all the king's domain'. The result of this policy seems to have been that Archbishop Athelm lost the right to issue silver pennies in his own name. From Jænberht to Plegmund every pontificate had been marked by the production of coins, normally by two moneyers concurrently, which bore the archbishop's name on the obverse (Figure 11). No such coins were produced for Athelm or for any subsequent archbishop, though Athelstan's code indicates that the profits from the work of two moneyers of the Canterbury mint continued to go to the archbishops. Henceforth, however, the coins that the archiepiscopal moneyers produced bore the king's name, and their design was indistinguishable from other English pennies.[68] This curtailment of the visible sign of the privileged status of the see of Canterbury serves as another indication of the precocious uniformity achieved by the tenth-century English state.

The political and military successes of the dynasty also brought a new widening of the territorial interests of the church of Canterbury. Some acquisitions continued to be made in Kent – such as the great estate of Reculver, which Archbishop Wulfred had fought to retain from Mercian royal hands but had lost to the West Saxons; King Eadred with the support of his mother, Eadgifu, granted the whole 26 sulungs of Reculver to the Cathedral Church in 949 in a charter, which was apparently written by Abbot Dunstan of Glastonbury himself.[69] Other Kentish estates were given by wealthy nobles, such as the bequest of the downland manor of Meopham by the king's thegn Byrhtric and his wife, Ælfswith.[70] But King Eadred's grant of Twickenham (Middlesex) in 948 (if we may accept a very strange charter full of continental features),[71] King Eadwig's grant of Ely to Archbishop Oda

[68] II Athelstan 14 (Liebermann, *Geseze*, i. p. 158); C.E. Blunt, 'The Coinage of Athelstan', *British Numismatic Journal*, 42 (1974), pp. 40–1, 64–5.

[69] BCS 880 (S 546); the critical view of its authenticity in Brooks, *Early History*, pp. 232–6, is withdrawn in id., 'The Career of St Dunstan', in N.L. Ramsay, M.J. Sparks and T. Tatton-Brown, eds, *St Dunstan: His Life, Times and Cult* (Woodbridge, 1992), pp. 1–23, at 17–18 (see below, pp. 173–4).

[70] D. Whitelock, *Anglo-Saxon Wills* (Cambridge, 1930), no. 11 (S 1511).

(possibly intended to provide a foundation for his monk-nephew, Oswald),[72] the bequest to Christ Church by Ealdorman Ælfgar of Essex of the reversion to an estate at Eleigh (Suffolk),[73] the gift of Vange (Essex) to Archbishop Dunstan by the king's thegn Ingeram,[74] and the acquisition of the huge manor of Pagham (Sussex), seemingly after a successful joint programme of forgery with the see of Chichester in the late 950s[75] – all are signs that the see and the community were profiting from the wider contacts made through the archbishop's regular participation in the meetings of the *witan*.

The renewed Viking threat in the closing decades of the tenth century restricted once again Canterbury's income from rents, drained its cash resources, and at times threatened the safety of archbishops and community directly. Viking armies are known to have been active in Kent and neighbouring shires in 991, 994, 999, 1006, 1011, 1013, 1014, and 1016. Their unchecked tactics of deliberate devastation in order to extort mounting payments of tribute disrupted the routine extraction of resources by great landlords. Thus in the autumn of 994 the 'pagan' army of Olaf Trygvason and Svein Forkbeard threatened to destroy the cathedral church by fire unless Archbishop Sigeric paid the sum promised to them. Unable to raise the sum from his own resources, Sigeric had to borrow 90 pounds of silver and 200 mancuses of gold (in all £115) from Bishop Æscwig of Dorchester in return for ceding to him an estate of 30 hides at (Monks) Risborough (Buckinghamshire).[76] In 1009 Thorkell's army landed at Sandwich and made straight for Canterbury: 'and would quickly have captured the borough if all the citizens had not still more quickly asked them for peace. And all the people of East Kent made peace with that army and gave 3,000 pounds.'[77] In September 1011 the cathedral and city were threatened for a third time, but on this occasion Thorkell's forces were not bought off. Admitted to the city, they captured Archbishop Ælfheah and other leading ecclesiastics and laymen, together with 'all those in holy orders'. They proceeded to sack and burn both the cathedral and the borough, before carrying off the archbishop as a hostage. Just how devastating a blow to English morale was the capture of the archbishop and the ransacking of the cradle of English Christianity is indicated by the huge

[71] BCS 860 (S 537); for the traditional view against its authenticity, see Brooks, *Early History*, p. 232.
[72] BCS 999/1347 (S 646).
[73] Whitelock, *Wills*, no. 2 (S 1483).
[74] BCS 1101 (S 717).
[75] Brooks, *Early History*, pp. 240–3.
[76] *Codex Diplomaticus Aevi Saxonici*, ed. J.M. Kemble, 6 vols (London, 1839–48), no. 689 (S 882); Brooks, *Early History*, p. 283.
[77] ASC, 1009 CDE.

tribute of £48,000 that had to be paid by the following Easter to secure peace. It seems that the money was not all gathered in time. Six days later, on 19 April 1012, Archbishop Ælfheah was battered to death by the pagan army in a display of festive and drunken barbarity. Regarded immediately as a Christian martyr, the Archbishop was said to have been killed because of his refusal to allow any money to be paid as a personal random.[78] What is clear, however, is that this further act of terrorism was effective. Full payment of the huge sum due to Thorkell's army was soon completed.

We do not know the size of the tribute due from the Canterbury estates in the winter of 1011–12, nor its share of other huge payments, which culminated in the £72,000 paid in 1018. A general impoverishment of English magnates, secular and ecclesiastical, has been suggested because of the use of baser metals in the extant metalwork of the period and because of the quantity of English silver found in Scandinavian hoards at this time.[79] But even these unsettled conditions were by no means entirely unfortunate for a major church like Canterbury. Thus the death of both Ealdorman Byrhtnoth of Essex (in the battle of Maldon in 991) and subsequently of his wife, Ælfflæd, without offspring, brought to Christ Church estates at Lawling in Essex and Monks Eleigh and Hadleigh in Suffolk.[80] Another heirless noble, Æthelric of Bocking, gave his patrimonial estate to the community, and Archbishop Ælfric was able to persuade the King to allow the bequest to stand despite the suspicions of Æthelric's treachery in 991.[81] The King's eldest son, the *ætheling* Athelstan, made a deathbed bequest of his Kentish estates at Hollingbourne and Garrington (in Littlebourne) to Christ Church in 1014, and successive archbishops – Ælfric, Ælfheah, and Lyfing – all bequeathed substantial estates to the community.[82] In times of violence and insecurity, belief in the efficacy of the prayers of the community for the souls of benefactors, lay and ecclesiastical, ensured a substantial flow of endowments.

The sources tell us more about the fortunes of the endowment than they do about the life of the community in the tenth century. One

[78] Ibid., 1011, 1012 CDE; Thietmar of Merseburg, *Chronicon*, ed. R. Holtzmann, MGH Script. Rer. Germ., NS ix (Berlin, 1935), vii. 42, trans. in *EHD*, no. 27.

[79] D. Hinton, 'Late-Saxon Treasure and Bullion', in D. Hill, ed., *Ethelred the Unready*, BAR British Series, 69 (Oxford, 1978), 135–58; for contrasting views of the authority of the Anglo-Saxon Chronicle's figures for the payments of 'Danegeld', see J. Gillingham, 'Levels of Danegeld and Heregeld in the Early Eleventh Century', *English Historical Review*, 104 (1989), pp. 373–85, and M.K. Lawson, 'Levels of Taxation in the Reigns of Æthelred II and Cnut', ibid. pp. 385–406.

[80] Brooks, *Early History*, pp. 285–6.

[81] Whitelock, *Wills*, no. 16 (i) and (ii) (S 1501, 939).

[82] Ibid., no. 20 (S 1503).

charter, which records the terms on which Archbishop Oda (941–58) and the Christ Church community leased their property at Ickham to a Kentish noble, gives us the names of three mass-priests, five deacons, one priest, and twelve others who are not given any rank.[83] But without comparable lists from the tenth or eleventh century it is not possible to trace changes in the community's composition. There is, however, evidence that in the second quarter of the tenth century the community acquired a few learned Continental scholars. The first was the author of an elaborate dedicatory poem entered into the richly but simply ornamented gospel-book (BL, Cotton MS Tiberius A. ii), which King Athelstan had received from the German King Otto I and his mother, Matilda, and had then given to Christ Church, seemingly in the closing years of his reign (*c.* 938 × 939). The poem, *Rex Pius Æthelstan*, celebrates in twenty lines of elegiac couplets the English king's conquest of fierce and proud kings and his gift to Christ Church of the gospel-book, which he had had adorned with golden letters and bejewelled covers.[84] This poet wrote excellent Latin, in the 'hermeneutic' style, aiming to display as many obscure and learned words as possible; he also used an elegant and practised continental Caroline minuscule script (Figure 13).

Another Continental scholar, Frithegod – or Freðegod, as he is called in the list of the community under Archbishop Oda – was a deacon at Christ Church and was remembered as a teacher of unique learning. His principal extant work, the *Breviloquium vitae Beati Wilfridi*, is a rendering of 'Eddius' Stephanus' *Vita Wilfridi* into 1,400 hexameters. It was written to honour the installation of the bones of St Wilfrid in an altar at Christ Church. The relics had been seized from their shrine at Ripon (along with the text of the *Vita*) in King Eadred's punitive sack of the monastic church there in 948. The poem survives in two manuscripts of the mid-tenth century: one a copy in which five Christ Church scribes, experimenting with the Caroline script, combined to produce a working text, the other in Frithegod's own hand incorporating his subsequent revisions of the text. Frithegod's poem is notable not only for obscuring the awkward fact that Wilfrid had been in constant conflict with Archbishops Theodore and Berhtwald, but also for the author's unequalled command of Greek vocabulary and syntax in coining new

---

[83] A.J. Robertson, *Anglo-Saxon Charters* (2nd edn, Cambridge, 1956), no. 32 (S 1506).

[84] The text of *Rex Pius Æthelstan* is printed and discussed by M. Lapidge, 'Some Latin Poems as Evidence for the Reign of Athelstan', *Anglo-Saxon England*, 9 (1981), pp. 61–98, at 93–7. For the history of the gospel-book see S.D. Keynes, 'King Athelstan's Books', in M. Lapidge and H. Gneuss, eds, *Learning and Literature in Anglo-Saxon England: Studies Presented to Peter Clemoes* (Cambridge, 1985), pp. 143–201, at 147–53.

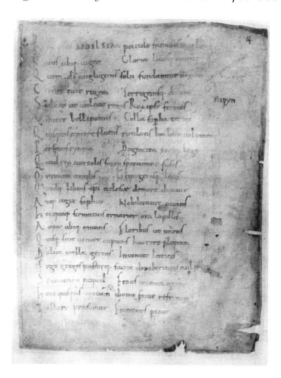

Figure 13. Verse dedication in elegiac couplets recording King Athelstan's gift of the Athelstan Gospels to Christ Church, written by a contemporary Continental scribe. (BL, Cotton MS Tiberius A. ii, fo. 15.) [By Permission of the of the British Library.]

Latin words from Greek roots in forms designed to meet the needs of his verse. This was indeed a virtuoso display of scholarly one-upmanship.[85]

The Caroline minuscule script was introduced at Christ Church by scholars such as this, and perhaps by others – such as the four clerks who were remembered as bringing relics of St Audoenus ('St Ouen') from Rouen in 957 x 958;[86] it was adopted gradually at Christ Church in the second half of the tenth century. Dunstan himself seems to have

[85] *Frithegod Monachi Breviloquium Vitae Beati Wilfridi et Wulfstani Cantoris Narratio Metrica de Sancto Swithuni*, ed. A. Campbell (Zurich, 1950). There is now a major critical study of Frithegod and his work in M. Lapidge, 'A Frankish Scholar in Tenth-Century England: Frithegod of Canterbury/Fredegaud of Brioude', *Anglo-Saxon England*, 17 (1988), pp. 45–65.

[86] Frithegod wrote a lost verse *Life of St Ouen* (Lapidge, 'A Frankish Scholar', p. 48); Eadmer's story of the four clerks arriving with the saint's relics of Edgar's court (presumably in Mercia) is in his *De Reliquiis Sancti Audoeni et Quorundam Aliorum Sanctorum quae Cantuarie in Aecclesia Domini Salvatoris Habentur*, ed. A. Wilmart, *Rev. des sciences religieuses*, 15 (1935), pp. 364–5.

Figure 14. Decorated initial U and the opening of book II of Julian of Toledo's *Liber Prognosticorum*. Written at Christ Church in a graceful English Caroline minuscule script at the end of the tenth century. (BL, Royal MS 12. C.XXIII, fo.23ᵛ.) [By Permission of the of the British Library.]

learned the Caroline hand when in exile at Ghent, in 956–7.[87] By the last decade of the tenth century, when we first have books surviving from the Christ Church library (as opposed to gospel-books and psalters which were kept on the altars of the church), the traditional 'insular minuscule' had been abandoned for all texts in Latin (though it was retained for the vernacular). By that time, there were twenty or more scribes at Christ Church trained to write a highly calligraphic English Caroline script and to ornament important initial letters with

[87] Brooks, 'Career of St Dunstan', pp. 1–23. Since this chapter was written a much-needed reassessment of the introduction of Caroline scripts at Christ Church has been provided by D.N. Dumville, *English Caroline Script and Monastic History* (Woodbridge, 1993), pp. 86–110, 141–5.

elaborate pen-drawn interlacing patterns of fronds and animals (Figure 14). In the first two decades of the eleventh century a substantial number of Christ Church scribes mastered this stately script, achieving what has been described as its 'possible limit of perfection'.[88]

The development of an outstanding scriptorium using the new script was one of the distinctive changes in the life of the Christ Church community in the tenth century, as it came under the growing influence of the English revival of monasticism. Archbishop Oda had himself received the monastic habit at Fleury (one of the principal offshoots from Cluny), probably when he visited the court of the Capetian Duke, Hugh the Great, in 936. Archbishop Dunstan (959–88) had been the first English reforming abbot to establish (at Glastonbury) a community of monks observing the Benedictine Rule. His successors at Canterbury – Æthelgar (988–90), Sigeric (990–4), Ælfric (995–1005), Ælfheah (1006–12), and Lyfing (1013–20) – had all been abbots of reformed houses before their elevation to the episcopate and their subsequent translation to the metropolitan see.[89] The reforms that Archbishop Wulfred had imposed upon the community in the ninth century, especially the common dormitory and refectory and the insistence on monastic discipline, would certainly have appealed to these monk-archbishops. Under Oda, the Canterbury clergy were clearly differentiated from monks by being ranked in the various clerical grades; to judge from continental parallels, they may also have worn better clothing and have continued to retain some private but inalienable property for their lives. But there is no evidence that they were an hereditary aristocratic body of married clergy, like that which caused Æthelwold such offence at Winchester. Stories of the expulsion of secular clerks from Christ Church by Archbishop Sigeric in 990, by Ælfric in 995 or 1006, or by Æthelnoth in 1021, all seem to be late monastic inventions from periods when the monastic chapter was under threat.[90] Rather, it is likely that successive archbishops encouraged a growing proportion of the community to follow their own example and take the monastic profession. Thus the balance in a mixed community of clerks and monks would gradually have swung to the monks.

Certainly in the extant altar-books we have evidence that the liturgical regime of the Christ Church community was increasingly Benedictine.

[88] T.A.M. Bishop, 'Notes on Cambridge Manuscripts, Part VII: The Early Minuscule of Christ Church, Canterbury', *Transactions of the Cambridge Bibliographical Society*, 3 (1959–63), pp. 412–23, at 416–17. See now the masterly survey in Dumville, *English Caroline Script*, pp. 111–39, 146–51.

[89] For the monastic careers of these archbishops, see Brooks, *Early History*, pp. 222–3, 278–80, and Brooks, 'Career of St Dunstan', pp. 1–23.

[90] For the context in which these stories were fabricated and the historical errors perpetuated, see Brooks, *Early History*, pp. 257–60.

Figure 15. Illustration and text of Psalm 26 from the Harley Psalter. The drawings were based on those in the Carolingian 'Utrecht Psalter', but the text is Roman rather than Gallican. Here the psalmist's enemies are shown encamped against him, whilst (above) the psalmist approaches the Temple (centre) and seeks to hide in the Lord's pavilion (right). Script and drawings are of the early eleventh century. (BL., Harl. MS 603, fo. 16.) [By Permission of the of the British Library.]

The Bosworth Psalter is a manuscript written by a scribe associated with Archbishop Dunstan and is prefaced by a calendar which adapts a Glastonbury model for use at Christ Church; it contains all the important texts of the Benedictine Office: the Roman psalter, with the divisions of particular psalms in accordance with the Rule, the canticles for daily singing, the hymns of the New Hymnary brought to England with the monastic reform movement, and the monastic canticles which belong to the third nocturn of the Office.[91] Both in this psalter and in

---

[91] BL., Add. 37517; P.M. Korhammer, 'The Origin of the Bosworth Psalter', *Anglo-Saxon England*, 2 (1973),pp. 173–89; E. Temple, *Anglo-Saxon Manuscripts, 900–1066*, Survey of Manuscripts Illuminated in the British Isles, 2 (London, 1976), no. 23 and plates 81–3. For the monastic canticles, see P.M. Korhammer, *Die monastischen Cantica im Mittelalter* (Münchener Universitäts-Schriften; Munich 1976), and for the hymnary, see H. Gneuss, *Hymnar und Hymnen im englischen Mittelalter* (Tübingen, 1968) and G.R. Wieland, *The Canterbury Hymnal* (Toronto, 1982). For the Roman and Gallican psalter texts in England, see C. and K. Sisam, *The Salisbury Psalter* (London, 1959), pp. 48–51.

Figure 16. St Benedict displays his *Rule* to the monks of Christ Church, while Eadui Basan at his feet, presents this Psalter (BL, Arundel MS 155, fo. 133). [By Permission of the of the British Library.]

the magnificently illustrated copy of the Utrecht Psalter (Fig. 15) that was produced at Canterbury at the turn of the century,[92] and in the Arundel Psalter, written by the Christ Church monk Eadui Basan about the year 1020, Christ Church practice remained loyal to the use of the Roman rather than the Gallican text of the psalms. Contemporary continental houses, both those of the Lotharingian and of the Cluniac reforms, knew only the *Gallicanum*. Increasingly in the eleventh century that was the practice of English reformed houses too. But at Christ Church the tradition of Roman authority remained supreme in matters liturgical. The deliberate compromise which this involved is apparent in

[92] BL, Harley 603; F. Wormald, *English Drawings of the Tenth and Eleventh Centuries* (London, 1952), pp. 44–5, 54–6; Temple, *Anglo-Saxon Manuscripts*, no. 64.

the Arundel Psalter, where a Winchester calendar is adopted (presumably replacing the Glastonbury model hitherto in use at Christ Church), but where the *Romanum* psalter text is none the less retained. That Canterbury found no difficulty in marrying Roman and Benedictine authority is vividly revealed in the superb illustration which Eadui Basan placed between the end of the psalms and the start of the monastic canticles in the Arundel Psalter (Figure 16).[93] The illustration shows the artist-monk kneeling in a position of humility and holding the psalter at the feet of St Benedict, who, authorized by the hand of God, delivers the Benedictine Rule to a group of genuflecting monks. Scholars have disagreed whether the model which Eadui was here adapting came from Æthelwold's Winchester or from Dunstan's Canterbury, but what is clear is that by 1020 the Christ Church community saw itself as avowedly Benedictine and bound by the terms of the Rule.

The surviving books from the pre-Conquest library at Christ Church tell very much the same story. Nothing remains from the Cathedral library of the days of Theodore, or even of Frithegod. But some sixty-two manuscript books, written at Christ Church seemingly during the period from *c.* 990 to 1066, are extant, mostly executed in the Christ Church version of the English Caroline minuscule script.[94] It is clear that a major effort was made, particularly in the early part of that period, to produce a library with copies of the works that were considered essential for the reading and instruction of the cathedral community. The Christ Church books are a characteristic example of what has been called 'the late Anglo-Saxon monastic curriculum'.[95] The reading of the community would seem to have concentrated upon the Gospels, the psalms, and monastic hymns, that is, on the core texts of the communal worship of the monastic Office. Prominent too were the works of Juvencus and Arator, which retold New Testament stories in Latin verse, the collections of moral maxims and exemplary stories of Prosper, Defensor, and Smaragdus, Aldhelm's prose and verse eulogies of the conventual life, collections of the lives and passions of saints and martyrs, as well as a number of individual monastic *vitae*. The intention of this library was clearly to provide the Canterbury monks with a good literary training from Christian or moralizing authors. Of Virgil and the

---

[93] BL., Arundel 155, fo. 133; for the hand, see T.A.M. Bishop, *English Caroline Minuscule* (Oxford, 1971), p. 24. The fullest discussions of the iconography of this important drawing are J. Higgitt, 'Glastonbury, Dunstan, Monasticism and Manuscripts', *Art History*, 2 (1979), pp. 275–90, and R. Deshman, '*Benedictus Monarcha et Monachus*: Early Medieval Ruler Theology and the Anglo-Saxon Reform', *Frühmittelalterliche Studien*, 22 (1988), pp. 204–40, at 211–16.

[94] Brooks, *Early History*, pp. 266–78.

[95] M. Lapidge, 'The Study of Latin Texts in Late Anglo-Saxon England: (i) The Evidence of Latin Glosses', in N.P. Brooks, ed., *Latin and the Vernacular Languages in Early Medieval Britain* (Leicester, 1982), p. 102.

pagan classical poets on whom Frithegod had drawn so freely, there is no trace. Remarkably, there are also very few of the fundamental theological, exegetical, and historical works of the Christian Fathers: Ambrose, Augustine, Eusebius, Isidore, Gregory, Orosius, nor even of England's own Bede. It was a library intended to produce devout and humble Benedictine monks, who would know the psalms and much of the New Testament by heart and who would appreciate the skills of Latin hexameters and hymns. It does not seem to have encouraged intellectual curiosity or, indeed, new writing. It is characteristic that neither of the two pre-Conquest Lives of St Dunstan was written at Christ Church. The first was written by 'B.', an Englishman and a former clerk of Glastonbury who had been abroad at Liège throughout Dunstan's archiepiscopate, and the second by Adelard, a monk of Ghent who also had no knowledge of the Archbishop's life at Canterbury.[96]

The Gathering Storm (*c.* 1020–66)

The accession of the Danish barbarian warrior Cnut to the English throne in 1016 brought an end to the long agonies of political and military disaster that had characterized the reign of Æthelred the Unready. Cnut was determined to rule as a lawful Christian ruler, not as a pagan conqueror, and he therefore relied heavily on the advice of his archbishops, whom he was prepared to reward. In 1018, when Archbishop Lyfing had returned from Rome with the *pallium*, the King and his new wife, Ælfgifu/Emma, the widow of Æthelred, visited Canterbury; they first granted to the archbishop a small property adjoining one of his manors in Sussex, and then, in a public ceremony in the cathedral, Cnut confirmed the privileges granted to Christ Church by earlier kings by taking the charters of freedom (*freolsas*) and laying them on the high altar. The shire court of Kent was notified of this demonstration of the king's support for the lands and rights of the church of Canterbury, and a record of this message was inserted by the monk and master-scribe Eadui Basan into one of the church's gospel-books.[97] One of the privileges which the king laid on the altar was evidently the forged charter of King Wihtred of Kent, purporting to

---

[96] For the Lives by B. and Adelard, see Stubbs, *Memorials of Saint Dunstan*, p. 1–68; M. Lapidge, 'B. and the *Vita S. Dunstani*', and A. Thacker, 'Cults at Canterbury: Relics and Reform under Dunstan and His Successors', in Ramsay et al., eds, *St Dunstan: His Life, Times and Cult*, pp. 247–59 and 221–45.

[97] BL, Stowe Charter 38 (S 950); *Anglo-Saxon Writs*, ed. F.E. Harmer (Manchester, 1953), no. 26 (S 985), which is entered into BL, Royal 1 D. ix, fo. 44v. See Brooks, *Early History*, pp. 288–90. For Cnut's benefactions to other English monasteries, see L.M. Larson, *Cnut the Great* (New York, 1912), pp. 175–8.

cede to the Kentish churches freedom from all secular burdens and to the archbishops control of the Kentish minster churches. The surviving text of this ninth-century forgery is a fair copy seemingly written for this occasion by Eadui Basan himself.[98] It seems unlikely that Cnut knew what he was confirming.

Just how far the King was prepared to dance to the monks' tune was made clear when Lyfing died, on 12 June 1020. In his place, on 13 November, there was consecrated Æthelnoth, who had previously been the 'dean' of the Christ Church community, that is to say, he had presided over the monastic chapter. This was the first time for a century that the incoming archbishop had not been translated from a southern see; it was also the first time since 805 (Archbishop Wulfred) that a member of the Christ Church community had succeeded to the archbishopric. We do not know whether Æthelnoth's elevation was the product of a free election by the monks of Christ Church, in accordance with the Rule and the provisions of the English *Regularis Concordia*.[99] But the monks clearly regarded it as an important precedent, since they entered documents connected with Æthelnoth's elevation into one of their gospel-books.[100] No other archiepiscopal succession was commemorated in this way, so it would seem that the election of their dean, however it had been achieved, was regarded as a triumph, which they intended should be remembered.

Other successes followed in 1023, when Æthelnoth returned from Rome with the *pallium*. In the summer of that year, King Cnut authorized the archbishop to remove the body of the martyred Ælfheah from St Paul's in London, where it had been taken in 1012 from Greenwich and where miraculous cures had already been reported. According to the post-Conquest monk Osbern, Archbishop Æthelnoth and a party of Christ Church monks – including Ælfweard the Tall and Godric, who was later dean of the community – broke open the tomb and removed the body as speedily as possible under the protection of a troop of Cnut's housecarls and against the wishes both of the clergy of St Paul's and of the citizens of London.[101] Removed from London on 8 June, brought to Canterbury in a cortège led by Queen Emma and her child, Harthacnut, on 11 June, the body was enshrined in the cathedral just on the north side of the altar of Christ on 15 June, in a ceremony attended

[98] BCS 91 (S 22); for the hand, see Bishop, *English Caroline Minuscule*, no. 24; for the context, see Brooks, *Early History*, pp. 289–90.

[99] *Regularis Concordia*, ed. T. Symons (Nelson's Medieval Classics; London, 1953), ch. 9.

[100] *Writs*, ed. Harmer, nos. 27, 28, which are entered into the MacDurnan Gospels (LPL, MS 771, fos 69, 114v). See Brooks, *Early History*, pp. 290–1.

[101] ASC, D 1023; Osbern, *Historia de Translatione S. Elphegi*, in Wharton, *Anglia Sacra*, ii. 143–7.

by several bishops. Thus the community acquired with maximum publicity the relics of a recent and already potent martyr. It cannot be said, however, that the pre-Conquest monks of Christ Church made the most of their acquisition. They neither produced a Life of Ælfheah while there were still contemporaries of the archbishop in the community to remember his deeds; nor did they commission a continental scholar to write one for them; nor did they collect details of miracles occurring at the tomb. In short, they failed to establish the cult of St Ælfheah – a failure which had to be remedied by the Anglo-Norman community in the closing years of the century.

Other important but somewhat uncertain royal gifts to the Cathedral church belong to the same year and probably to the same visit to Canterbury. Queen Emma donated a notable relic, an arm claimed to be St Bartholomew's, which she had purchased in Italy from the Archbishop of Bari;[102] King Cnut was claimed to have granted his gold crown, which he placed on the altar of Christ in the Cathedral, together with all tolls and rights in the port of Sandwich for the monks' food ('ad victum monachorum').[103] Sandwich was a major herring-port and its haven was the largest sheltered anchorage for naval fleets in eastern England. Control of Sandwich was therefore of vital strategic importance in the eleventh-century struggles for the English throne. To give it to Christ Church could be considered an act of foolish generosity; certainly Harold Harefoot was to repossess it in 1037.[104] Moreover, in the 1030s the abbey of St Augustine's acquired land on Thanet, on the northern bank of the Wantsum channel. For more than a century there were constant disputes between the two Canterbury houses over port dues and the unloading of cargoes on one bank or the other. The fact that none of the numerous extant single-sheet versions of Cnut's Sandwich diploma is in a pre-Conquest hand, and that the charter purports to give to the Christ Church monks a monopoly of revenues from the port and all landing-rights on *both* sides of the Wantsum therefore suggests that the extant diploma is a forgery. But the details of the witnesses and the formulation show that the forger had access to a genuine diploma of Cnut granted in 1023. It is probable that the King did grant the monks some rights in Sandwich in that year, but not as fully or precisely as the extant charter claims.

Cnut and Emma's astounding largesse may have been intended to ensure the church of Canterbury's support for their rule and for the succession of their only son, Harthacnut. Certainly Æthelnoth was to prove faithful to his benefactors, even refusing to crown the illegitimate

[102] Brooks, *Early History*, p. 292.
[103] *KCD* 737 (S 959); Brooks, *Early History*, pp. 292–4.
[104] *Charters*, ed. Robertson, no. 91 (S 1467).

Harold Harefoot in 1036. When Harold established his authority over the whole kingdom in 1037, he confiscated the port of Sandwich, doubtless in order to close it to Harthacnut's fleet. By that time, moreover, the tide of history was no longer running in the monks' favour. Since Cnut had attended the imperial coronation of Conrad II in Rome in 1127, he had developed his royal chapel on the imperial model as the chief route for ecclesiastical preferment in England. In the later years of his reign, he and Emma were grooming one of the king's priests, Eadsige, as Æthelnoth's successor. Eadsige became a monk for the purpose in 1035 and granted to Christ Church a series of properties on the edge of Romney Marsh in return for the community's 'staunch support and loyalty to him'. In the same year, Æthelnoth consecrated Eadsige as bishop, probably with a seat in St Martin's church in Canterbury, and Eadsige took over the Archbishop's role in the shire court of Kent.[105] In 1038, when Æthelnoth died, Eadsige succeeded to the metropolitan see without interference. Whilst the formality of promoting a member of the Christ Church community had thus been maintained, in reality Cnut had arranged for the succession of one of the priests of his chapel. It was a dangerous precedent, which ran counter to the canonical prohibition both of auxiliary bishops (*chorepiscopi*) and of bishops consecrating their own successors. In 1035–8 determined kings could ignore the canonical proprieties, but the age of reform was near.

Eadsige's archiepiscopate (1038–50) was remembered as an unhappy time at Christ Church because it coincided with the rise of Earl Godwine of Wessex. After the Conquest, when denigration of the Godwine family was politic, Eadsige was considered to have permitted Godwine to steal the monks' manor of Folkestone, to have lost to him the 'third penny' of shire revenues in Kent, which Æthelnoth was said to have received, and to have 'given' to Godwine Kentish properties at Richborough, Langport, Newenden, and Saltwood.[106] The reality seems to be that Christ Church estates were leased out to leading Kentish nobles, not only to Godwine but also to local men like Æthelric Bigga and his son, Osbern, for one or more lives.[107] It could always prove difficult to recover such estates from powerful sitting lords, and after 1066 it was particularly difficult to prevent the confiscation of estates that had been in the hands of those who had fought at Hastings.

[105] Fir Eadsige's relations with Cnut and with the community, see ibid., no. 86 (s 1465), BL, Stowe Charter 41 (S 976), and *Writs*, ed. Harmer, nos 29, 30 (S 987, 988); Brooks, *Early History*, pp. 295–6.

[106] Brooks, *Early History*, pp. 300–2.

[107] *Charters*, ed. Robertson, no. 101 (S 1471); BL, Cotton Augustus II 36, discussed and trans. in F.R.H. Du Boulay, *The Lordship of Canterbury* (London, 1966), pp. 38–41. For the general problem, see Brooks, *Early History*, pp. 301–2.

Godwine, however, may not have been the scourge of Christ Church whom it was later convenient to depict. Certainly, when Eadsige fell ill in 1044, the Earl seems to have co-operated with the archbishop in securing King Edward's consent that Abbot Siward of Abingdon should be consecrated as bishop to be his replacement, reportedly in order to prevent an unsuitable candidate from purchasing the office.[108] Though not a monk of Christ Church, Siward, as an abbot of Abingdon who had been trained at Glastonbury, had an impeccable monastic pedigree. In the event, Siward died before Eadsige, in 1048, and Eadsige consecrated a certain Godwine (of whose connections we know nothing) as 'Bishop of St Martin's' in his place. So far as we can tell, in these arrangements the initiative lay with Eadsige, and the Earl was co-operative.

When Eadsige died, on 29 October 1050, the community sought to continue this alliance by electing a monk of Christ Church, named Ælric, who was a kinsman of Godwine. But they had miscalculated the political situation disastrously, for King Edward the Confessor chose this moment to throw off the tutelage of the Godwine family. At a *witan* held at London in March 1051, the King forced through the translation to Canterbury of his Norman friend Robert of Jumièges, the bishop of London.[109] The recognition of Duke William of Normandy as the heir to the English throne, and the exiling of Earl Godwine and of all his sons soon followed. As archbishop, Robert set about recovering the Christ Church lands that had been in Godwine's hands. But in September 1052 the earl and his sons forced the king to restore their earldoms, and the Norman archbishop to flee to his homeland. In his place the *witan* nominated Bishop Stigand of Winchester, who had been the intermediary who had negotiated the Earl's return.[110]

For Christ Church the elevation of Stigand was a disaster. Stigand, despite his tenure of the monastic see of Winchester, was not a monk and showed no willingness to become one. He was already a pluralist, holding the sees both of East Anglia (Elmham) and of Winchester. Though in 1052 he seems to have passed Elmham on to his brother, Æthelmær, he retained Winchester, which, after Canterbury, was the richest see in England. He had also been involved in simony, as in the attempted promotion of Spearhafoc to London in 1051, which Archbishop Robert had quashed. In Edward the Confessor's eyes, Stigand was the man who had usurped the office of his friend Archbishop Robert. Royal benefactions to the see of Canterbury came to

[108] ASC, 1043 D, 1044 C; Brooks, *Early History*, pp. 299–300.
[109] ASC, 1050 C, 1051 E; *Vita Ædwardi Regis*, ed. F. Barlow (London, 1962), pp. 18–19.
[110] For Stigand's career, which is summarized here, see F. Barlow, *English Church, 1000–1066* (London, 1963), pp. 77–9, 217, and Brooks, *Early History*, pp. 304–10.

an end. As a pluralist and a simoniac, Stigand had no chance of securing a *pallium* from Pope Leo IX or from any of his reforming successors. Though the Tusculan pope Benedict X, who seized control of Rome for ten brief months (1058–9), did send a pall to Stigand, his acts were soon annulled by Pope Nicholas II. Except in 1058–9, English bishops therefore went abroad or to York for consecration. Stigand, it would seem, was neither excommunicated nor deposed by the reforming popes; he continued to be given first place among the bishops at meetings of the *witan*, even when the papal legates were present,[111] but was prevented from exercising authority as metropolitan of the southern province. The popes were apparently well aware that Stigand was a key figure in the balance of power between the King and the Godwine family and in the dispute over the English succession. Perhaps wisely, they seem to have decided not to choose between the claims of a Norman duke and an English earl to the throne of the childless Edward.

Stigand therefore survived in possession of the sees of both Winchester and Canterbury. He also amassed a huge personal lordship of estates, primarily in East Anglia, where his family interests lay, but also in Gloucestershire; there were no less than thirty-nine burgesses on his properties in Norwich, and numerous East Anglian freemen had taken him as their lord by commendation. The patronage of this successful operator was evidently worth having, and several major English churches (including Ely, St Alban's, St Oswald's, Gloucester, and the Old Minster at Winchester) leased properties to him, seemingly as a retainer for his political services and maintenance.[112] He must have cut a remarkable figure as a great lord, on a par with the greatest earls. But all this manipulation seems to have brought no advantage to the see of Canterbury or to the monks of Christ Church. In Stigand's eighteen years as archbishop (1052–70), Canterbury probably saw very little of him. Certainly the neglect of any record-keeping of the community's land transactions in these years, the virtual absence of new grants, and the declining output of books written in the Christ Church scriptorium[113] all speak of a community and a church that desperately lacked leadership, spiritual or political. It was Canterbury's misfortune that the most secular of all its archbishops should have proved so long-lived and that his notoriety in an age of ecclesiastical reform should have created

---

[111] 'Florence' of Worcester, *Chronicon*, i. p. 220; William of Malmesbury, *Vita Wulfstani*, ed. R.R. Darlington (Camden 3rd series, 40; 1928), pp. 16–18; ASC, 1060–1 D.

[112] Brooks, *Early History*, p. 308.

[113] Only eight out of the sixty-two books ascribed to the Christ Church in Brooks, *Early History*, pp. 266–70, were written in *saec. xi med.*, and most of them were probably from Eadsige's rather than from Stigand's archiepiscopate.

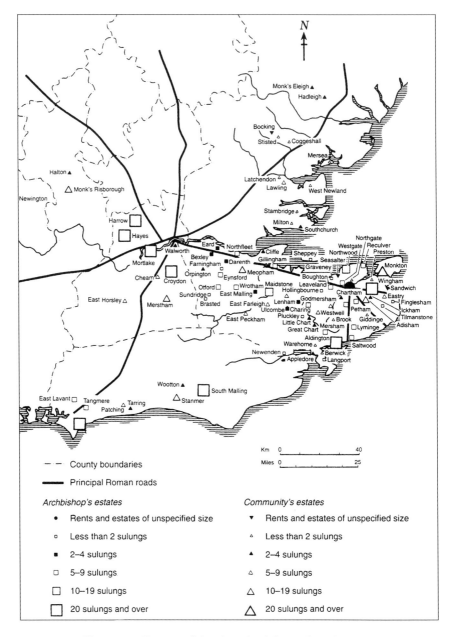

Figure 17. Estates of the church of Canterbury in 1066.

the false impression at the time of the Norman Conquest that both Canterbury and the Anglo-Saxon church as a whole were in need of a radical reform. His record should not obscure the achievement of his predecessors in securely establishing the metropolitan church with a monastic constitution and a landed endowment (Figure 17) that were to be its twin foundations throughout the Middle Ages.

The Pre-Conquest Cathedral

Nothing of the structure of the Anglo-Saxon cathedral survives above ground to this day. The church and most of the monastic buildings were gutted by a great fire on 6 December 1067, and the shell of the old buildings was soon demolished and totally replaced by Archbishop Lanfranc's new Norman cathedral. However, in the spring of 1993 traces of the foundations of the pre-Conquest cathedral were revealed when the need to renew the marble floor of the present nave and south transept provided an opportunity for limited archaeological investigations.[114] Combining this recent archaeological evidence with the scraps of information in pre-Conquest written sources and with the detailed account of the principal altars by the English monk Eadmer, based upon his childhood memories,[115] it is possible to establish the main features of the plan of the church (Figure 18).

The cathedral was remarkable in being bipolar, that is, in having apses and altars at both the east and west ends. Eadmer tells us that the principal altar, that of Christ, was in the raised sanctuary on the chord of the eastern apse, with the tombs of the archbishop-saints Ælfheah and Oda located immediately to the north and the south. A second altar, containing the relics of St Wilfrid, was at the extreme east end of this apse. Beneath this 'presbitery' (as Eadmer termed it) was the crypt, seemingly a ring-crypt, with a central passage leading to the tomb of St Dunstan, the principal Anglo-Saxon saint of the cathedral church.

Westward from the sanctuary steps stretched the choir, where the community could maintain the daily liturgical cycle of prayer and

[114] Through the kind co-operation of Paul Bennett of the Canterbury Archaeological Trust a provisional plan and interpretation is offered in advance of the publication of his excavations. [See now K. Blockley et al., *Canterbury Cathedral Nave: Archeology, History and Architecture*, (The Archaeology of Canterbury, new series 1, Canterbury, 1997), pp. 1–110, 211–1.]

[115] Eadmer, *De Reliquiis S. Audoeni*, ed. Wilmart, pp. 305–6. For Eadmer's age, see R.W. Southern, *St Anselm and His Biographer: A Study of Monastic Life and thought 1059–c. 1130* (Cambridge, 1963), pp. 231, 274–87. Full references to the written sources may be found in Brooks, *Early History*, pp. 37–59. Important earlier interpretations are H.M. Taylor, 'The Anglo-Saxon Cathedral Church at Canterbury', *Archaeological Journal*, 126 (1969), pp. 101–29, and F. Woodman, *The Architectural History of Canterbury Cathedral* (London, 1981), pp. 13–32.

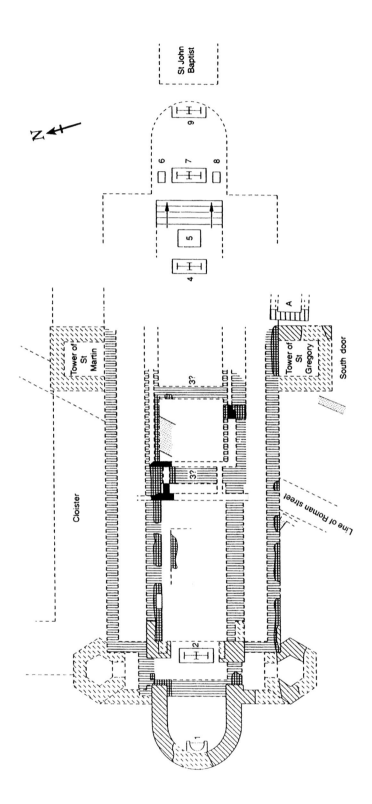

St John
Baptist

N

9

6   7   8

5

4

Tower of
St
Martin

Cloister

3?

3?

Tower of
St
Gregory

South door

Line of Roman street

A

2

1

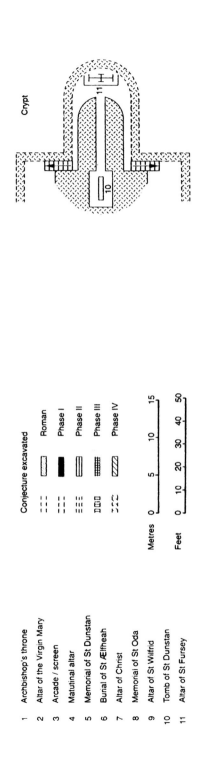

Crypt

1 Archbishop's throne
2 Altar of the Virgin Mary
3 Arcade / screen
4 Matutinal altar
5 Memorial of St Dunstan
6 Burial of St Ælfheah
7 Altar of Christ
8 Memorial of St Oda
9 Altar of St Wilfrid
10 Tomb of St Dunstan
11 Altar of St Fursey

Conjecture excavated

⠇⠇⠇ ≡≡≡ Roman
⠇⠇⠇ ─── Phase I
≡≡≡ ☰☰☰ Phase II
⫶⫶⫶ ▦▦▦ Phase III
⫶⫶⫶ ▨▨▨ Phase IV

Metres 0   5   10   15
Feet   0 10 20 30 40 50

Figure 18. Plan of the pre-Conquest cathedral and crypt. The eastern end of the church, the position of altars, tombs, memorials, choir screen, and of the archiepiscopal seat and the layout of the crypt are at present known only from written sources. The plan of the western half is reconstructed on the basis of the excavation of those fragments which have survived destruction by the foundations of both the Norman and the present cathedral and by the construction of tombs in subsequent centuries.

psalmody at the canonical hours, cut off from the laity by a screen. Here was the stone column or 'pyramid' erected immediately above the tomb of St Dunstan, and further to the west the matutinal altar for morning or 'Morrow' masses, which English practice had added to the Benedictine Office. Near the mid-point of the church were two towers: that of St Gregory on the south contained the south door, which was the main entrance to the cathedral; that of St Martin on the north gave access to the cloister. At the western extremity of the cathedral, at clerestory or first-floor level and accessible only by means of stair-towers at the western corners of the building, was the massive apisdal 'oratory of St Mary', containing an altar of the Virgin, and behind it, against the wall of the apse, the archiepiscopal *cathedra* or throne. This altar would seem to have been the one used for pontifical masses and for all rites involving the laity.

In the Anglo-Saxon period it was believed that this cathedral was indeed the same Roman church which Augustine had received from King Æthelbnerht and had recovered for Christian use. While that is certainly not true of those parts of the early cathedral revealed by the recent excavations, it remains possible that the most easterly portion of the Anglo-Saxon cathedral, where the high altar and the crypt were situated, had at its core a Romano-British church.[116] The excavations have brought to light four main phases in the cathedral's construction (Figure 18):

Phase I The early church of the seventh and eighth century, whether or not it embodied a Romano-British core, seems likely to have been of typical Kentish form. That is, it had an apsidal chancel and a simple nave, which had gradually come to be surrounded on the west, north, and south sides by porches (*porticus*).

Phase II A separate building, perhaps a baptistery-church, lay within 2 feet of the south-eastern corner of the nave of the early cathedral and had also been extended in subsequent periods.

Phase III A massive enlargement of the cathedral in the ninth or (more probably) the tenth century involved widening the foundations (presumably to permit a heightening of the walls), incorporating the *porticus* into side-aisles and virtually doubling the length of both church and aisles by extending them westwards. This had the effect of providing a nave that was distinct from the choir.

Phase IV The final westward extension, and the rebuilding of the west

---

[116] For the Roman core of the church of St Martin's, Canterbury, see T. Tatton-Brown, 'St Martin's Church in the Sixth and Seventh Centuries', in M.J. Sparks, ed., *The Paris of St Martin and St Paul, Canterbury: Essays in Memory of James Hobbs* (Canterbury, 1980), pp. 12–18.

end of the cathedral, involved the construction of a large western apse with the oratory of St Mary at clerestory level and with access by means of hexagonal stair-towers built at the western end of the church.

A provisional interpretation of the cathedral's structural history can therefore be essayed.

1. The early church is likely to have had a Roman core, to have been developed by Augustine as a simple building with a nave and apsidal sanctuary, and to have had a series of *porticus* added successively by later archbishops.
2. Archbishop Cuthbert (740–60) built a church dedicated to St John the Baptist as close as possible to the sanctuary of the cathedral church, with the intention that it should serve as a baptistery and as a place of burial for the archbishops. The latter function made subsequent extensions necessary.
3. Archbishop Wulfred (805–32) 'rebuilt, renewed and restored the holy monastery of the church of Canterbury' as part of his reform and reorganization of Christ Church. It seems that this programme may have concerned the monastic buildings alone.[117]
4. Archbishop Oda (941–58) restored the church, removing damaged roofs and beams, and taking down parts of the walls so that the walls could be raised in height by some 20 feet.[118] We should probably equate this reconstruction of the cathedral with Phase III of the excavated sequence, rather than with a subsequent reinforcement of the wall of the south aisle.
5. Some reorganization of the choir and of the crypt must have been necessitated by the construction of the tomb of St Dunstan in the years immediately after his death in 988.
6. Finally, the reconstruction of the western end of the cathedral, with the apsidal oratory of St Mary and its hexagonal stair-towers (Phase IV), seems most likely to have been the work of Archbishops Lyfing (1013–20) or Æthelnoth (1020–38) and to be associated with the widespread development of the cult of the Virgin Mary in Benedictine circles at that time.[119] The southern tower may probably be identified with the tower of St Gregory, which incorporated the south door, the main entrance to the cathedral.

By the end of the Anglo-Saxon period, the cathedral was a very substantial church indeed, measuring some 100 feet (31 m.) in width. The overall length is unknown (in the absence of excavations in the

---

[117] Brooks. *Early History*, pp. 153–60.
[118] Byrhtferth, *Vita S. Oswaldi*, in *Historians of the Church of York*, i. p. 407.
[119] M. Clayton, *The Cult of the Virgin Mary in Anglo-Saxon England* (Cambridge, 1990).

crypt) but, since the tower of St Gregory was near to the middle of the cathedral, may have reached almost 300 feet (95 m.). Canterbury cathedral is therefore likely to have been the largest church in England and would certainly have ranked among the major early medieval churches of northern Europe. Like many European churches of the ninth, tenth, and eleventh centuries, it had come to have a bipolar form, with both western and eastern apses. Here and in the arrangements of the eastern crypt it was reminiscent of, and doubtless in part modelled upon, the Constantinian basilicas of Rome and upon St Peter's in particular. Imitation of Rome, a liturgy that was becoming ever more elaborate and more explicitly Benedictine, and the burial of the growing number of venerable or saintly archbishops – these seem to have been the dominant ideas that ha shaped the cathedral's development over the five centuries that separated St Augustine from the Norman Conquest. Had any of the church's walls or decoration survived intact above ground, we might appreciate better how worthily the Anglo-Saxon cathedral had served these purposes.

8

The Career of St Dunstan

To ATTEMPT to assess the career of a great man on the millennium of his death is a daunting task, all the more so since Dunstan has been well studied by major scholars with a far deeper experience than my own of the communal worship and liturgy of major English religious institutions. The scholar who treads a path already well beaten by Bishop William Stubbs, Dean J. Armitage Robinson and Dom David Knowles seems destined to be a pygmy standing on the shoulders of such giants;[1] his sole advantage is the more powerful lens of recent scholarship on liturgy, palaeography and diplomatic with which to peer a little further into the world of Dunstan than they.[2] Moreover it has to be admitted that in recent scholarship Dunstan's role has waned as that of his younger contemporaries, Æthelwold and Oswald, has grown. No longer, for example, do we consider that Dunstan was the author of the *Regularis Concordia*, nor do we attribute to him the crucial development of the English coronation order. A reassessment is therefore overdue, but the difficulties of carrying it out critically but sympathetically have grown.

Stubbs, Robinson and Knowles provided a re-evaluation of the tenth-century reform movement that effectively countered the ignorance and prejudice of earlier positivist and militantly protestant interpretations with an analysis that was both scholarly and sympathetic to monastic ideals. They sought to integrate the sparse information

---

[1] W. Stubbs, ed., *Memorials of Saint Dunstan, Archbishop of Canterbury*, Rolls Series, 63 (London, 1874); J.A. Robinson, *The Times of Saint Dunstan* (Oxford, 1923); M.D. Knowles, *The Monastic Order in England* (Cambridge, 1949), pp. 31–57.

[2] *The Claudius Pontificals*, ed. D.H. Turner, Henry Bradshaw Society 97 (London, 1971 for 1964), pp. xxxi–xxxiii; J.L. Nelson, 'The Second English *Ordo*', in her *Politics and Ritual in Early Medieval Europe* (London, 1986), pp. 361–74; *St Dunstan's Classbook from Glastonbury*, ed. R.W. Hunt, Umbrae Codicum Occidentalium, 4 (Amsterdam, 1963); T.A.M. Bishop, *English Caroline Minuscule* (Oxford, 1971); E. John, 'The King and the Monks in the Tenth-Century Reformation', *Bulletin of the John Rylands Library*, 42 (1959), pp. 61–87, reprinted with related studies in his *Orbis Britanniae* (Leicester, 1966); P. Chaplais, 'The Anglo-Saxon Chancery: From the Diploma to the Writ', *Journal of the Society of Archivists*, 3 (1965–9), pp. 160–76, reprinted in *Prisca Munimenta*, ed. F. Ranger (London, 1973), pp. 43–62; S.D. Keynes, *The Diplomas of King Æthelred 'The Unready' 978–1016* (Cambridge, 1980).

from contemporary sources with nuggets gleaned from the various hagiographies of the three leading figures – Dunstan, Æthelwold and Oswald – and their findings have been widely accepted.[3] As a method of explaining the careers of the individual saints, however, this approach runs the risk of ignoring the circumstances under which particular *Vitae* were written. In consequence the crucial questions have too seldom been asked. Did their authors have access to accurate biographical information? Or were their stories invented to serve the needs of the communities that generated them?[4]

For the purpose of reconstructing Dunstan's career our principal authority is the earliest *Life,* that of the English priest 'B', who had indeed known Dunstan personally but whose work is none the less of limited value. B. is known to have been writing at about the turn of the century, that is between 995 and 1004.[5] Though he dedicated his work to Archbishop Ælfric, he had access to little or no information about Dunstan at Canterbury; indeed his personal knowledge of Dunstan's life is limited to the period before Dunstan returned to England having received the *pallium* in Rome in 960. B.'s stories about Dunstan's prophetic dreams and his miracles relate, in so far as they can be located, to Dunstan's early career at Glastonbury (940 × 946–56). B. seems to know no details of Dunstan's exile in Flanders in 956–7, but he may have accompanied the archbishop-elect to Rome in 960; thereafter B.'s career separated from Dunstan's. He seems to have established himself under the patronage of Bishop Ebrachar of Liège (959–71) as a secular canon; his subsequent attempts to secure a position at Winchester or Canterbury in the 980s and 990s culminated in the writing of the *Vita S. Dunstani*, but found no response in the face of the monastic hold on English patronage.[6] B. was therefore, as he claims, a first-hand authority for Dunstan's life at Glastonbury, but was writing after a break of some forty years in his knowledge of the holy man. He was presumably also seeking to please the recipient of his work at Canterbury, Archbishop Ælfric. Like any hagiographer, B.

[3] F.M. Stenton, *Anglo-Saxon England* (3rd edn, Oxford, 1971), pp. 446–7; among more recent works, see B. Yorke, 'Æthelwold and the Politics of the Tenth Century', in her *Bishop Æthelwold: his Career and Influence* (Woodbridge, 1988), pp. 66–8, and D.J. Dales, *Dunstan: Saint and Statesman* (Cambridge, 1988).

[4] For a more critical interpretation, see my *The Early History of the Church of Canterbury* (Leicester, 1984), pp. 245–6; M. Lapidge, 'B and the Vita S. Dunstani', in N.J. Ramsay M.J. Sparks and T. Tatton-Brown, eds, *St Dunstan: His Life, Times and Cult* (Woodbridge, 1992), pp. 247–60; A. Thacker, 'Cults at Canterbury: Relics and Reform under Dunstan and his Successors', ibid., pp. 221–46. This essay concentrates upon Dunstan's career until his elevation to the archiepiscopal see. For his work as archbishop, see Brooks, *Early History*, pp. 243–63.

[5] Stubbs, *Memorials*, pp. x–xi; Lapidge, 'B and the Vita S. Dunstani', p. 247.

[6] Lapidge, 'B and the Vita S. Dunstani', pp. 251–8.

sought to draw attention to events which could be interpreted as prophesying or demonstrating Dunstan's sanctity. Such factors need to be borne in mind before we use B. as a source for Dunstan's early career.

The later *Lives of Dunstan* – of Adelard of Ghent, Osbern, Eadmer and William of Malmesbury – attempt to make good some of B.'s deficiencies, but they were unable to counterbalance his ignorance of Dunstan's work at Canterbury. Osbern and Eadmer do indeed provide a splendid series of Canterbury miracles associated with the saint, but they are posthumous miracles, the vast majority of which purport to have occurred in the years around the Norman Conquest, that is when Osbern and Eadmer had been youths. Their few additions to our information about Dunstan's life inspire even less confidence. A typical example is Osbern's famous story of the young Dunstan at work at a forge in a Glastonbury cell seizing the devil (in the guise of a young woman) by the nose with his red-hot tongs. Clearly such stories tell us much about Anglo-Norman monastic conversation, but little about Dunstan. They are not 'Canterbury traditions', deriving either from Dunstan himself or from those who had known the archbishop's life there.[7]

Indeed the authors of the later *Lives*, or their informants, seem to have invented the historical circumstances of the miraculous and prophetic stories that they added to the Dunstan canon. Thus Adelard replaces B.'s story that Dunstan refused to be made bishop of Crediton on the death of Bishop Æthelgar (in 953) by a more elaborate account of his refusal of the (more important) bishopric of Winchester on the death of Ælfheah (951).[8] A similar 'development' of the legend concerns Dunstan's elevation to the episcopate. B. tells us that after Edgar had recalled him from exile, Dunstan was consecrated as bishop at a council at *Brandanford* and was only subsequently transferred to Worcester when Bishop Cenwald died (958); but Adelard develops this into a story of how Archbishop Oda of Canterbury, intending to consecrate Dunstan as bishop of Worcester, actually made a prophetic slip of the tongue by naming Dunstan's see as the metropolitan church of Christ of Canterbury in error for St Peter's, Worcester![9] When we recall that Adelard was writing for a Canterbury audience, namely for Archbishop Ælfheah (1006–12), who had been bishop of Winchester before his elevation to Canterbury, the motives for developing the Dunstan legend with alleged Winchester and Canterbury connections are not hard to seek. Stubbs' description of this development as one of

[7] Stubbs, *Memorials*, pp. 84–6; Thacker, 'Cults', pp. 222–3.
[8] Stubbs, *Memorials*, pp. 298–30, 56–7.
[9] Ibid., pp. 37, 60.

'luxuriant growth' may mask the surprising absence of any informed local tradition from Canterbury,[10] but it serves as a timely warning against accepting the testimony of Adelard, let alone of Obsern or Eadmer, when they contradict B.'s account or are unsupported by it. It is therefore very dangerous to follow Robinson, Knowles or Dales in reconstructing Dunstan's career with as many details from the later hagiographical sources as can be incorporated into a coherent conflated account.

Dunstan's Birth

According to B., Dunstan 'arose' (*oritur*) during the reign (*imperium*) of the glorious Athelstan, king of the English. Since he goes to describe the christening and naming of the infant and then to give an account of his childhood, there can be little doubt that B. meant that Dunstan was *born* whilst Athelstan was on the throne (924–39), as Osbern and the later hagiographers understood.[11] Modern scholars, however, have followed L. Toke and Armitage Robinson in supposing that Dunstan must in reality have been born in *c.* 909 or 910,[12] but this can only be accepted if we convict our earliest source of an error, presumably deriving from his ignorance of the succession dates of English kings before his own lifetime.

One principal reason for placing Dunstan's birth some fifteen years before Athelstan's accession was indeed the desire to conflate the information provided by B. with elements from Adelard's account. B. has Dunstan spend his childhood at Glastonbury and then as a *iuvenis* enter the entourage of Bishop Ælfheah of Winchester (934–51) and take the monastic profession through his influence; but Adelard has Dunstan leave Glastonbury during his adolescence and attach himself to the household of his paternal uncle, Archbishop Athelm (923–6), who is said to have commended him to King Athelstan and brought him to court. Only after he has been given Glastonbury by King Eadmund in Adelard's account is Dunstan made a monk and abbot.[13] Adelard, it would seem, was once again substituting an alternative

[10] Ibid., p. lx. Compare Thacker, 'Cults', p. 223.
[11] Stubbs, *Memorials*, pp. 6, 71, 165, 253, 325. For John of Wallingford's clear understanding of the difficulty of dating Dunstan's birth, see Robinson, *Times of St Dunstan*, pp. 92–3.
[12] L.A.St L. Toke, 'The Date of St Dunstan's Birth', in F.A. Gasquet and E. Bishop, *The Bosworth Psalter* (London, 1908), pp. 133–43; J.A. Robinson, *The Saxon Bishops of Wells*, British Academy Supplementary Papers, 4 (London, 1918), pp. 28–40.
[13] Stubbs, *Memorials*, pp. 13–14, 55–6.

version, which served to strengthen Dunstan's Canterbury connections. If we reject Adelard's alterations, we no longer need to squeeze
a period in Athelm's household into our account of Dunstan's career
or to suppose that Dunstan must already have been an adolescent by
the mid-920s.

Other reasons for pushing Dunstan's birth back before Athelstan's
accession might, however, be found in the overall pattern of the career
that B. describes: Dunstan is said to have received 'clerical tonsure'
(that is to have entered minor orders) at Glastonbury; to have later
rejected the prospect of marriage and become a monk at a time when
Ælfheah was bishop and Athelstan was still king (934 × 939); and
finally to have been installed as abbot of Glastonbury by King
Eadmund (939–46). His elevation to the abbacy could be dated more
precisely if a diploma of Eadmund of the year 940, preserved in the
Glastonbury cartularies and granting an estate at Christian Malford
(Wiltshire) to Abbot Dunstan, could be accepted as authentic.[14]
Though this charter has been shorn of its witness-list, its formulae
(including the dating clause) seem likely to derive from an authentic
diploma. But the surprising fact that this charter was not included in the
Liber Terrarum, the eleventh- or early twelfth-century Glastonbury
cartulary, which is now lost but whose contents are known,[15] raises the
possibility that a late forger may have substituted Dunstan's name in a
charter that originally had a lay beneficiary. Apart from the uncertain
Christian Malford charter, Dunstan does not appear as abbot in any
charter until the years 946 and 949.[16]

The silence of the charters might indicate that Abbot Dunstan did
not normally attend Eadmund's court, or else that the drafters of
charters, being accustomed only to record bishops among the ecclesiastical witnesses, did not record his presence; but we must also accept
that Dunstan may only have become abbot of Glastonbury towards
the end of Eadmund's reign (939–46). That could just allow
Dunstan's birth to post-date Athelstan's accession (924), as B.
believed. It would then follow that Dunstan had been a youth of at
most fourteen or fifteen when rejecting the attractions of the secular
life and choosing to be professed as a monk; he would have been a
young man of at most twenty-two when made abbot of Glastonbury.
We certainly do not need to suppose that in appointing to the major
churches of their kingdom, West Saxon kings were much concerned

[14] BCS 752 (S 466).
[15] The contents of this cartulary are known from the list in Cambridge, Trinity
College, R. 5. 33. For my understanding of this manuscript and of the significance of the
omission of the Christian Malford charter, I am indebted to Dr S.D. Keynes, who kindly
lent me a draft of his forthcoming study, *The Liber Terrarum of Glastonbury Abbey*.
[16] BCS 815 (S 520) of 946; BCS 880 (S 546) and BCS 883 (S 544) both of 949.

with canonical niceties in the early tenth century, any more than were their continental counterparts at that time. In the absence of direct evidence we are unable to determine whether B. failed to indicate Dunstan's youthfulness when he entered the monastic life and when he was made abbot, or whether he was misinformed about the time of his birth.

Family and Youth

B. tells us that Dunstan's parents were named Heorstan and Cynethryth, but tells us nothing of them except that they resided in the vicinity of the 'royal island' of Glastonbury. It was in that neighbourhood that the recorded events of his childhood all occur.[17] Thus it was to the churches of St Mary and St Peter at Glastonbury that the young Dunstan was taken by his father to pray and it was there that he is said to have had a vision of the monastic buildings that would be built in his day. It was there that his parents caused him to receive the clerical tonsure and that he spent the years of his puberty in prayer and in studying not only the scriptures but also the books brought there by Irish pilgrims. It was apparently from the 'royal island' that the bookish lad was driven out by his fellow *palatini* (that is, presumably, by other residents of the royal vill), many of whom we are told were his own kinsmen; they bound him and subjected him to a muddy humiliation in the nearby marshland so that, when he reached the house of a friend, only the dogs could recognize him.

After its beginnings at Glastonbury, Dunstan's career is portrayed by B. as developing through the influence of powerful relative. Bishop Ælfheah 'the Bald' of Winchester (934–51), himself a monk, was Dunstan's first patron and is said to have been Dunstan's *propinquus*. He persuaded Dunstan to reject the attractions of marriage and to take the monastic profession. We are then told how the two monks, going to the church of St Gregory in Winchester for compline, miraculously avoiding being crushed to death when a great piece of masonry fell to the floor between them.[18] Dunstan is also said to have been bound by ties of *propinquitas* to the matron Æthelflæd, a niece of King Athelstan; it was to her household at Glastonbury that Dunstan then returned. Finally Bishop Cynesige of Lichfield, with whom Dunstan was to be driven into exile by King Eadwig in 956, was also a

---

[17] Stubbs, *Memorials*, pp. 7–12. Stubb's marginal notes referring to Dunstan's presence at and expulsion from 'the Court' are misleading.

[18] Ibid., pp. 13–15.

blood relative (*consanguineus*).[19] With such kinsmen and kinswomen it would seem that Dunstan, even if we reject Adelard's assertion of his relationship to Archbishop Athelm, must have been drawn from the very highest ranks of the Anglo-Saxon nobility. Is his rise to eminence therefore to be explained by the fact that he had the right family connections and knew the right people?

We have to be cautious here. Hagiographers have a natural tendency to exalt the nobility of their subjects; the nobler a man's birth, the higher his material expectations and the greater his sacrifice in adopting a monastic way of life. B. certainly makes much of Dunstan's hesitations before taking the monastic profession and abandoning the attractions of the secular life and of marriage. Moreover, if Dunstan had really been drawn from the top rank of the Anglo-Saxon nobility, then we should expect his father Heorstan to have also been a prominent figure. Heorstan is a rare Anglo-Saxon personal name and it ought to be simple to identify Dunstan's father among the noble witnesses to the charters of Edward the Elder and Athelstan. But no man of that name occurs among the *duces* (ealdormen) or *ministri* (thegns) in the extant diplomas of these kings. Arguments from silence are seldom strong in the early Middle Ages and the absence of acceptable witness-lists for the period from 910 to 927 make this one particularly weak. That could have been exactly the period when Heorstan was at court. It is, however, at least, curious that the single occurrence of the name Heorstan in an Anglo-Saxon charter occurs among the eighty-two witnesses to a charter by which the *familia* of Winchester cathedral leased a twenty-hide estate at Chiseldon (Wiltshire) to Alfred, a thegn of King Athelstan, for three lives.[20] The lease certainly belongs to the early part of Athelstan's reign, that is to 925 × 933, and the absence of any bishop of Winchester from the document may point to its production towards the end of the life of Bishop Frithestan (909–31) or during a vacancy before the succession of Beorsnstan (931–4). The fact that no less than twenty-four of the witnesses are identified as *ministri* suggests that this Heorstan may not have attained that rank. Can this lowly Winchester Heorstan have been Dunstan's father, whom the *Vita S Dunstani* and modern historians have supposed so well connected?

---

[19] Ibid., pp. 17–18, 32. The first element of the name Cynesige could indicate a relationship to Dunstan's mother, Cynethryth. For the suggestion that Cynethryth is the Keondrud of the St Gall Confraternity Book, see ibid., p. lxxv. Names in Cyne- are, however, amongst the most common Anglo-Saxon personal names. See further *Councils & Synods, with Other Documents Relating to the English Church*, i, *AD 871–1204*, ed. D. Whitelock, M. Brett and C.N.L. Brooke (Oxford, 1981), pt i, pp. 40–3, no. 10.

[20] BCS 648 (S 1417). A Heorstan *minister* appears to attest BCS 605 of *c.* 900 (S 1443) but the earlier manuscript of his charter (BCS 1338) shows that the correct reading is Beornstan.

Given the fact that no other Heorstan is known to history, the possibility deserves careful consideration. We know from B. that within a year or two of this lease Dunstan himself was at Winchester in the company of Bishop Ælfheah, and that he had seemingly been driven from Glastonbury by the *palatini*. It is clearly conceivable that Heorstan had in fact brought his studious but unpopular son to Winchester to seek patronage (and perhaps library facilities) and that the father was of sufficient status to be considered a useful witness to the lease of this outlying Winchester property. That identification, however, would mean that we should have to minimize B.'s claim that Dunstan was a kinsman of Bishop Ælfheah and of Athelstan's niece, Æthelflæd, and of Bishop Cynesige. Either B. was making too much mileage out of relationships that were in reality very distant, or he was interpreting the adoptive kinship of the household of a bishop and of a noble widow as a real kinship; similarly he may have exalted Dunstan's shared exile into a blood relationship with Cynesige (*consanguineus*). Such an interpretation would be ironic but comprehensible in a writer whose letters of the 980s and 990s show him desperately seeking the patronage of successive archbishops of Canterbury – Dunstan, Æthelgar (988–90), Sigeric (990–94) and finally Archbishop Ælfric, to whom the *Vita S. Dunstani* was dedicated but to whom B. sadly admits that he was tied 'only by the bonds of charity' (*sola septus connexione caritatis*).[21]

If Dunstan's standing as a noble must remain uncertain, we do not need to doubt B.'s evidence that his career after he became a monk was assisted by the support of aristocratic widows. At a time when there was very little in the way of organized and communal religious life for women in England, noble widows who did not wish to enter a second marriage naturally sought the religious teaching and pious devotions of a holy man like Dunstan and proximity to an ancient church like Glastonbury. Athelstan's niece, Æthelflæd, had therefore welcomed the professed monk to the household that she had established to the west of the church of Glastonbury. There he was to attend her during her fatal illness, when she was able to interpret one of his visions.[22] The noble *matrona*, Æthelwynn, who commissioned him to design an ecclesiastical stole for her to embroider with gold thread and jewels, is likely to have been another widow attracted by the growing renown of the holy man.[23] Such ladies seem to be equivalent to the 'religious women of holy and monastic life' who received grants of bookland during the reigns of Eadmund and Eadred,

[21] Stubbs, *Memorials*, p. 5.
[22] Ibid., pp. 16–20.
[23] Ibid., pp. 20–1.

without being members of regular communities of nuns.[24]

We have one other means of understanding Dunstan's position during these years, namely by examining other members of his family. B. mentions the death of Dunstan's brother, named Wulfric, because when Dunstan was organizing the preparations for the funeral he miraculously escaped death from a 'heavenly missile', presumably a meteorite. Dunstan, we are told, had appointed Wulfric as reeve (*praepositus*) to be in charge of the monastery's scattered estates so that none of the monks would need to travel on secular business far from the monastery.[25] It is likely that Dunstan's brother can be identified with Wulfric, a king's thegn, who received in the 940s a huge landed fortune in Wiltshire and Surrey from Kings Eadmund and Eadred in a series of charters, which have been preserved in the Glastonbury cartularies:

940   Eadmund grant Wulfric 25 hides at Grittleton, Wiltshire (BCS 750; S 472)

940   Eadmund grants Wulfric 30 hides at Langley, Wiltshire (BCS 751; S 473)

944   Eadmund grants Wulfric 20 hides at Nettleton, Wiltshire (BCS 800; S 504)

947   Eadred grants Wulfric 5 hides at Idmiston, Wiltshire (BCS 829; S 530)

948   Eadred grants Wulfric a further 5 hides at Idmiston, Wiltshire (BCS 867; S 541)

949   Eadred grants Wulfric 20 hides at Merton, Surrey (BCS 878; S 551)

The texts of other grants by the same kings, conveying lands in Somerset (5 hides at Tintinhull, 10 hides at Yarlington) and Dorset (5 hides at Turnworth, 10 hides at Horton and *Cumbe*) to 'Wulfric' have not survived, though they are known to have been recorded in the lost Glastonbury *Liber Terrarum*.[26] Wulfric was believed to have granted some of these estates directly to Glastonbury; others initially supported

---

[24] The series begins with two charters of Athelstan in the last year of his reign: BCS 734 (S 449) for Wulfswith and BCS 743 (S 448) for Eadwulfu. Thereafter we have BCS 753 (S 464) of 940 for Æthelswith; BCS 763 (S 465) of 940 for Æthelthryth; BCS 768 (S 474) of 941 for Ælfflæd; BCS 775 (S 4485) of 942 for Wynflæd; BCS 778 (S 482) of 942 for Sæthryth; BCS 787 (S 487) of 943 for Ælfswith; BCS 795 (S 493) of 944 for Ælfgyth; BCS 868 (S 534) of 948 for Ælfthryth; BCS 869 (S 535) of 948 for Ælfwyn; BCS 903 (S 563) of 955 for Ælfgyth. There are also two as yet unpublished charters from Barking of Eadred in 946 to Æthelgifu and to Eawynn (S 517a, 517b), and three lost charters: of Edmund to Ælfswith (S 1720), of Eadred to Eawynn in 946 (S 1793) and of Eadwig to Ælfswith (S 1748).

[25] Stubbs, *Memorials*, p. 28.

[26] H.P.R. Finberg, *Early Charters of Wessex* (Leicester, 1964), nos 451, 453, 589, 647; S.D. Keynes, *The Glastonbury Liber Terrarum* (forthcoming).

his widow and the transfer was effected by their heir, Ælfwine, who
ended his days as a monk at Glastonbury; yet others seem to have first
passed into the hands of Ælfswith, the wife of Ealdorman Ælfheah.[27] If
all these grants were to a single Wulfric, then they show him being
established with lands amounting to at least 135 hides at much the same
period as his brother's abbacy at Glastonbury.

It may be possible to learn more about Wulfric's career from the
witness-lists of tenth-century royal diplomas. Unfortunately Wulfric is a
common name, but it seems likely that the majority of the attestations
of *ministri* with this name during the reigns of Athelstan, Eadmund,
Eadred and Eadwig belong to one of two thegns: either to Dunstan's
brother or to Wulfric Cufting, a thegn who acquired some 200 hides of
lands in Sussex, Hampshire and Berkshire in the 940s and 950s.[28] They
appear first in those charters of the years 931–4 which have the longest
witness-lists, that is those that have over twenty thegns attesting: a
single Wulfric (Wulfric I) appears in two diplomas of 931 and 932, but
both are already found in the two longest lists of 934.[29] There is then a
gap in the attestations (when the extant diplomas have shorter lists)
until 939–45 when the lists intermittently include one thegn named
Wulfric; these attestations may, however, refer to two separate individuals: Wulfric I, who climbs from a middle position among the thegns to
third place by 944, and Wulfric II who continues to occupy a low
position.[30] From 946, however, that is from Eadred's accession, both

[27] According to the *Liber Terrarum*, Tintinhull, Turnworth and Yarlington were given
by Wulfric directly to Glastonbury; Grittleton, Nettleton and Horton were passed on by
Ælfwine; Langley, Idmiston and Merton are shown to have been acquired by Ælfswith
in KCD 659, BCS 1259, 1196 (S 866, 775, 747).

[28] Wulfric Cufing is so named in D. Whitelock, *Anglo-Saxon Wills* (Cambridge,
1930), no. 4; his properties are listed at length in Edgar's charter of restitution of 960,
BCS 1055 (S 687). The charters for his Berkshire estates were preserved at Abingdon
and show him acquiring them between 944 and 958: BCS 796, 833, 866, 892, 902 and
1022 (S 503, 529, 542, 558, 575 and 577). For an earlier attempt (to which I owe
much) to establish his career and distinguish him from Dunstan's brother, see C.R.
Hart, *The Early Charters of Northern England and the North Midlands* (Leicester, 1975),
pp. 370–2.

[29] Wulfric I witnesses 15th out of 29 thegns in BCS 677 (S 416), 12/23 in BCS 689 (S
417), 24/52 in BCS 702 (S 425) and 15/25 in BCS 706 (S 427). Wulfric II appears 42/52
and 21/25 in the last two charters.

[30] It may be Wulfric I who witnesses 9/18 in BCS 743 (S 448) of 939; 8/15 in BCS
748 (S 470), 7/11 in BCS 757 (S 469), 9/18 in BCS 762 (S 461), 7/14 in BCS 763 and
767 (S 465, 476) all of 940; 7/14 in BCS 769 (S 478) in 941; 6/9 in BCS 783 (S 1811)
and 4/15 in BCS 784 (S 489) both of 943; 5/14 in BCS 791 (S 497), 6/15 in BCS 795 (S
493) and 3/13 in BCS 796 and 798 (S 503 and 494) all of 944. Wulfric II is perhaps the
thegn who attests 15/15 in BCS 774 (S 483), 11/12 in BCS 777 (S 480), 7/8 in BCS 778
(S 482) all of 942; 12/14 in BCS 780 (S 512), 12/12 in BCS 786 (S 488), 8/10 in BCS
787 (S 487), 10/11 in BCS 788 (S 486) and 15/17 in BCS 789 (S 491) all of 943; 8/11 in
BCS 792 (S 495), 15/17 in BCS 801 (S 496) and 8/10 in BCS 802 (S 500) all of 944.

Wulfrics appear in the same lists with increasing regularity and Wulfric II rises to occupy fifth or sixth place; from then until 951 both men were clearly amongst the select group of prominent thegns who regularly attended the meetings of the English *witan*. Thereafter Wulfric II appears to drop from sight, at least until 956, a year for which some sixty diplomas have survived and which marked the beginning of Eadwig's troubled reign:[31] only five of the extant charters (all from the early part of the year) are witnessed by two Wulfrics; Wulfric I attests regularly in second place those charters produced at a witan held in February, but very soon thereafter he dropped out of sight and is found in only one of the charters of Eadwig of 957 and in one of 958.[32] The second thegn Wulfric of 956 might be our Wulfric II, but is more probably a new man; he puts in an occasional appearance in a very low position among the thegns in charters for the rest of Eadwig's reign. He may perhaps be identified with Wulfric, the king's 'most renowned huntsman', who received an estate in Wiltshire early in 956.[33]

The problems of disentangling the thegns named Wulfric are typical of the difficulties of tenth-century English prosopography. It seems most probable that Dunstan's brother is our Wulfric II; the fact that he no longer attended court after 951 would fit with B.'s account of his death, seemingly during Dunstan's abbacy.[34] Wulfric I would therefore be Wulfric Cufing, who despite his wealth dropped from political prominence in the course of 956; it is not clear whether the confiscation of his properties occurred in Eadwig's last months or at Edgar's accession; although his lands were restored by Edgar in 960, he did not reappear at Edgar's court. What the evidence does show very clearly – owing to the fortunate preservation of many of Wulfric Cufing's charters at Abingdon and of Dunstan's brothers' charters at Glastonbury – is how these two thegns were massively enriched by royal patronage during the period from 940 to 950 when they became the trusted confidants and regular companions of kings Eadmund and Eadred. Royal favour, it would seem, transformed them from being minor local notables into two of the greatest nobles in the kingdom. We

---

[31] The following interpretation is based upon the analysis of the charters of 956 set out by S.D. Keynes, *The Diplomas of King Æthelred 'The Unready' 978–1016* (Cambridge, 1980), pp. 48–61.

[32] He attests first of the thegns in BCS 1004 (S 640) of 957 and in BCS 1028 (S 654) of 958.

[33] BCS 968 (S 637). The Wulfric *procer* or *princeps* who is the recipient of BCS 962 (S 635) and 926 (S 636) was presumably Wulric I, i.e. Wulfric Cufing, since these charters belong to the early part of the year when he was still prominent at court.

[34] Stubbs, *Memorials*, p. 28. B., however, mentions Wulfric's death before that of King Eadmund and his account of the accession of Eadred (in 946); that cannot be reconciled with the charter evidence.

thus obtain a welcome insight into the gulf that separated ordinary thegns from king's thegns in tenth-century England and into how this divide could be bridged by royal patronage.

What our sources do not specify, however, is whether Wulfric II's rise to prominence was by his brother's bootstraps or whether he rose by his own efforts and was then himself able to assist Dunstan. It is likely that Wulfric was the elder brother and that he had inherited the patrimonial estate near Glastonbury; for he had been appearing at court at least since 934 and he was to die some thirty years before Dunstan. Where Wulfric's career at court seems to have begun in the middle years of Athelstan's reign, it was not until Eadmund's accession, according to B., that the king chose to place Dunstan among his thegns and ealdormen at court (*inter regios proceres et palatinos principes*). By living a godly life there among the nobles of the royal household for a long period (*diu*), Dunstan won some friends but also made many enemies. The malicious intrigues of Dunstan's courtly opponents are said to have led the king to strip him of his rank and to order him to seek lordship (*senioratus*) outwith the kingdom. Eadmund's miraculous change of mind the very next day and his immediate appointment and installation of Dunstan as abbot of Glastonbury was attributed by B. to the king's admission that he had wronged Dunstan – a repentance purportedly brought about when he came near to being killed while hunting too close to Cheddar Gorge.[35] We should not be surprised that a hagiographer should seek a miraculous, rather than a political, explanation for this decisive change in Dunstan's fortunes. But B. has already indicated that Dunstan had some friends at court and it must surely have been helpful to have had a brother there with Glastonbury connections to plead his cause. It is also clear that the story fits a recurring pattern in Dunstan's life as portrayed by B.: the saint rejects the values and tastes of the secular nobility and is consequently expelled from their company; but with divine help his ecclesiastical career soon resumes its progress to even higher office. The pattern occurs in his youth at Glastonbury, here at Eadmund's court and again at the accession of Eadwig. We may suspect that the whole story of Dunstan's imminent expulsion, of the king's miraculous hunting escape and of Dunstan's consequent elevation is a tale that has much improved in the telling to fit this generic pattern.

Abbot of Glastonbury (940 × 946–956)

B. tell us that Eadmund repented of his expulsion of Dunstan when he saw both the stag that he was hunting and the hounds plunge to their

35 Ibid., pp. 23–4.

deaths down Cheddar Gorge and realised that his own mount was set to follow. Naturally he interpreted this as a sign of divine displeasure at his treatment of Dunstan. He did not, however, draw the obvious conclusion and recall Dunstan to court to reform its morals! Instead he is said to have immediately ridden to Glastonbury (twelve miles after his hazardous hunt) and placed Dunstan on the 'sacerdotal seat' there, declaring,

> Be thou the prince and powerful possessor of this seat and the faithful abbot of this church. Whatever you lack for the fulfilment of the sacred Rule, I will supply by royal gift.[36]

It may have been at this time that the 'royal island' at Glastonbury came into the possession of the abbey. By elevating Dunstan, the king had not only secured for himself the prayers and support of a man whose life had already shown him destined to be a holy man of distinction;[37] he had also rid his court of someone who had proved a disruptive influence. It is instructive that whilst the charters show Wulfric in Eadmund's household throughout the reign, his brother Dunstan cannot be shown ever to have been there. A king had not only to reward the ablest of his subjects, but he had also to manage men. The fact that Eadmund was to be buried at Glastonbury suggests that he regarded that house as very much his own creation and that there was never any serious rift between him and Dunstan. He may nonetheless have preferred to keep him at a distance.

Dunstan's appointment as abbot of Glastonbury may also have pleased the king's mother, Eadgifu, the third wife and widow of Edward the Elder. She had played no visible role in politics during Athelstan's reign, but is found at court in a prominent position from Eadmund's accession onwards. She was certainly later to be associated with the monastic reform movement in general and with Dunstan in particular.[38] B. does not attribute to her any hand in Dunstan's establishment as abbot, though she was prominent at court at the time. His only reference to Eadgifu comes later when her second son, King Eadred, sought her help in persuading Dunstan to accept the see of Crediton. That certainly suggests that she was felt to have some influence with the abbot and her fortunes certainly mirror his. Thus she witnesses many of the charters of her sons, either immediately after the king or in some other prominent position; like Dunstan she fell from favour early in the reign of Eadwig when all her estates were confiscated; like Dunstan she recovered her

---

[36] Ibid., p. 25.

[37] For the concept of the 'holy man', see P. Brown, *Society and the Holy in Late Antiquity* (London, 1982), pp. 103–65.

[38] C.R. Hart, 'Two Queens of England', *Ampleforth Journal*, 82 (1977), pp. 10–15, 54.

position and her properties at the start of Edgar's reign; and she then granted an estate at Cooling to Christ Church, Canterbury, where Dunstan was by then archbishop.[39] It is possible that she had been among those who had supported his appointment to Glastonbury; she may also have had some hand in the numerous grants that her sons made to 'religious women' in the 940s and 950s which come to an end when she was no longer at court. The evidence is indirect and inadequate but may suggest that Dunstan drew much of his support from the regiment of powerful women in early tenth-century Wessex and from Eadgifu in particular. We have only to look across the North Sea at Ottonian Germany for a contemporary society in which royal and noble widows linked to the royal house played a dominant role in determining the religious priorities of the age.[40]

Be that as it may, we can learn from B. something of the monastic life which Dunstan established at Glastonbury. The author describes him as 'following the most wholesome *institutio* of St Benedict' and as 'the first abbot of the English nation'. Though this verdict was to be enthusiastically reinforced by later writers of the monastic reform movement, like Ælfric, as well as by modern historians like Knowles (who began his *Monastic Order in England* with Dunstan at Glastonbury), it is doubtful whether B. meant more than that he was first in importance. Charters show no less than six English abbots attesting in 931 and 932, and in the first charter that Dunstan witnesses as abbot, he is accompanied by two others of the same rank.[41] We are not entitled to assume that the communal life in these contemporary houses was deplorable, or that the *Rule* was unknown in them. Since B. was himself a secular canon, he must be regarded as good authority for the particular devotion in which the Benedictine Rule was held at Dunstan's Glastonbury – he had no reason to exaggerate it. We also learn from Wulfstan and from Ælfric that St Æthelwold was one of those who joined Dunstan at Glastonbury and was received into the monastic order there. Several of B.'s stories, however, make clear that at Glastonbury there continued to be both clerks and monks under Dunstan's rule, and this is confirmed by the fact that when the young Æthelwold left Glastonbury to set up a more rigorous monastic life at Abingdon, he took with him three young *clerici*: Osgar, Foldbriht and Frithegar.[42] It would seem that Dunstan's

---

[39] F.E. Harmer, *Select English Historical Documents of the Ninth and Tenth Centuries* (Cambridge, 1913), no. 23 (S 1211).

[40] K.J. Leyser, *Rule and Conflict in an Early Medieval Society: Ottonian Society* (London, 1979), pp. 49–74.

[41] BCS 674, 675, 677, 680, 689, 690, 692, (S 412, 413, 416, 410, 417, 393, 418) of 931 and 932; BCS 815 (S 520) of 946.

[42] Ælfric, *Vita S Ethelwoldi*, ch. 7; Wulfstan, *Vita S. Ethelwoldi*, ch. 11; both in *Three Lives of English Saints*, ed. M. Winterbottom (Toronto, 1972), pp. 20, 41.

Glastonbury, like so many of its continental counterparts, began as a largely independent attempt to establish a more ascetic and more regular form of communal religious life. But it did not long satisfy all its younger brethren and it did not make the clear distinction, normal in the Frankish church since the reforms of Louis the Pious and Benedict of Aniane, between the regular and secular clergy; nor did it share the contempt for 'clerks' that came to typify the reformed houses of Æthelwold's tradition. In all these respects Dunstan at Glastonbury, as later at Canterbury, looked to an older and more insular tradition.[43]

The fortunes of the new house were consolidated during the reign of Eadred (946–55) in whose early years we have seen that Dunstan's brother Wulfric was rising rapidly in the order of precedence in the king's household. According to B.:

> Eadred loved the blessed father Dunstan with such great warmth of love that he hardly preferred any of his chief men to him.[44]

Following Stubbs, historians have often taken this to mean that Dunstan became Eadred's leading counsellor, even his 'prime minister'! But the passage need imply no more than that under Eadred Dunstan too found a place at court which he had not enjoyed under Eadmund – an interpretation which fits very much better with the record of Dunstan's attendance at court in the charters. B. goes on to tell us that Eadred demonstrated this affection and trust by committing to Dunstan,

> all the best of his goods, namely many title deeds and also the ancient treasures of preceding kings to be faithfully kept in the security of his monastery.

Some confirmation of this account may be found in Eadred's will in which substantial sums of money were to be deposited in leading churches – Christ Church, Canterbury (Archbishop Oda), Winchester (Bishop Ælfsige), Glastonbury (Dunstan) and Dorchester (Bishop Oscytel) – to be used for the benefit of the local shires for relief either from poverty or from the devastations of a heathen army. Of the four recipients Dunstan was to hold the smallest sum, namely £200 on behalf of the people of Somerset and of Devon.[45] It was not, however, to the terms of Eadred's post-obit bequests that B. was referring, but to the arrangements for the custody of his treasure during his reign. B.

---

[43] D.A. Bullough, 'The Continental Background of the Reform', in D. Parsons, ed., *Tenth-Century Studies* (London and Chichester, 1975), pp. 20–36; C.P. Wormald, 'Æthelwold and his Continental Counterparts: Contract, Comparison, Contrast', in Yorke, ed., *Bishop Æthelwold: Career and Influence*, pp. 13–42.

[44] Stubbs, *Memorials*, p. 29.

[45] Harmer, *Select Documents*, no 21 (S 1515).

knew that there were other custodians of the royal treasure apart from Dunstan, for he tells us that the dying king summoned them all to bring him a report of exactly what they had in custody so that he could make his final bequests of his movable and landed property. To what extent those who held his treasure and his charters were also those who advised the king on how he should dispose of his wealth, we cannot tell. But it was certainly a task that is likely to have created jealousies. For the king chose to give the vast bulk of his disposable landed fortune – the three ancient royal manors of Amesbury, Wantage and Basing and all his booklands in Sussex, Surrey and Kent – to his mother Eadgifu. That can scarcely have pleased Eadred's successor and nephew, Eadwig, who was not even mentioned in the will. It is indeed conceivable that the huge bequest given to Eadgifu was intended to be held on behalf of her second grandson, Edgar, who was under age. Be that as it may, B. does mention that Dunstan failed to arrive to present his account of his custodianship of Eadred's treasure before the king had died.[46] That failure may well have occasioned the sort of malicious rumour that Dunstan had attracted at court earlier in his career, perhaps to the effect that he had misappropriated some revenues in favour of Eadgifu and Edgar.

Exile

Eadred died on 23 November 955 and the succession passed to Eadwig, Eadmund's eldest son, a youth of just fifteen years. Because he fell out with Dunstan, Eadwig gets a deplorable press from B. which has coloured all subsequent interpretation of his brief reign. Not content on this occasion with vague references to Dunstan standing out against the immoralities and backbiting of the courtiers, B. provides a highly coloured account of scandal whereby a wanton noblewoman Æthelgifu and her voluptuous daughter, Ælfgifu, enticed the young king to their chamber when he should have been drinking and feasting with his nobles after his consecration as king. When Archbishop Oda of Canterbury sought to organize a deputation to summon the king back to his convivial duties, only the steadfast Dunstan and his 'kinsman' Bishop Cynesige of Lichfield dared to intervene:

> They found the royal crown, marvellously worked with gold, silver and gems, cast aside on the floor and the king repeatedly wallowing between the two women, in evil fashion as if in a vile sty.

---

[46] Stubbs, *Memorials*, p. 31. B. has Dunstan made miraculously aware of the king's death by an angel.

Dunstan therefore put the crown back on the king's head and dragged him back to the coronation feast, thereby arousing the lasting enmity both of Eadwig and of the two ladies. Dunstan was promptly deprived 'by the king's consent' of his office and his properties and he had rapidly to go into exile.[47]

It is very uncertain how adequate or how complete an explanation of Dunstan's fall from grace this is. Dr Keynes's analysis of the witness-lists of the numerous charters of the year 956 has shown that Dunstan and Cynesige did indeed attend the January meeting of the witan at Kingston-upon-Thames where the royal consecration took place; Dunstan attended once further in February, but neither he nor Cynesige attended any of the later meetings in that year.[48] Their disgrace was therefore real enough. Ælfgifu, however, the comely daughter, does not seem to have been the scarlet woman that B. portrays. She soon married Eadwig and was certainly recognized as queen both at Æthelwold's Abingdon and later at Winchester. After Eadwig's death she was given lands in Buckinghamshire and Oxfordshire by his successor Edgar. In her will she made in turn substantial bequests to Edgar, to his son and to his queen, as well as to a host of major West Saxon churches: Winchester (the Old, New and Nuns' minsters), Romsey, Abingdon and Bath.[49] She came from the highest West Saxon nobility, being the sister of the chronicler, Ealdorman Æthelweard; but she was also distantly related to Eadwig himself, seemingly being a third cousin once removed. In reforming ecclesiastical circles in the tenth century a mistaken interpretation of the canonical prohibitions had arisen which forbad the marriage of fourth cousins or anyone more closely related. Ælfgifu and Eadwig therefore fell foul of this interpretation and in 957 Archbishop Oda separated them on the grounds that they were *to gesybbe*, 'too closely related'.[50]

It is entirely possible that B.'s dramatic account of this court scandal is a partisan polemic deriving from his memory of the character assassination that attended a disputed marriage. There are likely to have been wider political and territorial interests in conflict. The young king's early marriage would inevitably affect the chances of Eadwig's younger brother, Edgar, of succeeding to the throne.

---

[47] Ibid., pp. 32–3.

[48] Keynes, *Diplomas of Æthelred*, pp. 49–68.

[49] Whitelock, *Wills*, no. 8 (S 1484); for Edgar's grants see BCS 1176 and 1189 (S 738, 737); for her acceptance at Abingdon and Winchester see her attestation of BCS 972 (S 1292) and her listing as an illustrious benefactor in the New Minster *Liber Vitae*, ed. W. de Gray Birch (Hants Record Society, 1892), p. 57.

[50] ASC, D 958: *Two of the Saxon Chronicles Parallel*, ed. C. Plummer (2 vols, Oxford, 1892–9), i, p. 113. For a fuller treatment of the problem of the relationship of Ælfgifu and Eadwig, see Brooks, *Early History*, pp. 225–6.

Moreover, since Ælfgifu's brother was Æthelweard, ealdorman of the western shires of Wessex, her family connections lay in Dunstan's own home territory. If we recall that Dunstan had earlier been driven out of Glastonbury as a boy by the *palatini* there and that he had subsequently fallen foul of the nobles at court during Eadmund's reign, there is an obvious possibility that he had already clashed with Ælfgifu's kin. Since B. tells us that even at Glastonbury there were those who abetted his fall, whilst those who remained his friends suffered the same fate as he,[51] it is clear that a court coup had been effected involving the disgrace of one group of Eadred's advisers. Among the group who were ousted must be counted Eadwig's grand-mother, Eadgifu, who was also deprived of her estates at this time. We cannot reconstruct all the alliances and the intrigues, which are so inadequately reflected in B.'s account. We do, however, know that in 956 Eadwig embarked on a programme of granting bookland to certain West Saxon nobles on an entirely unprecedented scale. As a result far more Anglo-Saxon royal diplomas have survived from the year 956 than from any other.[52] It has yet to be determined why Eadwig needed to secure the support of these men or how he could afford to give so much land away. It may be that Dunstan was one of those ousted in order to increase the king's resources and that B.'s account reflects the bitterness of the dispossessed.

B. seems to have known nothing of the circumstances of Dunstan's foreign exile. He vaguely asserts that the holy man, driven out by the threats of the wicked *populatrix*, came by sea to 'the region called Gaul', whose speech and customs he scarcely knew, and there found the favour of 'a certain prince of that land'. It is Adelard, not B., who tells us that Dunstan was received by Count Arnulf I of Flanders and that he was installed in the count's recently restored monastery of St Peter's, Ghent (Blandinium), where he set 'an example of light to be imitated'.[53] In this instance we may surely place some trust in Adelard, for Flanders was his homeland and Blandinium his own monastery. Moreover his account receives some support from a letter written in Arnulf's name congratulating Dunstan on his elevation to the archbish-opric, recalling their friendship and requesting the archbishop's support for an embassy to King Edgar. In other letters from the same collection Abbot Guy of Blandinium (981–6) sought Dunstan's generous support for a fund-raising embassy undertaken on behalf of St Peter's by a

[51] Stubbs, *Memorials*, pp. 33–4.

[52] Nearly sixty royal diplomas belong to the year 956, some three times the number attributable to any other year. See Sawyer, *Anglo-Saxon Charters*, passim. For an attempt to identify some of those whom Eadwig was promoting at this time, see Yorke, 'Æthelwold and Politics', in idem, ed., *Bishop Æthelwold*, pp. 78–80.

[53] Stubbs, *Memorials*, pp. 34, 59–60.

certain Leofsige.[54] We do not know the results of these requests, but the letters certainly indicate that both Arnulf and his monastery at Ghent believed that Dunstan was indebted to them.

Historians have often been tempted to identify Dunstan's stay at Ghent as the source of Lotharingian influence on the English monastic revival, its liturgy and culture.[55] Given the frequency of cross-Channel contacts in the tenth century, such arguments, however attractive, are incapable of proof. But Dunstan himself may have acquired a more personal skill during his year of exile. At some stage in his life he abandoned the native insular minuscule script which he would have learnt to write during his youth at Glastonbury and adopted instead Caroline minuscule which was the standard on the Continent. The corrections to manuscripts and the passages which have been attributed to Dunstan's Caroline hand cannot be closely dated. Palaeographers are clear that he wrote the script skilfully but hesitantly and with an idiosyncratic mixture of insular and continental features.[56] In short, his is exactly the sort of script that a middle-aged English abbot might adopt as a result of a year's enforced furlough in Flanders.

This chronology for the development of Dunstan's script draws support from the fact that we have one example of Dunstan's hand dated to the year 949, which shows him still writing insular square minuscule at a time when he was abbot of Glastonbury. Scholars, including the present writer, have long dithered over whether to accept or reject the authenticity of the famous charter, still preserved in the cathedral archives, by which King Eadred granted Reculver to the cathedral church of Canterbury in that year – a charter which claims to have been both composed and written by Dunstan (*dictitando conposui et propriis digitorum articulis perscripsi*).[57]

---

[54] Ibid., pp. 359–60, 386. Dunstan may not have spent the whole of his exile at Ghent. We do not know when he became a friend of Fulrad of St Vaast at Arras (ibid., pp. 383–4).

[55] T. Symons, 'The Sources of the *Regularis Concordia*', *Downside Review*, 59 (1941), pp. 14–36, 143–70, 264–89; *Regularis Concordia*, ed. and trans. T. Symons (London, 1953), pp. xlv–lii; idem, 'The *Regularis Concordia*: History and Derivation', in Parsons, ed., *Tenth-Century Studies*, pp. 37–59; P.E. Schramm, *A History of the English Coronation* (Oxford, 1937), p. 18.

[56] *St Dunstan's Classbook*, ed. Hunt, pp. xiv–xvi; T.A.M. Bishop, 'An Early Example of Insular Caroline', *Transactions of the Cambridge Bibliographical society*, 4, pt 5 (1968), pp. 396–400; Bishop, *English Caroline Minuscule*, pp. 1–2; H. Gneuss, 'Dunstan und Hrabanus Maurus', *Anglia*, 96 (1978), pp. 136–48. Their proposed dating (before 957, that is, Dunstan's ordination as bishop) ignores the fact that the 'Classbook' could have been annotated by Dunstan after his recovery of Glastonbury in 959.

[57] Canterbury, D & C Archives, Chart.Ant. R.14; BCS 880 (S 546). For recent discussion of this charter, see P. Chaplais, 'The Anglo-Saxon Chancery: from the Diploma to the Writ', *Journal of the Society of Archivists*, iii, pt. 4 (1966), p. 164; Brooks, *Early History*, pp. 232–67; M. Lapidge, 'Æthelwold as Scholar and Teacher', in Yorke, ed., *Bishop Æthelwold*, pp. 91–2.

However, there are compelling reasons for associating the charter's diplomatic with the abbey of Glastonbury during Dunstan's abbacy, since the earliest charters to share much of the same formulation are said to have been written on Dunstan's orders, whilst many of the later grants in this group (now known as the 'Dunstan B' charters) have explicit connections with Glastonbury or with Dunstan.[58] Moreover both the hand of the main text of the Reculver charter and that of the vernacular boundary clause on its dorse appear to be contemporary scripts of the mid-tenth century. The change of scribes and the unusual layout could have arisen because the boundaries of this Kentish estate were not available at Glastonbury when the charter was written;[59] but it is very difficult to imagine a forger adopting such a procedure. Once we appreciate that this script could be Dunstan's, even though it is distinct from his Caroline hand, we may thankfully abandon the increasingly tortuous attempt to suppose that the Reculver charter is a uniquely brilliant forgery of the later tenth, or early eleventh, century. Restored to its status as an authentic original written by Dunstan himself, it becomes an invaluable testimony to the development of his script and to the history of the manuscripts in which his Caroline script has been recognized. Dunstan's corrections and insertions in his new script should therefore be attributed to the period of his exile or to the years that followed.

---

[58] For the 'Dunstan B' charters, see Hart, *Early Charters of N. England and N. Midlands*, pp. 19–22, and Keynes, *Diplomas of Æthelred*, pp. 46–8. Apart from the Reculver charter the group includes charters of 946 and 951 written on Dunstan's orders (BCS 816, 889; S 509, 555), grants to Dunstan as abbot in 955 and as archbishop in 967 (BCS 904, 1198; S 568, 753), grants to Glastonbury in 966 and 973 (BCS 1188, 1294; S 743, 791), a grant to a Somerset layman witnessed by Dunstan and the Glastonbury community (BCS 931; S 571), a grant to Æthelflæd (? Dunstan's benefactress) with reversion to Glastonbury (BCS 817; S 513), the foundation charter establishing Dunstan's pupil, Æthelwold, at Abingdon (BCS 924; S 605) and charters enacted by Glastonbury in 960(?) and 975 (BCS 1048, 1315; S 670, 802). Apart from these there are five purported grants to St Peter's, Bath (BCS 1009, 1073, 1164, 1287 and *Codex*, ed. Kemble, no. 643; S 661, 694, 735, 785 and 854) whose reform was probably due to Dunstan's influence, two grants by Edgar in 958 as king of the Mercians when Dunstan was a bishop at his court (BCS 1036, 1037; S 678, 676) and two grants of land in Somerset (BCS 903, 923; S 563, 570). There are also nine charters with no evident connection with Dunstan (BCS 899, 900, 905, 908, 987, 1134, 1209, 1292 and 1314; S 561, 560, 565, 564, 574, 726, 750, 790 and 803) and two erroneously attributed to King Eadred (BCS 987, 1023; S 574, 579). In general the dating of these charters and the location of their estates encourages the view that they could have been produced by Dunstan or by one in his following, but a major study of their diplomatic and historical context is urgently needed. [This has now been provided by Prof. S.D. Keynes. See below, p. 206, no. 89.]

[59] Other tenth-century charters whose bounds follow the witnesses are BCS 816 and 1073 (S 509, 694) of the 'Dunstan B' group and also BCS 1056 (S 684).

Return

Dunstan's return to England to a position of power and influence in the English church was a direct result of a change of regime in England in the summer or autumn of 957. According to the Anglo-Saxon Chronicle, Edgar, the younger brother of Eadwig, 'succeeded to the kingdom of the Mercians', apparently at the age of thirteen or fourteen, and the boundary between his kingdom and that of his brother was fixed at the river Thames.[60] The Chronicle here studiously avoids any hint of a coup in favour of Edgar. St Æthelwold himself was to write at the height of the monastic revival in the preface to his translation of the *Rule of St Benedict* that Eadwig had 'through the ignorance of childhood dispersed his kingdom and *divided its unity*'.[61] That may suggest a degree of willing intent on Eadwig's part. To understand such brief statements correctly we need to recall just how new the English kingdom was in 957. Only three years previously Eadred had brought the Scandinavian kingdom of York under the rule of the West Saxon dynasty on the death of Eric Bloodaxe and it was less than forty years since Eadwig's grandfather, Edward the Elder, had annexed the Mercian kingdom. We therefore need not be surprised that when both brothers were of age the recently enlarged kingdom was divided in such a way that the patrimonial lands south of the Thames were held by the elder, whilst the younger ruled the more recent acquisitions to the north. Though this experiment was ended by Eadwig's death within two years, it is noteworthy, as Sir Frank Stenton pointed out long ago,[62] that the men whom Eadwig had appointed to the office of *ealdorman* on

[60] ASC 957 BC; *Two Chronicles*, ed. Plummer, i, p. 113. For the Thames as the frontier, see 'Florence' of Worcester, *Chronicon ex Chronicis*, ed. B. Thorpe, 2 vols (London, 1848–9), i, p. 137, and also B.'s *Life* (Stubbs, *Memorials*, p. 36). Edgar's age is determined by the *Chronicle*'s statement that he was 29 on 11 May 973 (*Two Chronicles*, ed. Plummer, i, pp. 118–19). My understanding of the circumstances of the division of the kingdom in 957 draws heavily upon a forthcoming study of Eadwig's reign by Dr S.D. Keynes, where the evidence for the political allegiances at this time is fully set out. I am most grateful for his generosity in sending me an early draft of this work and permitting me to anticipate his conclusions in so far as they relate to St Dunstan.

[61] *Councils & Synods, 871–1204*, I, ed. Whitelock, Brett and Brooke, pt i, pp. 142–54 at 146.

[62] F.M. Stenton, *Anglo-Saxon England* (3rd edn, Oxford, 1971), pp. 366–7. The point derives from the first edition of 1943. Little weight can be placed upon the dubious Worcester charter of 956 which Edgar attests as *regulus* (BCS 937; S 633) or upon the 'D' version of the *Anglo-Saxon Chronicle* which records the succession of both Eadwig to Wessex and Edgar to Mercia under the year 955 (*Two Chronicles*, ed. Plummer, i, p. 112), but they suggest that at Worcester and in the north there was no abiding memory of revolt against Eadwig.

both sides of the Thames – Byrhtnoth of Essex, Æthelwold of East Anglia, Ælfhere of Mercia and Ælfheah of Hampshire – remained in office under King Edgar. Such continuity amongst the greatest nobles makes it difficult to believe that the division of the kingdom was simply a coup against Eadwig and his supporters.

Dunstan's hagiographer, B., however, writing some forty years after these events and from across the Channel, naturally interpreted political changes in a very different light, that it as evidence that God had been at work in order to promote Dunstan's career. He therefore supposed that the Eadwig had been 'deserted' by the northern people (*a brumali populo relinqueretur*) because of his unwise government and 'his ruining of those who were wise and sagacious'.[63] In other words the expulsion of the holy Dunstan and of his friends revealed to the Mercians (though not apparently to the West Saxons!) that Eadwig was unfit to rule. B. does admit that the *publica res* of the two kings was divided at the Thames 'by the decision of wise men and with the witness of the whole people', but he asserts that it was by God's guidance that Edgar was chosen as king and by God's will that Dunstan was recalled from exile. Moreover, Eadwig's early and miserable death was the result of his having 'turned away from the just judgments of his God'. In consequence Edgar received the entire kingdom and restored to Dunstan 'the office which had been taken from him' – that is, presumably, the abbey of Glastonbury.

For B., therefore, history had shown what God did to those who slighted St Dunstan. Eadwig's loss of the territories north of the Thames and his premature death were themselves proof of Dunstan's sanctity. B. could no more resist deducting *post hoc ergo propter hoc* than a modern politician can resist attributing to government policies such favourable events as occur in his (or her) term of office. The later hagiographers of St Dunstan, notably Osbern and Eadmer, elaborated the story even further and claimed that the division of Eadwig's kingdom was the result of a full-scale rising in which the impious king was driven out and his 'wicked harlot' put to a gruesome death at Gloucester.[64] Faced with such fables, the historian can only assert that the division of the kingdom is very unlikely to have been provoked by Eadwig's treatment of Dunstan. The fortunes of the abbot of Glastonbury would scarcely have been a dominant concern of many of the Mercian nobility. The division may rather have already been planned in 955, when the early death of King Eadred made it inevitable that the recently enlarged kingdom would be ruled by an inexperienced youth.

---

[63] Stubbs, *Memorials*, pp. 35–6.
[64] Ibid., pp. 102, 194.

For Dunstan the division of the kingdom and its reunification under Edgar two years later were certainly very fortunate. B. tells us that Dunstan was recalled by Edgar and then elected bishop at a *sapientium conventus*, that is at a *witenagemot*, which Edgar held at *Brandanford*.[65] Initially Dunstan was not appointed to any specific see. The king's intention may have been to give him immediate authority and status in the Mercian court. When Bishop Cenwald of Worcester died, however, probably early in the year 958,[66] B. tells us that Dunstan was translated to that see and that he ministered so well to the needs of his flock that when the see of London also became vacant, Edgar appointed Dunstan there too.

It is difficult to know how fully we should trust B.'s account here. In reality London probably became vacant before Worcester. Bishop Byrhthelm of London was a supporter of Eadwig and attests his charters, not those of Edgar. His diocese, however, was in Edgar's kingdom, and Byrhthelm seems to have transferred to the see of Wells when the kingdom was divided in 957.[67] It may be that the young Edgar initially hesitated to intrude Dunstan into a see which already had a properly elected – if absentee – bishop, until it was quite clear that Byrhthelm's translation to Wells was secure and that he was not seeking to retain control of London as well. Were it not for the evidence of B., however, the natural interpretation of the episcopal lists and of the witness-lists of charters would be that Dunstan had first become bishop of London and had then received Worcester in addition. But, since B.'s account of Dunstan's ordination and subsequent acquisition of the sees of Worcester and London serves no evident hagiographic purpose, it should probably be accepted.

It is clear that already while Edgar was 'king of the Mercians' (957–9), he was committed to furthering Dunstan's career at every available opportunity. B. gives no hint of any earlier contact between them, but Edgar had been tutored by Æthelwold at Abingdon[68] and may have acquired from him a deep respect for Dunstan as monk, holy man and abbot. Eadgifu, who recovered her estates at the same time as Dunstan, may have been another of his advocates with her grandson, in view of Dunstan's ministry to the religious needs of royal and noble widows. Clearly, however, the young Edgar responded to Dunstan's

[65] Ibid., pp. 36–7. B. mistakenly places Dunstan's consecration as bishop after Edgar had acquired the whole kingdom, seemingly because for B. what was important was the recovery of Glastonbury.

[66] Cenwald attests BCS 1042 (S 675) of 958 along with Bishop Dunstan, but is not found in BCS 1036, 1037, 1040, 1043 (S 678, 676, 677, 674) of the same year.

[67] For a detailed discussion of the problems of identifying the careers of the bishops named Byrhthelm at this time, see Brooks, *Early History*, pp. 238–40.

[68] E. John, *Orbis Britanniae* (Leicester, 1966), pp. 158–60.

personality and was determined to make him his leading ecclesiastic. Once Eadwig had died on 5 October 959, Dunstan's career therefore resumed its upward course. The abbey of Glastonbury was restored to him despite his episcopal responsibilities. Moreover before the year was out he had also been installed in the archiepiscopal see at Canterbury in the place of Eadwig's nominee, Byrhthelm, who returned to his previous see of Wells.[69]

Thus Dunstan had reached the apogee of his career. By any reckoning in acquiring the sees of Worcester, London and Canterbury in addition to the abbey of Glastonbury, he had, momentarily at least, proved to be one of the most remarkable pluralists of the tenth century. Canon law prohibited not only the holding of more than one see, but also the translation of a bishop from one see to another. Such rules seem to have bothered neither Edgar nor Dunstan, nor indeed B., his hagiographer. King and archbishop were apparently determined to use the system that they found for the benefit of the revival of monasticism; they were not in any way anticipating the wider Gregorian movement of the reform of the whole church. Moreover unless Byrhthelm had had the political and financial resources to resist his ejection from Canterbury, Pope John XII was unlikely to raise objection. Dunstan followed the example of his tenth-century predecessors at Canterbury by travelling to Rome to receive the pallium in person from the pope, a practice that seems to have developed in England in order to get retrospective approval for the translation of a consecrated English bishop from his original see to the archiepiscopate. Dunstan's is the only English tenth-century pallium-privilege to survive, because it was copied as the opening text in his pontifical, the so-called 'Sherborne Pontifical'.[70] That may indicate that Dunstan had himself been particularly concerned to record the authority for his metropolitan rank. It is scarcely likely that Pope John XII from his papal glasshouse would have enquired rigorously into the circumstances of Dunstan's elevation. The filling of the sees of Worcester and London through the election of Oswald and Ælfstan in 961, within a year of Dunstan's return from Rome, should therefore be attributed to Edgar and Dunstan, not to papal pressure. So far as his tenure of these bishoprics was concerned, Dunstan's pluralism was therefore a temporary expedient until men of whom he approved could be appointed.

Glastonbury, however, the house where he had himself single-

---

[69] I have set out full details of the appointment of Dunstan to Canterbury and the ousting of Byrhthelm in my *Early History*, pp. 238–40, 243–4.

[70] H. Zimmermann, *Papstregesten 900–1024* (Vienna, 1969), no. 284; *Councils & Synods*, i, ed. Whitelock, Brett and Brooke, pt i, pp. 88–92, no. 25. For the pontifical, see J. Rosenthal, 'The Pontifical of St Dunstan', in Ramsay et al., eds, *St Dunstan*, pp. 143–64.

handedly revived the regular life, was probably a different matter. B. writes of Dunstan's recovery of his office and then of his premonitions ('visions') of the deaths of Glastonbury monks and of his ordering the construction of the church of St John the Baptist there. Such stories may suggest that Dunstan continued to rule the monastery while he was archbishop; certainly B. mentions no abbot of Glastonbury. Moreover Edgar's charters granting the monastery estates in Somerset in 966, 968 and 973 are drafted in such a way that their texts do not refer to any abbot; unfortunately the Glastonbury cartularies omit all the witnesses of these charters after Archbishop Dunstan, so we cannot be certain that the abbots had not appeared lower in the original lists. Glastonbury tradition, indeed, claimed an Abbot Ælfric as successor to Dunstan, but the only abbot of that name witnessing charters of the period seems to have been the abbot of St Augustine's, Canterbury. Not until the attestations of Sigegar in 974 and 975 do we have clear evidence of an abbot at Glastonbury.[71] It seems likely, therefore, that Dunstan retained Glastonbury in his own control for some years after his elevation to the metropolitan see. That may also have been his practice at Westminster, whose refoundation was achieved while Dunstan was administering the see of London (958–61). Certainly there is no trace of Abbot Wulfsige until 966; before then Dunstan seems to be looking after the territorial interests of the house. Edgar's charter granting the site for the reformed abbey in 959 or 960 only survives in mutilated, though contemporary form.[72] It is significant, however, that it was enacted at Glastonbury and that the house's liberty is granted to Archbishop Dunstan, not to Abbot Wulfsige. It would seem that Archbishop Dunstan was more concerned to retain control of his monasteries than of his bishoprics.

How, then, may we assess St Dunstan's career? In the eyes of his hagiographer this holy man had risen to the highest position in the English church is part through the help of his noble and ecclesiastical kinsmen, but above all through the protective hand of God which

---

[71] For Dunstan's Glastonbury visions, see Stubbs, *Memorials*, pp. 46–7. Edgar's charters to Glastonbury are BCS 1188, 1214 and 1294 (S 743, 764 and 791). For the problems of identifying the tenth-century abbots of Glastonbury, see J.A. Robinson, *Somerset Historical Essays* (London, 1921), pp. 1–15, and D. Knowles, C.N.L. Brooke and V. London, *The Heads of Religious Houses, 940–1216* (Cambridge, 1972), p. 50.

[72] BCS 1048 (S 670) which survives on a contemporary single sheet (Westminster Abbey Muniments, no. V; *O.S.Facs*, II, Westminster no. 4) but unfortunately with the final figure of the date illegible and with the witnesses cut off in an apparent attempt to make it appear that the charter had once borne a seal. Archbishop Dunstan's receipt of an estate at Cholden, Surrey (BCS 1198; S 753) and his participation in the litigation over properties at Sunbury and Send (A.J. Robertson, *Anglo-Saxon Charters* (1st edn, Cambridge, 1939), no. 44; S 1447) may have been intended from the start to benefit Westminster.

supported him whenever his devotion to God's work had brought him into conflict with secular powers and secular values. From the evidence available to us and within the explanatory terms acceptable to modern historians, we may prefer to question just how well connected Dunstan was, and in consequence to emphasize how his unusual devotion to a celibate and scholarly way of life and a regular religious observance marked him out as a holy man, whom the newly rich kings and nobles of the recently extended English state could well afford to support. His values were not those of secular courts; they appealed to wealthy widows and to those rulers who were more sensitive to spiritual needs or who were nearing the end of their lives, precisely because of their distinctiveness. Though the influence of his brother, Wulfric, at court and of other friends and patrons was doubtless crucial at critical moments, Dunstan may be seen as the man who gave expression to the conscience of his age. The unequalled landed wealth of the monastery at Glastonbury in late Anglo-Saxon England and the dominant role in the English church of the late tenth century played by monks trained by Dunstan at Glastonbury are an effective measure of the impact that he made.[73] His example helped to inspire a massive transfer of landed resources from the secular aristocracy to a religious aristocracy; it made possible a revival of scholarly, religious, pastoral and cultural standards in late-tenth-century England that gave a distinctively monastic character to the English church and hierarchy. Some of the results of that transformation are with us still; they justify the attempt to pierce the obscurities of the sources for Dunstan's life, even across the chasm of a thousand years.

[73] For the Glastonbury estates, see M.D. Costen, 'Dunstan, Glastonbury and the Economy of Somerset in the Tenth Century' in Ramsay et al., eds, *St Dunstan*, pp. 25–44, and S.C. Morland, 'The Glastonbury Manors and their Saxon Charters', *Proceedings of the Somerset Archaeological & Natural History Society*, 130 (1986), pp. 61–105. For the role of Glastonbury-trained monks, see F. Barlow, *The English Church, 1000–1066* (2nd edn, London, 1979), passim.

9

Anglo-Saxon Charters: Recent Work

1973 is an auspicious year for the study of the charters of the pre-Conquest period. At the time of writing,[1] the publication of Professor A. Campbell's *Anglo-Saxon Charters I, The Charters of Rochester* is imminent. This is the first volume in a series in which the entire corpus of pre-Conquest charters is to be edited with full critical apparatus, with detailed analysis of their diplomatic, palaeographical, topographical and linguistic features and with extensive glossaries and indices. Professor Campbell's volume is part of a collaborative enterprise organized by a committee of The British Academy and The Royal Historical Society. When the series is complete, historians will no longer need to reiterate W.H. Stevenson's famous dictum, 'It cannot be said that the Old English charters have yet been edited.'[2] One significant feature of the scheme deserves to be noted here; each volume will cover the charters of an archive that was in existence towards the end of the Old English period. Thus there will be one volume for Rochester, another for Christ Church, Canterbury, another for Exeter, another for Burton Abbey, and so on. Small archives will be grouped together with others from the same region or diocese to form suitable volumes. In this way the organization of the edition will itself reveal the local character of Anglo-Saxon charters which is no marked throughout their history. It will also bring to light the work of forgers for individual churches developing their claims to particular lands and rights by means of charters of apparently widely differing dates.

Any collaborative enterprise of this type takes many years to complete. It cannot be overemphasized that the full value of the edition will be realized only when the series is all in print. Here, then, is the task for this generation of pre-Conquest historians. Here is the ideal training for the best of our research students. When one considers the contribution made to early medieval studies on the Continent by historians trained by editing volumes of diplomata for the Monumenta Germaniae Historica, or for the Chartes et Diplomes series of the Académie des

---

[1] This review covers the twenty years up to the end of August 1973.
[2] *The Crawford Collection of Early Charters and Documents*, ed. A.S. Napier and W.H. Stevenson (Oxford, 1895), p. viii.

Inscriptions et Belles Lettres, the opportunities and prospects which the new series presents are clear. Few research subjects are so well defined, or so educative in the different disciplines that they involve, or so exciting in the discoveries that await the painstaking scholar, than the title-deeds of a single major beneficiary. The completion of the new edition will depend upon the willingness of today's scholars to take their part in the work, and to train and direct their research students to it.

In one sense, therefore, the last two decades may be seen as an inter-regnum in charter studies – a lull between the publication in 1952 of the late Miss F.E. Harmer's *Anglo-Saxon Writs*[3] and the start of the new edition of the entire corpus of pre-Conquest charters. But they have also been years in which much fundamental work has been done, and in which major differences in approach and interpretation have become apparent. It is not surprising that the pre-Conquest charters should have become the subject of controversies. The Anglo-Saxon royal diplomas are unique in Europe in bearing no outward signs of valida-tion, neither any seal, nor autograph subscriptions, nor autograph crosses, nor even the name of the scribe. Their form is not that of a public act issued from a 'public' or royal chancery, but of a private deed of a particularly primitive and peculiarly religious form. Their authen-ticity was purely religious and ecclesiastical – hence the pictorial and verbal invocations to God, and the pious preambles and anathemas, even in grants to laymen; hence too the use in the earliest charters of uncial and majuscule scripts that were normally reserved for sacred books, and the association of charters with gospel-books and with ceremonies at the altar of an important church. Such charters were the products of a large number of ecclesiastical scriptoria whose diplomatic needs to be studied separately. In the absence of a comprehensive and critical edition, the difficulty of establishing the authenticity of these texts, especially when the majority only survive in late and often corrupt copies, will be evident.

The novice may best be introduced to charter problems by means of Professor Whitelock's introduction to the 'Charters and Laws' and her translations and comments upon selected documents.[4] Sir Frank Stenton's more discursive survey of the Latin diplomas[5] demonstrates with *élan* how a combination of rigorous but wide-ranging criticism and a sympathetic and informed judgement can wring important historical evidence from the most unpromising materials. In addition to these general introductions there are now available a number of basic manuals, which help to clear the path of the scholar or of the layman,

---

[3] *Anglo-Saxon Writs*, ed. F.E. Harmer (Manchester, 1952).
[4] *EHD* (1st edn), pp. 337–55 and 440–556.
[5] F.M. Stenton, *The Latin Charters of the Anglo-Saxon Period* (Oxford, 1955).

who is interested in a particular charter or in those of a particular period or region. Professor Sawyer's *Anglo-Saxon Charters: An Annotated List and Bibliography*[6] is an invaluable work of reference. Every extant charter is listed (in addition to many 'lost charters'), and for each charter Professor Sawyer has provided a brief description of its content, a list of the surviving manuscripts (up to 1800), an estimate of the date of their scripts, references to all printed editions, translations and facsimiles, and a bibliography of all significant discussions of the charter, together with a brief indication of the gist of the views of most of the cited authors. The value of this handbook has been immeasurably increased by the inclusion of the judgements of N.R. Ker and T.A.M. Bishop on the date of the script of all 'apparent originals' and of Professor Whitelock on the authenticity of many of the most difficult documents. Properly used as a guide to the original sources and to the secondary literature, and not as an alternative to them, the *Bibliography* saves many hours of misguided searching in libraries and is a constant stimulus to effective research. It is to be hoped that scholars will respond to the editor's plea to send him corrections and additions, and that it will be possible to keep this manual up to date at regular intervals.

The second major enterprise of the last two decades and one that is still in progress has been the work of Professor Finberg and of his pupil, Dr Hart, in providing local historians with handlists, county by county, of all the pre-Conquest charters concerned with lands or rights therein, both charters that are extant and those that are known to have once existed. Beginning in 1953 with Devon and Cornwall, Professor Finberg has covered in turn the counties of the West Midlands and of Wessex; Dr Hart has been responsible for Essex and the counties of eastern England;[7] a volume for northern England and the north Midlands is promised, and it is to be hoped that a scholar will be found to take on the large tasks of calendaring the charters of the south-eastern counties. The great value of these lists lies in the amount of accurate and new topographical work they incorporate, and in the way they enable historians of the local society and economy to see at a glance how many of the estates in the pre-Conquest charters of their area have been located, and how much work in this field remains to be done. The opportunity has also been taken in each county list to publish usable texts of any charters that have hitherto been unprinted – something for which all pre-Conquest historians are in their debt. A

[6] Ed. P.H. Sawyer, (London, 1968).
[7] H.P.R. Finberg, *The Early Charters of Devon and Cornwall* (Leicester, 1953, 2nd edn 1963); Finberg, *The Early Charters of the West Midlands* (Leicester, 1961); Finberg, *The Early Charters of Wessex* (Leicester, 1964); C.R. Hart, *The Early Charters of Essex* (Leicester, 1957, 2nd edn 1971); and Hart, *The Early Charters of Eastern England* (Leicester, 1966).

controversial feature of the later volumes in the scheme has been the grading of the charters by a system of stars to indicate degrees of authenticity. Professor Finberg's belief that earlier scholars have been unduly critical and cautious in discussing the authenticity of the bulk of the pre-Conquest charters has led him to adopt a 'deliberately conservative and lenient standard of criticism'.[8] A glance at Professor Sawyer's *Bibliography* soon shows how frequently the handlists mark documents as authentic, or as in large part authentic, which have hitherto been considered spurious. It is a moot point, of course, whether the paralysis of research that may result from the over-critical condemnation of difficult charters is worse than the wasted effort and misguided conclusions that result from the acceptance as genuine of spurious and interpolated texts. Local historians would perhaps be better served if the remaining volumes in the series included references to Professor Sawyer's *Bibliography* and a brief indication of any considerations which have led the compiler to a more 'lenient' view of an individual charter.

One indispensable guide remains to be written, namely a manual of Anglo-Saxon diplomatic. Diplomatic has for so long been a neglected branch of English historical scholarship that it is not surprising that we lack an English Tessier, Dölger or Bresslau.[9] Until the charters have been re-edited, the scholar who attempted any such survey would indeed be sticking his neck out. But the need for this to be done is all the more acute since scholars of repute have questioned the methods of diplomatic and their applicability to pre-Conquest documents.[10] This is the more surprising since two model studies of all the 'apparent originals' of a limited period and category have shown what can be achieved even in well worked fields. T.A.M. Bishop and P. Chaplais, in their facsimile edition of all the royal writs of the eleventh century that survive on single sheets of parchment, built upon the foundations laid by Miss Harmer.[11] They emphasized that however much the pre-Conquest writs may take the form of administrative messages, they are in practice notifications of royal grants, which conferred title to rights and properties. Not only were writs therefore preserved in the beneficiary's archives along with his other title-deeds

[8] Finberg, *Wessex*, p. 20. Cf. Finberg, *West Midlands*, p. 14.

[9] G. Tessier, *Diplomatique Royale Française* (Paris, 1962); F. Dölger, *Byzantinische Urkundenlehre* (Munich, 1968); and H. Bresslau, *Handbuch der Urkundenlehre für Deutschland und Italien*, 3 vols, 2nd edn (Leipzig, 1912–31).

[10] F. Barlow, *The English Church 1000–1066* (London, 1963), p. 127, n. 2, and Finberg, *Wessex*, p. 199, and 'Fact and Fiction from Crediton', *West Country Historical Studies* (Newton Abbot, 1969), pp. 65–9.

[11] *Facsimiles of English Royal Writes to AD 1100*, ed. T.A.M. Bishop and P. Chaplais (Oxford, 1957).

but on occasion they were also written by a scribe of the beneficiary.[12] The assumption that Anglo-Saxon royal writs were *in toto* the products of a royal 'chancery' was thus shown to be false. Mr Bishop and Dr Chaplais also established that Edward the Confessor had but one royal seal (that hitherto known as his second seal), and that the other seals purporting to be his, and the documents to which they are attached, are forgeries. The abbey of Westminster was revealed as a prolific centre of forged seals and forged writs in the middle years of the twelfth century.[13]

The second work to show the value of meticulous attention to the extant originals consists of two volumes in the series Chartae Latinae Antiquiores in which Dr A. Bruckner has re-edited with facsimiles all the extant Anglo-Saxon charters whose script may be assigned to a date before 800.[14] In addition to providing an exact text of these charters with full critical apparatus, Dr Bruckner has surveyed the diplomatic of the extant originals in the introduction to volume 4. Following the practice of this series, this introduction carries no annotation, and scholars should therefore study the somewhat fuller version that Dr Bruckner has published with copious footnotes in the *Archivalische Zeitschrift*.[15] Particularly valuable is his attention to the evidence for the procedures by which the diplomas were produced and delivered, and his demonstration of how frequently the authenticity of 'apparent originals' can be placed beyond reasonable doubt by detecting and explaining changes of script or of ink, confirmatory endorsements, and traces of preliminary drafts. Though we may doubt Dr Bruckner's belief that some of the attestations in certain diplomas have autograph crosses, and may also regret the omission from the facsimiles of the endorsements that are later than 800, his work breaks new ground and serves as a reproach to the neglect of most British scholars. Only the sumptuous edition of the recently discovered will of Æthelgifu by Professor Whitelock, Dr Ker and Lord Rennell shows in a comparable way how much can be learnt when original documents are edited with full studies of their internal and external characteristics.[16]

The other major contribution to Anglo-Saxon diplomatic has been the revolutionary series of articles by Dr P. Chaplais, who may be said

[12] Ibid., pp. xii–xiii and plates xviii and xxiiib.

[13] Ibid., pp. xx–xxiii.

[14] *Chartae Latinae Antiquiores*, ed. A. Bruckner and R. Marichal iii and iv (Olten, 1963 and 1967).

[15] A. Bruckner, 'Zur Diplomatik de älteren angelsächsischen Urkunden', *Archivalische Zeitschrift* 61 (1965), pp. 11–45.

[16] *The Will of Æthelgifu*, trans. and examined by Dorothy Whitelock, with Neil Ker and Lord Rennell, for the Roxburghe Club (Oxford, 1968).

to have inherited the mantle of W.H. Stevenson.[17] Fundamental to all his work is the plea which he made in 1965 for an exact and rigorous terminology. A charter in which any attempt at deception can be detected, is called a 'forgery'. 'Original' is used only to refer to a charter in contemporary script on a single sheet of parchment and displaying no suspicious features. 'Copy' refers to a charter which also has no suspicious features, but which is not in a contemporary hand. Charters on single sheets, but which through insufficient palaeographical and diplomatic analysis cannot yet be placed in one of these categories, are termed 'apparent originals'.[18] The great merit of this classification is that it concentrates attention on the period and context in which the extant charters were produced rather than on their purported date. It also helps to discourage what in the absence of a critical edition must be regarded as the besetting sin of Anglo-Saxon historians, namely their use of those parts of spurious charters that fit their theories on the grounds that the anachronistic features of the document are 'later inter-polations' in a charter that is basically genuine.

Dr Chaplais's conclusions on how the authenticity of the earliest surviving diplomas can be established are notably similar to those reached at the same time by Dr Bruckner.[19] None the less it is startling to discover that there are still major discoveries to be made about such famous and well studied charters as King Hlothar's grant of 679 to the abbey of Reculver[20] (where Dr Chaplais shows that the witnesses were added by a different but contemporary scribe) or the grant of Œthelræd to Æthelburh, abbess of Barking, in March 687(?).[21] In this charter not only the list of witnesses but also the boundary clause was written by a later scribe, who alone used the late spellings *Œdel-* and *Hædde* whose presence in this charter once caused philologists such trouble. Both charters can now be accepted as originals – Hlothar's grant in its entirety, Œthelræd's as far as the unfinished corroboration clause 'Et ut firma et inconcussum sit donum'. The bounds and witnesses of Œthelræd's charter were added about a century later; they were

[17] P. Chaplais, 'The Origin and Authenticity of the Royal Anglo-Saxon Diploma', *Journal of the Society of Archivists* 3 (1965–9), pp. 48–61; 'The Authenticity of the Royal Anglo-Saxon Diplomas of Exeter', *Bulletin of the Institute of Historical Research*, 39 (1966), pp. 1–34; 'The Anglo-Saxon Chancery: from the Diploma to the Writ', *Journal of the Society of Archivists*, 3 (1965–9), pp. 160–76; 'Some Early Anglo-Saxon Diplomas on Single Sheets: Originals or Copies?', ibid., pp. 315–36; and 'Who Introduced Charters into England? The Case for Augustine', ibid., pp 526–42.

[18] Chaplais, 'Diplomas of Exeter', p. 3.

[19] Chaplais, 'Some Early Diplomas', passim.

[20] BL Cotton Augustus ii. 2; *Facsimiles of Ancient Charters in the British Museum*, ed. E.A. Bond (London, 1873–8) I, I, and BCS 45 (S 8).

[21] Augustus ii. 29; *BMFacs* I, 2 and BCS 81 (S 1171).

probably copied from a scribal memorandum on a separate piece of parchment stitched to the original. Dr Chaplais has drawn attention to the traces of stitching that can still be detected along the bottom edge of the charter.

Dr Chaplais's examination of the diplomatic of the earliest originals has led him to re-open the question of the date when 'landbooks' or charters were first introduced to England. He argues the case for Augustine as the originator, even though (like earlier scholars) he can find neither originals nor copies of authentic charters before the 670s.[22] The obvious objection to Dr Chaplais's theory – namely that it is inconceivable that churches would all be so negligent of their earliest deeds as to fail to copy them before they disintegrated through age and damp – is less powerful when one considers how few English churches have an uninterrupted history from before the age of Archbishop Theodore.[23] Consequently his case relies on the accumulation of indirect evidence. It might, however, have been strengthened had he discussed the purported grant of King Æthelberht to the church of Rochester in the year 604. W. Levison drew attention to the formulae drawn from Italian private deeds in this charter, though he found the unique address to the king's son, Eadbald, anomalous.[24] But the address to Eadbald may be a point in its favour rather than the reverse; we know too little of Kentish politics to reject the possibility that Eadbald had some authority in west Kent during his father's lifetime.[25] If the boundaries in English indicate that the charter as it stands is a forgery, their brevity suggests that it was an early one. And if forged, it is strange indeed that the forger resisted the temptation to record the presence of Augustine himself and to date the charter by the era of the incarnation. Whatever may be made of this Rochester charter, Dr Chaplais has an important point when he stresses that the form of Old English diplomas implies a very primitive secretarial organization, such as we might expect amongst the earliest missionaries. The absence of any means of validation and also the variety of formulae

---

[22] Chaplais, 'Origin and Authenticity', pp. 49–52, and 'Augustine', *passim*.

[23] The only churches to be considered are Canterbury, Rochester, London and Winchester and the monasteries of St Augustine's and Lyminge. The new edition, when it covers these churches, should show whether there are local archival reasons why authentic charters of the early seventh century have not been preserved in these houses.

[24] BCS 3; W. Levison, *England and the Continent in the Eighth Century* (Oxford, 1946), pp. 223–5. As Levison points out, the address to Eadbald is misleadingly printed by Birch. It consists simply of 'Ego Æthelberhtus rex filio meo Eadbaldo'. The following words belong to the proem.

[25] Compare the otherwise unknown King Æthelwald (*adulwaldi*) who was converted by Bishop Justus, and was probably a subordinate king in (west) Kent during the reign of Eadbald. See P. Hunter Blair, 'The Letters of Pope Boniface V and the Mission of Paulinus to Northumbria', in P. Clemoes and K. Hughes, eds (Cambridge, 1971), pp. 7–8.

amongst the earliest originals would be surprising if the diploma had been recently introduced by Archbishop Theodore, who is known to have had at least one notary, the aptly named Titillus, in his *familia*.[26]

Religious in form, the pre-Conquest charter was also, Dr Chaplais argues, ecclesiastical in production. He stresses that Anglo-Saxon diplomas were always written in monastic or episcopal scriptoria, and frequently drafted by high-ranking ecclesiastics. There were, of course, royal writers and king's priests, who could write letters for the king when required. But he challenges the view that any pre-Conquest English king ever had a royal 'chancery' – that is, a permanent central royal secretariat staffed by scribes who specialized in royal business. The demonstration that ninth-century royal diplomas were for the most part produced in episcopal scriptoria is welcome, and is likely to be reinforced when the new edition of the charters gets under way.[27] But it is for the tenth and eleventh centuries that Dr Chaplais's views are most revolutionary. He accepts the evidence accumulated by R. Drögereit that for about a generation from 931 many royal diplomas, even though they concern estates in widely separated parts of the kingdom, were produced in a single scriptorium. But he is unwilling to interpret this as a royal chancery, an organ of government reflecting the growing power of the West Saxon dynasty. Instead he has drawn attention to Dr Ker's demonstration that one of the so-called 'royal' scribes who wrote such 'chancery' diplomas was the Winchester writer responsible for the 951 annal in the Parker Chronicle (Cambridge, Corpus Christi College 173), and that the script of five of the other seven 'royal' scribes (Chaplais nos 2, 3, 5, 7 and 8) may together with the hand of the annals from 925 to 955 in the Parker Chronicle be regarded as the typical script of the Winchester scriptorium.[28] The concentration of charter-writing in the episcopal *familia* at Winchester was doubtless an administrative convenience, not least because there were so few other centres of literacy in the kingdom and because the bishop of Winchester would normally be in attendance at important meetings of the witan with some of his *familia*. But Winchester was never the only scriptorium which produced charters for the English kings. Indeed the first 'chancery'

---

[26] Titillus wrote the acts of the Synod of Hertford, preserved by Bede (*Historia ecclesiastica*, iv. 5); *Bede's Ecclesiastical History of the English People*, ed. B. Colgrave and R.A.B. Mynors (Oxford, 1969), p. 352.

[27] Chaplais, 'Origin and Authenticity', pp. 58–9. Evidence that the writing of ninth-century royal diplomas concerning lands in Kent was organized on a strictly diocesan basis was presented in my unpublished Oxford D.Phil. thesis, 'The Pre-Conquest Charters of Christ Church, Canterbury' (1969). See N.P. Brooks, *The Early History of the Church of Canterbury* (Leicester, 1984), pp. 167–74, 327–30 and below, pp. 207–8.

[28] Chaplais, 'Origin and Authenticity', pp. 59–61, and N.R. Ker, *Catalogue of Manuscripts Containing Anglo-Saxon* (Oxford, 1957), p. lix.

scribe who wrote originals of the years 931 and 934 used a very different script from the Winchester type, and his spelling of personal names and of the Old English bounds of the estates shows that he was not a West Saxon.[29] A group of charters concerning Mercian and East Anglian estates and ranging in date from 940 to 956, which are drafted in rhythmical and alliterative prose and in formulae quite distinct from those of the Winchester scriptorium, must be regarded as the products of a Midland writing-office.[30] Moreover Dr Chaplais has shown how, when the tenth-century reformation of monastic life got under way in England, royal diplomas began once more to be written in monasteries – at Glastonbury in the 950s and at Abingdon in the 960s.[31] No scholar has succeeded in proving the existence of a centralized chancery in the later decades of the tenth century, and it is to be expected that the volumes of the new edition will establish the activities of many local monastic and episcopal scriptoria in the last century of Anglo-Saxon England.

Dr Chaplais has also provided a new and far more satisfying inter-pretation of the development of the royal writ. Like Professor Barraclough, he is not willing to conclude that the royal writ was already in use under King Alfred from Alfred's reference to a man who receives his lord's 'ærendgewrit and hys insegel', and from his use in the preface to the *Pastoral Care* of an opening protocol that is close to the address and greeting of the writs of the eleventh century.[32] The 'lord's letter and his seal' may refer to a letter sealed 'close', but Dr Chaplais argues that it more probably means a letter and a loose seal carried by the bearer as a sign of credence. He does not deny that the formulae of the royal writs may be much older than the eleventh century, but explains their appearance in set form already in the earliest writs of certain authenticity – those of King Cnut for Christ Church,

---

[29] BCS 677 and 702; *British Museum Facsimiles* 111, 3 and 5. The dialect forms are more common in BCS 702 than in BCS 677, so it is possible that they are not a guide to the scribe's origin, but have been copied into BCS 702 from a scribal memorandum listing the bounds and the witnesses, which had been written in the region of the estate, i.e. in Sussex or Kent.

[30] BCS 746, 751, 771, 772, 773, 815, 876, 882, 883, 884, 890, 893, 909, 911, 937 and 1346.

[31] Chaplais, 'Anglo-Saxon Chancery', pp. 163–5.

[32] Ibid., pp. 166–76; Harmer (*Writs*, pp. 10–13) argued for writs in Alfred's time. G. Barraclough ('The Anglo-Saxon Writ', *History*, new series 39 (1954), pp. 193–215) understood *insegel* to mean a signet-ring carried as a sign of credence, and stressed that the use of comparable epistolary protocols does not prove that the royal writ as we know it later was already being used for the same purposes in Alfred's reign. The reference to 'your lord's *ærendgewrit* and his *insegel*' is from *King Alfred's Old English Version of St Augustine's Soliloquies*, ed. H.L. Haragrove, Yale Studies in English 12 (New Haven, CT, 1902), 23.

Canterbury – as the result of their long use for purely oral messages. He argues that the motive for recording the king's message to the courts in writing was not the king's desire for efficient government, but the beneficiaries' wish for a permanent record of their acquisitions. Thus the earliest authentic writs were written on spare leaves of gospel-books at Christ Church by contemporary Canterbury scribes.[33] There is no reason to suppose that these gospel entries are copies of sealed originals. They are rather the only record of notifications of the king's grants made orally in the shire court. Their authenticity was guaranteed by their presence in a gospel-book on the altar at Christ Church. Thus it is that none of the 'writs' that were entered into gospels have been preserved as sealed 'originals', and conversely the one Christ Church writ which has been preserved on a single sheet of parchment with the king's seal,[34] was not copied into any extant gospel-book. It did not need any authentication beyond the royal seal.

With this picture of the writ deriving its formulaic phraseology from generations of oral messages to the folk-courts, but being recorded in writing only with beneficiaries insisted upon a more permanent testimony than the memory of those present in the court, the last evidence for a royal 'chancery' in the Anglo-Saxon period disappears. Doubtless one of the members of the king's household had custody of the royal seal, which from Edward the Confessor's reign, and perhaps already from Cnut's[35] was being used to authenticate writs. Equally some of the king's priests may on occasion have been asked to write royal writs, though it is not until the very end of William I's reign that the extant originals provide clear evidence for a royal scribe. Until that time *Empfängerausstellung* seems to have been the general rule.[36] As Professor Barraclough observed, the development of the royal chancery from the

---

[33] Harmer, *Writs*, nos 26, 27, 28, 29, 30 and 35.

[34] British Museum, Campbell Charter xxi.5; Harmer, *Writs*, no. 33.

[35] Harmer (*Writs*, pp. 94–101) follows Bresslau in suggesting that the double-sided English royal seal originated with Cnut, who had two kingdoms, and that its design was modelled on the (one-sided) seal of Emperor Conrad II, whose coronation in 1027 Cnut attended. Dr Chaplais ('Anglo-Saxon Chancery', p. 175) draws attention to the numismatic evidence that Edward's seal may have been the work of the German engraver, Theodoric, who, it is suggested, made the dies for the coins of the later part of Edward the Confessor's reign. See R.H.M. Dolley and F. Elmore Jones, 'A New Suggestion Concerning the So-Called Martlets in the Arms of St Edward', in R.H.M. Dolley, ed., *Anglo-Saxon Coins: Studies presented to F.M. Stenton* (London, 1961), pp. 215 and 220. The two positions are not incompatible.

[36] Bishop and Chaplais, *Facsimiles*, pp. xii–xiii, xvi–xix and plates ix and xxva. Their tentative suggestion that the similar hands of BL, Cotton Augustus ii. 80 and Campbell Charter xxi. 5 (plates i and v) might represent 'the style of the royal chancery script' under Edward the Confessor is doubted by Dr Chaplais in his more recent article, 'Anglo-Saxon Chancery', p. 175.

royal chapel was a very slow one, scarcely complete before the thirteenth century.[37] Though some of the seeds of this development may be discerned in the reign of Edward the Confessor, we must beware of exaggerating the Anglo-Saxon administrative and bureaucratic capacity.

No other scholar has ranged so widely over the entire field of pre-Conquest charters as Dr Chaplais, and it is to be hoped that he will be persuaded to give us the manual of Anglo-Saxon diplomatic that he alone of present-day scholars is qualified to write. His judgements may on occasion be too severe. For example it is difficult to accept that the two papal privileges to King Cenwulf of Mercia, whose corruptions Levison corrected, are the work of a Winchcombe forger who somehow had access both to a genuine privilege of Pope Paschal I and to a copy of the papal formula-book, the *Liber Diurnus*; for a forgery which did not even name the estates which the monastery of Winchcombe wished to claim would not only be incompetent but also motiveless.[38] But to err on the side if rigour is a good fault if pre-Conquest diplomatic is to achieve a sure foundation.

The work of other scholars has been limited to particular aspects of the charters, to individual texts, or to groups or charters. Often important work has been incidental to research on much wider subjects. Thus the interests of German scholars in the concepts of kingship and of imperial rule has led to a series of studies of the regnal styles in English charters. R. Drögereit's attempt to show that the use of imperial styles by Anglo-Saxon kings was a chimera, on the grounds that styles using *imperator* and *imperialis* occurred only in spurious charters, was received with enthusiastic masochism in England.[39] But his analysis of the charters – wilful in its neglect and distortion of palaeographical evidence, in casting doubt by false associations, and in its failure to suggest any motive or occasion for the forgery of so many charters (most of them grants to laymen) from almost a dozen different archives – has been justly criticized by Mr E. John and by Dr E. Stengel.[40] Of particular

[37] Barraclough, 'Anglo-Saxon Writ', pp. 213–15.

[38] BCS 337 and 363; Chaplais, 'Some Early Diplomas', pp. 335–6. Compare Levison's judgement in *England and the Continent*, pp. 255–8.

[39] R. Drögereit, 'Kaiseridee und Kaisertitel bei den Angelsachsen', *Zeitschrift der Savigny-Stiftung für Rechtsgeschichte*, Germ. Abt. 69 (1952), pp. 24–73. Drögereit's arguments on the 'imperial' charters of the tenth century were summarized by H.R. Loyn, 'The Imperial Style of the Tenth-Century Anglo-Saxon Kings', *History*, new series 40 (1955), pp. 111–15.

[40] E. John, *Land Tenure in England* (Leicester, 1958), pp. 95–8; 'An Alleged Worcester Charter of the Reign of Edgar', *Bulletin of the John Rylands Library* 41 (1958), pp. 60–3; and *Orbis Britanniae* (Leicester, 1966), pp. 52–6; and E.E. Stengel, 'Imperator und Imperium bei den Angelsachsen', *Deutsches Archiv für Erforschung des Mittelalters* 16 (1960), pp. 15–72, reprinted in E.E. Stengel, *Zum Kaisergedanken im Mittelalter* (Cologne, 1965), pp. 289–342.

interest in view of Alcuin's rôle in the creation of Charlemagne's empire is Dr Stengel's demonstration of the links between the title 'divina largiente rector et imperator Merciorum regni' in a charter of King Cenwulf of 798 and the letters of Alcuin of the later 790s.[41] There will still remain doubt, however, about the significance of imperial titles in English charters. Are we really to understand them as proof of a non-Roman concept of empire among the Anglo-Saxon (let alone the Celtic) peoples of Britain? Do they imply rule over other kingdoms, or even a claim to universal rule within the *orbis Britanniae*? Or are they simply attempts to ring the changes among the various Latin words for royal lordship available to the drafters of charters? Hanna Vollrath-Reichelt has recently taught us to use the evidence for overlordship with care and precision.[42] Of particular note is her emphasis on the fact that after 785 King Offa ruled in Kent, not as overlord, but as king (of the Mercians); but her denial that Offa had ever claimed to control (or to confirm) the booking of land in Kent in the 760s and 770s, when there were still native kings on the Kentish throne, involves the rejection on quite inadequate grounds of the charters of 764 and 765 from the Rochester cartulary and is based upon an incomplete analysis of the evidence for Offa's quashing of the charters of King Egbert II of Kent.[43]

The land-law that lies behind the pre-Conquest charters, the nature and origin of 'bookland' and 'folkland', have again become subjects of controversy in recent years. Mr E. John has argued the relevance of Professor E. Levy's studies of Vulgar Roman law to a proper understanding of English bookright, and stressed that the creation of hereditary right and the power of alienation were the essence of the legal changes brought about in the 'booking' of an estate. But the deliberately 'disputatious' aim of his work, and the slipshod or too brief discussion of many of the key charters, antagonized his readers and did no service to his case.[44] His recent restatement of his view that folkland was land

---

[41] BCS 289; Stengel, 'Imperator', pp. 38–54 and 69–72. A better edition of this charter using ultra-violet photography is in Bruckner and Marichal, *Chartae* III (no. 191).

[42] H. Vollrath-Reichelt, *Königsgedanke und Königtum bei den Angelsachsen bis zur Mitte des 9 Jahrhunderts*, Kölner Historische Abhandlungen 19 (Cologne, 1971).

[43] Ibid., pp. 151–76. Miss Reichelt's rejection of BCS 195 and 196 is not based on any analysis of their diplomatic; neither the somewhat inflated style of BCS 195 nor the attestation of the otherwise unknown bishop, Badenoth, in BCS 196 constitutes grounds for suspicion. Her analysis of the 'Aldhun affair' involves a very forced interpretation of BCS 332 and she ignores the fact that Offa quashed not only Egbert's grants to Aldhun and to Christ Church (BCS 293) but also his grants to Rochester. Compare BCS 227 and 228 with BCS 257.

[44] John, *Land Tenure*. See the important reviews by D. Whitelock (*American Historical Review*, 66 (1960–1), pp. 1009–10, and further correspondence, ibid., 67 (1961–2), 582–4) and H.R. Loyn (*History*, new series 46 (1961), pp. 233–5).

which was held precariously and which reverted to the king at the death of the tenant is constructive, if regrettably brief, and a welcome challenge to pre-Conquest historians to re-examine their assumptions about early English society and land-law.[45] Another long-overdue contribution to this subject has been the attempt of Miss Vollrath-Reichelt to relate the evidence of the English charters to current German assumptions about the nature of early medieval lordship over land, and about the meaning of such terms as *folc* and freeman.[46] In accord with one school of thought she interprets folkland as *fiskalland*, that is land directly dependent upon the king in his capacity as leader of the *folc* and settled by *Königsfreien*, who owed services and dues to the king. And it is entirely typical of this school, with its delight in the paradoxes of unfree, and even semi-free, freedom, that she should argue, in the face of the evidence of numerous immunity clauses,[47] that the 'secular services' of the charters were not owed by all the people, the whole *gens*, but only by the king's (free) men on *fiskalland* (folkland). These works have demonstrated the need for a far more extended treatment of pre-Conquest land-law; it will need of course a deep knowledge of the English charters, but it will also have to take account of current continental scholarship on Germanic and Vulgar Roman law, and of the works of the adherents of the *Königsfreien* school and of their many Italian, French and German critics; it will need, too, to study the development of the Anglo-Saxon immunity, which so far as been systematically examined only in relation to the reservation of the three military burdens.[48]

Few aspects of charter studies have been advanced so much in the last twenty years as the study of the actual estates that are the subject of the grants.[49] Most Anglo-Saxon royal diplomas include a description of

---

[45] E. John, 'Folkland Reconsidered', *Orbis Britanniae*, pp. 64–127.

[46] Vollrath-Reichelt, *Königsgedanke*, pp. 65–8 and 192–225.

[47] The references from Anglo-Saxon diplomas were collected by W.H. Stevenson, 'Trinoda Necessitas', *English Historical Review*, 29 (1914), 689, n. 3. See also N. Brooks, 'The Development of Military Obligations in Eighth- and Ninth-Century England', in Clemoes and Hughes, eds, *England before the Conquest*, pp. 69–70 and 76–8; reprinted in Brooks, *Communities and Warfare, 700–1400* (London, 1999), pp. 32–47.

[48] E. John, 'The Imposition of Common Burdens on the Lands of the English Church', *Bulletin of the Institute of Historical Research*, 31 (1958), pp. 117–29, reprinted in *Land Tenure*, pp. 64–79, and Brooks, 'Development', pp. 69–84.

[49] Studies of the bounds of individual charters in the last twenty years are too numerous to be fully listed here. Amongst the more important are: T.R. Thomson, 'The Early Bounds of Purton and a Pagan Sanctuary', *Wiltshire Archaeological Magazine*, 55 (1954–5), pp. 353–63; 'The Bounds of Ellandune *c*. 956', ibid., 56 (19555–6), pp. 265–70; 'The Early Bounds of Wanborough and Little Hinton', ibid., 57 (1958–70), pp. 203–11; and (with R.E. Sandell) 'Saxon Land Charters of Wiltshire', ibid., 58 (1961–3), pp. 442–6; H.P.R. Finberg, 'The Treable Charter', *Devon and Cornwall*, pp. 20–31; 'The Hallow-Hawling Charter', *West Midlands*, pp. 184–96; 'Some Crediton Documents Re-examined', *Antiquaries Journal*, 48 (1968), pp. 59–86, reprinted with emendations as

the boundaries of the land granted, and careful topographical research can therefore reveal the extent and shape of a pre-Conquest estate, and hence can help to fill in our picture of the exploitation of the land and the development of settlement. Since the pioneering studies of Dr T.R. Thomson and of Professor Finberg, the principles of such topographical study and of its publication have gradually been clarified. Firstly, as Professor Finberg has justly emphasized, no Anglo-Saxon diploma has been correctly understood until the estate has been precisely located, its extent and character understood. His own works have repeatedly shown that the identifying of the boundaries of a charter may lead to a radically new understanding of the document's purpose.[50] Equally, however, the bounds of a charter cannot be studied in isolation from the diplomatic, the palaeography and the language of the charter. One of the more common forms of forgery of pre-Conquest charters was the addition of a lengthy set of boundaries to early charters, which originally had only the briefest indication of the neighbouring properties on north, south, east and west or had no boundary clause at all. It is hazardous to assume that a boundary clause, whose form and language are later than the purported date of the charter to which it belongs, none the less represents accurately an estate that was granted at the date borne by the charter. For on the rare occasions when both an original and a later version with modernized bounds survive the additions of the forger can be detected.[51] Two things are needed above all others by the student of Anglo-Saxon boundaries: the linguistic skill and knowledge to interpret them correctly, and a current knowledge of and access to the area, so that the difficulties of the bounds can be solved by repeated walking in various seasons and weathers. Work from maps, old and new, is an essential preliminary, but identifications based on map-work

'Fact and Fiction from Crediton', *West Country Studies*, pp. 29–69; and 'Two Acts of State', ibid., pp. 11–28; M. Gelling, 'The Boundaries of the Westminster Charters', *Trans. of the London and Middlesex Archaeological Society*, new series 11 (1954), pp. 101–4; C. Hart, 'Some Dorset Charter Boundaries', *Proceedings of the Dorset Natural History and Archaeological Society*, 86 (1964), pp. 158–63; and D.J. Bonney, 'Two Tenth-Century Charters Concerning Lands at Avon and Collingbourne', *Wiltshire Archaeological Magazine* 64 (1969), pp. 56–64.

[50] Finberg, 'Treable Charter', 'Hallow-Hawling Charter' and 'Some Crediton Documents'.

[51] As for example BCS 335 of the year 811, which survives in two versions: BL, Cotton Augustus ii. 10 of *saec. ix (1)* and BL, Stowe Charter 10 of *saec. x (2)*, which includes boundaries of two additional estates. An object lesson in the need to study the boundaries of charters in conjunction with the diplomatic, palaeographical and linguistic evidence (or with the collaboration of experts in these fields) is provided by the way in which Professor Finberg had had to retract the exciting conclusions that he first drew from the bounds of BCS 1331 and of the Treable charter of 976. Compare Finberg, *Devon and Cornwall*, pp. 20–31, with *West Country Studies*, pp. 44–61.

alone without field-work will always be incomplete and often mistaken. At the end of the day it is likely that there will still remain some points along a boundary that defy identification, where place-names have passed out of use or where the bounds themselves are trees that have long since died, or small ponds, swampy places, copses and the like, which have long since been drained or cut down and cleared away. It is therefore essential for the benefit of future workers in the field that accurate Ordnance Survey grid references are given for each bound that has been located, and that those that are positively identified should be distinguished from intermediate points whose location is dependent upon them. A willingness to admit the uncertain areas of an identification is vital. For the historian may reasonably doubt an identification which, for example, claims that the estate covers an area that was still assessed at the time of the Domesday Survey at a far larger number of hides than the assessment in the charter itself, more than two centuries earlier.[52] When an estate is eventually located therefore, it must make historical and geographical sense.

Pre-Conquest charters often contain essential information for solving the chronological problems of Anglo-Saxon history. Indeed they are often the only evidence for dating the pontificates of bishops and the reigns of kings. In recent years work on these problems has been resumed. Mary Anne O'Donovan has put all historians of the English church in the age before the monastic revival in her debt by setting out with exemplary clarity the evidence for the order of succession and the dating of the bishops of all the English sees of the southern province during the period from 850 to 950.[53] Kenneth Harrison has re-investigated the numerous

[52] Professor Finberg's identification of the bounds of the famous South Hams charter of 846 (BCS 451), by which King Æthelwulf booked twenty hides of land to himself, makes the estate cover an area which in 1086 was assessed at more than three times this number of hides. Yet there is evidence to suggest that the hidage assessment of Devon and of Cornwall was remarkably stable in the tenth and eleventh centuries, for the four Devon boroughs in the Burghal Hidage are given a garrison drawn from 1534 hides, which equals the combined assessment of Devon and Cornwall in Domesday Book. For the Burghal Hidage, see A.J. Robertson, *Anglo-Saxon Charters* (1st edn, Cambridge, 1939), p. 246. We can scarcely avoid the conclusion that men from Cornwall had to go to help defend and repair the boroughs in west Devon, and that the assessment of these shires remained unchanged over nearly two centuries. To maintain Professor Finberg's identification of the bounds of the South Hams charter, one would need to suppose that the assessment of this part of Devon was drastically increased between 846 and the early tenth century, when the Burghal Hidage was compiled. Evidence for such increases in assessment is entirely lacking.

[53] M.A. O'Donovan, 'An Interim Revision of Episcopal Dates for the Province of Canterbury, 850–950', *Anglo-Saxon England*, 1 (1972), pp. 23–44 and 2 (1973), pp. 91–113. See also Dorothy Whitelock, 'The Pre-Viking Age Church in East Anglia', *Anglo-Saxon England*, 1 (1972), pp. 1–22, esp. 19–22.

problems connected with the use of indictions and of the era of the incarnation. Of particular importance is his demonstration that use of the Year of Grace is not necessarily a cause for suspicion in charters earlier than Bede's *Ecclesiastical History*. Incarnational dating occurs in a small number of Mercian, Kentish and West Saxon charters associated with Bishop Wilfrid, all of which have features suggesting that despite some corruptions they may be copies of authentic texts.[54] Wilfrid, of course, had championed the Roman cause at the Synod of Whitby, when the Easter tables of Dionysius, based on the era of the incarnation, were adopted. Equally important is Mr Harrison's analysis of the dating clauses of the second half of the eighth century and of the ninth; he shows that the drafters of these charters began their incarnation year at Christmas, and that they seldom, if ever, made any allowance, when calculating the indiction, for the fact that the indiction properly began in September. It would seem that their normal practice was simply to read the indiction number from the Dionysiac Tables.[55] The effect of Mr Harrison's work is to reduce the significance of the indiction in England. But, in the view of the subsequent all-conquering rôle of the 'Bedan' indiction on the continent through the work of Anglo-Saxon missionaries and scholars, there remains much to be done to determine how and when the equinoctial indiction beginning on 23 or 24 September was transmitted from the east Mediterranean, where it is found until the mid-fifth century, to England in the seventh century or the eighth.[56] Indeed in the

[54] K. Harrison, 'The *Annus Domini* in some Early Charters', *Journal of the Society of Archivists*, 4 (1970–3), pp. 551–7. He discusses BCS 42, 43, 51 and 72. Only BCS 42 has no evident connection with Wilfrid. Yet it shows Wilfrid's friend and protector, King Æthelred of Mercia, intervening in Kent by force in January 691 ('dum ille infirmaverat terram nostram') at a time when the see of Canterbury was vacant. Wilfrid was by this time again running into difficulties with the Northumbrian king, and his biographer claims that he had been offered the succession to the see of Canterbury by Archbishop Theodore himself. See *Life of Bishop Wilfrid by Eddius Stephanus*, ed. B. Colgrave (Cambridge, 1927), pp. 86–92. The problem of the succession to the see of Canterbury after Theodore's death is discussed in Brooks, *Early History*, pp. 76–7.

[55] K. Harrison, 'The Beginning of the Year in England *c.* 500–900', *Anglo-Saxon England*, 2 (1973), pp. 51–70. I am grateful to Mr Harrison for showing me a typescript of his article in advance of publication.

[56] V. Grumel ('La Chronologie Byzantine', *Traité d'Études Byzantines*, ed. P. Lemerle 1 (Paris, 1958), 193–205) has the best discussion of the use of the autumn equinox as the beginning of the civil year, and hence of the indiction, in the eastern Roman Empire; he also shows its association with the feast of the conception of St John the Baptist (24 September in the west, 23 in the east), and with the birth of Emperor Augustus (23 September), and fixes as precisely as possible the change from the equinoctial indiction to that beginning on 1 September. Long after this change eastern liturgical calendars continued to record the beginning of the indiction and the conception of St John on 23 September. The most likely source of the transmission of the equinoctial indiction to English is, as Grumel suggests, a Roman calendar with some eastern entries. An English calendar of *saec. xi (2)* (Cambridge, University Library, Kk. v. 32) has under 24

light of the work of Levison, and more recently of Mr D.P. Kirby, Dr Chaplais and Mr Harrison, it is fair to question whether anyone seeking to comprehend *de novo* the dating of Archbishop Theodore's synods of Hertford and Hatfield would ever reach R.L. Poole's conclusion that they used the misnamed 'Greek' indiction, beginning on 1 September, and that they must therefore be dated 672 and 679 in preference to Bede's dates of 673 and 680.[57] If we could accept that the two synods used the equinoctial indiction and that Bede dated them correctly, then we no longer need to explain how the 'Bedan' indiction replaced the 'Greek' indiction in England and went on to triumph over it on the continent at a time when Mr Harrison has shown the indiction to have had little importance in England.

Charters, wills, writs and the like, written in the vernacular, and Latin charters with substantial Old English boundaries, are a vital, but as yet inadequately used, source for the development of English as a vehicle for written prose, for the analysis of the different English dialects, and for the dissemination of 'classical' West Saxon in the tenth century. A start has recently been made in the study of the syntax of the Old English charters,[58] but progress on the various dialects of the extant charters of the ninth and tenth centuries has been hampered by uncertainty about the provenance of charters. Sweet's analysis and classification of the charters extant in manuscripts earlier than *c.* 900 has remained in use, even though Sweet himself knew that it was inadequate.[59] He knew that the scribes

September an addition of *saec. xi–xii*, 'Hic incipiuntur indictiones et finiuntur'. See *English Kalendars before AD 1100*, ed. F. Wormald, Henry Bradshaw Society 72 (London, 1933), 78. The source may, however, have been Bede rather than calendar tradition.

[57] R.L. Poole, *Studies in Chronology and History* (Oxford, 1934), pp. 38–55. Levison (*England and the Continent*, pp. 265–79) and Harrison ('Beginning of the Year', pp. 55–9) have destroyed Poole's theory that Bede's Year of Grace began on 24 September. D.P. Kirby ('Bede and Northumbrian Chronology', *English Historical Review*, 78 (1963), pp. 517–18) has drawn attention to the difficulties of fixing the date of the Synod of Hatfield from the regnal years of the kings listed in the protocol; in particular he notes that Kentish charters (BCS 36 and 44) suggest that King Hlothere succeeded in 674 rather than 673. Cf. Bede, *Historia ecclesiastica*, iv.17. This, together with Bede's date for Æthelred of Mercia's succession (675; *Historia ecclesiastica*, v.24), points to the synod having taken place in 680 not 679. Chaplais ('Some Early Diplomas', pp. 324–5) emphasized that Bede's indiction both began *and ended* on 24 September, i.e. the change occurred on the 24th, probably at sunset; Bede could therefore regard an event which happened on 24 September as occurring on the last day of the old indiction, and he therefore dated the Synod of Hertford 673 rather than 672. Taken together these facts explain why Bede dated these councils 673 and 680, and suggest that he was right to do so. The only evidence for the 'Greek' indiction in England may therefore be a chimea.

[58] C. Carlton, *Descriptive Syntax of the Old English Charters* (The Hague, 1970).

[59] *Oldest English Texts*, ed. H. Sweet (London, 1885), 420–60.

of some charters that he had listed as 'Mercian-Kentish' and 'Saxon-Kentish' had also written some that he had listed as purely 'Kentish'.[60] It is therefore scarcely surprising that difficulties and doubts should have arisen over identifying and distinguishing the Mercian and Kentish dialects in the ninth century.[61] The new edition of the pre-Conquest charters will use diplomatic and palaeographical tests to identify the scriptoria where the charters were written. A new and firmly based classification of the Old English material in the charters will then be possible. Charters, of course, like books, could be written in one region in the dialect of another,[62] but when it has been established where they were written, one of the uncertainties in the study of dialects will have been removed.

If the study of the language of the vernacular charters has been hampered by inadequate analysis and classification, that of the Latin of the charters has been largely neglected. Yet there is a rich field of study here for any who will analyse the grammar and the orthography of the 'apparent originals'. No one who has examined those of the ninth century will doubt Alfred's statement that at his accession there were very few south of the Humber who could translate a letter from Latin to English, and that he could not recall a single one south of the Thames. Later, under King Athelstan, when Latinity had improved and had become inflated with 'hisperic' style, there is much to be learned, as Professor Bullough has recently demonstrated, from the study of its sources and vocabulary.[63] Here too the new edition should act as a spur to research by showing how varied was the Latin written in different centres throughout the Anglo-Saxon period. Indeed it will be possible to analyse not only the Latin styles of a number of English scriptoria but also the development of their script. At present the writings of E.A. Lowe, N.R. Ker and T.A.M. Bishop contain invaluable scattered clues to the provenance and date of charter hands, and to the scripts of individual houses at key

[60] Ibid., p. 424.

[61] Thus the charters describes by Sweet as 'Kentish' (ibid., pp. 443–53; nos 34 and 37–44) were regarded as pure West Mercian by R. Vleeskruyer (*The Life of St Chad* (Amsterdam, 1953), p. 47), but as Kentish with some influence of Mercian spelling by A. Campbell (*Old English Grammar* (Oxford, 1964), §§ 307 and 314, and *The Vespasian Psalter*, ed. D.H. Wright and A. Campbell (Copenhagen, 1967), 85–6), and as Kentish by R.M. Wilson ('The Provenance of the Vespasian Psalter Gloss: The Linguistic Evidence', *The Anglo-Saxons: Studies in some Aspects of their History and Culture presented to Bruce Dickins*, ed. P. Clemoes (London, 1959), pp. 302–4.

[62] K. Sisam, 'Canterbury, Lichfield, and the Vespasian Psalter', *Review of English Studies*, new series, 8 (1956), pp. 1–10 and 113–31.

[63] D.A. Bullough, 'The Educational Tradition in England from Alfred to Ælfric: Teaching *Utriusque Linguae*', *Settimane di Studio del Centro Italiano di Studi sull'Alto Medioevo*, 19 (1972), pp. 466–78.

periods;[64] may we look forward to the prospect of a series of studies of Anglo-Saxon scriptoria using charter evidence as their foundation?

One of the most profitable lines of approach to the charters in recent years, and one which itself anticipates the concept of the new edition, has come from the study of monastic cartularies and narratives. Since the bulk of purportedly pre-Conquest charters has been preserved only in such collections, it is essential to understand the occasion, the motives and the methods of their compilation. The pioneering work of Dr Ker of the late Professor Wormald on Hemming's cartulary and on the Sherborne cartulary set the standard in this field.[65] More recently Dr E.O. Blake has re-edited the *Liber Eliensis* with a foreword and critical notes by Professor Whitelock.[66] Book II of this work of the mid-twelfth century is based upon a wide range of pre-Conquest charters and vernacular records of various types, most of which there is every reason to accept as authentic. They provide an invaluable picture not only of the fluctuating fortunes of the Ely endowment but also of East Anglian administrative, legal and monetary practice. The preliminary studies of the cartulary of the cathedral priory of Winchester (BL Add. 15350) by Professor Finberg and Dr Hart have also stressed the importance of examining cartularies in their own right.[67] But the number of grants to laymen in this cartulary, which concern lands that have not yet been shown to have ever belonged to, or even to have been claimed by, Winchester, does not prove, as Dr Hart argues, that 'the royal archives' were kept at Winchester and that copies of all charters issued from a royal (Winchester) scriptorium were preserved in them. There is no evidence at all that royal diplomas were normally issued in duplicate in the Anglo-Saxon period, one for the donor and one for the donee. And charters that have no known connection with the house where they were preserved are not a problem unique to Winchester. On the contrary

---

[64] E.A. Lowe, *English Uncial* (Oxford, 1960), and *Codices Latini Antiquiores* ii: *Great Britain and Ireland* (2nd edn, Oxford, 1972); Ker, *Catalogue*; and T.A.M. Bishop, 'Notes on Cambridge Manuscripts', *Transactions of the Cambridge Bibliographical Society*, 2 (19654-8), pp. 185–99 and 323–36, and 3 (1959–63), pp. 93–5 and 412–23; 'A Charter of King Edwy', *Bodleian Library Record*, 6 (1957), pp. 369–73; and *English Caroline Minuscule* (Oxford, 1972).

[65] N.R. Ker, 'Hemming's Cartulary: A Description of the two Worcester Cartularies in Cotton Tiberius A.xiii', in R.W. Hunt, W.A. Pantin and R.W. Southern, eds, *Studies in Mediaeval History presented to F.M. Powicke* (Oxford, 1948), pp. 49–75, and F. Wormald, 'The Sherborne Cartulary', in D.J. Gordon, ed., *Fritz Saxl Memorial Essays* (London, 1962).

[66] *Liber Eliensis*, ed. E.O. Blake, *Royal Historical Society*, Camden 3rd series, 92 (London, 1962).

[67] Finberg, *Wessex*, pp. 16–18 and 214–48, and Hart, 'The *Codex Wintoniensis* and the King's *Haligdom*', *Land, Church, and People: Essays presented to H.P.R. Finberg, Agricultural History Review*, 18 Supplement (1970), pp. 7–38.

most major pre-Conquest churches have such charters, if they have preserved a substantial number of original charters or have a cartulary whose compiler did not restrict himself to grants to his own house. It is simpler to accept the traditional and well documented conclusion that laymen who received charters often placed them for safe-keeping in an important church[68] than to credit the Anglo-Saxon monarchy with bureaucratic procedures that would put them more than two centuries in advance of all other secular governments in western Europe.

The charters of the monasteries of the tenth-century reformation in England have been the especial interest of Mr E. John,[69] and they present particularly acute problems of criticism. On the one hand these monasteries themselves acted as scriptoria where charters were drafted and written,[70] so that arguments for and against their authenticity cannot necessarily be decided by appeal to the charters of other houses. On the other hand monastic reform, as Mr John has rightly stressed,[71] frequently involved a tenurial revolution which meant that the subsequent history of the house was one of endless litigation. In these circumstances there was always a motive for forgery, and we must regard with particular suspicion any 'apparent original' to a reformed monastery, whose script is later than its purported date. We should not therefore be surprised that Mr John's interpretation of many of these charters has proved controversial. In particular his attempt to prove that the cathedral community of Worcester was reformed in 964 along Æthelwoldian lines (i.e. by sudden and forcible ejection of recalcitrant clerks in favour of monks) rests upon his belief that a considerable genuine stratum can be distinguished in the forged BCS 1135, the so-called *Altitonantis* charter.[72] But Professor Darlington and Professor Sawyer have since shown in detail and beyond all reasonable doubt that this charter is a compilation of the twelfth century and that no part of it

---

[68] Stenton, *Latin Charters*, pp. 19–20. Compare Robertson, *Anglo-Saxon Charters*, no. 78, where a layman even gets the settlement of a land dispute entered into the gospel book of the local cathedral church (Hereford).

[69] E. John, 'An Alleged Worcester Charter of the Reign of Edgar', *Bulletin of the John Rylands Library*, 41 (1958), pp. 54–80; 'St Oswald and the Tenth-Century Reformation', *Journal of Ecclesiastical History*, 9 (1958), 147–68, reprinted in his *Orbis Britanniae*, pp. 234–48; 'The King and the Monks in the Tenth-Century Reformation', *Bulletin of the John Rylands Library* 42 (1959), pp. 61–87, reprinted in his *Orbis Britanniae*, pp. 154–80; 'Some Latin Charters of the Tenth-Century Reformation', *Revue bénédictine*, 70 (1960), pp. 333–59; 'Some Alleged Charters of King Edgar for Ely', *Orbis Britanniae*, pp. 210–33; and 'The Church of Winchester and the Tenth-Century Reformation', *Bulletin of the John Rylands Library*, 47 (1964–5), pp. 404–29.

[70] John, *Orbis Britanniae*, pp. 207–9 and 228, and 'Church of Winchester', pp. 405–7, and Chaplais, 'Origin and Authenticity', p. 60, and 'Anglo-Saxon Chancery', p. 165.

[71] John, 'King and Monks', *passim*.

[72] John, 'St Oswald', and 'The Altitonantis Charter', *Land Tenure*, pp. 162–7.

can be reliably used as evidence for the tenth. Professor Sawyer has further demonstrated that the witness-lists of Bishop Oswald's leases do not support any theory of sudden reform at Worcester.[73] On the contrary they show that the composition of the community was only gradually changed, that there were two main periods of recruitment – 964–5 and 969–77 – and that its members, even by the end of Oswald's life, were more frequently called clerks than monks.

With *Altitonantis* must also fall Mr John's interpretation of the military and judicial privileges of the liberty of Oswaldslow, which is dependent upon it.[74] Of greater value is his discussion of a group of charters granting wide privileges to a number of reformed houses, particularly those of Æthelwold's connection; they have formulae in common and have been usefully styled the *Orthodoxorum* charters from the first word in most of their preambles.[75] Such general grants of privileges, particularly when they are also *pancartae* – that is when they include general confirmations of listed estates – were always liable to alteration and improvement by forgers. Mr John admits that some of the *Orthodoxorum* group are, in Dr Chaplais's terminology, forgeries. But he makes a good case on diplomatic and historical grounds for the authenticity of Æthelred's privilege of 993 to Abingdon and of Edgar's privilege of 972 to Pershore.[76] If his conclusions can be supported by the necessary close examination of the script and of the external characteristics of these charters in the light of other charters and books from these houses, the diplomatic of the monastic reform movement will have received a welcome foundation in a sea of uncertainty. Mr John has also argued, against the view of Dr Blake and Professor Whitelock, that a case can be made out for the authenticity of the Ely 'foundation privilege', BCS 1266; his arguments have been strengthened by Professor Pope's demonstration that the style of the vernacular version of this charter leaves little room for doubt that it was composed by Ælfric.[77] This, of course, does not rule out the possibility that BCS 1266 is an early forgery, and we still need an adequate explanation of why, if Ely possessed an authentic

[73] R.R. Darlington, *The Cartulary of Worcester Cathedral Priory*, Pipe Roll Society, 76 (1962–3), pp. xii–xix, and P.H. Sawyer, 'Charters of the Reform Movement: The Worcester Archive', in D. Parsons ed., *Tenth-Century Studies: Essays in Commemoration of the Regularis Concordia* (Chichester, 1975), pp. 84–94, 228–9. I am indebted to Professor Sawyer for showing me a copy of his article before publication.

[74] John, *Land Tenure*, pp. 80–139.

[75] John, 'Some Latin Charters'. The charters are BCS 1046, 1047, 1187, 1282 and 1284 and KCD 684 (s 658, 673, 812, 786, 788, 876).

[76] KCD 684 and BCS 1282 (s 876, 786). Cf. Chaplais, 'Anglo-Saxon Chancery', p. 165.

[77] John, 'Some Alleged Charters'; *Liber Eliensis*, ed. Blake, pp. 414–15 (s 779); and J. Pope, 'Ælfric and the Old English Version of the Ely Privilege', in Clemoes and Hughes, eds, *England before the Conquest*, pp. 85–113.

original of 970, it was necessary for this to be redrafted in bilingual form as though that had been its original appearance.

Such doubts are unlikely to be resolved until the relevant volumes of the new edition of the pre-Conquest charters have appeared in print, with the necessary combination of diplomatic, linguistic, palaeographical and topographical analysis. In the meantime it is evident that sure progress in charter studies can come only from comparable collaboration between experts in these different disciplines. Thus few will be convinced by Professor Finberg's valiant attempt to salvage the credit of the charters of 844 and 854 purporting to belong to Æthelwulf's *decimatio* of his estates;[78] for Professor Finberg justifies setting aside the diplomatic evidence that these charters are full of formulae of the late tenth and early eleventh centuries by quoting Sir Frank Stenton in such a way as to make it seem that Sir Frank had believed that such analysis was valueless;[79] he fails to explain why the only charter of this series which survives as an 'apparent original' is in a hand of *saec. xi*, or why these charters contradict the evidence of the Anglo-Saxon Chronicle and of the Rochester *decimatio* charter, BCS 486, that the tithing occurred in 855. Solution of the problems of Æthelwulf's *decimatio* will be achieved only by combining detailed analysis of the diplomatic and palaeography of the charters with study of the history of the archives where they have been preserved, and with wider historical considerations, in particular with an examination of the comparable measures of Carolingian rulers, whose interpretation is, of course, equally controverted.

It is fitting, in view of the aims of this periodical, that a review of recent work on charters should end with a plea for collaboration between scholars in different disciplines, between diplomatists and topographers, palaeographers and linguistics. Few if any scholars have such mastery of all these skills that they can do without such expert help. It is only through collaboration that the new edition will be achieved, and that the more bitter controversies of the last generation will lead to constructive and sure conclusions in this most stimulating, but most difficult of fields.

Postscript: Anglo-Saxon Charters, 1973–1998

After a quarter century of further work the world of Anglo-Saxon charters now presents a very different appearance in some fields from

[78] Finberg, *Wessex*, pp. 187–213.

[79] Ibid., p. 199. The quotation comes from Stenton, *Latin Charters*, p. 15, where Sir Frank was criticizing Stevenson's hasty and unbalanced comments upon some of the Muchelney charters; but Stenton's overall appreciation of Stevenson's methods of detailed diplomatic analysis is shown on pp. 7–10 of the same work.

that of 1972–3; in others the foundations that were then being laid have produced more imposing structures. In the continued absence of any manual of Anglo-Saxon diplomatic it may therefore be helpful to survey the last twenty-five years' work on the charters. In particular this may serve as a guide both for those who only occasionally have to tackle charter evidence and for those who come to charter studies for the first time.

One volume, though published before 1973, needs to be mentioned first since it has proved to be the essential foundation for all modern research. Professor Peter Sawyer's *Anglo-Saxon Charters: An Annotated List and Bibliography* (1968) is an invaluable handbook with a convenient and robust numbering of the entire corpus for brief but clear identification and reference, providing scholars both with full details of the extant manuscripts and editions and a bibliography for each charter. No work has done more to reduce the arcane mystery of charter scholarship and to make the subject accessible throughout the world. Inevitably after thirty years the need for a second edition has become pressing, to take account both of the volume of subsequent work and of charters newly discovered since 1968. It is therefore wonderful news that a fully updated revision of the list and bibliography has been prepared by Dr Susan Kelly for publication in book form by the Royal Historical Society and that, pending completion of a fundamental organization of the final section on 'Lost and Incomplete' texts, where modern scholarship has most transformed the subject, it is available on the internet.[80] The internet will also provide a wonderful opportunity to keep this basic tool abreast of current scholarship hereafter, while not undermining the need of most scholars to have this essential *vademecum* of the subject to hand in book form.

The fundamental work of editing the charters to modern scholarly standards, commenced in 1966 by a joint committee of the British Academy and the Royal Historical Society, has made significant, though disappointingly slow, progress. Professor Campbell's edition of the charters of Rochester inaugurated the series with welcome despatch in 1973, but proved so deficient in its analysis of the language, the diplomatic and the boundary clauses of the charters as to require the committee to provide much stronger guidelines for editors.[81] Professor Peter Sawyer, the secretary to the committee

---

[80] P.H. Sawyer, *Anglo-Saxon Charters: An Annotated List and Bibliography*, Royal Historical Society, Guides and Handbooks, 8 (London, 1968); the revised edition, prepared for the British Academy's research project on Anglo-Saxon Charters is available as 'The Electronic Sawyer' on the web at <http//www.trin.cam.ac.uk/chartwww/>.

[81] A. Campbell, *Charters of Rochester*, Anglo-Saxon Charters, 1 (British Academy, 1973). See my review in *English Historical Review*, 40 (1975), pp. 626–7.

during its first sixteen years (1966–82), gave the series a more secure foundation with his volume on the charters of Burton Abbey (1979); this fascicule not only stands comparison with the best editions of diplomata by continental academies, but also provides a rich harvest of information on the late Anglo-Saxon society of the north Midlands. One of the advantages of the decision to publish the charters archive by archive, rather than reign by reign, was thus revealed. In the 1980s this progress was only maintained by Mary-Anne O'Donovan's edition of the Sherborne charters in a volume which included those of the dependent Horton Abbey (1988).[82] Recently, however, a welcome advance has been made by Dr Susan Kelly, whose editions of the charters of St Augustine's, Canterbury (1995), Shaftesbury (1996) and of Selsey (1998) have brought Anglo-Saxon diplomatic to new standards of expertise.[83] The same author's *Charters of Abingdon Abbey* is eagerly awaited, since it will be the first time that the new edition has published one of the larger archives, that is those with over 150 charters. Abingdon will therefore set an important example for the other major archives in the series (Christ Church, Canterbury; Old Minster, Winchester; and Worcester), but also, because of the huge number of tenth-century royal diplomas in the archive, it will provide a first opportunity to give the production of royal charters against the background of one of the major centres of the monastic reform movement. Other editors have produced draft volumes on the charters of New Minster, Winchester, of Exeter and of St Albans abbey for consideration by the charter committee, so a surge in publication of the series may be expected in the next few years.[84]

Somewhat surprisingly the corpus of known Anglo-Saxon charters has been enlarged significantly in the last twenty-five years; in part as the result of outstanding work by county archivists and record offices in fulfilling their role as local repositories, and in part as the product of a campaign of research by Dr Simon Keynes into the papers of the seventeenth- and eighteenth-century antiquarians and into the whereabouts of lost medieval cartularies. Pride of place must go to a series of eleven pre-conquest charters, connected archivally with Barking Abbey (Essex), preserved in the sixteenth-century cartulary of Ilford

[82] P.H. Sawyer, ed., *Charters of Burton Abbey*, Anglo-Saxon Charters, 2 (British Academy, 1979); M.A. O'Donovan, *Charters of Sherborne*, Anglo-Saxon Charters, 3 (British Academy, 1988).

[83] S.E. Kelly, ed., *Charters of St Augustine's, Canterbury*, Anglo-Saxon Charters, 4 (British Academy, 1995); idem, *Charters of Shaftesbury Abbey*, Anglo-Saxon Charters, 5 (British Academy, 1996); idem, *Charters of Selsey*, Anglo-Saxon Charters, 6 (British Academy, 1998).

[84] By Dr Sean Miller, Dr Charles Insley and Dr Julia Crick respectively.

Hospital, now at Hatfield House.[85] They include two charters of 693 × 709 in the name of King Swæfred and four new diplomas of King Eadred, two of them grants to 'religious women'. The nature of the discoveries that may still await us is perhaps better characterized by the Bollandist copy of a lost St Albans cartulary, which has not only preserved full transcripts of five Old English documents hitherto known only from inadequate Latin summaries, but also fuller texts of many well-known St Albans diplomas, including our first sight of the vernacular boundary clauses belonging to seven of them.[86] Almost as productive, though ultimately more tantalizing, have been Dr Keynes's investigations into the activities of the Strangeways family's antiquarian activities following their acquisition of the estates and archives of the eleventh-century monastery of Abbotsbury (Dorset) and his discovery of Sir Henry Spelman's extracts from the lost Abbotsbury cartulary in their possession. Significant segments of the texts of six royal diplomas of the tenth and eleventh centuries have been revealed.[87] The recovery at Taunton Record Office of the missing part of a transcript of the lost Athelney cartulary by the eighteenth-century antiquarian, George Harbin, has likewise made it possible to recover two diplomas in the name of King Alfred and another of Æthelred the Unready; and Lincoln's Inn is the source of transcripts of missing St Paul's charters of King Æthelbald of Mercia and of Edward the Elder, both of considerable historical interest given the scarcity of authentic records of those reigns.[88] Finally three remarkable charters of King Edgar, surviving independently as antiquarian transcripts, have proved of interest not only for the history of the estates in question, but also for showing Edgar's use of a

[85] H.H. Lockwood, 'One Thing Leads to Another – the Discovery of Additional Charters of Barking Abbey', *Essex Journal*, 25 (1990), pp. 11–13; K. Bascombe, 'Two Charters of King Suebred of Essex', in K. Neale, ed., *An Essex Tribute* (London, 1987), pp. 85–96. These charters will be included in C.R. Hart's *Charters of Barking Abbey*, Anglo-Saxon Charters (forthcoming); transcripts of these texts (with other newly discovered charters) are provided in a booklet prepared for editors of the charter series by Dr S.E. Kelly.

[86] S. Keynes, 'A Lost Cartulary of St Albans Abbey', *Anglo-Saxon England*, 22 (1993), pp. 253–79; idem, 'The Will of Wulf', *Old English Newsletter*, 26 (iii) (1993), pp. 16–21; Dr Crick's edition of *The Charters of St Albans Abbey* is in an advanced stage of preparation.

[87] S. Keynes, 'The Lost Cartulary of Abbotsbury', *Anglo-Saxon England*, 18 (1989), pp. 207–43.

[88] S. Keynes, 'George Harbin's Transcript of the Lost Cartulary of Athelney Abbey', *Somerset Archaeology and Natural History*, 136 (1992), pp. 149–59; S.E. Kelly, 'Trading Privileges from Eighth-century England', *Early Medieval Europe*, 1 (1992), pp. 3–28; S. Keynes, 'A Charter of King Edward the Elder for Islington', *Historical Research*, 66 (1993), pp. 303–16.

Mercian draftsman for one charter and of a Glastonbury charter-writer for the other two.[89]

Authoritative work on Anglo-Saxon diplomatic has to be built, wherever possible, upon an understanding of those charters that survive as 'apparent originals' on single sheets of parchment. Scholars therefore owe a considerable debt to Dr Simon Keynes for his superb volume of facsimiles which provides actual-size photographs of forty charters, which had been omitted from the great nineteenth-century facsimile volumes produced by the British Museum and the Ordnance Survey, together with some essential information about the script and provenance and the bibliography of each document.[90] With this tool comparative work on the script and layout of single-sheet charters has been made possible. To understand the earliest charters, however, extant 'originals' are a very rare luxury. As Patrick Wormald has shown, apparent originals and early copies do provide some foundation and context for a reassessment of the origins of charter formulation and of the underlying concepts of land-law involved, but only if they are seen against a critical review of the totality of the evidence, British and continental, early and late. Dr Anton Scharer's fine survey of the royal diplomas of the seventh and eighth centuries and his later study of royal titles of the same period were both founded securely in the long tradition of German and Austrian study of diplomatic.[91] They therefore reach very cautious estimates of the authenticity of charters, formulae or royal styles that are only witnessed in diplomas surviving in cartulary copies. He, like those who study areas with virtually no surviving single-sheet charters, such as Heather Edwards' pioneering study of the earliest West Saxon charters, can make only tentative progress until their work can be tested by a clear understanding of the nature of later archival contamination.[92]

---

[89] N.P. Brooks, M. Gelling and D. Johnson, 'A New Charter of King Edgar', *Anglo-Saxon England*, 13 (1984), pp. 137–55 for the grant of Ballidon (Derbyshire) in 963; S. Keynes, 'The "Dunstan B" charters', *Anglo-Saxon England*, 23 (1994), pp. 165–93 at 166–72 for the grants of Coundon (Warwickshire) in 958 and of Brickendon (Hertfordshire) in 974.

[90] S. Keynes, ed., *Facsimiles of Anglo-Saxon Charters*, Anglo-Saxon Charters, supplementary series I (British Academy, 1991).

[91] A. Scharer, *Die angelsächsische Königsurkunde im 7 und 8 Jahrhundert*, Veroffentlichungen des Instituts für österreichische Geschichtsforschung, 26 (Vienna, 1988); idem, 'Die Intitulationes der angelsachsischen Könige im 7 und 8 Jahrhundert', *Intitulatio III: Lateinische Herrschertitel und-titulatur vom 7 bis 13 Jahrhundert*, Mitteilungen des Instituts für österreichische Geschichtsforschung, 24 (Vienna, 1988).

[92] P. Wormald, 'Bede and the Conversion of England: The Charter Evidence', Jarrow Lecture 1984 (Jarrow, 1985), pp. 1–32; H. Edwards, *The Charters of the Early West Saxon Kingdom*, BAR, British Series 198 (Oxford, 1988).

Nonetheless some fundamental studies of early Anglo-Saxon diplomatic have been able to be based on the evidence of contemporary texts. Thus Susan Kelly has rested her case that the earliest Kentish charters were produced in the scriptoria of the Kentish minster churches not only upon the evidence of the late St Augustine's cartularies but also on a careful assessment of the comparatively plentiful single-sheet evidence for Kent.[93] Moreover the astonishing survival of fifty-four ninth-century charters from Christ Church Canterbury on single sheets of parchment has made possible the identification of the work of Christ Church scribes and the recognition of Canterbury formulas normally used for charters concerning estates in East Kent, which were quite distinct from the scripts and formulas used in charters produced at Rochester for West Kentish estates or at Worcester for properties in that diocese.[94] Palaeographical study of charters and of manuscript books has deepened our knowledge of the Canterbury scriptorium and of the work of related scribes, although the fortunes of the scriptorium in the face both of the Viking threat and of the decline of learning later in the ninth century have occasioned some controversy.[95]

In Wessex, by contrast, the charters issued in the names of King Æthelwulf (838–58) and of his sons (855–99) have been shown to belong to a single diplomatic tradition, no matter in what part of the kingdom or in what diocese the estates that they grant lay. The suggestion that the agency that produced these charters was the body of priests who served in the royal household is certainly a plausible, if not the only, interpretation; and it has been reinforced by the identification of a West Saxon version of Anglo-Saxon cursive minuscule, which was used both for the charters and for a small group of manuscript books.[96] Recent work on the diplomatic of the ninth-

[93] Kelly, *Charters of St Augustine's*, pp. lxxi–xciii.

[94] N.P. Brooks, 'The Pre-Conquest Charters of Christ Church Canterbury', (unpublished D.Phil. thesis, University of Oxford, 1968), pp. 129–92; idem, *The Early History of the Church of Canterbury* (Leicester, 1984), pp. 168–70, 327–30.

[95] M.P. Brown, 'Paris, Bibliotheque Nationale, lat. 10861 and the Scriptorium of Christ Church, Canterbury', *Anglo-Saxon England*, 15 (1986), pp. 119–37; J. Crick, 'Church, Land and Local Nobility in Early Ninth-Century Kent: the Case of Ealdorman Oswulf', *Historical Research*, 61 (1988), pp. 251–69. For an argument that the decline of learning in the Canterbury scriptorium and its association with the Viking threat should be minimized, see J.E. Morrish, 'King Alfred's Letter as a Source on Learning in England', in P.E. Szarmach, ed., *Studies in Earlier Old English Prose* (Albany, NY, 1986), pp. 87–107. This view has been decisively rejected in a masterly analysis of the latinity of the charters by M. Lapidge. 'Latin Learning in Ninth-Century England', in his *Anglo-Latin Literature, 600–899* (London, 1996), pp. 409–54, at 434–6 and 446–54.

[96] S. Keynes, 'The West Saxon Charters of King Æthelwulf and his Sons', *English Historical Review*, 109 (1994), pp. 1109–49; J. Crick, 'The Case for a West Saxon Minuscule', *Anglo-Saxon England*, 26 (1997), pp. 63–75.

century kingdoms may serve as a background to the great debate about the production of royal charters in the tenth and eleventh centuries. In 1980 Dr Simon Keynes challenged what had become the prevailing interpretation, namely that of Dr Pierre Chaplais, who had argued that Anglo-Saxon diplomas were normally produced by ecclesiastical scriptoria and very often by their beneficiaries. By contrast Keynes identified a dominant diplomatic tradition, first detectable in the charters of King Athelstan from the year 928, which continued with only minor interruptions throughout the tenth and early eleventh centuries.[97] Of fundamental importance is Keynes's analysis of the witness-lists as evidence of the actual assemblies or *witenagemots* where the lands were granted and the charters produced; he demonstrates that throughout the tenth and early eleventh charters that were issued on the same occasion for different recipients frequently shared many details of their formulation. The forty-eight surviving diplomas of the year 956 provided a superb demonstration of this method, since he was able to show convincing reasons for attributing them all to just four separate assemblies. In concluding that a single agency was responsible for producing most of the extant royal diplomas, Keynes was able to argue that a 'royal secretariat' formed an important part of English government, not only in the early tenth century, but throughout the reigns of Edgar, Æthelred the Unready and of their successors.

In the ensuing debate,[98] there is agreement both that the Anglo-Saxon royal diploma remains astonishingly consistent in its layout and external characteristics throughout the period from 928 to 1066, and that some charters were indeed drafted and even written by leading ecclesiastics, bishops or abbots, either as beneficiaries or at the king's request. There is also agreement that some groups of charters were produced by non-royal agencies, though the exact significance of charters where one of the ecclesiastics attests with the word *dictavi* (or some more elaborate phrase), often remains unclear. Thus a group of nineteen charters ranging in date from 930 to 956 and written in a distinctively alliterative and rhythmical Latin have been styled the 'Dunstan A' charters by Dr Roy Hart and attributed by him to the Glastonbury scriptorium, but by others to Bishop Cenwald of

---

[97] For Dr Chaplais's views, see above, Chapter 9, pp. ooo–o; S. Keynes, *The Diplomas of Æthelred the Unready* (Cambridge, 1980), pp. 19–153.

[98] P. Chaplais, 'The Royal Anglo-Saxon "Chancery" of the Tenth Century Revisited', in H. Mayr-Harting and R.I. Moore, eds, *Studies in Medieval History presented to R.H.C. Davis* (London, 1985), pp. 41–51; S. Keynes, 'Regenbald, the Chancellor (*sic*)', *Anglo-Norman Studies*, 10 (1988), pp. 185–222.

Worcester;[99] while another group of thirty documents ranging in date from 951 to 975, the so-called 'Dunstan B' charters, are accepted as being associated with Glastonbury under Abbot (and Archbishop) Dunstan.[100] If we bear in mind that Dr Chaplais's belief in the role of ecclesiastical scriptoria derived in part from his detection of distinctive features in the formulation of south-western diplomas (those of Exeter in particular) and that even in the reign of Æthelred II Dr Keynes has found authentic diplomas with features specifically associated with the New Minster at Winchester,[101] then it is clear that Anglo-Saxon arrangements for the drafting of charters were far more fluid than those of continental chanceries, royal or papal. It may be that our attention should focus upon the nature of the English *witenagemot*, where throughout the tenth and eleventh centuries kings met their leading lay and ecclesiastical subjects and granted charters with their consent. The same assemblies often took on a more ecclesiastical aspect as synods of the national church, and bishops and abbots were accompanied by clerical or monastic members of their households or communities. At such gatherings there would be many scribes capable, if requested, of drafting a royal diploma or of bringing a draft to the meeting; there would also be occasions for scribes to pass from the service of a bishop or abbot into the royal household for a stint as a 'king's priest' and for others to make the opposite transfer. The public ceremonies involved in the grant of the estate would help to ensure some agreement on the diploma's formulation and to maintain its fundamentally religious character. Both a royal secretariat of 'king's priests' and the followings of leading eccleasitics may have been more fluid and less formal bodies than the historians of governmental institutions have tended to assume.

Diplomas that survive on apparently authentic single sheets of parchment are crucially important evidence for students of early medieval

---

[99] For the attribution to Glastonbury, see C.R. Hart, 'Danelaw Charters and the Glastonbury Scriptorium', *Downside Review*, 90 (1972), pp. 125–32 and revision version in idem, 'Danelaw and Mercian Charters of the Mid-Tenth Century', *The Danelaw* (London, 1992), pp. 431–53 at 431–44; for the attribution to Bishop Cenwald, see P.H. Sawyer, ed., *Charters of Burton*, pp. xlvii–xlix and S. Keynes, 'King Æthelstan's Books', in M. Lapidge and H. Gneuss, eds, *Learning and Literature in Anglo-Saxon England: Studies presented to Peter Clemoes on the Occasion of his Sixty-Fifth Birthday* (Cambridge, 1985), pp. 143–201, at 157–9.

[100] C.R. Hart, *The Early Charters of Northern England and the North Midlands* (Leicester, 1975), pp. 19–22; Keynes, 'The "Dunstan B" Charters', pp. 165–93.

[101] P. Chaplais, 'The Origin and Authenticity of the Royal Anglo-Saxon Diplomas of Exeter', *Bulletin of the Institute of Historical Research*, 39 (1966), pp. 1–34; his arguments have been reinforced by his pupil, Dr C. Insley, 'Charters and Episcopal Scriptoria in the Anglo-Saxon South-West', *Early Medieval Europe*, 7 (1998), pp. 173–97; Keynes, *Diplomas of Æthelred*, pp. 92–4; the New Minster features will be discussed further in Dr Sean Miller's edition of the *Charters of New Minster* (in preparation).

palaeography, since they can provide exactly datable and even (where the scriptorium can be identified) locatable examples of script and thus form a framework on which a chronological and geographical ordering of manuscript books may be built. The work of T.A.M. Bishop on English Caroline minuscule pioneered the use of charters to anchor the different phases that he detected in the history of the script, and Professor David Dumville has revised and refined his account of the origins and development of the English forms of Caroline script. The close association of this script with the progress of monastic reform in the circles of Dunstan, Æthelwold and Oswald, and the dominance of the Canterbury scriptoria in the script's later elaboration are the dominant themes of this rich vein of work. Dumville has also turned his attention to surveying the development of English square minuscule from the late ninth century in a series of papers where the charters are repeatedly the chief evidence for the identification of the different phases, particularly those of the 940s and 950s.[102] Without the charters palaeographers could seldom claim greater precision in dating scripts than a half century.

Charters are, of course, in the first instance title-deeds for the ownership of land. They tell us principally of the endowment of their recipients, so it is not surprising that where they survive in quantity they can be used to help reconstruct the landed endowment of major churches and to map the accretion (or loss) of property in ecclesiastical hands across the early Middle Ages. But the record is often incomplete where (as at Canterbury cathedral) the earliest charters have been lost. Nonetheless it has been possible to use the charters to trace the relations of kings and nobles with the archbishops and the Christ Church community in considerable detail from the end of the eighth century. Hitherto little-known players, like Archbishop Wulfred (805–32), have emerged alongside (or indeed above) an Oda or a Dunstan as reforming champions of their church, not only struggling with royal and lay lords (even to the point of forgery), but also husbanding and developing the landed wealth of the see.[103] At Glastonbury, where the overburden of myth and of fabrication is even greater, Dr Abrams has preferred to found her fine study of that

[102] T.A.M. Bishop, *English Caroline Minuscule* (Oxford, 1971); D.N. Dumville, *English Caroline Script and Monastic History: Studies in Benedictinism, A.D. 950–1030* (Woodbridge, 1993); idem, 'English Square Minuscule Script: the Background and Earliest Phrases', *Anglo-Saxon England*, 16 (1987), pp. 147–79; idem, 'The Anglo-Saxon Chronicle and the Origins of English Square Minuscule Script', *Wessex and England from Alfred to Edgar* (Woodbridge, 1992), pp. 55–140; idem, 'English Square Minuscule Script: the Mid-Century Phases', *Anglo-Saxon England*, 23 (1994), pp. 133–64.

[103] N.P. Brooks, *Early History*, pp. 129–315; for an updated summary, see Chapter 7 above, pp. 101–54.

church's endowment on a detailed analysis of each individual estate, before essaying a sketch of its growth.[104] The volumes of the new edition of the Anglo-Saxon charters include sections of their introduction on the history of the particular church and of its endowment; already we have notable pictures of the very early landed wealth of St Augustine's and of Selsey to set alongside the enrichment of Shaftesbury by King Alfred and his descendants and Professor Sawyer's fascinating account of Wulfric Spot's creation of Burton Abbey at the start of the eleventh century.[105]

A high proportion of Anglo-Saxon diplomas, particularly those of the tenth century, are grants not to churches but to lay nobles. Moreover the witness-lists record, often at considerable length the names of those who attended the kings' courts. The history of the Anglo-Saxon nobility is therefore a viable subject. Thus Alan Thacker has traced the shifting terms for Anglo-Saxon nobles from the mid-seventh to the end of the ninth century very largely from charter evidence and Simon Keynes has detailed the contrasting relations of Mercian and West Saxon kings with the Kentish nobility in the ninth century through a sophisticated analysis of the attestations to the charters in relation to the places where charters were issued.[106] It is in the tenth century, however, that the prosopography of the English nobility comes into its own. Something of its potential for the greatest magnates was revealed in the pioneering studies of Roy Hart and by Ann Williams of Æthelstan 'Half-king' and of Ealdorman Ælfhere of Mercia. More typical is the reconstruction of, and distinguishing between the careers of two king's thegns, Wulfric the brother of Dunstan and Wulfric Cufing, whose rise to prominence under Eadmund and Eadred can be reconstructed with some probability.[107] The possibility of tracing the careers of nobles, whether ecclesiastical or lay, through their attestation of charters, has long been understood and scholars from W.H. Stevenson onwards have perforce had to reinvent the wheel by creating their own lists in order to establish the

[104] L. Abrams, *Anglo-Saxon Glastonbury: Church and Endowment* (Woodbridge, 1996), esp. pp. 42–265, 335–49.

[105] See Anglo-Saxon Charters, volumes 2, 4, 5 and 6 (above, pp. 000–00, nn. 2 and 3; for Selsey, see further S.E. Kelly, 'The Bishopric of Selsey', in M. Hobbs, ed., *Chichester Cathedral: An Historical Survey* (Chichester, 1994), pp. 1–10.

[106] A.T. Thacker, 'Some Terms for Noblemen in Anglo-Saxon England, c.650–c.900', *Anglo-Saxon Studies in Archaeology and History*, 2 (1981), pp. 201–36; S. Keynes, 'The Control of Kent in the Ninth Century', *Early Medieval Europe*, 2 (1993), pp. 111–31.

[107] N.P. Brooks, 'The Career of St Dunstan', in N. Ramsay, M. Sparks and T. Tatton-Brown, eds, *St Dunstan: His Life, Times and Cult* (Woodbridge, 1992), pp. 1–23, at 8–10.

authenticity of particular witness-lists or to trace the careers of particular individuals.[108] The need for a comprehensive handlist of all the
witnesses in the entire corpus has now been met by Simon Keynes's
superb *Atlas of Attestations* which presents tables, kingdom by
kingdom and reign by reign of all the æthelings, bishops, abbots,
earls/ealdorman, thegns and other ranks listed in the witness clauses of
the charters and of the order in which they are listed. Dr Keynes had
whetted our appetites with the pioneering tables in his studies of the
diplomas of Æthelred II and of Cnut's earls.[109] But he has now made
it possible for scholars and students, amateur and professional, under-
graduates and postgraduates, to test their own insights into the
workings of Anglo-Saxon politics and kin-groups. A notable example
of what is in store has been provided by Dr Andrew Wareham's investigation into the maternal and paternal kinsmen of Bishop Oswald of
Worcester from the evidence of the Worcester leases and the Ramsey
Liber benefactorum.[110]

On the donors of charters, there has perhaps been less concentrated
work. But much has been done to sort out the succession of the kings
of the East and South Saxons and those of Kent and to understand
the periods of joint-rule, very largely on the foundation of improved
understanding of the charters.[111] More rigorous use of charters has
also taught scholars, led by Patrick Wormald, to be much more
cautious in interpreting the evidence of the regnal styles of powerful
overkings (the so-called *Bretwaldas*) of the seventh and eighth
centuries as marking progressive accretions of power on the road
towards a single kingdom of the English: many of the key charters
have been shown to be later forgeries and others may tell us more of
the conceptions of their ecclesiastical draftsmen rather than of the

[108] A.S. Napier and W.H. Stevenson, eds, *The Crawford Collection of Early Charters and Documents* (Oxford, 1896), p. ix; C.R. Hart, 'Biographical Notes on the Burton Charters', in his *The Early Charters of Northern England and the North Midlands* (Leicester, 1975), pp. 253–80.

[109] S. Keynes, *An Atlas of Attestations in Anglo-Saxon Charters, c. 670–1066* (University of Cambridge, Department of Anglo-Saxon, Norse and Celtic, revised edn, 1998). It is intended that the *Atlas* will eventually be published as a volume in the British Academy's Anglo-Saxon Charter supplementary series. For earlier use of the tables, see Keynes, *Diplomas of Æthelred*, pp. 154–231, and idem, 'Cnut's Earls', in A. Rumle, ed., *The Reign of Cnut* (Leicester, 1994), pp. 43–88.

[110] A.F. Wareham, 'St Oswald's Family and Kin', in N.P. Brooks and C. Cubitt, eds, *St Oswald of Worcester: Life and Influence* (Leicester, 1996), pp. 46–63; see also V. King, 'St Oswald's Tenants', ibid., pp. 100–16.

[111] For Essex, see B. Yorke, 'The Kingdom of the East Saxons', *Anglo-Saxon England*, 14 (1985), pp. 1–36; for Sussex, Kelly, *Charters of Selsey*, pp. lxxiii–lxxxiv; for Kent, B. Yorke, 'Joint Kingship in Kent, c.560–785', *Archaeologia Cantiana*, 99 (1983), pp. 1–19, and Kelly, *Charters of St Augustine's*, pp. 205–14.

ambitions of their rulers.[112]

The chronological problems of Anglo-Saxon history have been less to the fore in the last quarter-century than hitherto. Patrick Sims-Williams did indeed show good reason for thinking that incarnational dating can be accepted in two seventh-century charters associated with Bishop Wilfrid, long before the system had been widely popularized by its use in Bede's *Ecclesiastical History* and by English synods.[113] But much of the heat of the debates on early Anglo-Saxon chronology has been removed by Dr Susan Wood's masterly demonstration that Bede did not start his incarnational years in September (with the indiction) but rather in January; and that he identified whole incarnation years in terms of the regnal years of kings, rather than calculating the kings' years from their actual accessions.[114] It is therefore no longer necessary to use the charters in order to 'correct' Bede's chronology, though it has yet to be determined how far the charters indicate that Bede's practices were general in the early Anglo-Saxon kingdoms.

Many extant charters record the course of legal disputes and sometimes their resolution. Patrick Wormald has led the way in listing and studying the pre-Conquest lawsuits and in explaining that the record that we have is very often a partisan account on behalf of one of the participants in the dispute; under his guidance some of the complexities of the long litigation over Westbury (Gloucestershire) and Snodland (Kent) find explanation and we are also introduced to the forgery of charters almost as soon as we have evidence of litigation. Alan Kennedy has used the charter narratives to prove the role of the shire courts in the resolution of disputes about bookland and has also begun to exploit the rich vein of evidence about East Anglian litigation in the Ely *Libellus Æthelwoldi*.[115] Particularly notable is Patrick

---

[112] P. Wormald, 'Bede, the *Bretwaldas* and the Origins of the *Gens Anglorum*', in P. Wormald, D. Bullough and R. Collins, eds, *Ideal and Reality in Frankish and Anglo-Saxon Society: Studies presented to J.M. Wallace-Hadrill* (Oxford, 1983), pp. 99–129; see also, B. Yorke, 'The Vocabulary of Anglo-Saxon Overlordship', *Anglo-Saxon Studies in Archaeology and History*, 2 (1981), pp. 171–200.

[113] P. Sims-Williams, 'St Wilfrid and Two Charters Dated A.D. 676 and 680', *Journal of Ecclesiastical History*, 39 (1988), pp. 163–83; C. Cubitt, *Anglo-Saxon Church Councils c.650–c.850* (Leicester, 1995).

[114] S. Wood, 'Bede's Northumbrian Dates Again', *English Historical Review*, 98 (1983), pp. 280–96.

[115] P. Wormald, 'A Handlist of Anglo-Saxon Lawsuits', *Anglo-Saxon England*, 17 (1988), pp. 247–81; idem, 'Charters, Law and the Settlement of Disputes in Early Medieval England', in W. Davies and P. Fouracre, eds, *The Settlement of Disputes in Early Medieval Europe* (Cambridge, 1986), pp. 149–68; A. Kennedy, 'Disputes about Bookland: the Forum for their Adjudication', *Anglo-Saxon England*, 14 (1985), pp. 175–85; idem, 'Law and Litigation in the *Libellus Æthelwoldi Episcopi*', *Anglo-Saxon England*, 24 (1995), pp. 131–83.

Wormald's re-examination of the long-disputed nature of pre-conquest judicial immunities and his demonstration that the exclusion of the sheriff and of all royal agents from the bishop of Worcester's triple hundred of Oswaldslow was the achievement, not of St Oswald, but of St Wulfstan after the Norman Conquest had brought new aristocratic pressures and new concepts of law.[116]

The identification of actual Anglo-Saxon estates by locating the bounds listed in individual charters has commanded the attention of a huge number of scholars and local historians, too numerous to list here. Let it suffice to draw attention to some highlights and some of the more wide-ranging studies. Dr Margaret Gelling devoted much of the third volume of her *Place-Names of Berkshire* to a systematic identification and mapping of the boundary clauses of that county, and she and Dr Hart added two further volumes to the series of *Early Charters* established by H.P.R. Finberg covering the Thames Valley and northern England.[117] A keen understanding of landscape history and of both topographical and cartographical evidence underlies the work of the geographer, Dr Della Hooke, in the West Midlands and in Devon and Cornwall; her identifications of charter bounds have set high standards by their exemplary maps and their provision of Ordnance Survey references throughout.[118] Her interpretations are therefore clear and scholars may build upon, or refute them. Few scholars will be able to profit from Dr Hart's advice to ride around the bounds (however much they might wish to do so!), but the value of an initimate knowledge of the local terrain has emerged again and again from these studies.[119]

---

[116] P. Wormald, 'Oswaldslow: An Immunity?', in Brooks and Cubitt, eds, *St Oswald of Worcester*, pp. 117–28, and a fuller exposition in idem, 'Lordship and Justice in the Early English Kingdom: Oswaldslow Revisited', in W. Davies and P. Fouracre, eds, *Property and Power in Early Medieval Europe* (Cambridge, 1995), pp. 114–36.

[117] M. Gelling, *The Place-Names of Berkshire*, iii, English Place-Name Society, 51 (Cambridge, 1976), pp. 615–799; idem, *The Early Charters of the Thames Valley* (Leicester, 1979); Hart, *Early Charters of Northern England and the North Midlands*. This series' coverage is now complete save for Sussex and Kent, but the publication of the charters of Selsey and of Rochester and the preparation of the Christ Church, Canterbury volume makes the final volume largely unnecessary.

[118] D. Hooke, *Anglo-Saxon Landscapes of the West Midlands: The Charter Evidence*, BAR, British series 95 (Oxford, 1981); idem, *The Anglo-Saxon Landscape: The Kingdom of the Hwicce* (Manchester, 1985); idem, *Worcestershire Anglo-Saxon Charter Bounds* (Woodbridge, 1990); idem, *Pre-Conquest Charter-Bounds of Devon and Cornwall* (Woodbridge, 1994).

[119] C. Hart, *An Autobiography and Personal Philosophy of a Retired Physician* (Lampeter, 1998), p. 101. Of many examples of the value of local knowledge I would cite H. Gough's superb 'Eadred's Charter of 949 and the Extent of the Monastic Estate of Reculver, Kent', in Ramsay et al., eds, *St Dunstan*, pp. 89–102. I have attempted to practise what I preached (above pp. 193–5) in Chapters 11 and 12 below.

The boundary clauses are also important as examples of Old English that have the unusual merit (if their authority can be established) of being both datable and localizable. For the history of English dialects (their phonology, their vocabulary and their syntax) the charters are therefore of fundamental importance. A series of ground-breaking articles by Peter Kitson, based upon study of the entire corpus of charter boundaries repay reading several times; he has begun to lay the foundations of a new understanding of how English actually developed in different regions.[120] His forthcoming *Guide to Anglo-Saxon Charter Boundaries* to be published by the English Place-Name Society, which will offer an interpretation of every perambulation informed by his linguistic expertise, is eagerly awaited. With this notable exception, the vernacular charters, wills and writs have been relatively little exploited by the current generation of philologists. Recent work by Kathryn Lowe on variant and later versions of Anglo-Saxon wills has, however, begun to show what a treasure chest awaits both for those constructing the linguistic atlas of England as for those seeking to understand the realities of Anglo-Saxon legal proceedings.[121]

It is evident then that the last twenty-five years have seen significant progress in the fundamental work of editing the charters and some major advances in understanding their contribution to Anglo-Saxon diplomatic, palaeography, political and ecclesiastical history, prosopography, law, linguistics, social and economic history, local history and topography. There is a great deal of basic work still to be done, and the need for collaboration between amateurs and professionals and between those whose expertise lies in different fields remains as great as ever. The prospect is exciting as new technologies spread both the information and the expertise to an ever widening circle of enthusiasts.

---

[120] P.R. Kitson, 'On Old English Nouns of More than One Gender', *English Studies*, 71 (1990), pp. 185–221; idem, 'Old English Dialects and the Stages of the Transition to Middle English', *Folia Linguistica Historica*, 11 (1992 for 1990), pp. 27–87; idem, 'Geographical Variation in Old English and the Location of Ælfric's and Other Literary Dialects', *English Studies*, 74 (1993), pp. 1–50; idem, 'Quantifying Quantifiers in Anglo-Saxon Charter Boundaries', *Folia Linguistica Historica*, 14 (1994), pp. 29–82; idem, 'The Nature of Old English Dialect Distributions, Mainly as Exhibited in Charter Boundaries', in J. Fisiak, ed., *Medieval Dialectology*, Trends in Linguistics, Studies and Monographs, 79 (Berlin and New York, 1995), pp. 45–135; idem, 'When Did Middle English Begin? Later Than You Think!', in J. Fisiak, ed., *Studies in Middle English Linguistics* (Berlin, 1997), pp. 221–69.

[121] K. Lowe, ' "As fre as thowt"?: Some Medieval Copies and Translations of Old English Wills', in P. Beal and J. Griffiths, eds, *English Manuscript Studies*, 4 (London and Toronto, 1993), pp. 1–23; idem, 'The Nature and Effect of the Anglo-Saxon Vernacular Will', *Legal History*, 19 (1998), pp. 23–61.

10

A New Charter of King Edgar

with M. Gelling and D. Johnson

THE DOCUMENT printed below, an early- or mid-seventeenth-century copy of a hitherto unrecorded charter of 963 by which King Edgar granted 5 hides at Ballidon in Derbyshire to a certain Æthelferth (see Figure 19), came to light early in 1983 among some manuscripts on temporary deposit at the Staffordshire Record Office. It is published by kind permission of the depositor. The account of the provenance of the charter and of the history of the estate, which follows, is the work of one author (D.A.J.), whilst another (N.P.B.) is responsible for the edition and the topographical analysis, and the third (M.G.) has contributed the discussion of the place-name forms.[1]

The document seems to be a competent transcript, on a single sheet of parchment, of an original charter. The handwriting, which may be that of an amanuensis, has not so far been identified.[2] The provenance of the document makes it almost certain that it was at one time in the possession of the Staffordshire antiquary John Huntbach (1639–1705) of Seawall in Bushbury and later of Featherstone in Wolverhampton. Huntbach was a nephew of Sir William Dugdale, who was his mentor in antiquarian studies,[3] and like Dugdale he came of a well-established gentry family. He had no known links with Ballidon, or indeed with Derbyshire, and he seems to have had no particular interests in Anglo-Saxon antiquities. The subjects of his researches were instead those dear to gentlemen antiquaries: the history of his own county (especially southern and south-western Staffordshire, which lay near to his home) and the pedigrees of its leading families. The Ballidon charter would

---

[1] The authors are grateful for much generous help received from Mr D.V. Fowkes, Mr M.W. Greenslade, Mr F.B. Stitt and Mr D.G. Vaisey on the problems of the manuscript's provenance, from Mr R.N. Smart on palaeographical matters, from Mr R.P.H. Green, Dr M. Herren and Dr M. Lapidge on the traces of verse in the proem, from Dr S.D. Keynes on diplomatic and from Mr P. Kitson on matters onomastic and topographical.

[2] It is not that of Dodsworth, of Spelman, or of any of the antiquaries mentioned below.

[3] For Huntbach, see M.W. Greenslade, *The Staffordshire Historians*, Staffordshire Record Society, Collections for a History of Staffordshire, 4th series, 11 (1982), pp. 69–72.

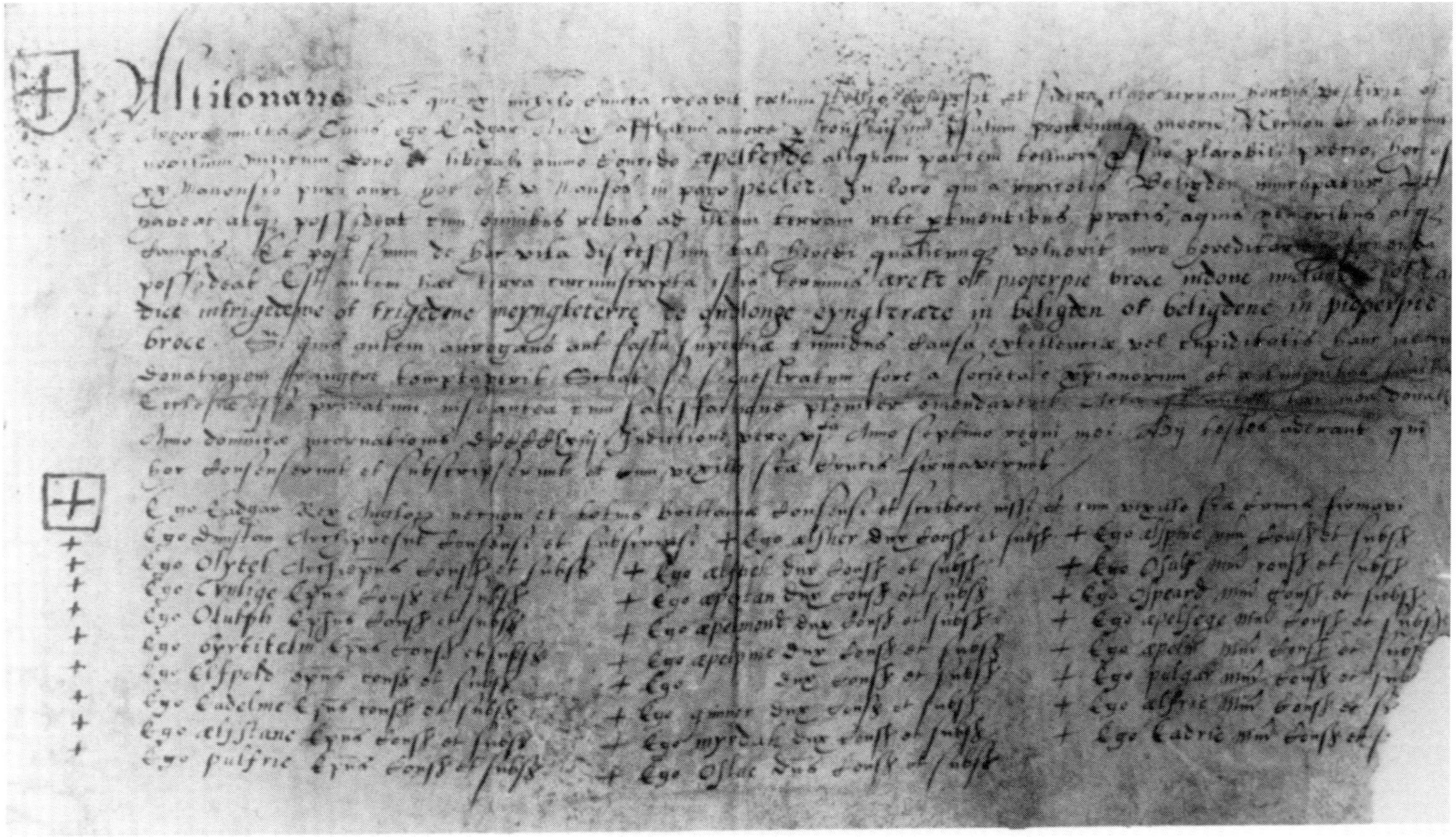

Figure 19. Stafford, Staffordshire Record Office, Temporary Deposit 1406: seventeenth-century copy of the Ballidon charter of King Edgar, 963 (reduced).

probably have interested him only as a curiosity, and the copy may indeed have been given to him as such. If so, the donor may have been Dugdale or one of the other midland antiquaries whom Huntbach knew – perhaps his friend Walter Chetwynd (1633–93), squire of Ingestre, Staffordshire, and author of an unfinished 'Short Survey' of Staffordshire, or the lawyer and author Sir Simon Degge (1613–1703), who collected material for the history of both Staffordshire and Derbyshire.[4]

Since it is not clear how Huntbach acquired the document, the story of the descent and ultimate fate of the single-sheet charter from which it was apparently copied remains a mystery. Edgar granted the estate to a layman. Ballidon was in lay hands in 1066 and 1086,[5] and remained in lay hands thereafter. By the late twelfth century it was held by the Harthill family, perhaps descended from the Colle who held Harthill, Derbyshire, in 1086 of Ralph fitzHubert of Crich, lord of Ballidon. In the late fourteenth century it passed by marriage from the Harthills to the Cokaynes; they held it until the early years of the seventeenth century, when Sir Edward Cokayne sold the manor.[6] If it could be assumed that Edgar's charter came into the hands of the Harthills or the Cokaynes, an apparently plausible link with Huntbach could be suggested: the charter might have been among the 'old evidences' belonging to Sir Aston Cokayne, grandson of Sir Edward, which seem to have been borrowed in 1651 by Sir Francis Nethersole and sent to Dugdale.[7] The assumption is, however, inherently unlikely. No surviving Anglo-Saxon royal diploma is known to have been preserved in lay hands continuously from the time of its writing. Moreover, if the charter had come to Dugdale (and there is no evidence that he knew of it), it was probably not from Sir Aston Cokayne's muniments; for the 'old writings' of Ballidon are known to have descended with the manor

[4] Ibid., pp. 37–48 and 72–7.

[5] BD i, fo. 277; see *Victoria County History of Derbyshire* i, ed. W. Page (London, 1905), p. 350.

[6] Ibid.; R. Hodges, M. Poulter and M. Wildgoose, 'The Medieval Grange at Roystone Grange', *Derbyshire Archaeological Journal*, 102 (1982), pp. 88–100, at 90–1; and A.E. Cockayne, *Cockayne Memoranda* (privately ptd, Congleton, 1873), pp. 162–3, citing BL, Add. 6675, p. 193.

[7] *The Life, Diary, and Correspondence of Sir William Dugdale*, ed. W. Hamper (London, 1827), pp. 256–7. For Sir Aston and his relationship to Sir Edward, see the entries in the *Dictionary of National Biography* for Sir Aston and Thomas Cokayne. If the Cokaynes owned the charter, an alternative route to Huntbach can be suggested. The Staffordshire antiquary Sampson Erdeswick (ob. 1603) was related to the Cokaynes (see E.A. Sadler, 'The Ancient Family of Cockayne and their Monuments in Ashbourne Church', *Derbyshire Archaeological Journal*, 55 (1934), pp. 18–19), and most of his collections came into Chetwynd's possession (Greenslade, *Staffordshire Historians*, p. 38). There is no trace of the Ballidon charter in Chetwynd's antiquarian manuscripts, now part of Staffordshire Record Office, D.649.

on Sir Edward's sale.[8] The 'evidences' which interested Dugdale in 1651 were probably those of Sir Aston's manor of Pooley, in Polesworth, which lay in Dugdale's own country of Warwickshire.

It is therefore more probable that the charter survived in the archives of a religious house. Two had links with Ballidon, but both were twelfth-century foundations. The Cistercian abbey of Garendon, Leicestershire, was granted land at Ballidon by the Harthills in the early thirteenth century and later established a grange there.[9] In 1205 the Augustinian priory of Dunstable, Bedfordshire, acquired the tithes of Ballidon from Geoffrey le Cauceis; a few years later Adam of Harthill granted Dunstable a messuage in Ballidon in lieu of his demesne tithes.[10] None of the surviving cartularies of Garendon and Dunstable mentions Edgar's charter and it was not among the Dunstable muniments in the early thirteenth century.[11]

The Staffordshire abbey of Burton is the only religious house which is known to have preserved the texts of pre-Conquest charters concerning Derbyshire estates in its archives; it is also the only house which was holding land in Derbyshire in 1066.[12] Although Burton had no interests in Ballidon, then or later, it had been extensively endowed with property in the county by its founder, the prominent Mercian thegn Wulfric Spot (who died in or shortly after 1002).[13] At the Conquest Ballidon was held by Leofric and Leofnoth, who were probably brothers and whose other estates in Derbyshire and Nottinghamshire included lands which had once belonged to Wulfric. How they had acquired Ballidon is not known; there is no evidence that it had ever been held by Wulfric, and their relationship to him (if any) is unknown.[14] But it is possible that they or their predecessors at Ballidon might have used Burton Abbey as a suitable local repository for a royal charter. More than one member of Wulfric's family seems to have deposited charters there.[15] Such charters were not necessarily of interest to the abbey itself. About half the surviving Burton archive

---

[8] A.E. Cokayne, 'South Notes on the Cokayne Family', *Derbyshire Archaeological Journal*, 3 (1881), p. 130. The author of the article is the A.E. 'Cockayne' of n. 6 above.

[9] Hodges et al., 'Roystone Grange', pp. 89–90.

[10] G.H. Fowler, *A Digest of the Charters Preserved in the Cartulary of the Priory of Dunstable*, Bedfordshire Historical Record Society, 10 (1926), nos 238–9.

[11] G.R.C. Davis, *Medieval Cartularies of Great Britain* (London, 1958), nos 320–2 and 431–2, and BL, Harley 1885, 4–6v, esp. 6. In the early seventeenth century the Harthills' charters to Garendon could not be found (Hodges et al., 'Roystone Grange', p. 89).

[12] *VCH Derbyshire* i, ed. Page, pp. 298–9 and 327–55.

[13] *Charters of Burton Abbey*, ed. P.H. Sawyer (Oxford, 1979), pp. xxxix–xl and xliv–xlvii.

[14] Ibid., p. xliii, and *VCH Derbyshire* i, ed. Page, pp. 305–6 and 350.

[15] *Burton Charters*, ed. Sawyer, p. xlviii.

of pre-Conquest charters concerns estates which did not belong to Wulfric and have no known connection with Burton Abbey; one such charter records the grant of 10 hides at Parwich, Derbyshire – the parish immediately to the west of Ballidon – to a certain Ælfhelm, possibly Wulfric's brother.[16] The Ballidon charter might thus have survived in the abbey's archives, and have passed with them at the Dissolution to Sir William Paget, who built up a great estate in Staffordshire.[17] But it would have been of no interest to the Pagets as a title-deed, and therefore might easily have strayed from their muniments. One at least of the abbey's single-sheet pre-Conquest charters, now lost, fell into the hands of the antiquary William Burton (1575–1645) of Fauld, near Tutbury, Staffordshire; he printed it in 1622 and gave the original to the eminent lawyer Sir Edward Coke.[18] Some of Burton's notes and papers passed after his death to Huntbach's friend, Walter Chetwynd.[19] They may have included the Ballidon charter.

There is, however, one major objection to such a theory. The Ballidon charter is not mentioned in any surviving Burton Abbey cartulary;[20] above all it is not included in the thirteenth-century cartulary which forms part of the Burton miscellany, now Aberystwyth, National Library of Wales, Peniarth 390. Every extant single-sheet pre-Conquest charter from the Burton Abbey archive was copied into Peniarth 390.[21] If the Ballidon charter was also at Burton, why then was it not also included in the cartulary? The only explanation that might be offered – that it had been mislaid at the time the cartulary was compiled – carries us even further into the realms of speculation and special pleading. Whilst, therefore, the probability must be that the Ballidon diploma was a Burton charter, proof is entirely lacking.

---

[16] Ibid., p. xiii and no. 21.

[17] Ibid., p. xiv.

[18] W. Burton, *The Description of Leicestershire* (London, 1622), pp. 209–10, and *Burton Charters*, ed. Sawyer, no. 12.

[19] Greenslade, *Staffordshire Historians*, p. 38. See also the entry for William Burton in the *Dictionary of National Biography*.

[20] For the Burton cartularies containing pre-Conquest charters, see *Burton Charters*, ed. Sawyer, pp. xiv–xv.

[21] *Burton Charters*, ed. Sawyer, nos 14, 17, 23, 26, 27, 28/9 and 32. A medieval scribe numbered each of these charters on their dorse in chronological sequence, corresponding to the order in which they are entered into Peniarth 390 (ibid., p. xiv). Thus ibid. no. 17 of 956 is endorsed 'XVII' and no. 23 of 968 is endorsed 'XXIII'. Since Peniarth 390 has five charters of intermediate date (i.e. between 956 and 968), it would seem that the original of the Ballidon charter was not available in the archives for numbering in this series. It is, however, possible that the numbering was contemporaneous with, or preparatory to, the compilation of the cartulary.

Edition[22]

Kind Edgar grants 5 hides at Ballidon, Derbyshire, to Æthelferth. AD 963

B. Stafford, Staffordshire Record Office, temporary deposit 1406: single-sheet copy, parchment, s. xvii, 205 × 323 mm. Text in thirteen lines, king's attestation in another, followed by the rest of the witnesses in three columns of nine, nine and eight lines. Old English names and bounds written in a larger and less cursive script. Manuscript slightly eaten by mice along part of the right-hand and bottom edges.

Printed from B

+ ALTITONANS dominus qui ex nihilo cuncta creavit cælum stellis composuit^a et sidere^b claro . terram herbis vestivit et arbore^c multa . cuius ego Eadgar anax^d afflatus amore per consensum presulum procerumque meorum . necnon^e et aliorum nobilium militum dono et liberali animo concedo Æþelferde aliquam partem telluris pro suo placabili pretio . hoc est .xx. mancusis^f puri auri . hoc est .v. mansos in pago Pecset . in loco qui a ruricolis Beligden nuncupatur . ut habeat atque possideat cum omnibus rebus ad illam terram rite pertinentibus . pratis . aquis . nemoribus atque campis . et post suum de hac vita discessum tali heredi qualicumque voluerit iure hereditario [. . .]^g perfruendi possideat . Est autem hæc terra circumscripta istis terminis . ærest^h of pioperpic broce in ðone miclan dic . of ðam dice in frigedene^i . of frigedene in cyngstræte^j . ða^k ondlong^l cyngstræte^m in beligden . of beligdene in pioperpic^n broce . Si quis autem arrogans aut fastu superbiæ tumidus causa extollentiæ vel cupiditatis hanc meam donationem frangere temptaverit . sciat se sequestratum fore a societate christianorum et a liminibus sanctæ sanctæ ecclesiæ esse privatum nisi antea cum satisfactione pleniter emendaverit. Acta est autem hæc mea donatio anno dominicæ incarnationis . dcccclxiii . indictione vero vi^{ta} . anno septimo regni mei . Hii testes aderant qui hoc consenserunt et subscripserunt et cum vexillo sanctæ crucis firmaverunt .

+ Ego Eadgar rex Anglorum necnon et totius Brittaniæ consensi et scribere iussi et cum vexillo sanctæ crucis firmavi .

+ Ego Dunstan archipresul consensi et subscripsi

---

[22] The editorial conventions of the British Academy and Royal Historical Society's edition of Anglo-Saxon Charters have normally been followed. Standard abbreviations have been expanded silently; the capitalization has been modernized; the punctuation of the manuscript has been emended by the elimination of commas (inappropriate to a tenth-century exemplar) and the provision, where the sense requires, of a few additional *punctus*; the spelling follows that of the manuscript, though obvious scribal errors are corrected in the text (and the reading of the manuscript recorded in the apparatus).

+ Ego Oscytel[o] archiepiscopus consensi et subscripsi
+ Ego Cynsige episcopus consensi et subscripsi
+ Ego Osulf[p] episcopus consensi et subscripsi
+ Ego Byrhtelm[q] episcopus consensi et subscripsi
+ Ego Elfþold episcopus consensi et subscripsi
+ Ego Eadelm[r] episcopus consensi et subscripsi
+ Ego Ælfstan[s] episcopus consensi et subscripsi
+ Ego Ƿulfric episcopus consensi et subscripsi

+ Ego Ælfher[t] dux consensi et subscripsi
+ Ego Ælfheh[u] dux consensi et subscripsi
+ Ego Æþestan dux consensi et subscripsi
+ Ego Æþelmund[v] dux consensi et subscripsi
+ Ego Æþelƿine[w] dux consensi et subscripsi
+ Ego [ ][x] dux consensi et subscripsi
+ Ego Gunner[y] dux consensi et subscripsi
+ Ego Myrdah dux consensi et subscripsi
+ Ego Oslac dominus consensi et subscripsi
+ Ego Ælfƿine[z] minister consensi et subscripsi
+ Ego Osulf minister consensi et subscripsi
+ Ego Osþeard minister consensi et subscripsi
+ Ego Æþelsege[aa] minister consensi et subscripsi
+ Ego Æþelm minister consensi et subs[cripsi][bb]
+ Ego Ƿulgar minister consensi et sub[scripsi][bb]
+ Ego Ælfric minister consensi et su[bscripsi][bb]
+ Ego Eadric minister consensi et s[ubscripsi][bb]

[a] MS composit [b] MS sidera [c] MS arbora [d] MS arax
[e] MS Necnon [f] MS manensis [g] *Several words appear to be omitted here, such as*: derelinquat . et quamdiu vivat libertatem
[h] MS æreft [i] MS frigedeme [j] MS eyngleterre *or* eyngseterre
[k] MS ðe [l] MS ondlonge [m] MS eyngstræte [n] MS ƿioperƿic
[o] MS Osytel [p] MS Osulph [q] MS byrtibelm [r] MS eadelme
[s] MS ælfstane [t] MS ælsher (*? an error for* Ælfhere)
[u] *Probably a 'Mercian' form for* Ælfheah [v] MS æþelmond [w] MS æþelƿnie
[x] *Blank space in MS* [y] MS gunnor [z] MS ælsþnie
[aa] *Possibly a 'Mercian' form for* Æþelsige [bb] *Reading supplied where MS is eaten*

As may be seen from Figure 19, the seventeenth-century copyist made no attempt to imitate tenth-century letter-forms. Instead he used the standard 'set', or 'engrossing', secretary script of his own day for the Latin text, and a larger, even less cursive, version of it for the English names and boundaries. None the less he does seem to have reproduced some of the features of his exemplar; hence the use of parchment of a size and shape typical of Anglo-Saxon royal diplomas; hence the use of a display script for the opening word of the proem; hence perhaps also the emphasis on the cross at the beginning and on that before the king's attestation by enclosing one in a shield-shaped box, and the other in a square one;[23] hence too the lay-out of the witnesses, with one column of bishops, another of *duces* and a third of *ministri*. The copyist seems to have had little difficulty in transcribing the Latin, though he was probably responsible for the omission of five or six words in the important clause giving the recipient the power to enjoy the estate in his lifetime and to bequeath it as he wished thereafter; but otherwise he just made a few careless slips at the beginning (*composit* for *composuit*, *sidera* for *sidere*, *arbora* for *arbore*), and had problems only with unfamiliar words – *anax*, a rare word deriving from Greek αναξ, 'lord', hence 'king', which is used by at least one other tenth-century Anglo-Latin writer,[24] and *mancusis*, 'mancuses'. He was far less successful in transcribing the Old English, both the personal names and the boundary clause. Though he wrote these parts in an enlarged and more careful script, his ignorance both of the language and of Anglo-Saxon minuscule script led him to see no distinction between þ and *p* and to confuse both with *p*, to confuse ð and *d*, *s* and *l*, and *s* and *f*. Fortunately the boundary clause is not only brief, but also repeats most of the boundary marks; the copyist's second attempts at a word are sometimes a marked improvement upon his first. Thus it would have been difficult to determine what English name might lie behind *in eyngleterre*, had not the ensuing *ondlonge eyngstræte* betrayed that it must be *cyngstræt(e)*. By such means it is possible to reconstruct with some confidence the text that the seventeenth-century copyist had before him.

There would seem to be no room for doubt that the Ballidon charter which he copied was an authentic diploma of Edgar. Not only is it difficult to see in whose interest the forgery of a grant to an unidentified layman could possibly be, but the diploma passes every test of its authority that we can devise for a late copy. The witnesses fit the year 963 and no other; yet the same combination of names is not found in any other extant diploma. The diplomatic is quite different from the standard formulation of Edgar's charters at this time, but links instead with a very small group of the king's diplomas which have specifically Mercian connections.

---

[23] There appear to be no comparably enclosed crosses in the extant single-sheet Anglo-Saxon diplomas.

[24] As Dr Michael Lapidge has pointed out to us, Æthelweard uses *anax* three times of King Edgar, in his version of the poem on the king's coronation at Bath in 973: see *The Chronicle of Æthelweard*, ed. A. Campbell (London, 1962), pp. 55–6.

The witness-list is one of the fullest sets of names that we have for the year 963. The nine bishops can most easily be checked; all fit the year 963.[25] Indeed 963 was the last year in which Bishop Cynesige of Lichfield witnessed charters,[26] and the first in which Bishop Eadhelm of Selsey appears.[27] The presence of just one Bishop Byrhthelm (presumably of Wells) suggests that this well-attended assembly took place between the death of Byrhthelm of Winchester and the consecration of his successor, Æthelwold, on 29 November 963.[28] Of the ealdormen present, Ælfhere of Mercia, his brother Ælfheah of Hampshire, Æthelwine of East Anglia and Æthelstan (sometimes known as *rota*, 'the Red', who probably had authority in some part of Mercia) were all regularly in attendance at Edgar's court.[29] Æthelmund, who had been appointed ealdorman – apparently also in some part of Mercia – as early as 940, was by 963 only occasionally at court.[30] The missing sixth ealdorman – perhaps the seventeenth-century copyist found his exemplar illegible here, or perhaps the exemplar itself had a gap or an unfilled erasure – is likely to have been either Ealdorman Edmund or, more probably, Ealdorman Byrhtnoth of Essex. The last three witnesses in the column of *duces* (Gunner, Myrdah and Oslac), however, are all men who were very rare visitors to Edgar's court; all seem to have been subordinate earls in some part of northern England. Gunner *dux* had appeared fleetingly as a witness of two charters of 958, but otherwise does not appear until 963 when he witnessed a grant of lands in Yorkshire and was himself the recipient of an estate at North Newbald in the same

[25] Dunstan, archbishop of Canterbury (959–88); Oscytel, archbishop of York (956–71); Cynesige, bishop of Lichfield (949–63); Osulf, bishop of Ramsbury (950–70); Byrhthelm, bishop of Wells (956–8 and 959–73); Ælfwold, probably the bishop of Crediton (953–72) rather than of Sherborne (*c.* 964–78); Eadhelm, bishop of Selsey (963–80); Ælfstan, probably the bishop of Rochester (*c.* 961–95) rather than of London (964–96); and Wulfric, ? bishop of Dorchester (*c.* 958–70).

[26] He attests BCS 1112, 1119 and 1121 (= S 712, 723 and 713); his successor, Wynsige, already attests in 964 (BCS 1134 (S 726)).

[27] Eadhelm attests BCS 1101 (S 717), 1112 (S 712) and 1125 (S 714).

[28] For Æthelwold's consecration, see ASC, 963 A, E (*Two of the Saxon Chronicles Parallel*, ed. Charles Plummer (Oxford, 1892–9) i, pp. 114–15). For the complex careers of the two bishops named Byrhthelm in the years 956–63, see N.P. Brooks, *The Early History of the Church of Canterbury* (Leicester, 1984), p. 238–9.

[29] Their careers and family connections can now be conveniently studied in C. Hart, 'Athelstan "Half King" and his Family', *Anglo-Saxon England*, 2 (1973), pp. 115–44, and A. Williams, '*Princeps Merciorum Gentis*: The Family, Career and Connections of Ælfhere, Ealdorman of Mercia', *Anglo-Saxon England*, 10 (1982), pp. 143–72.

[30] In 963 he attests only BCS 1119 (S 723) and 1112 (S 713); for his career, see C.R. Hart, *Early Charters of Northern England and the North Midlands* (Leicester, 1975), pp. 287–8.

shire.[31] Myrdah *dux* witnesses only one other royal diploma, a grant
to the see of York in 958; his name is an English spelling of Old Irish
Muiredach (cf. modern Scots Murdoch), and it is possible that he
was an earl among the Hiberno-Norse (or perhaps Scotto-Norse)
settlers of north-western England.[32] Oslac, uniquely styled *dominus*,
is presumably the man who was to be appointed earl of southern
Northumbria when the earldom was divided in 966;[33] but it is difficult to be certain whether *dominus* is intended as an equivalent for
some such term as *hold* or high-reeve, or whether it is simply a scribal
error for *dux*; for Oslac certainly already attests one charter of 963
and three of 965 as *dux*.[34] The thegns (*ministri*) are less easy to
identify and locate. But Ælfwine and Æthelsige are revealed in the
charters as the two most consistent of Edgar's attendants; they are
known to have held office in the king's household as *discifer* and
camerarius (steward and chamberlain), and they seem to have been
the sons of Ealdorman Ælfhere and Æthelstan 'Half-King' respectively.[35] By contrast, Oswulf and Osweard (who are known to have
been brothers), and Æthelm and Ælfric, appear only intermittently in
the charters,[36] whilst Wulfgar and Eadric do not appear in any other
charter of 963 – though the first had appeared in 962 and Eadric in
961.[37] It is therefore clear that the witness-list of the Ballidon charter
has no anachronistic names, and that it is a record of an important
meeting of the king's *witan* with a particularly strong Mercian and
northern element.

The formulation of the charter, however, is highly unusual and
utterly distinct from the standardized phrases of the majority of Edgar's

[31] BCS 1043 (S 674), 1044 (S 679), 1121 (S 712) and 1113 (S 716); he may be the
same man as the unranked Gunner in BCS 882 (S 550) of 949 and the thegn of BCS
937 (S 633) of 956; and he was probably the father of the Thored who ravaged
Westmorland in 966. See D. Whitelock, 'The Dealings of the Kings of England with
Northumbria in the Tenth and Eleventh Centuries', in P. Clemoes, ed., *The Anglo-
Saxons: Studies . . . presented to B. Dickins* (London, 1959), pp. 70–88, at 78.

[32] Myrdah's other attestation is in BCS 1044 (S 679); for Norsemen from western
Scotland rather than from Ireland, see A.P. Smyth, *Scandinavian York and Dublin* i
(Dublin, 1975), pp. 78–89.

[33] Whitelock, 'Dealings', pp. 77–8.

[34] BCS 1113 (S 716), 1169 (S 734), 1171 (S 732) and 1172 (S 733).

[35] For Ælfwine, see Hart, *Early Charters of Northern England*, pp. 277–8; for
Æthelsige, see Hart, 'Athelstan "Half King" ', pp. 132–3.

[36] Oswulf and Osweard appear in 963 only in BCS 1121 (S 713) and 1123 (S 722);
they are stated to be brothers in a charter of 959 (H.P.R. Finberg, *The Early Charters of
Wessex* (Leicester, 1964), no. 483 (S 652)); Æthelm only witnesses BCS 1119 (S 723) in
963, and Ælfric BCS 1120 (S 719), 1124 (S 708) and 1125 (S 714).

[37] BCS 1093 (S 705) and 1076 (S 695); for possible reconstructions of their careers,
see Hart, *Early Charters of Northern England*, pp. 318 and 366.

charters of the years 960–3.[38] Its *proem*, royal style (*anax*) and much of its anathema are indeed unique; but it shares other features – notably the dating clause, the attestation formulas and elements of the *dispositio* – with a small group of three charters: BCS 1119 (S 723), a grant of land in Shropshire to a thegn Wulfric in 963; and BCS 1040 (S 677) and BCS 1041 (S 667), two charters of Edgar issued in 958 when he was king in Mercia but not yet in Wessex. One of these (BCS 1040) survives on a single sheet of parchment written in a contemporary hand; it provides an instructive parallel to the Ballidon charter.[39]

Both the Ballidon charter and BCS 1040 commence with a cross rather than with a decorative chrismon; in both charters the witnesses are arranged in three columns (bishops, ealdormen and thegns), and all attest with the old-fashioned formula '+ Ego . . . consensi et subscripsi'. The Ballidon charter shares with BCS 1040 and 1119 a very unusual feature – the recipient's name is in the English dative case (*Æthelferde*, *Ealhstane*, *Wulfrice*), rather than being undeclined. It also shares with BCS 1040 the reckoning of the payment for the estate in mancuses of pure gold. Ballidon is said to be 'in pago Pecset' (that is, in the district of the *Pecsæte*, the 'Peak-dwellers'), whilst BCS 1040 is a grant of an estate 'in pago Magesætna' and BCS 1119 'in provincia Þrocensetna'. No other tenth-century diplomas use these old Mercian tribal districts. (Indeed, were it not for the new charter we might have supposed that the *Pecsæte*, otherwise known only from the Tribal Hidage, had passed from history in the seventh or eighth century.)[40] All four charters (Ballidon and BCS 1040, 1041 and 1119) share a virtually identical clause to introduce the English boundaries, and Ballidon (like BCS 1119) uses the Mercian (or rather Anglian) form *ondlong* where a West Saxon would normally have written *andlang*. All four charters also use essentially the same formulas for the dating clause and for the highly distinctive clause introducing the witnesses. It is instructive too that both the Ballidon charter and BCS 1119 are dated in the 'seventh' year of Edgar's reign; that is, they reckon

---

[38] For the standard diplomatic at this time, see S.D. Keynes, *The Diplomas of King Æthelred 'the Unready' 978–1016* (Cambridge, 1980), pp. 70–4.

[39] Wells, Dean and Chapter, Cathedral Charter 1: W.B. Sanders, *Facsimiles of Anglo-Saxon Manuscripts*, Ordnance Survey (Southampton, 1878–84) 11, Wells. BCS 1040 is translated in *EHD*, no. 109. See also Keynes, *Diplomas*, p. 69 and n. 137.

[40] For the Tribal Hidage, see BCS 297; and for its date and manuscript transmission, see W. Davies and H. Vierck, 'The Contexts of Tribal Hidage: Social Aggregates and Settlement Patterns', *Frühmittelalterliche Studien*, 8 (1974), pp. 223–41 and 288–92. Bakewell is said to be 'on Peac lond' in ASC 924 A (= 920) (*Two Chronicles*, ed. Plummer i, p. 104). It remains uncertain whether the Mercian tribal districts (*Pecsæte*, *Wrocensæte* and *Magesæte*) were archaic by 963 and had already been replaced by the shire system. As late as 1016 we hear of the flight of Ealdorman Eadric with the *Magesæte* in ASC 1016 (*Two Chronicles*, ed. Plummer i, pp. 1522–3). See, further, F.M. Stenton, *Anglo-Saxon England* (3rd edn, Oxford, 1971), pp. 336–7.

his reign from his accession in Mercia in 957 rather than in Wessex in 959.

It would therefore seem that Edgar had the Ballidon charter drawn up by a writer whom he had used when he was king of Mercia alone, and that this writer's practice was consistently distinct from that of the scribe (or scribes) who had written most of his more recent diplomas and indeed from the traditions of the writers who had served the West Saxon and English kings for a generation. The Ballidon charter's links with diplomas issued in Edgar's name as king of Mercia from 957 to 959, its use of the Mercian administrative districts and of Mercian rather than West Saxon dialect in the boundary clause (and perhaps in the witness-list as well[41]) suggests instead that the writer was a Mercian. Probably BCS 1119 was drafted by the same man at the same time, but we can only guess why the king's regular writer was not used.

One other feature of the drafting of the Ballidon charter deserves comment. The proem and the opening of the *dispositio* are full of poetic cadences. Thus 'Altitonans dominus' could well be the opening two and a half feet of a hexameter, while 'cuncta creavit' is a well-known line ending.[42] Similarly 'sidere claro', 'arbore multa', 'afflatus amore' and 'procerumque meorum' could all serve as the ends of hexameters. At the very least, therefore, it is clear that the drafter was repeatedly ornamenting his prose with the resonances of hexameters. That he was attempting rather more than that might be suggested by his preference for the poetic singular *arbore multa*, 'with many a tree', which would balance 'sidere claro', rather than the plural 'arboribus multis', which would have been natural in unadorned prose ('He clothed the land with plants and with *many trees*'); it might also be suggested by the fact that the manuscript has an otherwise inexplicable capital N as the initial letter of *necnon*, which marks the point where the poetic cadences cease. The problems in such an interpretation became clear, however, if we print the opening of the charter as verse:

Altitonans dominus qui ex nihilo cuncta creavit	1
caelum stellis composuit et sidere claro .	2
terram herbis vestivit et arbore multa;	3
cuius ego Eadgar anax afflatus amore	4
per consensum presulum procerumque meorum . . .	5

As they stand these are not hexameters, since every line has false

---

[41] See above, textual notes *u* and *aa*.

[42] Michael Lapidge has drawn our attention to the occurrence of this familiar phrase first in Lucretius, *De Natura Rerum* ii.1147, then in Christian poets such as (pseudo-) Paulinus of Nola, *Carmen* xxxii.217, and Prosper, *Epigrammata* lv.1, and in Aldhelm, *Carmen de Virginitate* 35, and *Enigmata* xci.1 etc. He also points out that hexameter cadences are found in the same draftsman's BCS 1041 (S 667), such as the hackneyed 'spes unica mundi', first found in Caelius Sedulius, *Carmen Paschale* i.60.

quantities and several lack an adequate caesura.[43] None the less, lines 1, 2 and perhaps 5 might seem to be attempted hexameters. Lines 3 and 4 are a mess as they stand; both lack a foot – unless we suppose not only that elision is not practised (although it is necessary in line 1) but also that several short syllables have been scanned as long. It would indeed be possible to 'improve' these lines somewhat by emendation:

> terram herbis vestivit et *induit* arbore multa;
> cuius ego Eadgar anax afflatus amore *benigno* . . .[44]

But we are here on a slippery slope, made the more hazardous by our ignorance of the draftsman's intentions: there is room for doubt whether what we have is simply richly ornamented prose, or very rough or unfinished verse. That it should be read as ornamented prose is suggested by the apparent use of the rhythms of the medieval accentual *cursus* in its *clausulae* (that is, the sequences of syllables which conclude individual sentences and clauses).[45] Thus after a suitably sonorous opening (*Àltitónans*) we find, as in much tenth-century rhythmic prose, a clear preference for the *cursus planus* and the *planus* variant ('cúncta creávit', 'sidere cláro', 'hérbis vestívit', 'árbore múlta', 'afflátus amóre', 'procerúmque meórum') with just a single example of the *cursus tardus* 'stéllis compósuit'). In so short a passage with only a single sentence ending, it is not possible to apply the standard tests to establish that these rhythms are not accidental;[46] but we may be encouraged to suppose them deliberate when we find a closely similar pattern of rhythmic *clausulae* in the arenga of one, but only one, of the three charters whose diplomatic has been shown to have links with the Ballidon charter. Thus the proem of BCS 1041 is replete with the

[43] In line 1 *nihilo* is an anapaest, but needs to be a dactyl or a spondee (? read as *nilo*); in line 2 there is no caesura and the *-it* of *composuit* needs to be long but is short; line 3 lacks a foot; line 4 lacks both a foot and a caesura; and in line 5 there is again no caesura, and the first *u* of *presulum* has to be long, whereas it is short.

[44] We owe this suggestion and much of our understanding of the complexities of this passage to the kindness of Dr Michael Herren.

[45] The fundamental works on the *cursus* are now G. Lindholm, *Studien zum mittellateinischen Prosarhythmus* (Stockholm, 1963), for the period to *c.* 850 AD, and T. Janson, *Prose Rhythm in Medieval Latin from the 9th to the 13th Century*, Studia Latina Stockholmiensia, 20 (Stockholm, 1975). A major study of the use of rhythmic prose in Anglo-Latin is urgently needed; but see the pioneering work of M. Winterbottom, 'Aldhelm's Prose Style and its Origins', *Anglo-Saxon England*, 6 (1977), pp. 39–76, esp. 71–3, and P. Chaplais, 'The Letter of Bishop Wealdhere of London to Archbishop Brihtwold of Canterbury: The Earliest "Letter Close" Extant in the West', in M.B. Parks and A.G. Watson, eds, *Medieval Scribes, Manuscripts and Libraries: Essays presented to N.R. Ker* (Oxford, 1978), pp. 3–23, esp. 18–19. We are indebted to Dr Chaplais for drawing our attention to the possible use of the *cursus* in this charter.

[46] In order to achieve a consistent basis for comparison between authors, Janson's tests are limited to the ends of sentences (*Prose Rhythm*, pp. 14–21).

planus and *planus* variant ('cónditor órbis', 'lustrándo percúrrit', 'spléndore cómit', 'concédens donávit', 'repándi precépit') and has otherwise just a single *velox* ('evangélicum paradígma'). The use of rhythmic prose has not hitherto been detected in an Anglo-Saxon royal diploma; but it may prove to be an important diagnostic tool in Anglo-Saxon diplomatic, and should be recorded by charter students wherever it is found or suspected.

The Æthelferd or Æthelferth who is the recipient of the Ballidon charter is not given any rank and therefore cannot be identified with certainty. None the less, a man receiving 5 hides of land is likely to have been (or thereby to have become) a thegn; so it is possible that Æthelferth was the thegn of that name who witnesses, in a lowly position, an authentic diploma of Edgar of the year 960, and who would seem to have been a very occasional and junior visitor to the king's court.[47]

Despite the difficulties which the seventeenth-century scribe had in transcribing Old English, his copy of the Ballidon charter has preserved important forms of the Derbyshire place-names Ballidon, Friden and Parwich, and of the folk-name *Pecsæte*, which add to the materials available to Kenneth Cameron in his *Place-Names of Derbyshire*. The sources for the Middle English spellings of these names quoted below may be ascertained there.[48] Ballidon and Parwich had previously been discussed by Eilert Ekwall.[49]

The charter form *Beligden* validates the etymology given by Ekwall and Cameron for Ballidon. The name is a compound of *denu*, 'valley', with *belg*, modern belly, which in Old English meant 'bag'. Forms of this word differ according to dialect and date. The form evidenced in *Beligden* is on record: the part of the Rushworth Gospels which is a Mercian text has *beligas*, 'wine-skins'. In the place-name, *belig* may refer to the rounded embrasure in which the village lies, which is cut into the side of a longer valley. The use of a noun rather than an adjective as the qualifying term may indicate that it is not the overall shape of the longer valley that is being described. The Domesday Book spelling, *Belidene*, faithfully represents the charter form. Most subsequent spellings have

---

[47] BCS 1055 (S 687: BL., Cotton Augustus ii.40; E.A. Bond, *Facsimiles of Ancient Charters in the British Museum* (London, 1873–8) iii, p. 22), where he attests last of 25 *ministri*. He also attests the spurious BCS 1046 and 1047 (S 658 and 673); he is 17th out of 19 thegns in BCS 1176 (S 738) and 14th out of 20 in BCS 1189 (S 737), both of 966; he is 14th out of 20 in BCS 1221 (S 758) and 1225 (S 760), 13th out of 19 in both BCS 1222 (S 757) and 1224 (S 759), and last of 14 in BSC 1226 (S 769) – all of the year 968.

[48] K. Cameron, *The Place-Names of Derbyshire*, 3 vols., English Place-Name Society, 27–9 (Cambridge, 1959) i, p. 1–2, and ii, 343, 369 and 403–4.

[49] *The Concise Oxford Dictionary of English Place-Names* (Oxford, 1936), pp. 23 and 341 (4th edn, Oxford, 1960), pp. 24 and 358.

Bal-, and the *-a-* of these could reasonably be ascribed to the common Anglo-Norman confusion of *-a-* and *-e-*.

piowerwic broce is probably to be translated 'Parwich brook'. When confronted by the phonological problems raised by this form, one is tempted to dissociate the name in the charter bounds from Parwich by postulating a different distribution of the letters *p*, *þ*, and *p* in the original The name copied could be assumed to have been *Wiowerwic or *Wioþerwic instead of *Piowerwic*. A hypothetical *Wioþerwic could be associated with the lost place called Weatherwick, recorded in Wirksworth parish from 1276 to *c.* 1750. But 'Parwich brook' is the sensible rendering in relation to the probable location of the boundary, and *Piowerwic*, however obscure, is probably the genuine Old English form of Parwich. There is little point in trying all the possible combinations of *p*, *w* and *th* in order to avoid this conclusion.

Parwich has hitherto been considered a compound of the settlement term *wīc* with a pre-English river-name (British **Pebro-*, Primitive Welsh *Pebr, Welsh *Pefr*) meaning 'the bright one', which has become Peover, Cheshire, the first part of Perry, Shropshire, and Peffer, the name of several streams in Scotland.[50] There is another charter spelling for Parwich, *Peuerwich* in BCS 1175 (S 739),[51] but this charter is not certainly authentic and is only preserved in the mid-thirteenth-century cartulary, Peniarth 390; the *-wich* of the place-name certainly reveals post-Conquest influence. The form in the new charter takes precedence over this. From 1086 onwards Parwich is well recorded, the first element appearing as *Pever-*, *Pevre-*, *Pewer-*, *Peure-*, until the fourteenth century, when the shortened forms with *Per-* and *Pere-* start to appear. Forms with *Par-* as first noted in 1382.

The new spelling *piowerwic* renders derivation from a river-name *Peþr difficult to maintain. It is never possible to be certain whether intervocalic *-v-* and *-u-* in Middle English spellings represent the consonant *-v-* (from earlier *-f-*) or the vowel *-u-*. In the light of the new spelling, the two Middle English forms for Parwich which have *-w-* in the first element (*Pewerwike* 1281, *Pewerwyz* 1284) look especially significant. It now seems likely that Parwich never contained an *-f-*. The Old English sound may have been the semi-vowel *-w-*, which was vocalized to *-u-* in most of the Middle English forms.

Neither the *-w-* nor the *-io-* of *piower-* is to be expected in an Old English form derived from *Peþr*. Primitive Welsh *e* is regularly represented by OE *e*. If the *-f-* which is normal in English names from *Peþr* (and from the analogous river-name (*Duþr*, modern Dover) had suffered interchange with *-w-*, a diphthong *io* / *eo* might be ascribed to the effect

[50] W.F.H. Nicolaisen, *Scottish Place-Names* (London, 1976), p. 164.
[51] *Burton Charters*, ed. Sawyer, no. 21.

of this following -*w*-. But as there is no trace of interchange between -*f*- and -*w*- in names which certainly derive from *Peƀr* and *Duƀr* there is no warrant for assuming such a development in the present name. (Nor, incidentally, is there any sign of substitution of -*w*- for -*f*- in the pre-Conquest spellings for names such as Pevensey and Beverley, where -*f*- occurs in Old English words or personal names. The development of Pewsey, Wilts. from OE *Pefesige*, *Pevesige* is probably due to Middle English vocalization of -*v*-.) The modern -*eo*- spelling of Peover, Cheshire, is not an indication that the name contained a diphthong.

It would perhaps be better to abandon the derivation of Parwich from the primitive Welsh river-name *Peƀr*, and to seek an Old English origin for *piower*-; but there is at present no suggestion available which seems worth offering. The etymology of Parwich should be regarded as an open question.

The name *frigedene* is represented on the modern map by Friden, and the charter spelling triumphantly validates Professor Cameron's suggestion that this is 'valley of the goddess Frīg'. Middle English and early modern references (*Stanifridenmuth* early thirteenth-century, *Frydendale-Mouth* 1533, *Frydon Mouthe* 1599), by mentioning the 'mouth' of the valley and equating *denu* with ME *dale*, indicate that the topographical feature is a well-marked one. The name is a welcome addition to the corpus of English place-names which make reference to heathen deities. It has long been recognized that Woden and Thunor occur, but possible references to the goddess Frig have not been regarded as unequivocal. Ekwall, who listed a number of possible occurrences of her name in 1935,[52] gives the correct nominative as *Frēo*, *Frīge* being the genitive. He did not know of this Derbyshire name, and Professor Cameron did not claim it as a proven example because of the limited documentation available in 1959. Whatever conclusions may be reached about the other place-names put forward by Ekwall as containing possible references to the goddess, there is now no reason for rejecting Friden. Recent studies have considerably reduced the number of authentic 'pagan' place-names, and a paper published in 1983 has deleted Thurstable, Essex, from the canon,[53] so it is very pleasing to have gained a 'valley of the goddess Frēo' from this charter. Friden is a bare six miles west of Wensley, the other Derbyshire name of this type.

The remaining place-name in the charter which requires comment is

[52] E. Ekwall, 'Some Notes on English Place-Names Containing Names of Heathen Deities', *Englische Studien*, 70 (1935), pp. 56–9.

[53] L.J. Bronnenkant, 'Thurstable Revisited', *Journal of the English Place-Name Society*, 15 (1982–3), p. 9–19. The most recent general survey of pagan references in English place-names is M. Gelling, 'Further Thoughts on Pagan Place-Names', in F. Sandgren, ed., *Otium et Negotium: Studies in Onomatology and Library Science Presented to Olof von Feilitzen* (Stockholm, 1973), pp. 109–28.

the district-name *Pecset*. This is formed in a manner specially character-istic of the West Midlands by the addition of the plural suffix -*sǣte*, 'dwellers', to the name of a prominent feature of the landscape. The genitive of -*sǣte* was -*sǣt(e)na* and a new nominative, -*sǣtan*, was formed from this. Group-names often appear in the genitive in Old English texts (as in *Myrcna landes . . . W[r]ocen setna . . . Westerna . . . Pecsǣtna* in the Tribal Hidage)[54] and are frequently cited with -*n* in modern historical writing; but -*sǣte*, which may be presumed to lie behind *Pecset* in this document, is the primary form of the nominative. The omission of the final -*e* in *Pecset* is paralleled in the form *Beligden*, which lacks the -*e* almost universally found in Old English spellings of names containing *denu*. Mr P. Kitson remarks that if the manuscript readings here reproduce the charter of 963 accurately, they are evidence for the sporadic loss in place-names in late Old English of unaccented elements whose morphological function was no longer appreciated, a phenomenon not usually reflected in spellings until a much later date.

It remains to identify the Ballidon estate of 963 on the ground and on the map (Figure 20). The estate, being assessed at 5 hides, was evidently substantial. Moreover, the boundary-clause is extremely brief; it can therefore only record the cardinal points of the boundary, not follow every bend and natural feature in detail. In such circumstances it is reasonable to start by looking at the parish boundaries of the area as they can first be detected in the mid-nineteenth century, since the bounds preserved in Anglo-Saxon diplomas often prove to coincide wholly or in part with those of ecclesiastical parishes. Ballidon, however, was not an ancient parish, but a chapelry of the huge medieval parish of Bradbourne. From 1866 the former chapelry of Ballidon was recog-nized as a separate (civil) parish in its own right.[55] Although continuity between the civil parish of 1866 and the medieval chapelry of Ballidon is probable, the relationship of the chapelry to early medieval estates had hitherto been entirely unknown. It is therefore of interest that the parish of 1866 seems to have shared several, and perhaps all, of its boundaries with those of *Beligden* in 963. Pre-Conquest charter bounds most commonly start in the south-western or south-eastern corner of an estate and proceed in a clockwise direction; it can scarcely be a coinci-

[54] BCS 297.

[55] For the ancient parishes, see J.C. Cox, *Derbyshire Churches* iii (Chesterfield, 1877), pp. 427–45. The parish boundaries established in the title maps of the 1840s and 1850s are conveniently plotted on the first edition of the Ordnance Survey 1-inch-to-the-mile maps in the *Index to the Tithe Survey*, Ordnance Survey (London, 1878). The Poor Law Amendment Act of 1866 stipulated that chapelries and other units in which separate Poor Law rates had been levied should be called parishes thereafter. From that time OS maps record Ballidon as a separate parish. Margaret Poulter and Miss J. Sinar have kindly provided expert guidance on parochial development.

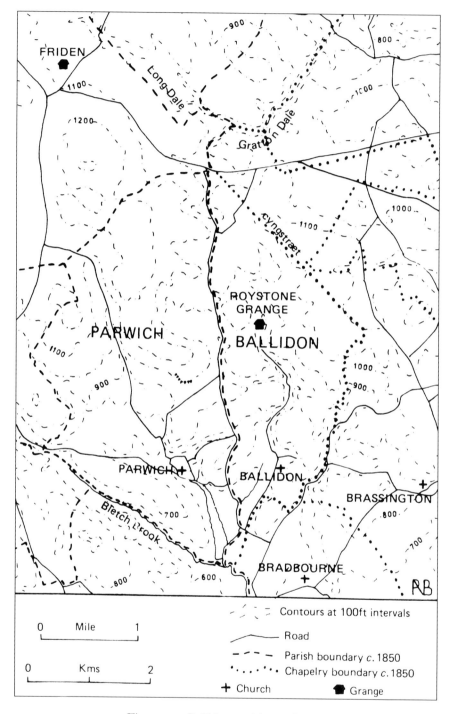

Figure 20. Ballidon and its environs.

dence, therefore, that the southern tip of the civil parish is defined by the stream that flows from Parwich, whilst the charter boundary starts from *piowerwic broce*, 'Parwich brook'. Moreover, the north-western limit of the civil parish follows the course of the Roman road from Buxton (*Aquae Arnemetiae*) to Little Chester (*Derventio*), near Derby,[56] and this road must surely be the *cyngstræt* of the charter, for *stræt* is the normal Old English term for a Roman road. Since we have seen that the charter's *frigedene* and *beligden* have given rise to the modern names Friden and Ballidon, the general course taken by the survey is clear, though the details must remain uncertain:

1 *First from Parwich brook*
The stream that flows through Parwich forms the boundary of the civil parish of Ballidon from SK 195529 to SK 195531.

2 *to the big dyke* (or *ditch*)
In the high limestone terrain of the Peak, much of it over 1000 feet and with excellent drainage, substantial ditches are not needed and linear earthworks are very rare. Property boundaries are formed by stone walls, constructed by different techniques at various times between the Roman Iron Age and the seventeenth century or the eighteenth.[57] Since the charter does not state that the boundary goes along the big dyke (in contrast to its reference to *cyngstræt*), it may be that *miclan dic* was a linear feature which crossed or abutted the Ballidon boundary. Field-work undertaken by Dr R. Hodges and Mr M. Wildgoose has revealed traces of an earthwork bank of Roman or pre-Roman date, now very largely ploughed out, to the north of Parwich (Figure 20). If (as is possible) this once extended up to or beyond the Parwich/Ballidon boundary, then it is likely to have been the *miclan dic*. An alternative suggestion, which we owe to Mr Kitson, is that the road which forms the Parwich/Ballidon boundary (Highway Lane, Backhill Lane and Parwich Lane) may preserve the line of the *miclan dic*. Recent field-work along this route has not, however, revealed any sign of an early boundary bank and ditch, nor has the systematic study of the field and property divisions of the medieval Roystone Grange, whose eastern boundary runs along part of this road.[58]

3 *from the dyke to Friden*

---

[56] I.V. Margary, *Roman Roads in Britain* (3rd edn, London, 1973), no. 71a.

[57] Hodges et al., 'Roystone Grange', pp. 96–9.

[58] R. Hodges and M. Wildgoose, 'Roman or Native in the White Peak: the Roystone Grange Project and its Regional Implications', *Derbyshire Archaeological Journal* 101 (1981), pp. 42–57. We are most grateful to Dr Hodges for organizing further field-work in the search for *miclan dic*, to supplement the preliminary investigation of the line of the parish boundary carried out by one of the authors (N.P.B.).

Friden is today the name of a small hamlet, a brickworks and a large house (Friden Grange, formerly Friden House) at SK 172607, the focus of an estate. The house and settlement lay some 3000 yards (2700 m) north-west of the northern tip of the civil parish of Ballidon. The head of a narrow dry valley, known at least since 1744 as Long Dale,[59] passes within 500 yards of the modern settlement of Friden. This valley, which stretches from SK 173615 to the point where it joins Gratton Dale at SK 196599, is the only candidate for the original 'valley of the goddess Frēo'. Indeed, Mr Kitson (who first made the identification) believes that the name *Frigedenu* may have applied to the whole complex of Gratton Dale as well as Long Dale. The head of Gratton Dale stretches up to the vicinity of Pikehall (SK 192592), the northern tip of the civil parish of Ballidon. On this interpretation, the *frigedene* of the charter may be here defining the northern end of the modern parish. Even if the name *frigedene* already by 963 applied to the site of the modern settlement of Friden, it is possible that the charter was referring to the boundary of an estate centred on Friden rather than to the settlement itself. It is therefore by no means certain whether the estate of the charter extended any further north than the present parish.

4 *From Friden to kingstreet*

The parish boundary joins the Roman road at SK 193591. (Beyond Ballidon parish to the north, this road has marked the boundaries of a series of ancient parishes almost as far as Buxton itself.)

5 *then along kingstreet to Ballidon*

The parish boundary follows the course of the Roman road in a south-easterly direction to the point (SK 217567) where the road changed its alignment in order to begin a descent over difficult terrain. The 'to Ballidon' of the charter is too imprecise for certainty as to whether the estate of 963 stretched as far south as the boundary of the modern parish, or whether it left the Roman road at a more northerly point and extended down the principal valley into the centre of the hamlet of Ballidon itself.

6 *from Ballidon to Parwich Brook*

Back to the starting-point.

As defined in the new charter, the estate of Ballidon in 963 seems to have had much the same boundaries and to have been about as large as the civil parish of 1866. Further work in the field, from the air or in local archives may establish the identification of *miclan dic* more certainly and therefore fix the line of the western boundary. It is important to bear in mind, however, that the 5-hide estate of 963 may have

---

[59] Cameron, *Place-Names of Derbyshire* ii, p. 395.

been larger than the 4 carucates held by Leofric and Leofnoth in 1066;[60] it may have been the Domesday estate, rather than that of 963, whose boundaries were fossilized in those of the medieval chapelry and of the later civil parish.

Despite such uncertainties, this newly discovered charter throws light on a dark corner of the Peak District and its nomenclature in the tenth century. It records a large assembly of the king's *witan* with a strong northern and midland representation; and it confirms the existence of a Mercian tradition of charter writing in Edgar's reign that is quite distinct from that of the king's regular writers. The discovery of a new Anglo-Saxon charter is a very rare event. Staffordshire, where the Ballidon charter was found and where five single-sheet diplomas of the tenth century and the eleventh came to light in 1941,[61] has a unique record in modern times. But, whilst the likelihood that further originals will be found is perhaps remote, the discovery of the Ballidon charter serves as a welcome pointer to the treasures that may still await identification amongst the papers of sixteenth- and seventeenth-century antiquaries.

---

[60] *VCH Derbyshire* i, ed. Page, p. 350, incorrectly attributes 3 carucates to the Domesday estate of *Belidene*. Dr R.F. Hunnisett and Margaret Condon of the Public Record Office have kindly confirmed that the reading of the manuscript (277r) is *iiij car'* (as printed in 1783).

[61] *Burton Charters*, ed. Sawyer, nos 17, 23, 26, 27 and 32. These texts had, however, been known previously from the versions in the Burton cartulary, Peniarth 390. [For subsequent discoveries of Anglo-Saxon diplomas, see above, pp. 204–6.]

11

The Micheldever Forgery

T HE MUNIMENTS or archives of Winchester College preserve the records of the administration of the school and of its properties over the last 600 years. How odd therefore that the four oldest documents date not from 1382, but from some four centuries before the school's foundation. They are charters of the tenth and early eleventh centuries conveying lands, not of course to the college, but to the monastery in Winchester known as the New Minster, which in late Anglo-Saxon times lay immediately adjacent to the cathedral (the Old Minster). These four diplomas are the only pre-Conquest charters from the New Minster to survive in what purports to be original form; the texts were printed three times in the later nineteenth century with varying standards of accuracy and were facsimiled by the Ordnance Survey in 1884.[1] Yet they have received very little scholarly attention since that time, apart from the pioneering work of G.B. Grundy on the boundaries of the estates.[2] There has however been some consensus among experts in diplomatic (the study of the formulaic phrasing of the charters) and in palaeography that three of the charters – the lease by the community of New Minster to the thegn Alfred of an estate at Chiseldon in Wiltshire (925 × 933), King Eadmund's grant of Pewsey in the same county to New Minster in 940, and Cnut's restoration of Drayton in Hampshire to the monks in 1019 – are authentic documents written in scripts that have every appearance of being contemporary with the date they bear.

There has been no such agreement about the first of the charters in the muniments – the purported grant to the New Minster by Edward

---

[1] *Liber Monasterii de Hyda*, ed. E. Edwards, Rolls Series, (London, 1866), pp. 85–97, 138–44, 147–50, 324–6; W.B. Sanders, *Facsimiles of Anglo-Saxon Manuscripts*, 3 vols, Ordnance Survey (Southampton, 1878–84), iii, Winchester College 1–4; BCS 596, 648, 748. Birch's edition was never taken beyond documents of the year 975, so he did not edit the Drayton charter, which has been translated in *EHD*, no. 132.

[2] G.B. Grundy, 'The Saxon Land Charters of Hampshire with Notes on Place-Names and Field-Names', *Archaeological Journal*, second series, 28 (1921), pp. 140–2 [for Candover]; 31 (1924) pp. 63–5 [for Curdridge]; ibid., pp. 82–5 [for Durley]; ibid., pp. 119–20 [for *Rige leah*]; 33 (1926), pp. 232–6 [for Micheldever], ibid., pp. 305–8 [for Cranbourne]; idem, 'The Saxon Land Charters of Wiltshire', *Archaeological Journal*, second series, 26 (1919), pp. 247–51 [for Pewsey].

the Elder of one hundred hides of land at Micheldever in Hampshire in the year 900. The late Professor H.P.R. Finberg, who habitually took a less sceptical view of Anglo-Saxon charters than most scholars, calendared it as an original.[3] But the prevailing scholarly opinion seems to have been that of W.H. Stevenson, who dismissed it as a forgery of the early eleventh century; the leading palaeographers T.A.M. Bishop and N.R. Ker date the script of the charter to that period, and Professor Dorothy Whitelock has lent her authority to those who suspect the document.[4] But since none of these scholars has given the reasons for their views on this particular charter, it is not surprising that at Winchester considerable uncertainty should reign about the status of the Micheldever charter. If Finberg were right, the charter would not only be the oldest document in the muniments, it would also be the only diploma of Edward the Elder to survive in original form anywhere; it would provide unimpeachable evidence for the antiquity of the division of Hampshire into 'hundreds' for administrative and legal purposes at that early date and would have much to tell us about the early development of the New Minster and of its estates. If however it is a forgery, we need to know the motive for, and the occasion of, the forgery and then to see what the document has to teach us of Micheldever and the New Minster at that time. It has therefore seemed appropriate to include a fully study of the Micheldever charter in this volume in order to test its claims to be the college's oldest document and to try to set it in its proper context. To save the reader from requiring access to early editions and to improve upon them, an edition of the charter is appended which adopts *mutatis mutandis* the conventions and standards of the new edition of Anglo-Saxon Charters being published by the British Academy and the Royal Historical Society, of which two volumes have so far appeared at the time of writing.[5] Those sections of the charter that are in Old English are translated in the course of this study.

It is perhaps best to start by explaining the presence of the Micheldever charter and of the other three Anglo-Saxon charters in the college muniments at all. Why were they not lost at the time of the Reformation and of the dissolution of the monasteries like other charters from New Minster? The four charters are not concerned with lands which ever formed part of the college estates, so they have not been preserved as

---

[3] H.P.R. Finberg, *Early Charters of Wessex* (Leicester, 1964), no. 34.
[4] References to these views on the charter are given in Sawyer, *Anglo-Saxon Charters* (S 360).
[5] A. Campbell, *Anglo-Saxon Charters*, i, *Charters of Rochester*, ed. A. Campbell (Oxford, 1973); *Anglo-Saxon Charters*, ii, *Charters of Burton Abbey*, ed. P.H. Sawyer (Oxford, 1979).

title-deeds to college manors. Nonetheless the charters are numbered in the muniments amongst the Woodmancott documents and when they were first brought to light in the nineteenth century they were kept in the Woodmancott drawer.[6] Woodmancott (Woodmancote) was one of two New Minster manors that the college acquired in 1543 by an exchange with Henry VIII: and it is clear that as a result of the exchange the college acquired a miscellaneous mass of deeds, court-rolls, and accounts from Hyde Abbey – as the New Minster was called after its move to Hyde just outside the city walls.[7] It would not seem, however, that the Anglo-Saxon charters were acquired by the college immediately in 1543. For they all bear the signature, in a sixteenth-century hand, of John Fisher (Fyssher). Fisher was related by marriage to Richard Bethell who was not only the tenant of Woodmancott in 1543 but had also emerged in 1538 with the reversion of the site of Hyde Abbey and of its demesne lands. Fisher himself acquired the neighbouring manor of Chilton Candover in 1562. It seems likely that it was John Fisher's antiquarian thieving from the Hyde Abbey archives in 1538 that secured these four charters and much else. For when John Leland visited the site in 1539 hoping to collect manuscripts and chronicles, he drew a blank.[8] Fisher also acquired the sixteenth-century Hyde cartulary, now in the British Library (Harley 1761) and his descendants extracted copies of Micheldever and Woodmancott documents from it. We therefore cannot be sure whether the college acquired these four priceless documents from Fisher himself or from his descendants at Woodmancott. It would seem that they have been preserved by a happy mixture of accident, opportunism, and neglect. Certainly their more recent nineteenth-century history in the college archives – during which they were lost at least once and eventually rediscovered in various parts of the Warden's Lodgings – has not been out of keeping with their earlier fortunes.

Turning to the Micheldever charter itself, we find a manuscript written in a neat and developed form of Anglo-Saxon 'square minuscule'. There can be no doubt that this hand could not belong to the year 900 when square minuscule was in its infancy. Features such as the use of a smaller script for the Old English boundary clauses, the use of

---

[6] WCM 12090 (Micheldever), 12092 (Chiseldon), 12091 (Pewsey), 12093 (Drayton); *Liber de Hyda*, ed. Edwards, passim; W.H. Gummer's manuscript catalogue of the college muniments, ii.59, 63.

[7] J.H. Harvey, 'Hyde Abbey and Winchester College', *Proceedings of the Hampshire Hants Field Club and Archaeological Society*, 20 (1956), pp. 48–55. For what follows on the fortunes of the charters I am particularly indebted to the notes of Herbert Chitty (College Archivist, 1927–49) which are kept in the folder with the charters and to Edwards, *Liber de Hyda*.

[8] J. Leland, *Itinerary*, 1535–43, (2nd edn, 1906–10), iii.86.

majuscule **s** in the Latin script, and the long-backed form of ð all suggest a later date and account for the verdict of Dr Ker and Dr Bishop that this is a hand of the first half of the eleventh century.[9] Careful imitative scripts such as this are notoriously difficult to date; indeed the ð may indicate a date in the middle or even the second half of the century. Moreover the scribe's avoidance of any letter-forms drawn from Caroline minuscule which by the eleventh century was normally used in solemn Latin documents, suggests a desire to give the script a deliberately archaic appearance, so that the charter could pass muster as an original diploma of Edward the Elder. Technically the charter is probably therefore a forgery. What then of the contents of the document? Are these also spurious? Or did the New Minster monks simply provide themselves with a fair copy of an authentic document that had been damaged or had decayed? Here we run into difficulties. In the reign of Edward the Elder (899–924) there is a gap in the sequence of Anglo-Saxon royal diplomas. We do not have a single Latin charter of Edward that survives in a contemporary manuscript, so we lack a reliable yardstick by which to judge our charter. However, the Micheldever charter does not share any of its phrasing with the few charters of Edward the Elder which have been shown to be worthy of some credence.[10] Its drafting is indeed highly unusual, though it sometimes reflects tenth-century usage. Thus the immunity clause:

> Proinde sit terra predicta ab omni seruitio mundana semper libera exceptis tribus causis hoc est expeditione et pontis arcisue constructione.

is a particular version of a formula that was in common use in charters for much of the tenth and early eleventh centuries.[11] But the exact wording of this clause and of the formulae of the rest of the charter are found again in two other texts purporting to be grants by Anglo-Saxon kings. Our suspicions are aroused by the fact that both are New Minster charters: the first is the so-called Golden Charter which (though we only have a sixteenth-century copy of it) was apparently originally written in golden ink and was intended to be a formal foundation charter by which Edward the Elder in 903 confirmed all the estates that he had granted to his new foundation; the second purports to be a

---

[9] Sawyer, n. 4 above. I am grateful to Dr Ker for advice on the charter's script. He later preferred a date of *s.xi med.* or even *s.xi²*, but considered that the scribe made 'rather a good job of writing the letters used in the tenth century, but very much letter by letter, without any fluency'.

[10] BCS 595, 600, 603, 607, 613.

[11] Compare the formula common from the 940s: *Sit* autem *praedict*um rus *liber ab omni mundi*ali obstaculo . . . *except*o istis *tribus expeditione et pontis arcisve constructione*/coaedificatione (BCS 734, 741, 749, 753, 757, 758, 759, 764, 767, 781, 789, 808, 821, 824 etc.).

grant by King Eadwig of an estate at Heighton in Sussex to the New Minster in 957.[12]

This group of three New Minster charters is highly anomalous; they do not fit any more easily amongst the numerous authentic charters of Eadwig's reign than they do amongst the few scraps from Edward the Elder's. It is difficult to be sure whether they were all three produced at one time. The Golden Charter, with its anachronistic description of King Alfred as the 'first crowned king of the whole of England' (*Anglie*) may be a confection of the twelfth century or later, based upon our Micheldever charter. For it is surely too much of a coincidence to suppose that Edward's principal grants to the New Minster were both made when meeting his councillors at (Sout)hampton in 900 and then in 903, that the identical body of thirty-nine lay and ecclesiastical nobles should have witnessed both grants, and that the scribes of the charters should have mistakenly dated each to the fourth indiction.[13] Whether both charters were forged at the same time or whether one is based on the other, we can be sure that neither of these two New Minster charters nor the Heighton charter was composed before the very last years of the tenth century, for they all share one feature that is very uncommon in Anglo-Saxon royal diplomas – a notification clause:

> Ego Eaduueardus (Eadwyus) . . . cunctis gentis nostrae fidelibus innotesco quod pro salute animae meae . . . benigne confero.

Though this precise wording is not found elsewhere, Dr Simon Keynes pointed out that such notification clauses, though common in continental documents, first came to be used in English charters in texts of the mid-990s and remained in common use for some two decades.[14] It is therefore very unlikely that the Micheldever charter would have included a notification clause, had it been composed any earlier than the 990s.

The evidence of the diplomatic form of the Micheldever charter therefore agrees well with that of its script, that it was produced in the eleventh century, though we cannot yet define the date more precisely. What, then, can we learn from the content of the document itself about the motive for its production? At first sight the charter appears to be a straightforward grant of a single estate named Micheldever – albeit a very large one since it is assessed at one hundred hides. No exceptional privileges or powers are granted in the charter, so we might suppose that the forger's purpose was to provide the monks of New Minster with better title to the land in question. But the detailed perambulations

---

[12] BCS 602, 1000 (s370, 648).
[13] AD 900 should be the third indiction, 903 the sixth.
[14] *The Diplomas of King Æthelred 'The Unready'* (Cambridge, 1980), pp. 111–12.

of the boundaries recorded in English in the text show that the hundred hides called Micheldever in fact comprised seven separate estates in Hampshire: at Micheldever itself, Cranbourne, Curdridge, Durley, *Rige leah*, Candover, and Worthy (i.e. Abbot's Worthy). These properties, or the bulk of them, formed in the Middle Ages the 'hundred of Micheldever', and there can be no doubt that this charter was intended to be the monks' title to their private hundred. The division of Hampshire, like the rest of Wessex, into administrative and judicial districts called hundreds goes back at least to the mid-tenth century; from that time the English kings began in their law-codes to impose duties not only upon their agents, the hundredmen or hundred-reeves, but also upon all the free inhabitants of every hundred who owed suit at the hundred court.[15] But the disparate collection of estates surveyed in the Micheldever charter owes nothing to the king's administrative needs or indeed to the realities of geography; rather it would seem to serve only the tenurial convenience of the abbot and monks of New Minster. As Sir Richard Hoare lucidly put it long ago, 'The lord of a private hundred will wish to connect other lands to the hundred and compel attendance at his court.'[16] Indeed we can see the abbey doing this at Micheldever, for by the time of the Domesday survey the hundredal manor of Micheldever had grown from the 100 hides of the charter to 106 hides; the increase by 1086 was doubtless largely accounted for by the addition by then of Drayton, which is not in the charter but is known to have been restored to the New Minster by King Cnut in 1019.[17]

On this interpretation the Micheldever charter, though forged, is a particularly important witness of that association of private estate or manor with one hundred hides of land which Professor Cam has elucidated in her researches into the origins of the private or seignorial hundred.[18] For the bulk of the evidence for hundreds in the hands of lay or ecclesiastical lords before the Norman Conquest comes only in Domesday Book. Apart from the Micheldever charter we have a small number of diplomas in the names of English kings from Edward the Elder to Edgar which seem to be grants of hundredal areas; we also

[15] H.R. Loyn, 'The Hundred in England in the Tenth and early Eleventh Centuries', in H. Hearder and H.R. Loyn, eds, *British Government and Administration: Studies presented to S.B. Chrimes* (Cardiff, 1974), pp. 1–15.

[16] *Modern History of Wiltshire* (1822), i.74.

[17] WCM 12093; *Liber de Hyda*, ed. Edwards, pp. 324–6; Sanders, ii, Winchester College 4.

[18] H.M. Cam, 'The "Private" Hundred in England before the Norman Conquest', in J. Conway Davies, ed., *Studies presented to Sir Hilary Jenkinson* (Oxford, 1957), pp. 50–60; idem, 'Manerium cum hundredo: the Hundred and the Hundredal Manor', *English Historical Review*, 47 (1932), pp. 353–76.

have a tiny number of royal writs granting rights over hundreds in the name of Edward the Confessor.[19] But most of these diplomas and writs are forgeries and none survives in a pre-Conquest manuscript. At Micheldever, however, our charter takes the history of the private hundred at least back to the era of the Domesday Survey. We need not accept its claim that the widely spread estates amounting to one hundred hides had been granted as a unit by Edward the Elder, that is before the hundredal system was itself in being. But we can use the boundary clauses of the charter to reconstruct the hundred that the monks were claiming a century and a half later. Only when the constituent portions of the hundred have been precisely located can we hope to understand how the hundred of Micheldever may really have come into being, or why it was necessary to produce a forged charter.

Tracing the boundaries of an Anglo-Saxon charter on the modern map and on the ground is one of the most rewarding forms of research. The excitement of discovering how a particular landscape has changed, or remained the same, over a thousand years cannot easily be equalled. But it is difficult to present the results of such work without suppressing the uncertainties and difficulties that must remain. In proposing identifications of the six perambulations in the Micheldever charter, I have therefore adopted the following procedure:

1 An accurate translation of the Old English text of each boundary clause is provided in accord with the findings of modern place-name scholarship.[20]
2 In order that the reader may check my identifications on the ground, full Ordnance Survey grid references are given to each suggested identification.
3 To give a more immediate impression of the estates, they are also mapped in the context of their physical and administrative setting. The roads, woodland, and river-courses shown are those of today, except that easily identifiable modern changes (such as motorways)

---

[19] Diplomas claiming to grant (or confirm) 100 hides of land: BCS 596, 620, 690, 801, 917, 1135, 1149; writs granting rights over hundreds: F.E. Harmer, *Anglo-Saxon Writs* (Manchester, 1952), nos 5, 9–10, 41–2. Those with the best claim to be copies of authentic documents are BCS 801 and 917 and Harmer, 9. A number of other diplomas grant estates of less than 100 hides which may be coterminous with the later hundreds of the same name: BCS 625 (Overton), 629 (Crawley ? = Buddlesgate Hundred), 887 (Pucklechurch), 927 (Tidenham), 1307 (Crondall); none of these survive in pre-conquest manuscripts.

[20] Particularly valuable are A.H. Smith, *English Place-Name Elements*, English Place-Name Society, 25, 26 (Cambridge, 1956) and M. Gelling, *The Place-Names of Berkshire*, iii, English Place-Name Society, 51 (Cambridge, 1976). I am most grateful to Mrs Gelling and to Mr P. Kitson for their kindness in correcting and improving my translations; I am alone responsible for any errors that may remain.

are omitted, as are most minor roads. Parish boundaries are shown as they can first be identified in the early nineteenth century.
4 To allow the reader to follow my reasoning, I have distinguished carefully:
  (a) Those boundary-marks which can be *positively identified*, i.e. where the Old English term has survived as an identifiable place-name on modern maps. These identifications provide the initial framework for the interpretation of each perambulation.
  (b) boundary-marks that can be located because they fit the topographical requirements of the term or because they recur in the perambulations of other charters.
  (c) bounds whose identification can only be conjectured from their relation to other points in the circuit.

By this procedure the reader or field-worker who wishes to build on, or to amend, my work will know where they stand. Too often in the past 'solutions' of charter boundaries have been propounded so baldly that it is impossible, without an inordinate amount of research, to know whether the results are reasonable or not. Sometimes the needs of the layman who has the time to fill in the details by walking (or riding) the bounds of a charter in his locality have even been neglected through failure to provide map references. I have used the Ordnance Survey 2½ inch (1:25,000) series throughout, but have supplemented its information from the Title Award maps of parishes in the Hampshire Record Office, from the first (1856–75) edition of the OS 6 inch series, and from early estate maps of Candover and of Micheldever.[21]

The Old English section of the Micheldever charter makes clear that the hundred hide estate comprised seven separate properties. Detailed bounds are given only for the first six; they are here interpreted in turn.

I Micheldever (Figure 21)

Five of the twenty-eight boundary points in the circuit can be positively identified:

  i *myceldefer* (3) is the Micheldever river which has given its name to the settlement, estate, and hundred of Micheldever. Until the boundary changes and amalgamations of parishes in the last

---

[21] There is a series of early-sixteenth-century estate maps in the college muniments drawn up to illustrate disputed grazing rights in Brown Candover and Woodmancott: WCM 21443–6. Estate maps of parts of the central area of the hundred of Micheldever, in particular of Micheldever Southbrook in 1730 and of East and West Stratton i 1770 have been consulted in Hampshire Record Office, nos 2 M51/3 and 38/M48/196.

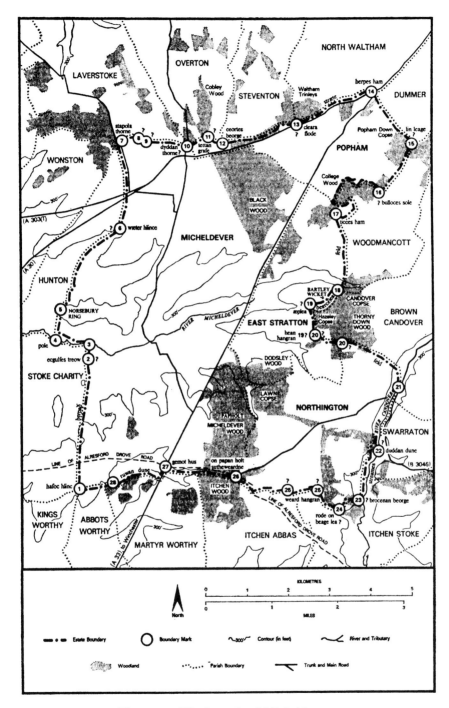

Figure 21. The bounds of Micheldever.

century,[22] the river formed for a short length the southern boundary of Micheldever and the northern boundary of the parish of Stoke Charity.

ii *næsan byrig* (5) is the hill-fort, now called Norsebury Ring at SU 490401, which lay on the parish boundary of Micheldever and Hunton. In a charter concerned with an estate at Hunton it is simply called *þære byrig*, the fort.[23]

iii *bearcelea* (18) survived as the place-name Bartley Wicket, recorded on the 6 inch Ordnance Survey at SU 555404. There is still a birch copse here, which now lies on the parish boundary between Micheldever and the Candovers, but until parish amalgamations in 1932 lay on that between East Stratton and Brown Candover.

iv *kendefer* (21) is the stream which has given its name to the settlements of Brown Candover, Preston Candover and Chilton Candover, and is a tributary of the river Alre. The Candover still forms the boundary between the parish of Northington on the west and the Candovers (formerly Brown Candover and Swarraton) on the east.

v *papan holt* (26) is Papholt which was noted by Gover as the old name for Micheldever Wood.[24] The southern side of this wood, as specified in the charter, still forms the southern boundary of the parish of Micheldever.

As is common in the study of charter boundaries we find an astonishing correspondence between the Anglo-Saxon bounds and parish boundaries as first mapped in the nineteenth-century Tithe Awards. All these five points coincide with parish boundaries that until the nineteenth century also formed the boundary of Micheldever hundred. At the very least it is clear from these five boundary marks that *myceldefer* in the charter enclosed much of the nineteenth-century parishes of Micheldever, Northington, and East Stratton. In the absence of any certainly identified points on the north and north-east sides of the boundary, we cannot be certain the same is true of that section. But since the parish of Popham was always part of the hundred of Micheldever and is not recorded as a separate estate, we may adopt the

---

[22] I have consulted the 1874 OS 6in. sheet and the Title Award maps in the Hampshire Record Office and the 1878 Index to the Tithe Survey in the map room of the British Library. There is now an indispensable guide to changes in administrative districts over the last 400 years in F.A. Youngs jnr, *Guide to the Local Administrative Units of England*, i, *Southern England*, Royal Historical Society, Guides and Handbooks, no. 10 (London, 1979), to which I am heavily indebted.

[23] BCS 629.

[24] A typescript of J.E.B. Gover's unpublished *Place-Names of Hampshire* may be consulted in the Hampshire Record Office.

working hypothesis that Popham is also included and that the charter circuit coincides with the boundaries of the nineteenth-century parishes of Micheldever, Popham, East Stratton, and Northington. These were the central parishes which at least from the thirteenth century formed the core of the hundred of Micheldever. The hypothesis is confirmed by the fact that two of the bounds in this section, *cleara flode* (13) and *herpes ham* (14), recur as consecutive bounds in a charter concerned with North Waltham.[25] Since North Waltham is the parish immediately to the north of Popham, it is reasonable to locate these bounds at the ends of their mutual boundary. We may therefore attempt to identify the Micheldever survey's twenty-eight boundary-marks in the order that they are described. In order to facilitate reference to the text printed at the end of this paper, the bounds, here translated from Old English, are given numbers (which are not, of course, fund in the manuscript).

These are the boundaries of the estate at Micheldever:

1 *First to hawk lynch ('ridge' or 'bank');*
   The boundary seems to begin at the south-west corner of the parish of Micheldever at SU 494358, and then proceeds in a clockwise direction.

2 *then along the army-path to Ecgulf's tree;*
   The tree may have marked the change of direction in the boundary at SU 496390 after which the *herepað* is represented by a modern road. Alternatively it may have marked the point where the Alresford Drove Road crosses the boundary at SU 494365.

3 *then along the army-path as far as the Micheldever [river];*
   The boundary joins the river at SU 497393.

4 *then along the Micheldever, then from the Micheldever to the pool;*
   There is still a large pool at SU 488393 where the parish boundary leaves the river and heads northwards.

5 *then from the pool to Norsebury;*
   The parish boundary passes around the western side of the fort, leaving it at SU 491402.

6 *then from Norsebury to water-lynch ('water-bank');*
   Perhaps where the boundary changes direction at SU 505420.

7 *then from water-lynch to the staple-thorn;*
   Apparently a thorn tree, marked (or supported?) by a post or 'staple'. In the bounds of Hunton (BCS 629) we find 'the thorn where the staple stands' apparently at the most northerly point of the parish, which coincides with the north-west corner of the parish of Micheldever at SU 505442.

---

[25] BCS 625.

8 *then from staple-thorn to [the] muddy way;*
The next four boundary points, for which locations may only be conjectured most tentatively, are either rather close together, or the boundary had been adjusted before the early nineteenth century.

9 *then from the muddy way to the dried-up (?) 'pill' ('pool', 'intermittent stream');*
The meaning of *forscæðan* 'to boil away' ought to give an adjectival form **forsodenan*.

10 *then from the dried-up pill to Dydda's thorn;*
The thorn may have stood at the angle in the boundary at SU 521439 where the parishes of Micheldever, Laverstock, Overton, and Popham all met.

11 *then from Dydda's thorn to Tetta's grove (or 'grave', 'ditch');*
The boundary turns a sharp angle by a copse at SU 526443.

12 *then from Tetta's grove to Ceort's barrow;*
A prominent bowl barrow at SU 529441 marks the junction of the parish boundaries of Popham, Steventon, and Overton.

13 *then from Ceort's barrow to the Clere spring (or 'intermittent stream');*
Cleara flode, which recurs as a boundary-mark of North Waltham (BCS 625), presumably marked the junction of the boundary of that parish with that of Popham and the hundred of Micheldever at SU 548445. No spring or stream is recorded at this site on modern maps, but there is a series of small springs along the boundary to the west, on the north side of the A30. *Cleara* is a pre-English river name which has also given its name to the various Cleres in Hampshire.

14 *then from the Clere spring along the street to Herp's enclosure;*
The boundary joins the London–Exeter road (A30) at SU 547445 and follows it to SU 566453, the northern corner of the parish of Popham, which was probably the site of *herpes ham*, which recurs in the bounds of North Waltham. At this corner the boundaries of Popham and North Waltham part company.

15 *then from Herp's enclosure to lin-lea ('flax-meadow');*
lin-leah was presumably at the next corner in the boundary at SU 575441.

16 *then from lin-lea to [the] bullock's wallowing-place;*
Perhaps at SU 567428.

17 *then from bullock's slough to Ticc's enclosure;*
This lost settlement may have been at SU 558423 or at SU 555427.

18 *then over the field ('open land') to birch-lea ('birch copse');*
The boundary of Micheldever with Woodmancott (formerly East Stratton and Woodmancott) still passes over open arable land before meeting a birch copse (Bartley) where the boundary changes course at SU 557406.

19 *then from birch lea on to apple-lea ('apple wood');*
Either the copse at SU 551403 or (if the birch-lea stretched to that
point) at SU 562395. Owing to the compression of detail between
points 18 and 19 on Figure 21, a mistaken impression is given that
estate and parish boundaries diverge here. The estate boundary is
the true line.

20 *then from apple-lea on again to high hanger ('wood on steep slope');*
Perhaps the copse known as Thickthorn Wood in the eighteenth
century at SU 564394, or else part of the modern Thorny Down
Wood.

21 *then over the field ('open country') to [the] Candover [river];*
The parish boundary passes over open downland and meets the
Candover at SU 572386.

22 *then along the Candover to Dudda's down;*
It is not clear whether Totford Down, Northington Down or
Abbotstone Down is meant.

23 *then along the stream to [the] broken barrow;*
Apparently continuing along the Candover. The boundary leaves
the river at SU 564356, though there is no trace of a robbed barrow
today.

24 *from [the] broken barrow, into the clearing in the ring-lea ('lea of the
rings');*
The planted woodlands around The Grand Park have probably
obscured all trace of the clearing and *beaga lea* which may have been
sited in the angle of the boundary at SU 557354.

25 *from the clearing to the midst of ward-hanger ('sloping wood of the
watch', or 'look-out'?);*
Perhaps at SU 553359.

26 *from ward-hanger on again to the south side of Papholt ('Papa's wood'
or perhaps 'pope's wood');*
The boundary joins the southern end of Papholt at SU 532362 and
leaves the wood at SU 524364.

27 *then to the moot-house;*
The next change in the boundary's course occurs at the cross-roads
of the Winchester-Silchester Roman road with the Alresford drove
road. An important cross-roads is of course an ideal site for the
meeting place and court-house of the hundred.

28 *then over [the] rough down;*
The down known in 1730 as Micheldever Sheep Down.

29 *then back to hawk lynch (= 1).*

In proposing 'solutions' to Anglo-Saxon boundary perambulations,
there is always a dangerous temptation to claim greater certainty and
precision than is possible where so many of the boundary marks are

ephemeral natural features such as trees, clearings and woods. Nonetheless in walking the Micheldever bounds it is encouraging: to find a pool at the correct place in the circuit (4); to find a prominent round barrow by the boundary where the charter seems to speak of *Ceortes beorge* (12); to find that the 'street' (14) coincides with the only place where the boundaries of these parishes follow the most important road running through the estate, namely the main road from London to the south-west, now the A30; to find the only birch trees for miles around in a copse where the place-name Bartley Wicket suggests the charters *bearcelea* to have lain (18); to find open, treeless arable land where the charter mentions *feld* (between 17 and 18 and between 20 and 21); to find that the 'court-house' was situated at the most important cross-roads in the estate (27); and finally to find that 'the rough down' of the charter was still the open sheep down of Micheldever parish in the eighteenth century (28). There are some short sections of the perambulation (nos 28–1,–4, 8–11, 15–17, 23–5) where further work from maps or in the field may correct some of the locations suggested here, but it is difficult to believe that the line will differ significantly from the boundaries of the four parishes in the nineteenth century. Only where the parish boundary of Popham excludes the hamlet and woods of Woodmancott do we seem to lack sufficient boundary marks in the charter to describe the boundary adequately.

II Cranbourne (Figure 22)

The second boundary survey in the Micheldever charter concerns an estate at Cranbourne. Cranbourne is not, and has never been, a parish in its own right, so we cannot expect parish boundaries to be so helpful to us. But within the parish of Wonston there are a considerable number of estates which today include Cranbourne in their name: Cranbourne Lodge, Cranbourne Grange, Lower Cranbourne Farm, Upper Cranbourne Farm, a second Cranbourne Lodge, and Cranbourne Wood. Together these properties form a long strip of territory on the eastern side of the parish with boundaries consistently some 800 yards wide stretching from the northern wooded end of the parish as far as the Micheldever river. The boundaries of these properties alone might suggest that they are all fragments of what was once a unitary estate named Cranbourne. In fact, though some of the bounds require extensive field-work (which I have not been able to undertake for this particular circuit), before locations can be suggested, it is clear that the charter's perambulation of *cramburnan* is describing exactly this unitary estate. Grundy's belief[26] that

---

[26] *Archaeological Journal*, 33 (1926), pp. 305–8.

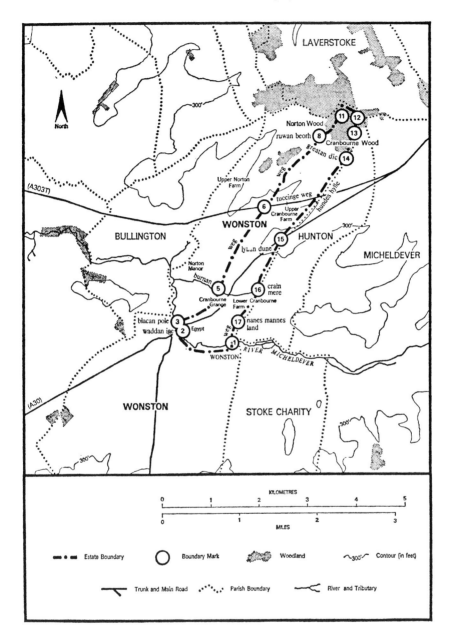

Figure 22. The bounds of Cranbourne.

the survey covered not only the properties named Cranbourne but also all the rest of Wonston parish that lay to the north of the Micheldever does not commend itself. Norton Manor (together with Upper Norton Farm and Norton Wood) has a quite separate history from Cranbourne, and forms a larger and more important unit.[27] It is therefore unlikely that had Cranbourne and Norton ever been combined they would have been called Cranbourne.

Only two of the seventeen boundary marks can be positively identified:

i The starting point of the circuit is *myceldeferes stream* (1), the Micheldever river, and the further specification 'over against the churchyard at *wynsiges tune* (Wonston)' enables us to fix the point as the place the boundary of the parishes of Wonston and Hunton met the river.

ii *hundes hylle* (15) can scarcely be other than the hill or down that lies above *hundatun* (Hunton), namely the hill that is now called Hunton Down.

Three of the boundary marks of this charter also recur in a charter by which King Edward the Elder is purported to have granted Hunton to the Old Minster at Winchester in 909,[28] namely the (red) 'pill' among the chalk pits (13), the *Crammere* (16), and 'the way' (18) which is called 'the green way' in the Hunton charter. Since the present eastern boundary of the various Cranbourne properties is the former Hunton–Wonston parish boundary, it is likely the later stages of the circuit of Cranbourne in our charter are following that boundary. If so it is clear that the survey proceeds around the bounds in a clockwise direction, as is indeed usual in Anglo-Saxon charters:

These are the boundaries of the estate at Cranbourne:
1 *First to the Micheldever steam over against the churchyard at Wonston;*
   Wonston churchyard adjoins the Micheldever Brook at SU 479396.
2 *along the stream to Wadda's island;*
   Perhaps the island at SU 467399 from which the settlement of Egypt takes its name.
3 *from Wadda's island along the stream to [the] black pool;*
   Of the various pools downstream from Egypt, that at SU 465400 seems most likely.

---

[27] *Nortune* in Barton Stacey hundred is listed amongst the land of the king's thegns in Domesday Book: in 1066 it had been held by Fulchi and assessed at 5 hides (DB, i, fo. 49b).
[28] BCS 629.

4 *from [the] black pool to whelp's-dell (or 'pit');*
There is no narrow valley nor any surviving pit in the vicinity.
Perhaps at SU 472404.

5 *from whelp's-dell to the bourne;*
The boundary of the Cranbourne properties crosses the
Cranbourne itself at SU 474407.

6 *from the bourne north along the way to Tuccinge way;*
Mr P. Kitson has suggested to me that *tuccinge weg* may be an old
track to Tufton (in Whitchurch), which the boundary crosses at SU
477416, and not the A303 as shown on Figure 22. North of the
bourne a farm track perpetuates the 'way' of the charter.

7 *from Tuccinge way, along the way to [the] great dyke;*
The *greatan dic* recurs in (14). From the downland terrain it is more
likely to have been a dyke rather than a ditch and, as Grundy
suggested, should be identified with the 'Devil's Dyke' recorded as a
field-name to the south of Cranbourne Wood on the Tithe Award
map.

8 *from the great dyke to rough barrow;*
A large round barrow is situated very close to the boundary at SU
495438. L.V. Grinsell noted that this identification had also been
made on the 6 inch OS maps kept at Southampton in a hand-
written note by O.G.S. Crawford.[29]

9 *from rough barrow through the wood to [the] chalk quarry;*
The boundary enters the wood almost immediately. The following
four or five boundary marks around Cranbourne Wood are very
close together. Without fieldwork the locations suggested on Illus.
22 are highly conjectural.

10 *along the path to Friday;*
'Friday' is a nickname for unproductive land.

11 *from Friday to the north end of the dirt-way;*
There are several paths or tracks in Cranbourne Wood.

12 *from the north end of the dirt-way, along the eastward way to the
narrow path;*

13 *from the narrow path out through [the] chalk pits to the red pill
('stream', or 'pool');*
The equivalent mark in the Hunton charter reads *innan cealc graf on
þonne pyl* 'within the chalk pit to the pill'.

14 *from the red pill along the furrow within the great dyke to the narrow
dell ('valley', 'pit');*

15 *from the narrow dell out to little down on the hound's hill (Hunton
Down);*

---

[29] L.V. Grinsell, 'Hampshire Barrows', *Proceedings of the Hampshire Field Club*, 14
(1938–40), p. 32.

The little down is probably the lower part of Hunton Down at SU 487417.

16 *from Hunton Down along the way to Cram mere ('heron's pool');*
Cram mere has now been drained, but its recurrence in the bounds of Hunton locates it at the source of the Cranbourne, which the parish and estate boundary meets at SU 482407.

17 *from Cram mere along the way to no man's land;*
The zig-zags in the boundary beginning at SU 478402 suggest that no man's land may have comprised the headlands of the plough acres of an arable field.

18 *from no man's land along the way, back into the Micheldever (= 1);*
The way is the 'green way' in the Hunton charter.

Once again then it is possible to reconstruct a late-Saxon estate with some confidence. Cranbourne as possessed by the monks of the New Minster is seen to have been a long narrow estate with its share of woodland and downland in the north and its arable fields and meadow land nearer the Micheldever Brook. It was separated from the main hundredal manor of Micheldever by the parish of Hunton which in late Anglo-Saxon times was a property of the Old Minster at Winchester.

III Curdridge (Figure 23)

With the next perambulation the Micheldever charter moves to a quite different part of Hampshire, to an area within a few miles of the urban sprawl of modern Southampton. The parish of Curdridge [*Cuthredes hricgce*, 'Cuthred's ridge'] lies on the east bank of the river Hamble at the point where the estuary ceases to be tidal. Though it is now an ecclesiastical and also a civil parish, it has been so only since 1838 and 1894 respectively.[30] Until 1838 Curdridge was a chapelry in the parish of Bishop's Waltham. We cannot therefore expect that modern parish boundaries will necessarily help to elucidate the Anglo-Saxon survey. Moreover only one of the ten boundary marks in the circuit can be positively identified.

i *syle forda* (9) has left its name not only in Silford Copse (SU 535125), but also in the field-name Lockhams Silfords.[31]

---

[30] Youngs, *Guide*, p. 204. In my interpretation of the bounds of Curdridge, I have been saved from major error by Mr P. Kitson who kindly put his own unpublished work at my disposal; he would favour a circuit enclosing a larger area on the north-east side of the estate.

[31] *Archaeological Journal*, 31 (1924), p. 65.

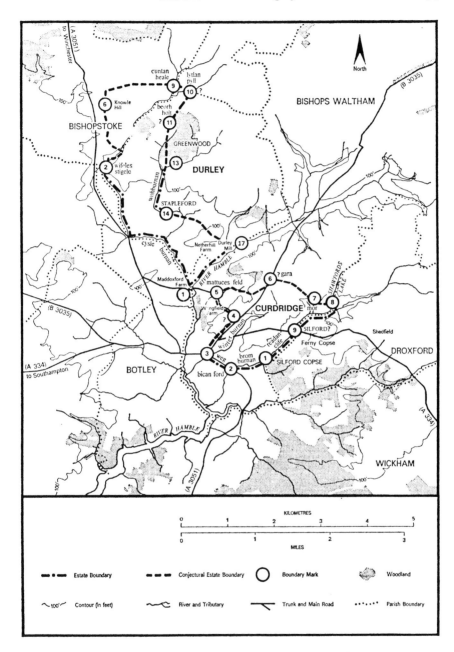

Figure 23. The bounds of Curdridge and Durley.

It is likely that *syle forda* was a ford across the stream that is now called Shawfords Lake and which forms the northern boundary of Silford Copse; this stream would be the *brom burnan* (8) of our charter. There is independent confirmation of this identification, as Grundy noticed: for most of its length Shawfords Lake is the present boundary between Curdridge parish and Shedfield; until the nineteenth-century changes it was the boundary between the parishes of Bishops Waltham and Droxford, and we have a detailed perambulation of the boundaries of Droxford in a charter of King Athelstan, which includes *brom burnan* at this stage in its circuit.[32] *Brom burnan*, then, is Shawfords Lake and this in turn provides a clue to the location of *bican forda* (10 and 2), which was reached in a single stage from Silford (9). *Bican ford* and *syle ford* were evidently both fords across the *brom burnan*. Today Shawfords Lake is crossed by just two roads, the A3051 (the Botley–Swanwick road) at SU 525127 and the A334 (the Botley–Wickham road) at SU 539135. Both bridges are about a half mile from the present Silford Copse. Unless field-work can establish the existence of a lost early mediaeval road and of a ford closer to the present copse, we must work on the assumptions that the two fords in our survey, were the predecessors of the present bridges and that the circuit is (as normal) progressing in a clockwise direction. On this basis we may attempt to elucidate this survey:

1 *First from the red cliff;*
   Probably where Droxford–Bishops Waltham parish boundary joins the *bron burnan* at SU 532128.
2 *on to Bica's ford;*
   The Botley–Swanwick road crosses Shawfords Lake at SU 525127.
3 *along the way to [the] winter-bourne;*
   The way would be the A3051, and the *winter burnan* the tiny stream reached at SU 521129.
4 *from [the] winter-bourne to the ferny hill;*
   Probably some part of the hill on which Curdridge stands, perhaps at SU 527138.
5 *from the ferny hill out to mattock's field (or 'open country');*
   The first element of this name is found in Maddoxford farm, situated close by a crossing of the Hamble at SU 517144, so *mattuces feld* ('land needing to be worked by pick') was possibly in the vicinity of Wangfield Farm.
6 *from mattock's field up to the gore, to the twisled ('forked') tree;*
   The *gara* may have been the triangle of land formed by the intersection of minor roads at SU 534146.

---

[32] BCS 742; Grundy, *Archaeological Journal*, 31 (1924), p. 64.

7 *from the twisted tree to the marsh;*

Several small watercourses leading to Shawfords Lake in the vicinity of SU 543138 may represent the draining of the *mor* in modern times.

8 *and over the marsh by the east of the marsh to [the] broom-bourne;*

A footpath, which seems to fit the topographical requirements and meets Shawfords Lake at SU 547141, may perpetuate the line of the boundary.

9 *along the broom-bourne to Silford;*

The ford may have been close to the present bridge at SU 539135.

10 *from Silford back to Bica's ford (= 2).*

IV Durley (Figure 23)

The fourth estate whose bounds are surveyed in the Micheldever charter is Durley, which lies immediately to the north of Curdridge. Indeed the river Hamble which forms the boundary between the Durley and the modern parish of Curdridge forms the southern boundary of the estate at Durley in our charter. The main problems of the bounds have been well tackled by Grundy.[33] Following his work two of the eighteen boundary-marks can be positively identified:

i *stapol forda* (14) is represented today by Stapleford Farm (SU 512160) where the footpath from Durley crosses the Durley Brook.

ii *hamele* (17, 18 and 1) is the river Hamble.

Other bounds can be located with some confidence even though the names have not survived. The identification of Stapleford establishes that the *wohburnan* (13, 14) is the modern Durley Brook which flows past Stapleford Farm. Two of the bounds, *wifeles stigele* (2) and *cuntan heale* (9) recur as consecutive boundary marks in the perambulation of Bishopstoke in a charter of King Edgar;[34] until the division of the parish of Bishopstoke in 1871 the brook now known as Ford Lake was for about two miles the boundary between Durley and Bishopstoke. It therefore seems likely that *wifeles stigele* and *cuntan heale* marked the two ends of the joint boundary. Moreover the *cysle burnan* which flowed from *wifeles stigele* (2) into the Hamble (1) can be identified as the modern Ford Lake. With these clues we may attempt to define the bounds of *Diorleage.*

---

[33] *Archaeological Journal*, 31 (1924), pp. 82–5.

[34] BCS 1054.

These are the boundaries of the land at Durley:

1 *First to the chisel-bourne ('gravelly-stream') in the Hamble, [that is] where the chisel-bourne first enters it;*

The present confluence of Ford Lake and the Hamble is at SU 517144, but the course of the Durley parish boundary suggests it may once have been slightly further north.

2 *up along the chisel-bourne to Wifel's stile;*

Presumably at SU 498169 where the Bishopstoke boundary joins that of Durley parish.

3 *from Wifel's stile to the red-leafed tree;*

4 *from the red-leafed tree on to the old stock (or 'stump');*

5 *from the old stock by the west of the bourne to the green way;*

6 *from the green way along the narrow path to knoll-gate;*

It would seem that we are here moving to the west of the modern parish of Durley. *Cnoll gete* would seem to be connected in some way with Knowle Hill (SU 499183).

7 *from knoll-gate on to the white tree;*

8 *from the white tree to the north-bent tree;*

9 *from the north-bent tree to cunt-hollow;*

Again from its recurrence in BCS 1058 *cuntan heale* must be placed at SU 514187 where the Bishopstoke boundary separates from that of Durley.

10 *from cunt-hollow to the little stream ('spring', 'well');*

A small stream crosses the Durley boundary some 350 yards east of *cuntan heale.*

11 *from the little stream on over barrow-holt;*

beorh holt is probably the high part of the modern Greenwood.

12 *to the tall birch;*

13 *from the tall birch into [the] crooked bourne;*

There can be no certainty where the estate boundary joined the *wohburnan.* A convenient footpath joins it at SU 511169.

14 *along the crooked bourne to Stapleford;*

The ford across the *wohburnan* is at SU 512160.

15 *up from Stapleford to the awl-shaped wych [elm];*

16 *from the awl-shaped wych-elm into the marsh in the hollow;*

17 *along the marsh in the hollow into the Hamble;*

It seems likely that the boundary joins the Hamble either at Durley Mill (SU 525152) or at Netherhill Farm (SU 523151).

18 *along the Hamble to where the chisel-bourne enters the Hamble (= 1).*

Unless early maps are found preserving some of the relevant place-names, it is unlikely that it will be possible to resolve the remaining uncertainties in the boundaries of *Diorleage* (i.e. nos 3–8, 11–12, 15–16). For despite many hours of pleasant fieldwork it is not possible to establish thereby the position of eleventh-century trees nor the particular identity of 'green ways' or 'small paths'. Nonetheless it is at least clear that the estate of Durley described in the charter comprised only a part of the medieval and modern parish, that is a strip of land along the western boundary with the addition of a significant chunk of territory outside the parish in the direction of Knowle Hill. The estate was low-lying and for the most part comprised rich arable land.

V Rige leage (Figure 24)

The name *rige leage* ('rye meadow') does not survive on the modern map, and since none of the boundary marks in the survey of this property in the Micheldever charter can be positively identified with surviving place-names, there must remain doubts about its location. Nonetheless Grundy was probably correct to equate *rige leage* with the one outlying member of the hundred of Micheldever that is otherwise unaccounted for, namely the manor of Slackstead in the southern part of the ancient parish of Farley Chamberlayne, some five miles west of Winchester.[35] For two of the boundary-points recur in other late Anglo-Saxon charters in the bounds of estates that adjoined Farley Chamberlayne. I have not been able to discover any old maps of this estate, nor to undertake fieldwork there; my interpretation of the bounds therefore largely follows that of Grundy, with only minor emendations.

These are the boundaries of the land at Rige leage ('rye-meadow'):
1 *First to the pit of the knives;*
   This mark recurs in the bounds of a property (*wic*) north of Ampfield (BSC 629). There is a pit at the most northerly point of the mutual parish boundary at SU 391255. The name is difficult to interpret and Mr P. Kitson has suggested to me that it may rather refer to the pond on the boundary at SU 393252. Sharp-edged reeds might explain the name, and this location would allow more space for the next two boundary-marks.
2 *from the pit of the knives to the hollow ash;*
3 *from the hollow ash to trind-lea ('fenced meadow'? or 'circular wood'?);*
   Trinde leage is a common name in West Saxon charter boundaries, whose meaning needs further research.
4 *from trind-lea to the dense oak;*
   The *fæstan æc* is also mentioned as one of the bounds of

[35] *Archaeological Journal*, 31 (1924), pp. 119–21.

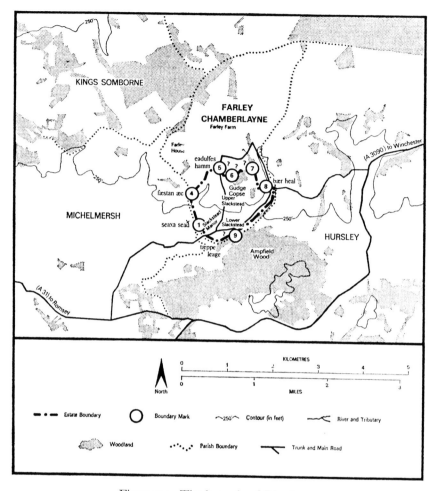

Figure 24. The bounds of *Rige leage*.

Michelmarsh in a charter of King Æthelred II.[36] It must therefore
have been on the Michelmarsh boundary, perhaps where it joins
that of Slackstead at SU 389262, rather than Grundy's suggested
SU 395267 which is too far within the parish of Farley
Chamberlayne.

5 *from the dense oak to Eadulf's enclosure;*
Perhaps at SU 395267.

6 *from Eadulf's enclosure to the red ditch (or dyke);*
The boundary in Gudge Copse follows a ditch.

---

[36] KCD 652.

7 *from the red ditch to the lea ('wood', 'meadow', 'clearing');*
Perhaps the copse at SU 403 267 whose western boundary is then followed southwards.

8 *from the lea to [the] barley-hollow;*
The hollow would be the re-entrant at SU 406263 where the boundary of the manor of Slackstead rejoins that of the parish of Farley Chamberlayne. The name *bær heal* may recur in Berryhill Copse in Braishfield Parish; it may also be related to the nearby Berry Down (SU 402275).

9 *from the bare hollow to tap-lea ('wood where spigots are obtained');*
Tap-lea was perhaps the copse at the southern end of the boundary (SU 398253); it recurs as boundary-mark of Chilcomb hundred in *CS* 620.

10 *from tap-lea back to the pit of the knives (= 1).*

VI Candover (Figure 25)

With the last circuit in the Micheldever charter we reach more secure ground once more. The estate named *kendefer* proves to be a narrow strip of land along the eastern boundary of the parish of Brown Candover. Though the rest of Brown Candover (like the neighbouring Chilton Candover) was part of the hundred of Mainsborough, this estate was administered as a detached part of the hundred and parish of Micheldever until the nineteenth century,[37] thus continuing the association set out in our Micheldever charter. Consequently the first edition of the Ordnance Survey six inch map (1874) provides an accurate survey of the estate-boundary. Moreover the fortuitous survival of a series of early sixteenth-century estate maps of Brown Candover in the college muniments[38] makes it possible to locate several of the bounds [*stan cistele* (2), *bican hyrste* (4), *widan herpaðe* (6), *trindlea* (11)] with precision and consequently to establish beyond doubt the identity of this detached portion of Micheldever hundred with the estate of *Kendefer* of the charter. Consequently we can dispense with our usual procedure of fixing the positive identifications on the map first, and seek instead to tackle the entire circuit immediately:

These are the bounds of the six hides of land at Candover:
1 *First from the bourne-stowe (i.e. 'bathing', 'watering', or 'washing place'?);*

---

[37] It is so recorded on Ralf Treswell's map of 1588 in the college muniments (WCM 21443); but on the 1874 OS 6 in. Hants sheets 26 and 34 it is assigned to Northington parish, a change which can probably be dated to 1847 (Youngs, *Guide*, p. 216).

[38] WCM 21443–6.

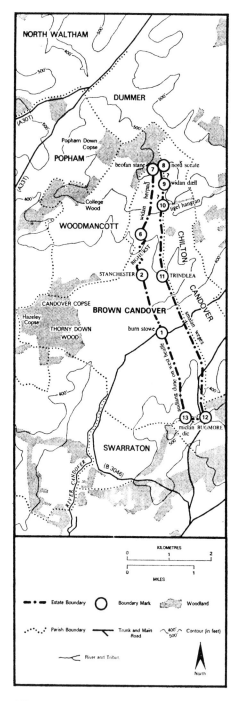

Figure 25. The bounds of Candover.

The boundary starts at the site of a well still in existence in the 1874 six inch map in the valley of the Candover at SU 585397.

2 *to [the] stone-heap;*
stan cistele is still recorded as a visible site, named *Stancheste(r)*, in the early sixteenth-century estate maps and was depicted as a rectangle of ruinous stone walls. *Ci(e)stel* is probably a diminutive of *ceas*, 'heap', rather than of *ceaster*, 'fort' or 'walled town'. But a substantial Roman building has been identified (at SU 58044108 in a field still named Stanchester) on many occasions in the last century from the scatter of foundation debris, tiles, wall-plaster, glass and pottery of the first to fourth centuries;[39] it was probably a Roman villa.

3 *and thence to the great thorn;*
4 *and then on to Bighurst to [the] wood;*
The name Bighurst or Bickhurst (Down) was applied in the sixteenth and nineteenth centuries to the whole area of downland in the northern third of the estate; it survives in corrupt form today as Becket's Down. The northern part of the estate was much more heavily wooded in the sixteenth century than today, but the wood of this point in the circuit had already disappeared. The irregular boundary between points 2 and 6 was then marked by piles of stones in unfenced open downland.

5 *and so from there to [the] rough barrow (or 'hill');*
6 *and thence to the wide army-path ('highway');*
The boundary joins the path at SU 579419. On Ralph Treswell's map of 1588 it is called 'The wide law path'.

7 *and so straight to Beofa's stone;*
Presumably a boundary stone where the path crosses the Woodmancott-Brown Candover boundary at SU 584435.

8 *to the north shot ('angle', 'projection' or 'corner') to the wood;*
The northmost tip of the estate at SU 585435 now marks the beginning of the dense woodland, but in the sixteenth century this extended further south.

9 *and through the wood into the midst of the wide dell ('pit');*
Perhaps the large chalk pit beside the boundary at SU 586431.

10 *thence out through tile-hanger ('sloping-wood where tiles are made');*
The belt of trees at SU 585427 formerly crossed this estate as well.

11 *and after that out through trind-lea ('fenced pasture'?);*
Trindlea is a term that has so far defied definitive interpretation though it is common in West Saxon charters. 'Trindley' is marked

---

[39] *Victoria County History of Hampshire*, i (1900), p. 306; *Proceedings of the Hampshire Field Club*, 14 (1941–3), p. 240; 18 (1953–4), p. 137. I am grateful to C.F. Wardale of the Archaeology Branch of the Ordnance Survey for providing information about this site.

on the sixteenth century maps at SU 585410, and is depicted as a rectangular fenced enclosure. No trace is visible today.

12 *so along the narrow way to Bugmore, [and] to the big dyke (or ditch);*

The *smalan weges* is represented by a track as far as the Candover Valley and then by a modern road to the high point of *bucgan oran* ('Bucga's bank'), the modern Bugmore Hill, which forms the southeast corner of the estate at SU 595377. The *miclan dic* which formed the southern boundary is largely obscured by the road along its course.

13 *and so finally along the west side of the down to the bourne-stow (= 1) which we named before at the start.*

The field boundaries along the western boundary, where they have not now been ploughed out, make use of the contours yet achieve a direct course to the *burn stowe*.

No bounds are given for the seventh estate that completed the hundred of Micheldever. Instead the Old English section of the charter is completed with the following passage:

> And the seven hides at Worthy belong to the hundred hides at Micheldever, even as the land-boundaries surround it round about; and one weir on the Itchen, and half the white cliff, and the southmost mill in Winchester within the wall.

It is difficult to understand the charter's phase *eall spa ða land gemæra hit on butan belicgeað.* The compiler of the charter seems to be excusing himself from providing a perambulation of Abbot's Worthy, but his reason is not clear. He does not say (as charter-writers sometimes do) that the bounds are well known, and it is therefore natural to interpret the phrase to mean that the series of six *land gemæra* (Micheldever, Cranbourne, Curdridge, Durley, *Rige leah,* and Candover) which he has just written out, provide the boundaries on all sides. But our identification of the bounds of these six estates makes clear that they do not adjoin and surround Abbot's Worthy, which has King's Worthy on the west, Martyr Worthy on the east, and the river Itchen on the south. The New Minster estate at Worthy could never have had its boundaries effectively described in the course of perambulations of the other parts of the Micheldever hundred. Only on the north was there a joint boundary with Micheldever hundred (see Figure 21). Either then we have a statement which can be translated but makes no sense, or we must deduce that this section of the charter has been copied from a different document, presumably one concerned with all the Worthies.

There are other indications that the compiler of the Micheldever charter drew upon several documents to provide the perambulations of the component estates of the hundred. For there are consistent

differences in the drafting of the boundary clauses of some of the
estates. Thus in the bounds of Micheldever each section commences
with the words *þonne of* ('then from'); whereas in the bounds of
Cranbourne, Curdridge, Durley, and *Rige leah* each stage begins
simply with *of* ('from'); whilst the sixth boundary clause, that of
Brown Candover, is quite different in that each stage is begun with
one or two Latin words: *Primitus . . . ac deinde . . . indeque . . . sic
deinceps . . . illincque . . .* etc. It would seem likely that the forger used
various different charters concerning these six estates that he found in
the New Minster archives to provide the boundary-clauses he needed.
For we have no evidence that the monks' claim to any of these
properties was ever disputed and certainly they possessed the entire
hundred by the time of the Domesday survey.

There is therefore no reason to doubt that the New Minster had been
given all these properties at some time in the tenth or early eleventh
centuries. Moreover the forger presumably had at least one text of the
reign of Edward the Elder to provide the list of witnesses, perhaps a
charter of 901, the year of the fourth indiction. His purpose may rather
have been to justify the administration of a disparate group of estates as
a single unit of 100 hides. The difficulty of dating the charter's imitative
script prevents us from establishing the occasion of the forgery. A
plausible context could be envisaged at any time from the early eleventh
century (when the second age of Viking assaults necessitated some
reorganization of hundredal boundaries and assessments)[40] to the reign
of William the Conqueror. Certainly it would be a great convenience
for the abbot of the New Minster to be able to meet the monastery's
obligations from these estates assessed as a single unit, and to be able to
require the inhabitants to come to a single hundredal court rather than
having to look after the interests of the abbey's men in four or five
different courts, each meeting once a month. As a forgery the
Micheldever charter seems to have been successful, since Hyde Abbey
possessed the hundred of Micheldever uncontested throughout the
Middle Ages. This is perhaps not surprising since the only persons who
would suffer from the creation of this hundred would be those tenants
of the outlying portions who now had a long journey of fifteen miles to
court (Figure 26), and perhaps also the victims of thieves who evaded
capture and justice by escaping into parts of the hundred that were now
distant from the control of the hundred-reeve at Micheldever.

Finally we may ask what we can learn from the charter about the
origin of the hundred of Micheldever. Micheldever is known to have
been a *regalis villa* in the mid-ninth century, when King Æthelred I and

[40] *Anglo-Saxon Chronicle*, trans. D. Whitelock (1961), *s.a.* 1008; Harmer, *Writs*, pp.
266–8.

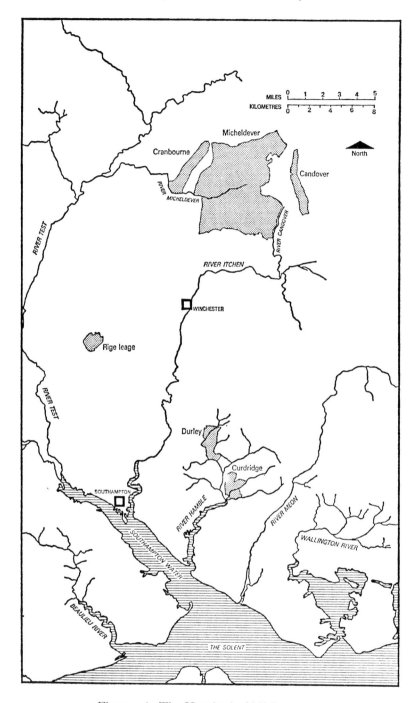

Figure 26. The Hundred of Micheldever.

his West Saxon court met there in or about the year 865.[41] Historians who have sought to discover what sort of administrative districts existed in Wessex, as elsewhere in England, before the establishment of the hundredal system in the tenth century, have found evidence in mediaeval sources of significant groupings of hundreds which seem to be of great antiquity and which were normally centred upon an important royal manor, *cyninges tun* or *regalis villa*.[42] It is possible that the ninth-century royal 'vill' of Micheldever was the centre of just such a district or *regio*, which in Kent would be called a lathe, in Sussex a rape, and in northern England a shire. We cannot tell how large this district might have been, but there is a clear indication in the bounds of the Micheldever charter that it was larger than the central core of the later hundred and presumably (in origin at least) was a consolidated territory. For as we have seen the bounds of the first estate surveyed, that of Micheldever itself, include a *gemot hus* at an important crossroads on the Roman road leading north from Winchester. This is the only reference that we have to a hundredal court building, since hundreds seem normally to have met in the open air, often by some prominent landmark. But the cross-roads site of the moot-house is typical of hundredal meeting places,[43] except that it is situated on the boundary of the hundred rather than within it. A meeting place at this site looks as though it is a relic of an older, larger district. At the very least such an early district would have included the tiny hundreds of Bountisborough (comprising the parishes of Itchen Abbas, Itchen Stoke, Swarraton, and Godsfield) and of Mainsborough (comprising the parishes of Brown and Chilton Candover and of Woodmancott). As Anderson has suggested,[44] these two have all the appearance of being relics left high and dry by the creation of a separate administrative unit for the New Minster properties. What further territories may once have 'belonged to' the royal vill of Micheldever can only be a matter of pure conjecture. The association of all or much of the hundred of Barton Stacey would, however, draw into a consolidated territory several of the outlying territories of the later

---

[41] BCS 504. I assume that the date 862 borne by this charter is a mistake for 865 or 867, since Æthelred's reign lasted from 865 to 871. In that event the attestation of Swithun must either be an interpolation or he did not die in 862. The formulae of the charter are those of ninth-century West Saxon texts and there is no evident motive for Abingdon to forge a charter to a layman.

[42] H.M. Chadwick, *Studies on Anglo-Saxon Institutions* (Cambridge, 1905), pp. 241–62; H.M. Cam, 'Early Groups of Hundreds', in J.G. Edwards, ed., *Historical Essays in Honour of James Tait* (Manchester, 1933), pp. 13–26; F.M. Stenton, *Anglo-Saxon England* (3rd edn, Oxford, 1971), pp. 292–8; G.W.S. Barrow, 'Pre-feudal Scotland: Shires and Thanes', in idem, *The Kingdom of the Scots* (1973), pp. 1–68.

[43] O.S. Anderson, *English Hundred-Names: South-Western Counties (Lunds Univ. Arsskrfit*, n.f. Avd. i, Bd. 35 no. 5, 1939).

[44] Ibid., xvii.

hundred of Micheldever – Cranbourne, Drayton and Abbot's Worthy – and perhaps might explain how the strange sentence about Abbot's Worthy found its way into the charter, since the combined hundreds would indeed surround Abbot's Worthy.

Even though the Micheldever charter may be the earliest evidence that we have for a private hundred, we cannot be certain whether the hundred was already private from the establishment of the hundredal system in Hampshire, or whether it represents a usurpation of royal or public authority by a wealthy ecclesiastical community in the eleventh century. Professor Cam has argued persuasively that the private hundred and the mediaeval franchise (immunity) were not the result of the alienation of royal authority but rather the natural product of the long-standing authority exercised by secular and ecclesiastical lords over land; as the royal government grew in its reach and its complexity during the tenth and eleventh centuries so lords needed to define their rights more closely.[45] The Micheldever forgery could then be seen as one lord's answer to the new need to define its traditional authority in up-to-date terms. But this is not the only possible model. Across the channel in the French kingdom the early eleventh century was, as the researches of Duby, Dhondt, and others have shown,[46] the time par excellence when the public authority of the counts disintegrated and powerful lords, lay and ecclesiastical, carved out new lordships and new feudal immunities for themselves. In England the weakness of royal power did not last so long as in Western Frankia; but it is by no means improbable that between the reign of Æthelred the Unready and the Domesday survey powerful lords should have taken the opportunity to usurp hundredal rights for their own estates and, in the Micheldever charter, to bolster their usurpation by forgery.

Such are the possibilities that the identification of the hundred hides of the Micheldever charter opens up. To the reader who enjoys walking in the downs of Hampshire this author would recommend a perambulation of the hundredal boundaries that is organized to finish at the *gemot hus*. For the only building now at the crossroads is a public house called Lunways Inn; it does not take the local brew long to convince the weary walker that the inn may perpetuate some of the more social aspects of the court meetings of a thousand years ago![47]

[45] H.M. Cam, 'The Evolution of the Medieval English Franchise', *Speculum*, 32 (1957), esp. 428–33.

[46] G. Duby, *La Société au XIᵉ et XIIᵉ siècles dans la région mâconaise* (Paris, 1953); Y. Bongert, *Recherches sur les cours laiques du Xᵉ au XIIIᵉ siècles* (Paris, 1949), pp. 37–78; J. Dhondt, *Etudes sur la naissance des principautés territoriales en France, IX–X sièces* (Bruges, 1948).

[47] My thanks are due to Mr Robin Gibb of the St Andrews University cartographic unit who drew all the maps working from my detailed notes. Any advance that they make in the mapping of early mediaeval estates is the product of his skill and care.

Edition

King Edward grants one hundred hides (*cassati*) at Micheldever [comprising Micheldever, Cranborne, Curdridge, Durley, *Rigeleah* and Candover], Hampshire, to the New Minister, Winchester. AD 900.

Manuscripts
A WCM 12090: single sheet, parchment, saec.xi, 365 × 503 mm. *Endorsements*: (1) *by the scribe of the charter*: + to myceldeuer (2) *in a hand of s.xii, around the previous endorsement*: Eaduua[r]dus fundator istius loci[ ].c. cassatos. Ceseldene.xx. cassatorum. Anna .xv. cassat' . (3) *in a hand of s.xiii (?)*: Privilegium regis Edwardi primi de mucheldevora. (4) *in a medieval hand*: Micheld' anno regis . primi j⁰. *Note on face: signature, s.xvi*: J. Fyssher.
B Earl of Macclesfield, Shirburn Castle, Liber Abbatiae, fos 13v–15: copy of A, s.xiv.

Editions
BCS 596 from A.
Edwards, *Liber de Hyda*, 85–97 from B.

Listed
S 360.

Facsimile (of A)
Sanders, *Facsimiles*, ii, Winchester College no. 1.

Printed from A

Omnipotentia diuine, maiestatis ubique presidente et sine fine cuncta gubernante; EGO EADUUEARDUS. ipso largiente rex Anglorum cunctis gentis nostrę fidelibus innotesco quod pro salute anime, meae quendam fundum quem indigene. Myceldefer. appellant .centum. cassatorum quantitatem continentem benigne confero monasterio Sancte, Trinitatis quod UUentana situm est ciuitate Nouumque appellatur; Huic autem libertati fautores et consiliarii mei fuerunt duces et magnates qui me ad hanc largitatem incitauerunt. qui etiam omnes unanimiter constituerunt ut donatio ista firma in æternum permaneat. neque a quolibet seu superiore uel inferiore commutetur. et quisquis uiolare presumpserit excommunicetur a societate Dei et sanctorum eius. Proinde sit terra predicta ab omni seruitio mundana semper libera exceptis tribus causis hoc est expeditione et pontis arcisue constructione; Limites autem que, etᵃ superdictam pertinent terram subsequens manifestat stilus anglicus hoc modo; Ðis syndon þa land gemæra to Myceldefer. Ærest on hafoc hlinc¹ þonne spa ⁊lang herpaðes oð

ᵃ *Error for* ad.

ecgulfes treop.[2] þonne 7lang herpaðes oð myceldefer.[3] þonne 7lang
myceldefer. ðonne of myceldefer to ðam pole.[4] þonne of ðam pole to
næsan byrig.[5] þonne of næsan byrig to pæter hlince.[6] þonne of pæter
hlince to stapola ðorne.[7] þonne of stapola ðorne to horgan þege.[8] ðonne
of horgan þege to forsæðan pylle.[9] ðonne of forsæðan pylle to dyddan
þorne.[10] ðonne of dyddan þorne to tettan grafe.[11] þonne of tettan grafe
to ceortes beorge.[12] þonne of ceortes beorge to cleara flode.[13] þonne of
cleara flode 7lang stræte on herpes ham.[14] þonne of herpes ham to lin
leage.[15] ðonne of lin leage to bulloces sole.[16] ðonne of bulloces sole to
ticces ham.[17] þonne ofer ðone feld to bearcelea.[18] þonne of bearcelea
forð on æplea.[19] þonne of æplea spa forð on hean hangran[20] þonne
ofer ðone feld on kendefer.[21] þonne 7lang kendefer on duddan dune.[22]
þonne 7lang streames to brocenan beorge.[23] of brocenan beorge innan
ða rode on beaga lea.[24] of ðære rode on middepeardan peard
hangran.[25] Of peard hangran spa ford on papan holt suðepeardne.[26]
þonne on ðæt gemot hus.[27] þonne ofer rupan dune.[28] þonne eft on
hafoc hlinc;[29]

Þis syndon ða land gemæra to cramburnan; Ærest on myceldeferes
stream fornangean ðone cyric stede on þynsiges tune[1] 7lang streames
on paddan ige.[2] of paddan ige 7lang streames on ðone blacan pól.[3] of
ðam blacan pole. on hpelpes dell.[4] of hpelpes delle on ðone burnan.[5] of
ðam burnan norð 7lang þeges on tuccinge þeg.[6] of tuccinge þege. 7lang
þeges on greatan díc.[7] of greatan dic on rupan beorh.[8] of rupan beorge
þurð þone puda on cealc grafan[9] 7lang paðes on frigedæg.[10] of
frigedæge on horpeges norð ende.[11] of horpeges norð ende 7lang þeges
eastpeard on ðone smalan pæð.[12] of ðam smalan pæðe ut ðurh cealc
grafas on ðone readan pyll.[13] of ðam readan pylle 7lang fyr innan
greatan dic on þæt smale dell.[14] of ðam smalan delle ut to lytlan dune
on ðæs hundes hylle.[15] of ðæs hundes hylle 7lang þeges on cram
mere.[16] of cram mere 7lang þeges on nanes mannes land.[17] of nanes
mannes land 7lang þeges eft innan myceldefer;[18]

Þis syndon ða land gemæra to Cuðredes hricgce. Ærest of ðam readan
clife[1] in to bican forda[2] 7lang þeges to pinter burnan.[3] of pinter burnan
on ða fearnigan hylle.[4] of ðære fearnigan hylle ut on mattuces feld.[5] of
mattuces felda up to ðam garan on þæt tpyslede treop.[6] of ðam
tpysledan treope to ðam more.[7] 7 ofer þone mor be eastan ðan more on
brom burnan.[8] 7lang brom burnan to syle forda.[9] of syleforda eft to
bican forda;[10]

Ðis syndon ða land gemæra to Diorleage. Ærest on cysle burnan innan
hamele þær cysle burnan ærest ingæð.[1] up 7lang cysle burnan to pifeles
stigele.[2] of pifeles stigele on þæt read leafe treop.[3] of ðam read leafan
treope on ðone ealdan stocc.[4] of ðam stocce be pestan burnan on þone
grenan þeg.[5] of ðam grenan þege 7lang ðæs smalan paðes to cnoll gete.[6]
of cnoll gete on þæt hpite treop.[7] of þam hpitan treope on ðæt norð

healde treop.[8] of ðam norð healdan treope to cuntan heale.[9] of cuntan heale on ðone lytlan pyll.[10] of ðam lytlan pylle forð ofer beorh holt[11] on ða langan byrce.[12] of ðære langan byrce innan pohburnan.[13] ꝥlang pohburnan to stapol forda.[14] up of stapol forda to apelpican.[15] of apelpican into ðam holan more.[16] ꝥlang ðæs holan mores innan hamele[17] ꝥlang hamele þær cysle burnan gæð into hamele;[18]

Þis syndon ða land gemæra to Rige leage. Ærest on seaxea sæð.[1] of seaxe seaðe on þone holan æsc.[2] of ðam holan æsce on trinde leage.[3] of trinde leage on fæstan æc[4] of fæstan æc on eadulfes hamm.[5] of eadulfes hamme on ða readan díc.[6] of ðære readan díc on þa leage.[7] of ðære leage on bær heal.[8] of bær heale on tæppe leage.[9] of tæppe leage eft on seaxe seað;[10]

IN NOMINE IHesU CHRistI. Þis syndon ðæra syx hida land gemæra æt Kendefer. Primitus. fram ðære burn stope.[1] to ðam stan cistele.[2] Ac deinde. on ðone greatan þorn.[3] Indeque on bican hyrste to puda.[4] Sic deinceps. to rupan beorge.[5] Illincque to ðam pidan herpaðe.[6] Sicque promtim. to beofan stane[7] to norð sceate to puda.[8] ꝥ ðurh ðone puda inn on pidan dæll middeperd.[9] Ex hoc ut ðurh tigel hangran.[10] et de post. ut ðurh trindlea.[11] spa ꝥlang ðæs smalan peges to bucgan oran on ða miclan dic.[12] Sic denique ꝥlang dune on pest healfe to ðære burn stope ðe pe ær on fruman nemdan;[13] ꝥ ða seofan hida æt porðige hyrað to þam hund hidan to mycel defer. eall spa ða land gemæra hit on butan belicgeað. ꝥ an per on ycenan ꝥ healf þæt hpite clif ꝥ seo syðemyste mylen on pinteceastre binnan pealle;[14] C[elebr]ata[b] est igitur hec regalis institutio in pago qui dicitur Hamtun, anno dominice incarnationis .dcccc. indictione [quarta sub testi]monio[b] [et]b auctoritate gentis nostrae principum quorum uocabulo hic cernuntur.

[+ Ego Eadp]eard[b] rex	+ Þihtbrord minister
[+ Ego Plego]mund[b] bisceop	+ Deormod minister
[+ Ego Æðelp]eard[b] filius regis	+ Beorhtsie minister
[+ Ego Denep]ulf[b] bisceop	+ Ocea minister
[+ Ego Þi]ferð[b] bisceop	+ Æðelstan minister
+ Ego Þulfsige bisceop	+ Þulfhelm minister
+ Ego Asser bisceop	+ Alla minister
+ Ego Þighelm bisceop	+ Beornstan minister
+ Ego Ceolmund bisceop	+ Þulfhelm minister
+ Ego Eadgar bisceop	+ Beornstan minister
+ Ego Þimund bisceop	+ Tata minister
+ Ego Beornelm abbas	+ Þulfred minister
+ Æðelstan	+ [Eadulf]b
+ Beorhtulf presbyter	+ Þulfhelm

b *MS damaged, reading supplied from B.*

+ Beornulf diaconus   + Þulfsige
+ Eadstan diaconus
+ Eadulf
+ Ælfstan
+ Æðelstan
+ Þighelm
+ Þulfstan
+ Þulfric
+ Ealhstan
+ Þynsige

12

Romney Marsh in the Early Middle Ages

Introduction

The evolution of Romney Marsh has been such a fertile ground for antiquarian conjecture and controversy over the last century and a half that armchair historians might have learnt to leave well alone. But in the last generation major advances in our understanding of the technical processes by which the marsh has been formed have at last provided a more secure framework into which the historical evidence needs to be fitted. The work of W.V. Lewis in the 1930s and more recently of J. Eddison has transformed our knowledge of the shingle beaches that comprise the Dungeness headland and of the way that changes in sea-level have contributed to the formation of the headland.[1] The second crucial contribution was made in 1968 when R.D. Green published for the Soil Survey of Great Britain his final and full report on the area to seaward of the Royal Military Canal. For the first time the complexity of the marsh soils was revealed, defined and mapped; their stratigraphical relationship was established, and many of the technical problems of the variations in land-levels within the marsh and of the relics of former creeks and water courses were solved.[2] Then in 1980 Professor Cunliffe used these major contributions, together with scattered nuggets of archaeological, geological and historical information, to propound a bold interpretation of the geomorphological changes that have occurred since neolithic times. As his synthesis claimed to be no more than a 'preliminary' model, which required testing and refinement,[3] it may be

[1] W.V. Lewis, 'The Formation of Dungeness Foreland', *Geographical Journal*, 80 (1932), pp. 309–24; W.V. Lewis, 'The Formation of Dungeness and Romney Marsh', *Proceedings of the Transactions of the South East Union Scientific Society* (1937), pp. 65–70; W.V. Lewis and W.G.V. Balchin, '1940: Past Sea-Levels at Dungeness', *Geographical Journal*, 96 (1940), pp. 258–85; J. Eddison, 'The Evolution of the Barrier Beaches between Fairlight and Hythe', *Geographical Journal*, 149 (1983), pp. 39–53.

[2] R.D. Green, *Soils of Romney Marsh*, Soil Survey of Great Britain, Bulletin 4 (Harpenden, 1968).

[3] B.W. Cunliffe, 'The Evolution of Romney Marsh: A Preliminary Statement', in F.H. Thompson, ed., *Archaeology and Coastal Change* (London, 1980), pp. 37–55, at 47.

worth setting out some of the historical evidence that can help to deepen and to delimit our knowledge of the development of the landscape of the marsh.

Of all the marshland areas of Britain Romney Marsh offers the best prospect for the historian to work alongside the geologist and the archaeologist because it is uniquely well documented. In the Middle Ages the archbishops and the cathedral community of Canterbury were the dominant landowners in Romney Marsh proper, that is the marshland to the north-east of the Rhee Wall, where they held no less than 7140 out of the 17,300 acres of land; they also had extensive properties in Walland and Denge Marshes and around their manors at Appledore and the Isle of Oxney. Other Kentish monastic houses, such as St Augustine's, Canterbury, and Bilsington Priory, were also major lords in the Marsh.[4] The charters and estate-records of these houses, published and unpublished, provide an enormous corpus of material concerning the development of drainage and the many forms of land-use in Romney Marsh from the mid-twelfth century. Supplemented from the thirteenth century by the records of royal statute and central government and by the archives of the Cinque Ports, there is material here to keep several research students busy for many years. As yet the surface has only been scraped.[5] Detailed and well-documented studies of the development of the marsh landscape from the mid-thirteenth century or earlier are certainly both possible and urgently needed.

Romney Marsh is also surprisingly well documented in the early Middle Ages. The archives of Christ Church, Canterbury, and to a lesser extent of St Augustine's have preserved a series of charters concerning lands in the Marsh from the late seventh century onwards. Many of these charters were studied by the great Kentish topographer, Gordon Ward, in a series of articles published in *Archaeologia Cantiana* between 1931 and 1952.[6] When we recall that Ward was working

---

[4] R.A.L. Smith, *Canterbury Cathedral Priory* (Cambridge, 1943); N. Neilson, *Cartulary and Terrier of Bilsington Priory, Kent* (London, 1928).

[5] W. Dugdale, *History of the Imbanking and Draining of divers Fens and Marshes* (2nd edn, London, 1772); W. Holloway, *The History of Romney Marsh* (London, 1849); M. Teichman Derville, *The Level and Liberty of Romney Marsh, Kent* (Ashford, 1936); Smith, *Canterbury Cathedral.*

[6] G. Ward, 'Saxon Lydd.', *Archaeologia Cantiana*, 43 (1931), pp. 29–37; idem, 'Sandtunes Boc.', ibid., pp. 39–47; idem, 'The River Limen at Ruckinge', *Archaeologia Cantiana*, 45 (1933), pp. 129–32; idem, 'The Saxon Charters of Burmarsh', ibid., pp. 133–41; idem, 'The Wilmington Charter of A.D. 700', *Archaeologia Cantiana*, 48 (1936), pp. 11–28; idem, 'Discussion', in Lewis and Balchin 'Past Sea-Levels at Dungeness', pp. 291–2; idem, 'The Saxon History of the Town and Port of Romney', *Archaeologia Cantiana*, 65 (1952), pp. 12–25.

without any of the guides and handbooks that ease the path of the modern scholar through the difficult field of Anglo-Saxon charters,[7] it is astonishing how far his enthusiasm and his eye for detail enabled him to seize upon the significance of the topographical and economic information in the charters. Inevitably, however, there were mistakes; moreover Ward never attempted any synthesis of the whole body of the charter evidence in the light of the evidence of place-names and of the Domesday survey and related documents. Now that Green and Cunliffe have confirmed some of Ward's findings and challenged others, it is time for the evidence to be examined afresh.

Fundamental to any understanding of Romney Marsh in the early Middle Ages is Green's distinction between the 'Calcareous' or New

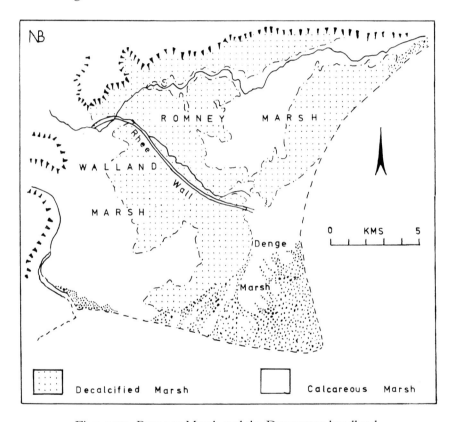

Figure 27. Romney Marsh and the Dungeness headland.

---

[7] F.M. Stenton, *Latin Charters of the Anglo-Saxon Period* (Oxford, 1955); D. Whitelock, *EHD*; P.H. Sawyer, *Anglo-Saxon Charters*; Brooks, 'Anglo-Saxon Charters: The Work of the Last Twenty Years', see above, pp. 181–215.

Marshland, which has been subjected to inundation by the sea within historic times, and the 'Decalcified' or Old Marshland from which the calcium has largely leached away after centuries of natural drainage (Figure 27). Green and Cunliffe have argued from good evidence that some or all of the old marshland already existed as land available for colonization between the first century BC and the first century AD.[8] With a change in environmental conditions, this old marshland itself came under threat in late Roman times. For Green detected in the decalcified marsh an elaborate system of tidal creeks which seems to be related to the routes taken by the rivers Brede, Tillingham and the two arms of the *Limen* (Rother) towards a wide estuary which made its way to the sea past the Roman fort at Lympne.[9]

It is also argued that the reclamation of the areas of Calcareous (New) Marsh did not all occur at one time: that of the Hythe estuary is attributed to the Middle- or Late-Saxon period, that of Walland and Denge Marshes to the late Middle Ages and early modern period.[10] Another significant proposal was indicated in Green's mapping of the alluvial beds of two supposed former courses of the northern branch of the river Rother: one finding its way to the sea at West Hythe, the other at Romney. Green identifies these two branches with the two courses of the river *Limen* recorded in pre-conquest charters.[11] Their meandering courses establish that both are natural watercourses; but it should be observed that the Romney branch cuts through the Old Decalcified Marshland, whilst the northern branch runs through New Calcareous Marshes. It has still to be determined whether this difference has any implications for their relative chronology.

Mention must also be made of the extensive layer of peat, deposited in the second half of the second millennium BC, which extends over much of the western half of the marsh, most thickly just to the south of Appledore.[12] It is possible that a medieval rise in the level of the sea, together with the desire to improve the marsh pastures, led to more and more elaborate drainage-schemes. Drainage in turn would have caused the peat to contract and the level of the land to drop. As a result of one or more of these factors, sea- and river-walls had to be built even higher. The familiar vicious circle of peat-marsh management provides one possible explanation for the growing concern shown in the

[8] Green, *Soils of Romney Marsh*, pp. 18 and 27; Cunliffe, 'Evolution of Romney Marsh', pp. 43–4.

[9] Ibid., figure 19.

[10] Green, *Soils of Romney Marsh*, pp. 30–44; Cunliffe, 'Evolution of Romney Marsh', pp. 47–52.

[11] But cf. Eddison, 'The Reclamation of Romney Marsh; Some Aspects Re-considered', *Archaeologia Cantiana*, 99 (1983), pp. 47–58, at 54–6.

[12] Green, *Soils of Romney Marsh*, pp. 14–15.

medieval records with the ancient and customary obligations of marsh-landowners to build up the banks of sea-defences and of water-courses. This *lex marisci* is already mentioned in charters from the early twelfth century.[13] It may have been that the subsidence of the land caused by effective drainage made this part of the marsh so vulnerable, especially when it was combined with changes in the barrier beaches and possibly with a gradual rise in sea-level.[14] The great inundation that had long been feared culminated in the disastrous storms of 1287–8: the sea broke through the defences; Old Winchelsea and the township of Broomhill were washed away; sea-water flooded much of the marsh to the west and south of the Rhee wall and created a new estuary of the rivers Brede, Tillingham and Rother (both the branch to the south of the Isle of Oxney and that to the north) that now flowed south past Rye. These dramatic changes made necessary a long and chequered process of medieval reclamation over the next three centuries. The extent of the areas that had to be regained from the sea since the thirteenth century is indicated by the extent of the calcareous soils in Walland and Guldeford marshes and in the vicinity of Romney Haven.

Parish Boundaries (Figure 28)

One approach to the problems of Romney Marsh in the early Middle Ages is to examine the parish boundaries that existed at the time of the Tithe Awards of the early nineteenth century. Elsewhere in England it is common to find that the parish boundaries that existed until the adjustments of the later nineteenth century coincide more or less precisely with estates surveyed in Anglo-Saxon royal charters of the tenth and eleventh centuries. In the Marsh, however, we know that some of the boundaries must be of more recent origin, namely where they traverse land reclaimed from the sea in late medieval or in early modern times. None the less it may be noticed that most of the parish churches in Romney Marsh are already recorded in the late eleventh century in the *Domesday Monachorum*:[15] moreover the four unidentified churches listed there as being dependent upon Lympne (*Siwoldescirce, Mertumnescirce, Kyngestun* and *Swirgildancirce*) may well account for some of the churches that seem to be omitted (Snargate, Snave, Burmarsh, Fairfield, Brookland, Hope).[16] We may therefore suspect

---

[13] Holloway, *History of Romney Marsh*, p. 66f.

[14] Eddison, 'Evolution of the Barrier Beaches'.

[15] C.C. Douglas, *The Domesday Monachorum of Christ Church Canterbury* (London, 1944), p. 78.

[16] But see T.W.T. Tatton-Brown, 'The Topography of the Walland Marsh Area between the Eleventh and Thirteenth Centuries', in J. Eddison and C. Green, eds, *Romney Marsh: Evolution, Occupation and Reclamation* (Oxford, 1988), pp. 105–12.

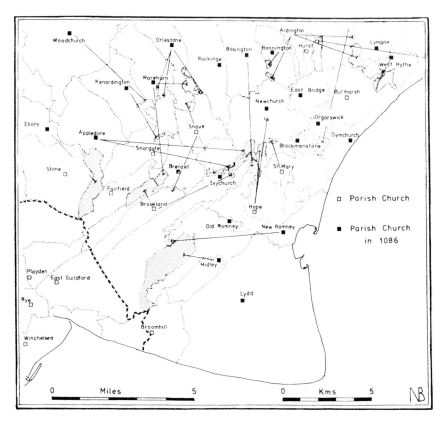

Figure 28. Parish boundaries of Romney Marsh. The boundaries are those of the nineteenth-century Tithe Awards; the coastline is derived from the first edition of the Ordnance Survey 1 inch survey (1816).

that Figure 28 reflects in part boundaries in existence since the early Middle Ages. Certainly the shape of the parishes seems to reveal some fundamental distinctions in the settlement pattern. To the north a series of villages is situated on the much eroded cliff overlooking the marsh, and their parish boundaries extend south so that an area of marshland is included in each of their territories – Appledore, Kenardington, Warehorne, Orlestone, Ruckinge, Bilsington, Bonnington Hurst and Lympne. The parishes that lie wholly in the marsh divide clearly into two types: north-east of the Rhee wall, in Romney Marsh proper, despite innumerable minor irregularities, the parishes form consolidated blocks, very approximately circular in shape with the parish church in a central position (Burmarsh, Eastbridge, Newchurch, Blackmanstone, Orgarswick, St. Mary-in-the-Marsh, Hope, Snave); but south-west of the Rhee wall the parishes are predominantly of long, narrow form with straight boundaries which follow the lines of the water-channels and embankments of the medieval 'innings' or marsh reclamations. The parish churches for the most part lie at the north-east end of these elongated parishes, that is in that portion of the parish that lies in the Old Decalcified Marshland; the relative regularity of their boundaries by contrast with the parishes of the north-eastern half of the marsh is therefore a product of the medieval and post-medieval reclamation of Walland Marsh as it progressed to the Kent-Sussex boundary.[17]

An interesting feature of the parish boundaries is their relationship to the various river courses of the Rother or *Limen*. Ward was the first to see that the fact that the parish boundaries totally ignore the Rhee Wall was one of a number of proofs that that work could not be of Roman origin as had hitherto been thought. This massive artificial water-channel had been constructed by the mid-thirteenth century in a direct line across all the existing ecclesiastical, manorial and hundredal boundaries[18] in a vain attempt to save the port of Romney. More remarkable however is the fact that the parish boundaries are equally independent of the Romney branch of the northern *Limen* that may have preceded the Rhee: at no point, save in the vicinity of Old and New Romney where the river-bed detected by Green's soil survey widens to form a broad estuary, do their courses coincide. It seems clear that the parish boundaries are older than the river-course that cuts through them, just as they are older than the artificial Rhee Wall. By contrast the northern branch of the *Limen*, which Green and Ward each detected by their different methods, coincides with the parish boundaries of Newchurch Eastbridge and Burmarsh where they adjoin Ruckinge, Bilsington, Bonnington, Hurst and Lympne. Since this is an area of new marshland which in late Roman times had been a wide tidal estuary[19] it is likely that reclamation of the estuary and the definition of estate and parish boundaries proceeded *pari passu* in the early Middle Ages.

A feature of the parishes of the Marsh (as they existed until the early nineteenth century) was the large number of detached portions that lay at considerable distances from the parishes to which they belonged (Figure 28). Some of these outlying members, such as the detached portion of the parish of Ebony, may represent marsh reclamations of the fifteenth or sixteenth centuries. Indeed most of them are situated in the New or Calcareous Marshland. But in reality many of them have a

---

[17] See Tatton-Brown, 'Topography of the Walland Marsh Area'.

[18] W.A. Scott Robertson, 'The Cinque Port Liberty of Romney', *Archaeologia Cantiana*, 13 (1880), pp. 261–80; Ward, 'Discussion'; Brooks, 'The Unidentified Forts of the Burghal Hidage', *Medieval Archaeology*, 8 (1964), pp. 74–90, at 82, n. 31, reprinted in Brooks, *Communities and Warfare, 700–1400* (London, 1999); Green, *Soils of Romney Marsh*, pp. 37–42; Eddison, 'Reclamation of Romney Marsh', pp. 53–6.

[19] Cunliffe, 'Evolution of Romney Marsh', pp. 43–5.

simple tenurial explanation of much greater antiquity. Thus the detached members of the parish of Aldington are clearly some of the holdings in the marsh of the great archiepiscopal manor of Aldington; one of them, lying between the parishes of Lympne and Burmarsh, is already mentioned in the boundary survey of a charter of King Eadmund of the year 946.[20] Even more ancient is the outlier of Sellindge parish that lay between Blackmanstone, Orgarswick and Dymchurch; Ward showed with some brilliant topographical detective work that there was a strong probability that this detached member was the pasture for 300 sheep called *Rumining seta* given to the minster of Lyminge by King Wihtred of Kent in the year 697 or 700.[21] Already at that early date this land was the 'Romney enclosure' (or 'enclosed pasture belonging to Rumen') attached to an inland estate at *Pleghelmestun* (now Wilmington) which was later part of the manor of Sellindge. At that time it was not uncommon for manors in central and even northern Kent to have distant sheep pastures in Romney Marsh. Thus we know that in the eighth century Ruckinge belonged to Ickham and Denge Marsh to Wye.[22]

The county boundary between Kent and Sussex also deserves some notice, for it makes little sense in terms of the marshland rivers as they have existed in the last six or seven hundred years. The boundary follows the old course of the southern branch of the river Rother passing south of the Isle of Oxney, but then departs from it at the point where the Rother now turns south towards Rye, as it has done since the storms of 1287–8. Very shortly thereafter, where the county boundary forms the northern limit of Guldeford Level (the parish of East Guldeford), it follows a straight and clearly artificial line across land that remained tidal marsh for many years after 1287–8. It resumes an irregular course as soon as it approaches the Old Decalcified Marshland. At this point the county boundary bisects the parish of Broomhill, so that astonishingly half of the parish is in Kent and half in Sussex. Since, as we shall see, the Kent–Sussex boundary was already on or close to the modern line here in the mid-eighth century, an explanation of the division of this parish is needed. The course of the boundary through Broomhill parish might repay detailed geological investigation.[23] The Brede or Tillingham rivers, or even the southern

[20] BCS 813; S 510; Ward, 'Saxon Charters', pp. 133–7.

[21] BCS 98; S 21; Ward, 'Wilmington Charter', pp. 20–7; P. Chaplais, 'Who Introduced Charters into England?', *Journal of the Society of Archivists*, 3 (1969), pp. 526–42, at 538–40.

[22] BCS 141, 214; S 1180, 111; Ward, 'River Limen'.

[23] See now Eddison, 'Evolution of Barrier Beaches', pp. 41–4; M. Gardiner, 'Medieval Settlement and Society in the Broomhill Area, and Excavations at Broomhill Church', in J. Eddison and C. Green, eds, *Romney Marsh: Evolution, Occupation and Reclamation* (Oxford, 1988), pp. 112–27.

branch of the Rother, may once have forced their way to the sea at this point. Alternatively it may be that the whole parish was originally in one county and that a storm such as those of 1287–8, which inundated the township of Broomhill, left only the eastern part of the parish intact. Thereafter it may have been inconvenient to reckon this tiny fragment as part of Sussex, since it now lay at the extremity of a marsh that was otherwise entirely in Kent.

The Domesday Survey of 1086 (Figure 29)

The evidence of boundaries that survived into the nineteenth century can be supplemented by the evidence of the Domesday survey and of the contemporaneous *Domesday Monachorum*. By 1086 there were four 'hundreds' whose territory lay entirely in the Marsh: Worth, Newchurch, Aloesbridge and Langport. As elsewhere in Kent, and indeed in Wessex as a whole, the hundreds are likely to have been the product of a major reorganization of local government carried through in the mid-tenth century.[24] The choice of hundredal centres is therefore of interest. Newchurch is the only Domesday hundredal centre situated on the New or Calcareous Marshland. Its name, which was applied to settlement, parish and hundred, implies that the church was for some time the dominant feature of the landscape and that there were other older churches nearby. We cannot be certain when the church was 'new', but it was certainly in existence by the date of the establishment of the hundredal system. By that time the colonization of this area of new marshland was sufficiently far advanced for Newchurch to be chosen as the hundredal centre in preference to Bilsington which is situated upon the upland. Some of the parish churches in the vicinity are certainly of later date: thus the church at Eastbridge, which is also in the Calcareous Marshland, is called *Ælsiescirce* in the *Domesday Monachorum* after Ælsi (Ælfsige) the pre-Conquest tenant of Eastbridge; nearby both the settlement at Blackmanstone and its church (*Blacemannescirce*) were named after the Englishman, Blaceman, who had held the land in the 'time of King Edward'; Orgarswick and its church *Orgarescirce* are likely to have been similarly named after a founder called Ordgar, and Dymchurch (*Demancirce*) from a judge (OE *dema*.[25] These names point not only to the building of private churches and the creation of the parochial system

---

[24] J.E.A. Jolliffe, *Pre-Feudal England: The Jutes* (Oxford, 1933), pp. 121–2; H.R. Loyn, 'The Hundred in England in the Tenth and early Eleventh Centuries', in H. Hearder and H.R. Loyn, eds, *British Government and Administration: Studies presented to S.B. Chrimes* (Cardiff, 1974), pp. 1–10.

[25] Douglas, *Domesday Monachorum*, p. 13; J.K. Wallenberg, *Place-Names of Kent* (Uppsala, 1934), pp. 461–3.

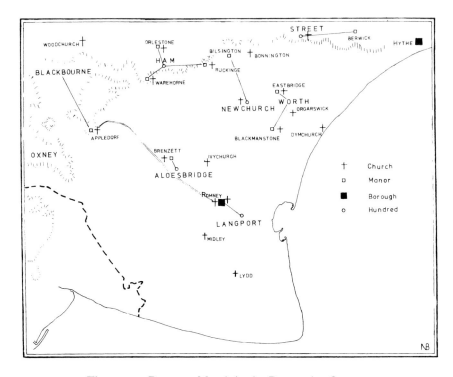

Figure 29. Romney Marsh in the Domesday Survey.

in this area of the marsh in the late-Saxon period, but also to the existence of prosperous and significant settlements in and on the fringes of the 'new' marshland at much the same time.

The other Domesday hundred names are less suggestive. We do not know the identity of the Æthelwulf who gave his name to Aloesbridge hundred, but Wallenberg's plausible suggestion that the hundred meeting-place was near Sumner House would locate Æthelwulf's bridge as a crossing of the supposed Romney branch of the northern *Limen* at TR 008272. Langport hundred probably took its name ('long market' or 'harbour') from an extension of the settlement or harbour of Old Romney; the name suggests that it may have been an attempt to solve the recurring problem of the silting of the Romney estuary by siting a new harbour nearer the sea.

Though there are several small estates and a number of churches in the Domesday records which cannot now be identified, it is striking that the locatable manors, churches and hundreds are all (apart from Midley and Lydd) in Romney Marsh properly so-called, that is they are all north-east of the Rhee Wall). Of course many estates in the Marsh are not named in the Domesday survey because they were subsumed in the record of the large 'discrete' estates of which they formed part, such as the great manors of Aldington, Wye and Ickham. But it is unlikely that the distribution of estates would be very different even if it were possible to include them all. For the Domesday evidence is strikingly complemented by the wider evidence of place-names. Kent is unfortunately one of the counties not yet covered by the English Place-Name Society's surveys. But the extensive researches of the Swedish scholar J.K. Wallenberg provide a corpus of evidence that is almost as comprehensive.[26] North-east of the Rhee Wall names found in pre-conquest charters abound. South-west of the 'wall' they are found only in the parishes of Lydd, Midley and Old Romney. Indeed in the parishes of Fairfield and Brookland and in those portions of Snargate, Brenzett, Ivychurch and New Romney that lie to the south-west of the Rhee Wall, Wallenberg found no single place-name evidenced before the thirteenth century – with the possible exception of Misleham in Brookland parish, if it is correctly identified as the *Mistanham* granted to Christ Church in the mid-ninth century.[27]

The contrast between the settlement history of the two halves of the marsh is therefore clear enough. Place-names and boundaries both point to the antiquity of the colonization of Romney Marsh proper and to the late date of the development of Walland Marsh. The contrast between the form of the drainage channels in the two halves of the Marsh is equally apparent. South-west of the Rhee Wall the straight 'sewers' and drainage cuts of medieval and modern reclamation abound; north-east of the wall the water-courses are predominantly irregular, being the survivors of natural creeks and streams.

Anglo-Saxon Charters (Figure 30)

For a more accurate picture of developments in the Marsh during the early Middle Ages we must turn to the surviving pre-Conquest charters. Unusually a majority are charters of the eighth and ninth centuries. Most of these diplomas came from the archives of the 'double-minster' of Lyminge, whose lands and archives passed to Christ Church, Canterbury in the ninth or tenth centuries. Lyminge was of course the minster of the lathe of the *Limenwara*, the 'Limen-dwellers', so it was natural that the monastery should have extensive lands in the marsh. Whilst it is invaluable to have early information about the Marsh, the brevity of the charters' descriptions of the estates means that their

---

[26] J.K. Wallenberg, *Kentish Place-Names* (Uppsala, 1931); Wallenberg, *Place-Names of Kent*.
[27] BCS 408; S 1623; Wallenberg, *Kentish Place-Names*, pp. 170–5.

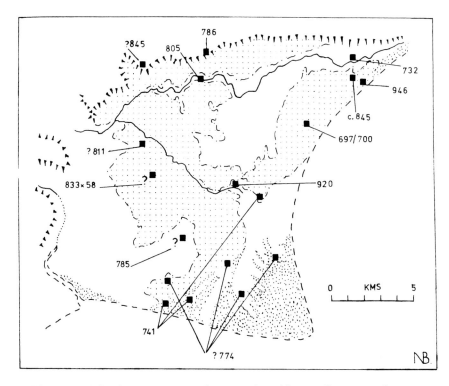

Figure 30. Marsh estates granted or mentioned in pre-Conquest charters.

topographical implications are not always clear. None the less, if we map all the identifiable estates granted or mentioned in pre-Conquest charters, we find that most of them are consistent with the findings of the soil scientists (Figure 30). For with exception of the *Sandtun* charter of 732, the Lydd charter of 774 and the Ruckinge charter of 805 (*CS* 1336; S 39),[28] all the estates recorded in the charters were situated in or on the edge of the Decalcified or Old Marshland.

The Northern Branch of the Limen (Figure 31)

The charters are most informative in locating one of the branches of the river Rother. The present name of the river is a modern invention, perhaps as late as the sixteenth century. It is a back-formation from the Sussex village- and hundred-name, Rotherfield (from OE *Hryðera-feld,* 'open land of the cattle') near its source, in exactly the same way as the river of the same name in West Sussex is a back-formation from

[28] BCS 148, S 23 (*Sandtun* charter); BCS 214, S 111 (Lydd charter); BCS 1336, S 39 (Ruckinge charter).

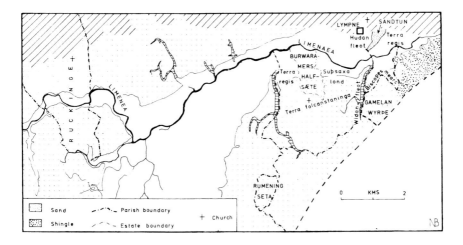

Figure 31. The northen branch of the *Limen*.

Rotherbridge, 'cattle-bridge'.[29] The previous name of the eastern Rother throughout its entire length in both Sussex and Kent was the *Limen*, which is a common Celtic river- and lake-name (**Lemana*) found in the rivers Leam, Leven, Lemon, Lyme and Lymn, in the lochs Lomond and Leven, and on the continent in Lac Leman. When it is found in the Kentish Anglo-Saxon charters the river-name has the suffix *-ea* (OE 'river'), which must have been attached at a time when the knowledge that the British name also meant 'river' had been lost. It is likely that the name *Limenea* was used for any of the branches into which the river split as it neared Romney Marsh and its shingle barrier beaches. If we can therefore locate a river named *Limenea* in the Marsh from the early charters, we cannot assume that it was necessarily the only, or even the principal, branch of the river.

In 732, in what seems to be an authentic and contemporary charter, King Æthelberht II of Kent confirmed to the priest-abbot Dun (of Lyminge) the grant that he had made to Dun's predecessor, Hymbra, of a quarter sulung of land beside the river *Limen* to serve as a saltern (*sali coquenda accommoda*); he also added a new annual gift of 120 cartloads of timber 'for cooking the salt' and a further 100 acres of the same property at *Sandtun*.[30] The site has been convincingly identified as the lost Sampton in West Hythe (TR 122338), situated on an ancient sand dune in the midst of the new marshland immediately beneath and south-east of the Roman 'Saxon Shore' fort of Lympne (*Portus Lemanis*),

[29] J. Mawer, F.M. Stenton, J.E.B. Glover, eds, *The Place-Names of Sussex*, 2 vols (Cambridge 1929–30), pp. xlvi, 7.

[30] BCS 148; S 23.

whose name also derives from the river.[31] The charter shows that the calcareous marsh to the east of *Sandtun* was royal property (*terra regis*), whilst on the north and west where once had been the anchorage of the Roman fort was now a creek named *hudan fleot*, 'Huda's fleet' (which was not detected by Green); the southern boundary was the river *Limen* (*Liminaee*), apparently already following the course detected by Green which runs immediately south of Sampton and is represented today by the Lower Wall. *Sandtun* surely is that rare phenomenon, a well-dated early medieval industrial site that would certainly repay further archaeological investigation; Birchell and Ward's unpublished excavations there in 1947 revealed occupation levels of middle-Saxon and of Saxo-Norman date with both imported and English pottery and with important assemblages of iron tools and of animal bones.[32] The material, now in the British Museum, still awaits systematic study, and the site must still have much to tell us of the fortunes of coastal and estuarine salt manufacture, as well as of the development of the Marsh, in the early Middle Ages.

The northern *Limen* as defined by Green recurs in other early charters. In 805 King Cuthred of Kent gave to Ealdberht and his sister, Abbess Selethryth (of Lyminge), 2 sulungs of land at Ruckinge 'on either side of the river *Limen*'.[33] Ward's identification of this estate at the southern end of the parish of Ruckinge has been strikingly confirmed by Green's demonstration that the northern *Limen* does indeed cut through the parish on the line now followed by the Sedbrook sewer.[34] In the same vicinity must have lain the sulung 'about the river *Limen*' which Æthelberht II had given in 724 during the last year or two of his father's reign to abbess Mildryth of Minster-in-Thanet;[35] for this property had formerly belonged to those who dwelt in Ickham, and we have other evidence that Ruckinge had once belonged to Ickham.[36] It deserves to be noticed that estates of one or two sulungs are (in Marsh terms) very substantial ones. The fact that the *Limen* passes through these estates, rather than forming their boundary, indicates that the river (*flumen*, *fluvius*) was not a significant barrier to farming in the Marsh; evidently we are here dealing with a bridgeable stream or small river, not with a great tidal estuary. Similar conclusions result from a

[31] Ward, 'Sandtunes Boc.'; Green, *Soils of Romney Marsh*.
[32] G.C. Dunning et al., 'Anglo-Saxon Pottery: A Symposium', *Medieval Archaeology*, 3 (1959), pp. 1–78, at 21; D.M. Wilson, The Archaeology of Anglo-Saxon England (London, 1976), pp. 258, 312, 376, 382 and 437; B.W. Cunliffe, 'Excavations at the Roman Fort at Lympne, Kent, 1976–8', *Britannia*, 11 (1980), pp. 227–88, at 228.
[33] BCS 1336; S 39.
[34] Ward, 'River Limen'.
[35] BCS 141; S 1180.
[36] Ward, 'River Limen'.

mid-ninth century private charter by which a certain Eadbald sold his half-pasture at Burmarsh to a certain Winemund.[37] The *Limen* formed the northern boundary of this estate and the channel of the *Limen* identified by Green still forms the parish boundary of Burmarsh. Ward's identification of the bounds of this charter and of the neighbouring estate *aet Gemelanwyrthe* granted by King Eadmund in 946 to two brothers, Ordhelm and Ælfwold[38] is also corroborated by the fact that Green has detected a substantial creek-relic exactly in the place where Ward placed the *widan fleot* ('wide creek') of the latter charter[39] – that is at the junction of Dymchurch, Burmarsh and West Hythe parishes. Taken together these charters of the eighth, ninth and tenth centuries indicate that the northern *Limen*, as detected by Green, was in existence when these transactions took place but that it was a river of minor importance, not the main course of the Rother. Moreover the charters give no hint at all that any of the calcareous marshland was still salt-marsh in need of reclamation, except for the few remaining tidal creeks or 'fleets'.[40] These relics should not obscure the fact that by the middle Saxon period the calcareous marshland in this part of the Marsh had already become dry land available for settlement.

One further important, though very local, change to the landscape of this area of the Marsh can be more precisely dated within the early medieval period, namely the collapse of the clay cliff on which the late-Roman fort of Lympne (*Portus Lemanis*/Stutfall Castle) had stood. Archaeologically it has been shown that the southern gate, walls and bastions of the fort broke up and slid into the Marsh at a time when the deposition of calcareous silt was still in progress there.[41] But the presence of 'Huda's fleet' at this spot in 732 means that we cannot suppose that this process was complete by the early eighth century. Indeed there are hints that the fort's collapse occurred much later. In the ninth century Lympne served as the centre where food-rents from the archbishop of Canterbury's properties in the vicinity were collected;[42] yet by the time of Domesday Book these estates were administered from the nearby Aldington. Moreover Lympne was a mint (and therefore perhaps also a borough) in the tenth century. A single coin of Athelstan's reign (924–39) is followed (when mint-signatures become the rule) by coins of every type from Edgar's reform of 973 to

---

[37] BCS 837; S 1193.

[38] BCS 813; S 510.

[39] G. Ward, 'The Saxon Charters of Burmarsh', Archaeologia Cantiana, 45 (1933), pp. 133–41.

[40] *hudan fleot* in BCS 148, S 23; 'wide fleet' in BCS 813, S 510.

[41] Cunliffe, 'Excavations', pp. 244–7 and 288.

[42] F.E. Harmer, *Select English Historical Documents of the Ninth and Tenth Centuries* (Cambridge, 1914), no. 1.

Cnut's 'short cross' issue of *c.* 1030–1035.[43] Thereafter the Lympne mint ceased production altogether. We do not, of course, know that either the archbishop's estate-centre or the mint had been situated within the Saxon Shore fort. But had they been in the modern village of Lympne, it is difficult to understand why they should have then needed to be moved elsewhere. There is therefore reason to suspect that the Roman defences of Lympne may have survived into the early eleventh century and have collapsed between the years 1030 and 1035 or very soon thereafter. By the reign of Edward the Confessor a new mint and a new port to replace Lympne had been established at Hythe, some two miles to the east.[44]

The Borough and River of Romney

The emergence of Romney as a significant port and urban settlement may have occurred about the time that the mint was established there in *c.* 1000.[45] Though the town's population was probably still small in 1086 when Domesday Book records just 156 burgesses at Romney, it is clear that it was already an important source of naval ships and crews. That was why both the Godwin family in 1052 and William the Conqueror in 1066 took good care to secure Romney.[46] Pre-conquest sources know only of a single settlement called Romney and are presumably always referring to Old Romney. The name of the town, recorded on coins as *Rume, Rumene, Ruman* and *Rumn*[47] and in the *Anglo-Saxon Chronicle* in 1052 as *Rumenea*, is not a settlement-name at all but a river-name. The suffix is OE *-ea*, 'river'; the first element may be a pre-English river-name, so that the whole would be parallel to *Limin(a)ea*, 'the river *Limen*'. If the reference is to the branch of the northern *Limen* whose course to Romney from Appledore was detected

[43] C.E. Blunt, 'The Coinage of Athelstan', *British Numismatic Journal*, 42 (1974), pp. 35–160, at 77–9; D.M. Metcalf, 'The Ranking of Boroughs: Numismatic Evidence from the Reign of Æthelred II', in D. Hill, ed., *Ethelred the Unready* (Oxford, 1978), pp. 159–212, at 211; Sylloge of the Coins of the British Isles, 13 (1970), nos 1499–1503.

[44] B.E. Hildebrand, *Anglosachsiska mynt i svenska kongliga myntkabinettet* (2nd edn, Stockholm, 1881), p. 245; ASC, s.a. 1052. See also J. Hutchinson et al., 'Combined Archaeological and Geotechnical Investigations of the Roman Fort at Lympne, Kent', *Britannia*, 16 (1985), pp. 209–36; J. Hutchinson, 'Recent Geotechnical, Geomorphological and Archaeological Investigations of the Abandoned Cliff Backing Romney Marsh at Lympne, Kent', in J. Eddison and C. Green, eds, *Romney Marsh: Evolution, Occupation and Reclamation* (Oxford, 1988), pp. 88–90.

[45] Metcalf, 'Ranking of Boroughs', p. 211.

[46] ASC, 1052; William of Poitiers, *Histoire de Guillaume le Conquérant*, ed. and trans. R. Foreville (Paris, 1952), p. 211.

[47] V.J. Smart, *Cumulative Index to SCBI, vols. 1–20*, Sylloge of the Coins of the British Isles, 28 (London, 1981), p. 103; Hildebrand, *Anglosachsiska mynt*, p. 134.

and mapped by Green,[48] derivation of the first element from OE *rum*, 'wide, broad' seems improbable for this narrow winding channel.

The earliest references to the river, however, are found centuries before the first mention of the town. Kentish antiquaries have long recognized that a charter of Æthelberht II of the year 741, which survives in an eighth-century manuscript, should probably be understood as referring to the Romney branch of the *Limen*:[49] Æthelberht granted to the church of Lyminge a fishery (*capturam piscium*) at the mouth of the river *Limen*, together with the part of the estate on which the oratory of St Martin and the fishermen's houses were situated, and also a quarter sulung of land round about; in addition the king conveyed a pasture for 150 draught cattle (*jumentorum*) at the south-west boundary of the Marsh, which had formerly belonged to Romanus *presbyter*. This charter does not refer explicitly to Romney and there must remain doubt whether the fishing settlement at the mouth of the *Limen* with a church of St Martin should indeed be identified with St Martin's church at New Romney. The present church is Norman in origin, and is listed in the *Domesday Monachorum*; its antiquity may be suggested by the fact that at least from the thirteenth century it was the meeting-place of the hundred and liberty of New Romney.[50] There is no difficulty in supposing that a fishing settlement and a church should have existed long before the creation of a borough at New Romney. If this charter is correctly interpreted, it provides evidence that by the first half of the eighth-century the river had a mouth at New Romney in addition to the (minor) northern course which disgorged into the sea in the vicinity of Hythe.

Unequivocal evidence of the Romney river is found in an authentic charter of the year 920 by which Archbishop Plegmund leased for three lives 80 acres of land at *Wæringc* marsh next to the river *Rumenesea*.[51] This awkward form of the name, which occurs twice in the charter, is more than a century older than any other full spelling of either the town or river. As Wallenberg (who was not normally disposed to derive place-names from personal-names if he could avoid it) came to recognize, the genitival form of the first element would suggest that it should be taken as a personal-name, were it not highly unusual for a river to be named after an individual. Moreover, it is at least a remarkable coincidence that a priest Romanus (OE *Ruman or *Rumen) is recorded as a former landowner in the Marsh in the charter of 741.[52] Romanus may

[48] *Soils of Romney Marsh*, pp. 39–42.

[49] BCS 160; S 24.

[50] W.A. Scott Robertson, 'Destroyed Churches of New Romney', *Archaeologia Cantiana*, 13 (1880), pp. 237–49, at 237–8; Ward, 'Saxon History', pp. 13–14.

[51] BCS 638, S 1288.

[52] Cf. Wallenberg, *Place-Names of Kent*, pp. 485–6 with idem, *Kentish Place-Names*, pp. 236–7.

reasonably be identified with the priest of that name 'from Kent' who played an important part in Northumbrian affairs as chaplain to King Oswy's wife, Eanflaed, in the years leading up to the synod of Whitby in 664.[53] For Eanflaed's mother was the Kentish princess, Æthelburh, who after the death of King Edwin in battle in 633 had returned to Kent with her daughter and founded the monastery of Lyminge, to which so many marsh properties (including that of Romanus) were given. Since none of the later forms of the name Romney have the medial -s-, we have no means of knowing whether a false etymology from Romanus was already current by 920, or whether the origin of the name *Rumenesea* was forgotten and the river-name normalized as *Rumenea* in subsequent centuries. The small pasture for 300 sheep called *Rumining seta* or *Rumening seta* which, as we have seen, was given to Lyminge in 697 or 700, could be based on *Rumen* whether it were a river-name or a personal-name. But since this property is so far distant from the Romney *Limen* it seems most likely to mean 'the enclosure which had once belonged to Rumen'; otherwise we should need to suppose that the Romney river had already given its name to the whole marsh on its north-eastern bank by the beginning of the eighth century.

Lydd and Denge Marsh (Figure 32)

Two early charters, Æthelberht II's grant to Abbot Dun in 741 and a purported grant of Lydd by King Offa in 774, throw light on the south-eastern portion of the Marsh.[54] Included among Æthelberht's grants to Lyminge in the first charter was grazing for 150 cattle 'next to the marsh called *biscopes uuic*, as far as the wood called *ripp* and as the bounds of Sussex (*Suthsaxoniae*)'. This is the property that had once belonged to the priest Romanus. As Wallenberg and Ward showed, the name *ripp* survives in the modern East and West Rype and in The Midrips; it refers to the stretches of shingle banks extending from the shore northwards to Lydd.[55] An extensive wood of holly trees (hence *Holm*stone) still grows on the shingle and on Poker's map of 1617 is shown extending from 'The Rype' (TR 030196) to the marsh known as 'The Wicks'.[56] It is therefore reasonable to identify the *biscopes uuic* of 741 with The Wicks, and to interpret the boundary clause to mean that the Sussex boundary formed the western limit of the pasture and The Wicks the eastern as far north as the holly-wood on the Rype. These

<hr/>

[53] Bede, *Historia ecclesiastica*; *Bede's Ecclesiastical History of the English People*, ed. B. Colgrave and R.A.B. Mynors (Oxford, 1969), iii.25.

[54] BCS 160, 214; S 24, 111.

[55] Wallenberg, *Kentish Place-Names*, pp. 37–8; Ward, 'Saxon Lydd.', pp. 35–7.

[56] Green, *Soils of Romney Marsh*, plate X.

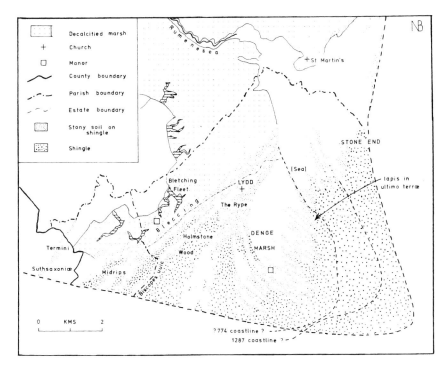

Figure 32. Romney, Lydd and Denge Marsh.

bounds in fact delimit the saltings now known as The Midrips, still used for rough grazing to this day.

Offa's purported grant of Lydd to Archbishop Jaenberht of Canterbury in 774 is more problematic. The charter survives on a single sheet of parchment which was not written at its purported date but in the second half of the tenth century. The formulae of the Latin text are highly distinctive and are under suspicion of having been doctored in the tenth century. Strictly therefore this charter cannot be taken as evidence for the boundaries of Lydd before the late tenth century. None the less it is clear from the witness-list and from much of the text that the forger or interpolator of this diploma did have a charter of 774 before him; and the brevity of the Latin boundary clause encourages us to believe that the bounds formed part of the authentic charter he was using. By the late tenth century, and perhaps therefore already in 774, the three sulungs at Lydd were bounded on the north and east by the sea, on the south by the '*terra regis aduui* called Denge Marsh *usque in lapidem adpositum in ultimo terrae*', and on the north and west by the king's boundary at *blecting*. Fortunately *blecting* can be recognized as the old name for the manor of Scotney (named from the family in possession from the late thirteenth century); the identification is confirmed by the survival into the later nineteenth century of Bletching Fleet (TR 020207), immediately north-east of Scotney and Scotney Court – a creek relic whose full extent has been detected and mapped by Green.[57] The other bounds of Lydd have, however, occasioned some difficulty. Ward interpreted the fact that the sea is named as forming the boundary on the north and east to mean that a wide tidal estuary of the river *Limen* separated Lydd from Old Romney. But this would be a curious way to refer to the estuary and in fact the phrase need mean no more than that the sea formed the north-eastern boundary of Lydd, which would fit very well with the north-easterly direction of the earlier shore-lines detected by Lewis in the shingle of the Dungeness headland and with the mouth or haven of the Romney *Limen* revealed by Green's soil survey.[57]

Lydd's southern boundary (Denge Marsh) was certainly misunder-stood by Ward[59] who sought to make the *terra regis aduui* into an estate of an unknown Kentish King (E)adwi(g). But since Denge Marsh is known in the Middle Ages to have been an outlying part of the manor of Wye at least from the time when Wye was given by King William I to Battle Abbey in 1071;[60] the phrase means no more than that Denge Marsh was a 'royal property (belonging) to Wye'.

It is also difficult to interpret the rather clumsy statement that Denge Marsh formed Lydd's southern boundary 'as far as the stone (*usque in lapidem*) situated at the end of the land (*adpositum in ultimo terrae*)'. Ward[61] was surely correct in taking *lapidem* to refer to the shingle as in the names Littlestone, Greatstone, Holmstone – which are all in the immediate vicinity of Lydd – rather than as a reference to a particular standing monument. Moreover it should be observed that the parish boundary of Lydd (Figure 32) reaches the shore at Greatstone, whose name at least until the seventeenth century was 'Stone End'. This is the name, for example, found on Cole's engraving (*c.* 1737) of Poker's map of the marsh in 1617.[62] The charter should therefore be understood to mean that Denge Marsh formed Lydd's southern boundary as far as Stone End, though we must allow that 'Stone End' will itself have moved progressively north-eastwards with the development of the Dungeness headland.

[57] Wallenberg, *Kentish Place-Names*, p. 56; idem, *Place-Names of Kent*, p. 481; Ward, 'Saxon Lydd.', p. 33.

[58] Ward, 'Saxon History', pp. 13–14; Lewis, 'Formation of Dungeness Foreland'.

[59] 'Saxon Lydd.', p. 33.

[60] H.W.C. Davis, *Regesta Regum Anglo-Normannorum, 1, 1066–1100* (Oxford, 1913), no. 62; E. Searle, *Lordship and Community: Battle Abbey and its Banlieu 1066–1538* (Toronto, 1964)

[61] Ward, 'Saxon Lydd.', p. 33.

[62] Green, *Soils of Romney Marsh*, plate X.

Since the principal elements of the boundary of the archiepiscopal estate of Lydd as it existed in the later tenth century (and perhaps already in 774) can be established with some confidence, we can be certain that Denge Marsh was already by that time a marshland estate attached to the royal vill of Wye. Here, however, the historical evidence conflicts with recent interpretations of the geology of the Marsh. For Green has defined the whole of Denge Marsh as Calcareous New Marshland which he suggests was first won from the sea after the storms of the late thirteenth century.[63] Yet this cannot be correct. The records of Battle Abbey do not speak of their manor of Denge Marsh being newly won from the sea in the later Middle Ages: on the contrary they regarded Denge Marsh as one of their original possessions going back to the Conqueror's foundation of the monastery.[64] It would seem therefore that either the definition or the chronology of the calcareous marshland in this area needs re-examination. It may be that the manor suffered from temporary inundation after 1287–8, and that this has affected the classification of the Denge Marsh soils.

Walland Marsh (Figure 33)

We have already seen how the shape of parish boundaries and of drainage channels suggests that the settlement of Walland Marsh has been fundamentally different from that of the rest of the Marsh. The distinction is made sharper or the absence of Domesday settlements and the scarcity of names recorded in Anglo-Saxon charters in Walland Marsh. However, an estate named *Mistanham* is listed amongst a number of properties in the vicinity of Romney Marsh which are said in the cartularies of Christ Church, Canterbury, to have been given to the community by King Æthelwulf of Kent at some date between 833 and 858. As Wallenberg pointed out,[65] there can be little doubt that this name can be identified with Misleham in Brookland parish, though there has apparently been Norman confusion of 'l' and 'n' either in the cartulary form of the name or in the subsequent medieval and modern spellings.

Equally it is possible that the property 'intertorrentem heorat burnan et haganan treae' ('between the stream hart-bourne and Hagana's tree') granted in 785 by King Offa to the *comes* Ealdbeorht and his sister, Selethryth (the later abbess of Lyminge), was indeed the manor of Agney as the monks of Christ Church later supposed.[66] One might

---

[63] Green, *Soils of Romney Marsh*, p. 43; Cunliffe, 'Evolution of Romney Marsh', p. 47.

[64] Searle, *Lordship and Community*.

[65] BCS 408; S 1623. Wallenberg, *Kentish Place-Names*, pp. 171–2.

[66] BCS 247; S 123; and cf. Brooks 'Unidentified Forts', p. 84, cited in n 18.

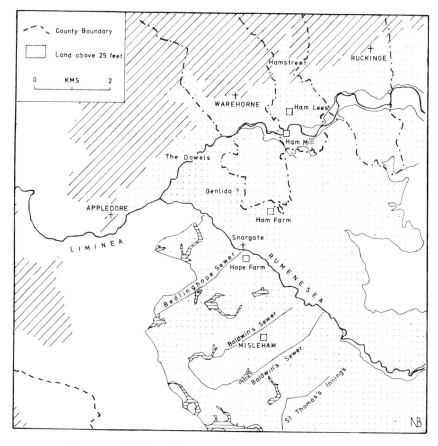

Figure 33. Walland Marsh and the branches of the *Limen.*

argue that the stream-name *heorat burnan* has been lost because its course ran in the new marshland which was overrun by the sea at some date subsequent to the charter. But names terminating in -bourne do not recur elsewhere in the Marsh, and since the charter gives no other indication of the estate's location, we should not build any theory on the monks' identification of the property as Agney.

The question therefore has to be asked whether the area of Old or Decalcified Marshland that lies to the south-west of the Rhee Wall is indeed older than the areas of New Calcareous Marshland around Newchurch and in Denge Marsh that we have found in occupation at least from the tenth century and possibly as early as the eighth. In this connection attention needs to be drawn to the series of water courses and sea defences in this area that bear the names of medieval archbishops of Canterbury. It was the nineteenth-century engineer

Elliott[67] who first suggested that these works represent the first 'innings' in Walland Marsh and attributed them to the initiative of Archbishops Thomas Becket (1162–70), Baldwin (1184–90), Boniface (1240–70) and Pecham (1279–92). We should hesitate, however, before attributing too much initiative to the archbishops. Baldwin's wall and Baldwin's sewer which enclose Misleham and Brookland must surely be related not to the archbishop of that name, but to the charter of *c.* 1150 by which the prior Wibert of Christ Church, Canterbury, gave Baldwin Scudaway 'as much land about Misleham as he could inne at his own expense against the sea'.[68] There is an urgent need for a new search of the cartularies of Christ Church for other twelfth- and thirteenth-century charters to enable us to date the construction of the drainage channels and sea walls in this area of the Marsh.[69]

Green was right, however, to resist the argument that all this decalcified marshland was first won from the sea at that time. For there are two pre-conquest charters which throw some light on conditions in this area of 'old' marshland. In 811 King Coenwulf of Mercia granted a number of estates to Archbishop Wulfred in return for a handsome payment of gold.[70] Nothing is said in the contemporary manuscript of this charter of any estate in Romney Marsh. But a tenth-century version of the same charter has an interpolation which includes one sulung of land in the Marsh whose bounds are as follows: on the east, *æla mearc*, on the south *byttlinc hopa* in the marsh, on the west the king's boundaries, and on the north *frodeshammespend* (or *flothamespynd*).[71] The name *byttlinc hopa* is preserved in Bedling Hope Sewer which runs close to the western limit of the decalcified marshland. We cannot be certain exactly where *byttlinc hopa* lay in relation to the sewer, but there must be a strong probability that it lay towards its north-eastern end at Hope Farm (TQ 992283), just south of the Rhee Wall at Snargate. Since *byttlinc hopa* was the southern boundary of the property, the estate must have comprised, or at least included, the area of the settlement of Snargate, a name which is first recorded in *c.* 1200[72] and which clearly refers to a medieval sluice-gate (perhaps intended to admit sea-waters to the Romney branch of the northern *Limen* at high tide). It is instructive too that *frodeshammespend*, the northern boundary of this estate, must have lain very close to the *flothammas* (*flodhamman*) of BCS 396 (S 282); Wallenberg convincingly argued on the basis of later forms

[67] Eliott's maps and views are found in T. Lewin, *The Invasion of Britain by Julius Caesar* (London, 1862).
[68] Holloway, *History of Romney Marsh*, p. 66.
[69] Tatton-Brown, 'Topography of the Walland Marsh Area'.
[70] BCS 335; S 168.
[71] BCS 336; S 1617.
[72] Wallenberg, *Place-Names of Kent*, p. 478.

that *frodes-* is a corrupt form for *flodes-*,[73] and that the first element is either OE *flod* 'flood', 'stream', *flode* 'channel', 'gully', or *flot* 'deep water' or 'sea'. The second element of the name, OE *hamm* 'enclosure', 'meadow' or 'dry ground in a marsh', is found in several local names: in Ham Farm (TQ 997296), and also in Ham Lees Farm (TR 003320) and Ham Mill Farm (TR 002316), both just in the neighbouring parish of Ham Street (TR 001334). The final element is OE *pynd* 'pound', 'dam', 'embankment'. Whether the whole name refers to an embanked river-channel (presumably of the river *Limen* or one of its branches), to a stock-pound in a water-meadow or to an embanked enclosure subject to flooding is important, for the name might mean that by the tenth century artificial water-channels or embankments were already being constructed in this corner of the marsh. Equally intriguing are the *confinia regis* which formed the western boundary of this unnamed sulung in the Marsh. If the 'king's boundaries' are simply those of an unnamed royal estate, it would seem to have lain in the calcareous marsh south-east of Appledore; if on the other hand they are perhaps some form of linear boundary-dyke it may be that in late Saxon times the king had already played a role in attempting to protect the Marsh and the river *Limen* from the inroads of the sea.

That the area north of Snargate was already under threat from the inroads of the sea is confirmed by a charter attributed to King Egbert of Wessex but bearing the date 845, which is impossible since Egbert died in 839.[74] The charter, which purports to be a grant to a layman of Warehorne and *Flothammas* (Ham?) survives in an eleventh-century manuscript and may therefore be taken as some guide to the topography at that time at least. On the west of Warehorne and Ham was *Genlida* (OE *gægnlad*), literally a 'counter-channel'. Green has not reckoned any part of 'The Dowels' to be amongst the calcareous soils, though some of the creek-ridges in the area have calcareous subsurface horizons and may yet prove to preserve the form of this channel.[75] The presence of a tidal channel or of an artificial river-course here in the eleventh century suggests that the whole branch of the *Limen* that flowed around the north of the Isle of Oxney was already endangered from the encroachment of the sea from the south and would already have needed extensive sea defences. The future of Romney as a harbour kept clear of silt and shingle by the current of fresh water was therefore already at risk, and once again the question of the antiquity of the embankments in this vicinity is brought into focus. A programme of planned excavation on the embankments and sea-defences of the marsh could alone resolve the uncertainties of their date and chronology.

[73] Wallenberg, *Kentish Place-Names*, pp. 114–15 and 165.
[74] BCS 396; S 282.
[75] Green, *Soils of Romney Marsh*, pp. 107–8.

Narrative Accounts

Early medieval narrative sources have sometimes been held to throw light on the Marsh. But we may surely discount the ninth-century description in the 'British Marvels' attributed to 'Nennius' of a 'lake *Lumonoi*' with sixty (340) islands each with an eagle's nest, and with sixty (340) rivers entering it but with only one (named *Lemn*) leaving it to the sea.[76] The reference is rather to one of the Scottish lochs – Lomond or Leven – whose name (like *Limen*) is also based on the Celtic root **Lemana*, but which fit the rather fanciful description of lake, islands, eagles and rivers very much better than does Romney Marsh. Some manuscripts indeed specify that Loch Leven *in regione Pictorum* is intended. By contrast, in the *Anglo-Saxon Chronicle* account of the arrival of the great Danish army at the mouth of the *Limen* in 892 with 200 (250) ships, we do have a strictly contemporary account of high authority and whose Kentish location is certain.[77] The Chronicler describes how the Viking fleet came into the mouth or estuary of the *Limen* and then rowed their ships four miles up river to a half-built fortress which they stormed; thereafter the Danes built for themselves their own winter-camp at Appledore, which is described in the next annal as being on the mouth (estuary) of the *Limen*. It is clear that in terms of the Romney or Hythe branches of the *Limen*, Appledore was already some seven or twelve miles up river and could scarcely be described as *on Limenemuthan*. Moreover if the half-built *burh* of 892 is correctly identified as Castle Toll, Newenden[78] then the chronicler's 'four miles' up-river would be a pardonable exaggeration if the mouth were at Appledore (six or seven miles) but a gross error had it been at Romney or Hythe. The conclusion seems clear. At least at high tide, the bulk of the calcareous area of Walland Marsh must have been covered by sea water, so that a huge fleet could be based at Appledore. Such a tidal lagoon might also explain the presence of the *genlida* or counter-channel on the west boundary of Warehorne and Ham, perhaps some early version of the Rhee channel designed to take in sea water at high tide. If we therefore picture Walland Marsh as already an area of tidal mud-flats in the ninth century, then we must recognize that the northern branches of the *Limen* must already have been under threat from the sea at that time. The surprise is perhaps that it took so long for

---

[76] Ibid., p. 18; Cunliffe, 'Evolution of Romney Marsh', pp. 48–9; Nennius, *Historia Brittonum*; *British History and the Welsh Annals*, ed. J. Morris (Chichester, Phillimore, 1980), c. 67.

[77] ASC, s.a. 892.

[78] B.K. Davison, 'The Burghal Hidage Fort of Eorpeburnan: A Suggested Identification', *Medieval Archaeaology*, 16 (1972), pp. 123–7.

the sea to capture the *Limen* in a definitive course to Rye. The traditional obligations of the *lex marisci* in the Appledore area that involved contributing to the work of building sea walls and water channels must have been just as necessary in the ninth century as they were when first recorded in the twelfth.

Conclusion

This survey of the extant historical evidence for Romney Marsh in the early Middle Ages must therefore raise as many questions about the current understanding of the geomorphological development as it answers. We need to bear in mind that the surviving charters do not record the date of the first settlement or colonization of a particular area of the Marsh, but merely tell us of the ownership and the boundaries of Marsh estates on particular occasions when they happened to change hands. The charters show that in Romney Marsh proper the decalcified marshland estates had boundaries that are recognizable on the ground today. Moreover much of the calcareous marshland here and in Denge Marsh was also already settled and farmed at various times between the eighth and tenth centuries. By contrast the calcareous marshland of Walland Marsh may have been inundated, at least at high tide, by the late ninth century: it was not to be reclaimed until the later Middle Ages, whilst the decalcified area of the Dowels contained a tidal channel at least by the eleventh century. We therefore need to question how far the geological evidence can accommodate these contrasts and apparent contradictions.[79] For the future, the need is clear. Historians, geologists and archaeologists must work in collaboration if the problems of the Marsh's evolution are to be solved.

---

[79] C.P. Green, 'Palaeography of Marine Inlets of the Romney Marsh Area', in J. Eddison and C. Green, eds, *Romney Marsh: Evolution, Occupation and Reclamation* (Oxford, 1988), pp.167–74.

Index of Charters

[Note: this is an index to significant discussions of the form or content of individual charters; it does not include every reference to such documents.]

BCS

3	(S1):	187
45	(S8):	186
81	(S1171):	186
91	(S22):	142–3
98	(S21):	282
141	(S1180):	282, 288
148	(S23):	287–8
160	(S24):	291–3
214	(S111):	293–5
227	(S35):	192
228	(S36):	192
247	(S123):	295–6
257	(S130):	192
289	(S153):	191–2
293	(S155):	112–3n, 192
335	(S168):	297
337:		191
342	(S1265):	115
363:		191
370	(S186):	117
373	(S187):	117
384	(S1436):	117–19, 10
396	(S282):	297–8
400	(S188):	121
421	(S1438):	122–3
451	(S298):	195 n.52
504	(S335):	269 n.41
596	(S360):	239–74
602	(S370):	242–3
638	(S1288):	291
648	(S1417):	161
677	(S416):	189
702	(S425):	189
752	(S466):	159
813	(S510):	289

860	(S537):	132–3
880	(S546):	57, 132, 173–4
1000	(S648):	242–3
1048	(S670):	179 n. 72
1119	(S723):	227–8
1135	(S731):	200–1
1040	(S677):	227
1041	(S667):	227
1198	(S753):	179 n. 72
1336	(S39):	288

KCD

684	(S876):	131
689	(S882):	133
715	(S914):	19
737	(S959):	144

Harmer, SEHD

9:		124
21	(S1515):	169

Harmer, Writs

27	(1386):	143
28	(S986):	143

Robertson, Anglo-Saxon Charters

32	(S1506):	134–5
44	(S1447):	179 n. 72
52:		58

S

712a:	217–37
1622:	116

Whitelock, Wills

8	(S1484):	171

Index

[All numerals refer to page numbers, save those in bold print (**11**) which indicate the Figures. The following abbreviations are used: arcbp = archbishop; bp = bishop; ct = count; dk = duke; kg = king; n = note; st = saint. Note that archbishops are of Canterbury unless otherwise specified.]